Making Competitive Cities

Making Competitive Cities

Edited by

Sako Musterd
Department of Geography, Planning and International
Development Studies, University of Amsterdam

Alan Murie
Centre for Urban and Regional Studies
School of Public Policy
University of Birmingham

WILEY-BLACKWELL

A John Wiley & Sons, Ltd., Publication

Library of Congress Cataloging-in-Publication Data

Making competitive cities / edited by Sako Musterd, Alan Murie.
    p. cm.
   Includes bibliographical references and index.
   ISBN 978-1-4051-9415-0 (hardback : alk. paper)   1. City planning.   2. Community
development, Urban.   3. Urban policy.   4. Urban economics.   I. Musterd, Sako.
II. Murie, Alan.
HT166.M246165 2010
307.1′16094—dc22

                                                                                    2009048119

A catalogue record for this book is available from the British Library.

Set in 10/13 pt Trumpmediaeval Roman by MPS Limited, A Macmillan Company

1 2010

Contents

Foreword

In the present age of hyperglobalisation, neo-liberalism and intense competition among places to attract investment, urban policy makers everywhere are seeking to find approaches to foster development. About every 5 years, a new formulation comes along, and leaders hop on the bandwagon, hoping that they have found a path to growth. Along with the traditional emphasis on infrastructure, we have witnessed promotion of subsidies to firms, deregulation of land use controls, creation of enterprise zones and urban development corporations, and fostering of science parks, sectoral clusters, office mega-projects, festive retail malls, iconic architecture and tourism development; most recently attracting the 'creative class' through developing social diversity and cultural amenities has become the most prominent tactic. Sako Musterd and Alan Murie have drawn together a group of scholars from a number of 'ordinary' European cities to test whether any of these strategies did, in fact, contribute to urban competitiveness. They especially looked at the creative class hypothesis.

Whereas traditional scholarship identified the decisions of firms as determining the location of industries, recent location theorists have placed a greater emphasis on the choices of individuals possessing skills in creative and knowledge-based industries. In addition to Richard Florida's identification of individual creativity as the fount of development, human capital theorists have contended that the presence of a highly educated stratum offers the key to growth in a post-industrial age. There is a certain chicken and egg problem: Does employment follow firms or do knowledge workers generate industrial development? The answer seems to be both, but the authors in this volume regard firm location as the dominant factor. In particular, they emphasise that political and business leadership and historical forces matter more than the city's appeal to footloose knowledge workers.

One of the problems for proponents of the various strategies mentioned above is that different contexts call for different approaches. Once every place follows the same strategy, cities lose their individuality and the market becomes saturated. In other words, convention centres may stimulate economic activity when there are relatively few of them, but when every city has one, very few will have sufficient draw to benefit their locales. Thus, policy makers need to figure out what makes their city distinctive rather than picking out a one-size-fits-all formula.

The great strength of this collection of essays is that it takes into account both the particular and the general in relation to the causes of competitiveness. By rigorously following a similar methodology in a number of European cities, the authors are able to select characteristics that seem to apply generally and those that depend on the specific path followed by each city. They also point to the tension between focusing on knowledge-based development and sustaining those large sectors of the population that do not have the skills to participate in the knowledge economy. In other words, dependence on elite activities can foster greater inequality. Furthermore, creative and financial sectors display considerable volatility, meaning that a narrowly based economy focused on these sectors can result in long-run instability.

To the extent that the authors find general causes of competitiveness, they are largely in the traditional determinants of attractiveness: the personal circumstances of workers and the available job opportunities rather than the urban environment. Amenities seem to be the icing on the cake – less drivers of growth than consequences of it. Rather than relying on either anecdotal evidence or regression analysis, this book employs carefully developed comparative case studies to discover the attributes that have allowed cities to prosper under new circumstances. In its excellent blend of empirical investigation and theoretical argument, *Making Competitive Cities* reveals the challenges presented to cities by the changing global economy and the disparate ways in which cities are transformed.

Susan S. Fainstein
Harvard University
Cambridge, MA

Preface

Making Competitive Cities has been developed on the basis of a large-scale international comparative research programme, called ACRE.[1] This is the acronym for Accommodating Creative Knowledge. The subtitle of that programme – Competitiveness of European Metropolitan Regions within the Enlarged Union – shows our ambition to learn more about the urban conditions that are seen as essential to enhance the competitiveness of urban regional economies across Europe.

Despite the ambitious title of this book, our aim is to provide balanced and grounded knowledge which contributes to the understanding of what makes urban regions more or less attractive for essential economic activities. We are aware of the fact that the field we address is wide and multidimensional and we would also like to stress that regional contexts vary a great deal. Therefore, we decided to limit the economic sector focus to creative and knowledge-intensive industries, and within these subsectors additional selections were made to enable comparison between the regions. We also put limits on the scope of this project by including 'only' 13 European regions.

However, writing a book is more than presenting research material. The extra efforts require strong commitment. That is what we got from all of the researchers who were involved in the wider project. Thirteen highly enthusiastic and 'driven' research teams from a similar number of European urban regions have contributed to this volume. All of them swiftly responded to our comments on earlier versions of manuscripts, and therefore, our acknowledgements go to them in the first place. But others also played a very important role in bringing the writings further. We would like to mention Olga Gritsai, who did not stop reminding contributors what the deadlines and limits were; and Puikang Chan, who was of tremendous help in making the texts of all chapters more uniform and technically readable. We also would like to thank Pieter Musterd for shooting the wonderful cover photos, and Christian Smid and Hans de Visser (UvA-map makers) for smoothly producing the graphics.

Sako Musterd and Alan Murie

[1] The programme was funded under priority 7 'Citizens and governance in a knowledge-based society' within the Sixth Framework Programme of the European Commission (contract 028270). Over a 4-year period, various surveys were carried out and a large series of publications have been written on aspects of urban economic development. Published results and more information about that research programme can be found on the ACRE website http://www2.fmg.uva.nl/acre/.

Contributors

Elena dell'Agnese (elena.dellagnese@unimib.it) is Associate Professor of Geography, and teaches in Political Geography and Geography of Development at the University of Milan Bicocca.

Austin Barber (a.r.g.barber@bham.ac.uk) is a lecturer in Urban Development and Planning at the Centre for Urban and Regional Studies (CURS), University of Birmingham.

Marco Bontje (m.a.bontje@uva.nl) is Assistant Professor in the Department of Geography, Planning and International Development Studies of the University of Amsterdam.

Julie Brown (j.brown.1@bham.ac.uk) is a research fellow at the Centre for Urban and Regional Studies (CURS), University of Birmingham.

Joachim Burdack (j_burdack@ifl-leipzig.de) is Professor of Geography at the University of Leipzig and a senior researcher at the Leibniz-Institute for Regional Geography (IfL).

Caroline Chapain (c.a.chapain@bham.ac.uk) is a research fellow at the Center for Urban and Regional Studies, University of Birmingham.

Veronica Crossa (veronica.crossa@ucd.ie) is a lecturer in the School of Geography, Planning and Environmental Policy at University College Dublin.

Evgenii Dainov (edainov@csp-sofia.org) is Professor of Politics at the New Bulgarian University, Sofia.

Denis Eckert (eckert@univ-tlse2.fr) is a senior researcher at the French National Center for Scientific Research (CNRS) and Head of the Interdisciplinary Center for Urban Studies (LISST-Cieu), University of Toulouse.

Tamás Egedy (ege6727@mail.iif.hu) is a senior research fellow at the Geographical Research Institute of the Hungarian Academy of Sciences (GRI HAS) and a lecturer at the Budapest Business School.

Vassil Garnizov (vasil_garnizov@abv.bg) is Professor of Social Anthropology, New Bulgarian University, Sofia.

Sabine Hafner (sabine.hafner@uni-bayreuth.de) is a lecturer and researcher at the Department of Geography of the University of Bayreuth.

Kaisa Kepsu (kaisa.kepsu@helsinki.fi) works as a researcher at the Department of Geography at the University of Helsinki.

Zoltán Kovács (zkovacs@iif.hu) is a scientific advisor at the Geographical Research Institute of the Hungarian Academy of Sciences (HAS-GRI) and Professor in Human Geography at the University of Szeged.

Bastian Lange (b_lange@ifl-leipzig.de) is a postdoctoral researcher at the Leibniz-Institute for Regional Geography in Leipzig, Germany.

Philip Lawton (philip.lawton@ucd.ie) is a post-doctoral research fellow in the School of Geography, Planning and Environmental Policy, University College Dublin.

Hélène Martin-Brelot (hmb@univ-tlse2.fr) is a research fellow at the Interdisciplinary Centre for Urban Studies (LISST-Cieu), University of Toulouse.

Michal Meczynski (micmec@amu.edu.pl) is a lecturer and researcher in the Institute of Socio-Economic Geography and Spatial Management at the Adam Mickiewicz University in Poznan.

Manfred Miosga (manfred.miosga@uni-bayreuth.de) is Professor of Urban and Regional Development at the Institute of Geography in the Faculty of Biology, Chemistry and Geosciences, University of Bayreuth.

Silvia Mugnano (silvia.mugnano@unimib.it) is a lecturer in Urban Sociology at the Department of Sociology and Social Research at the University of Milan Bicocca.

Alan Murie (a.s.murie@bham.ac.uk) is Emeritus Professor of Urban and Regional Studies at the Centre for Urban and Regional Studies, University of Birmingham.

Enda Murphy (enda.murphy@ucd.ie) is a lecturer in the School of Geography, Planning and Environmental Policy at University College Dublin.

Sako Musterd (s.musterd@uva.nl) is Professor of Urban Geography at the University of Amsterdam and Director of the Centre for Urban Studies in the same university. He coordinated the ACRE research programme, which formed the basis for this volume.

Robert Nadler (r_nadler@ifl-leipzig.de) graduated in Geography, Sociology and Business Administration at the University of Leipzig. He is currently working in the international PhD programme 'URBEUR – Urban and local European studies' at the University of Milan-Bicocca.

Marianna d'Ovidio (marianna.dovidio@unimib.it) is a research fellow at the Department of Sociology and Social Research of the University of Milan Bicocca.

Montserrat Pareja-Eastaway (mpareja@ub.edu) is Associate Professor at the Faculty of Economics and Business of the University of Barcelona.

Heike Pethe (h.a.a.pethe@uva.nl) is a post doctoral researcher in the Department of Geography, Planning and International Development Studies of the University of Amsterdam.

Marc Pradel i Miquel is Assistant Professor in the Department of Sociological Theory in the Faculty of Economics and Business of the University of Barcelona.

Arnis Sauka (asauka@sseriga.edu.lv) is a lecturer in Entrepreneurship and a research fellow at the Stockholm School of Economics in Riga, TeliaSonera Institute.

Krzysztof Stachowiak (krst@amu.edu.pl) is a lecturer and researcher in the Institute of Socio-Economic Geography and Spatial Management at the Adam Mickiewicz University in Poznan.

Anne von Streit (anne.vonstreit@lmu.de) is a researcher and lecturer at the Department of Geography, Ludwig-Maximilians-University of Munich.

Tadeusz Stryjakiewicz (tadek@amu.edu.pl) is Professor in the Institute of Socio-Economic Geography and Spatial Management, Adam Mickiewicz University in Poznan, and Head of the Department of Regional Policy and European Integration.

Mari Vaattovaara (mari.vaattovaara@helsinki.fi) is Professor in Urban Geography at the Department of Geography, University of Helsinki.

Part I

Introduction

1

Making Competitive Cities: Debates and Challenges

Sako Musterd and Alan Murie

Debates and challenges

From the start of the twenty-first century, challenging debates have taken place about the essential conditions for the development of new economic activities in advanced economies. In particular these have included the conditions that enable the development of creative and knowledge-intensive industries in urban or metropolitan environments. The key questions addressed in this book in 'Making Competitive Cities' are about how to facilitate the rise of so-called 'creative knowledge cities' and how to anticipate and address issues associated with this.

Best-selling books by authors including Landry and Florida – 'The Creative City: a Toolkit for Urban Innovators' (2000), 'The Rise of the Creative Class' (2002) and 'The Flight of the Creative Class' (2005) – have shaped new debates about knowledge and creative cities. They have done this, in the first place, through sophisticated marketing of the books. But, because they have also suggested that successful urban economies could easily be established or engineered by local governments and other actors, they have attracted attention from beyond the academic and research communities. The messages in these books are that it is crucial to nurture the qualities of cities and urban environments that attract 'the creative class'. Cities that do this successfully benefit from the intelligence and creativity of that class and these cities perform better, achieve higher rankings on the 'creative index' and increase their competitive advantage. Whereas previous policy preoccupations were with the formation, retention and attraction of firms and what influenced the location decisions of firms the new theoretical orientation has switched attention to creative individuals and how attracting and retaining them underpins economic success. In a nutshell, the basic argument is that cities should create conditions to attract talent and when that talent – the creative class – is there, economic activity will follow. To be able to attract talent, cities should be attractive places to live in, they should be tolerant places and their urban residents should be open to new initiatives and to diversity. Although arguments about the importance of associations between urban amenities and economic growth are not new (Hall, 1998; Clark et al., 2002), the new presentation of an old argument and of the concept of creativity and the way the argument is 'sold' has resulted in increased attention to the economic geography of cities, particularly in more affluent sections of the world.

However, especially from within the academic world, the robustness of the arguments advanced about creative cities has been challenged. Critical commentaries have been published in academic and other journals and have presented both conceptual and empirical critiques (Hall, 2004; Peck, 2005; Markusen, 2006; Storper and Manville, 2006). These commentaries argue that the research evidence mobilised to justify the emphasis placed on urban conditions is very thin. In addition, from a historical point of view, and unrelated to any short-term boom and bust-related fluctuations in cities' performance, there is nothing new in the argument that cities will be centres of creativity and innovation. This has been the case throughout history as Hall (1998) and Simmie (2005) have noted. Markusen (2006) has also argued that the connection between 'being creative' and 'being successful' is not straightforward. And perhaps the urban attributes referred to are more a consequence of city growth than a cause? Moreover creative cities or regions can hardly be created 'out of thin air' (Hall, 2004) and not all cities can aspire to become creative cities by adopting the approach recommended by Florida and others. A final set of criticisms levelled at some accounts of competitiveness and notably at Florida's contribution is that at best they pay scant regard to wider impacts on social inequality and at worst are recipes for increased social polarisation. They are preoccupied with attracting the creative class and ignore other citizens or assume that they will benefit from trickle-down effects.

Against this background debate, there remain good reasons for a contemporary focus on the conditions for *Making Competitive Cities*. Perhaps modern competitive cities should indeed be referred to as creative knowledge cities. In advanced urban economies, there has been an ongoing loss of employment in manufacturing and related industries, especially in labour-intensive sections of these industries. Yet, simultaneously, in cities that are thriving – and during economic upswings – there has been a growth in knowledge-intensive economic activities, for example in advanced producer services and high-tech firms, where high-skilled employees have become the dominant category of labour. In conjunction with that, as well as driven by changing consumer behaviour, creative industries have gained importance in advanced urban economies. This pattern of change may, in turn, have been driven by structural and global forces. More flexible forms of production, combined with a significant increase in the variety of products – even though the variety was frequently only superficial – gave way to increasing demand for the products of creative industries, including design, music, architecture and others. This has reflected a growing demand for 'distinction': building on the work of Bourdieu (1984), consumers are distinguished on the basis of their class position as indicated by the amount and orientation of their cultural, social and economic capital. Consumers distinguish themselves from each other – or are driven to do so – by consuming different products, including places to settle, on the basis of their class positions.

So, developing sufficient knowledge-intensive and creative industries within a city is of key concern for government and other urban stakeholders. Consequently, there are good reasons to make efforts to understand the conditions that are relevant for the development of these industries in urban areas and to understand how these changes in production and consumption impact on both economic and social life in cities (Scott, 2006).

Sectors

This book aims at contributing to the understanding of how to facilitate urban economic development, specifically focusing on creative and knowledge-intensive industries. Much of the debate hitherto has involved exchanging plausible assertions with or without evidence that appears selected to support the argument advanced. This book seeks to at least partly address the lack of robust empirical evidence. We report research findings from a major study in 13 European cities and urban regions that are introduced in Chapter 2. The research carried out has deployed a common methodology and referred both to creative and knowledge industries in general and to specific sectors within these broader categories. We will not embark on the discussion about the concept of 'creativity' and its meaning as such. Instead, we are interested in the varying developments of specific economic activities in (selected) creative or cultural industries and (selected) knowledge-intensive industry sectors. The objective is to contribute to the understanding of why cities and urban regions develop differently. This does not mean we do not see problems of definition. As Gibson and Kong (2005) have stated for the concept of 'cultural economy' (which is related to the concept of 'creative economy'), there are multiple ways in which that economy can be defined. In their critical review of the literature, they discussed various different approaches. Their conclusion after discussing these approaches was: 'What this discussion illustrates is that the polyvalent nature of cultural economies means that there are myriad conceptions in the literature, and the productive task ahead is not to sink into endless efforts at defining…, but acknowledge the polyvalency and address specific research agendas from there'. (p. 546). We have followed that recommendation and also taken account of other previous work including that of Pratt (1997) and Kloosterman (2004).

We have adopted a 'sector approach' in which we pragmatically define the creative industries (such as arts, media, entertainment, creative business services, architects, publishers, advertising, designers) and knowledge-intensive industries (such as ICT, R&D, finance, law). In comparisons where the wider categories of creative and knowledge-intensive industries are regarded as important, in particular when studying pathways and the policies, we tend to refer to these creative and knowledge-intensive industries in aggregate. However, where the appropriate evidence relates to opinions, attitudes and behaviour we tend to make more specific comparisons, because the wider sectors are internally very heterogeneous.

For the creative industries we have focused on the most creative of creative industries, and within certain sectors, like advertising, this means the most creative parts of advertising and not standardised activities, such as the production of weekly broadsheets providing details of 'dwellings for sale'. Following analysis of contemporary statistics for each of the urban regions involved, three sub-sectors of creative industries were identified as most important. Two out of these three were then chosen for further research by all teams. These were:

- creative parts of computer gaming, software development, electronic publishing, software consultancy and supply;
- motion pictures, video activities, and radio and TV activities.

A third important creative industries sector in the urban region was then chosen. This was advertising if it was among the most important sectors but was another sector when advertising was not important.[1]

A similar research strategy was followed for the knowledge-intensive industries. Here all research teams focused on:

- law, accounting, book keeping, auditing, etc.,
- finance;
- R&D;
- higher education.[2]

The research carried out on these specific sectors also took into account the size and location of the firm, and where we sampled to identify respondents for parts of the study we adopted a sampling procedure to include self-employed persons and persons in small (1–5 tenured staff) and larger

---

[1] NACE codes 722, 921, 922 and 744.
[2] NACE codes 741, 65, 73 and 803.

(more than 5 tenured staff) firms. We also sampled to include locations in the core of the metropolitan area and in the urban region beyond the core.

Questions and theories

The key questions or challenges in this book are derived from the wider public debates on how to foster economic development in urban regions and include the following very general question: 'What makes cities competitive?' Since we have based this book on rich empirical material which allowed for multiple comparisons between the urban regions, we have transformed the initial question into the following manageable research question: 'What are the key conditions for urban economic development in different regions?' Subsequently, we reformulated the question in greater detail: 'What are the conditions for specific creative industries and specific knowledge intensive industries in different metropolitan regions?' These questions implied an investigation of the development of the economic sectors, what has nurtured them and what will help to develop them further.

We applied four theoretical approaches and also referred to three different categories of actors that were regarded as of crucial importance for the understanding of economic development.

- The first theoretical approach includes a view of development which puts so-called classic location theory in the central position. We call this the 'hard' conditions or classic conditions theory. Here the availability of capital and of labour with adequate skills, proper institutional context, tax regimes, up-to-date infrastructure and accessibility are the factors that are regarded as playing the major role in explaining the development of firms in urban regions.
- A second and strongly related theoretical approach is associated with theory about economic clusters. In this field, agglomeration economies play a major role and it is assumed that activities cluster together where they use the same infrastructure, have linkages to each other and to the same environment and profit from each other's presence and the enhanced image of the cluster. The development of clusters gets special salience in debates on pathways that urban regions have followed over time. This also relates to debates about path dependence of urban economic development.
- A third field of theory refers to the importance of networks. Personal networks of employees, entrepreneurs and managers may play a crucial role in the decision-making process determining where to start a business and also where to expand. These networks can have different characteristics, ranging from very personal to business related, from small to large and from local to regional or global.

- A fourth theoretical approach, finally, includes views on economic development that are strongly related to 'soft' conditions. This is a field of thought that is nearest to the work done by Florida and followers and what seems to have become the 'New Conventional Wisdom', as Buck et al. (2005) have called it. The suggestion is that creating the proper conditions for the settlement of creative talent will be the key to successful development. The focus is on a range of urban amenities that are attractive to individuals – including factors such as quality of life, quality of environment and urban atmosphere, well-functioning housing markets that provide alternative types of attractive housing, and factors related to levels of tolerance, openness and diversity.

We believe it makes sense to draw on all of these theories and use them in more rigorous empirical studies in order to reverse the current trend in some segments of economic geography where there is 'more talk than test'. A narrow theoretical foundation and a thin empirical basis will, in the end, have serious implications for the development of urban policies aimed at enhancing the competitiveness of urban regions. It is our ambition with this book to come up with a broader theoretical foundation and more solid empirical testing of the crucial assumptions, thus providing the elements for developing better understanding and in turn better policies aimed at enhancing urban economic positions in the longer run.

As well as benefitting from a wide theoretical scope in this book, we believe that it helps to learn from the opinions and experiences of various actors in the field, as well as from policymakers and policy documents. We refer to three particular groups of actors selected because of their position in relation to key questions about the development of knowledge and creative sectors of the economy. These are:

- The managers of selected firms operating within the creative and knowledge-intensive firms under consideration. These managers potentially have power to make decisions about where to (re) locate and some will at least have some impact on crucial settlement decisions. What factors drive their decisions? What were the most important dimensions they considered?
- Since, increasingly, we are talking about globally connected economic activities, we also investigate what the opinions and motives and considerations are of transnational migrants who are employed in the creative and knowledge-intensive industries we focused upon. Why did they choose to live and work in a certain place? Was it because the jobs were there? Was it because they could earn most there? Or was it because of the soft conditions? Or was there some other reason?
- Finally, high-skilled and highly educated employees play a crucial part in some accounts of the development of the sectors we focus on. They can

tell us whether the soft factors identified in the literature had a major influence on their decisions over where to live and work. They can also tell us what kinds of considerations were important in their decisions and can clarify what conditions carried the most weight.

Information about the last category of actors (high-skilled employees and graduates) was collected through a survey. A total of 2,751 responses were obtained based on structured interviews (on average slightly over 200 per urban area). The survey data were collected in 2007. Apart from the common sector, size and location selection strategy that has already been referred to, we also agreed a common approach to the collection of information from respondents. This should not be taken as meaning that there was no variation between cities in the implementation of the approach. Of course, when working with many different urban and national contexts there are differences between the settings that should not be denied. These include sample frameworks, but also different local cultures that impact on some elements of the entire strategy. For example, in some contexts high-skilled employees in firms can be approached directly, whereas in other contexts the approach can only go via the management of the firm. Other issues included the variation arising from whether certain economic activities were present in each city. Although we chose sectors where some comparison could be achieved, the selected sectors are not equally distributed across all urban regions and this resulted in minor distortions of the 'ideal' strategy. Other locally specific issues also had some impact on the information we collected. Detailed data collection reports and response overviews for each urban region have been reported in ACRE reports 5.1–5.13.[3] The researchers involved in the data collection in each of the urban regions expressed their confidence over the quality of the data, but also considered that the number of responses for specifically defined sub-sectors may be too small to generalise the results to all of those who belong to such a sub-sector. We believe that in general it would be unwise to treat the data as entirely representative for the sub-sectors we deal with. Even the combined larger data set, where some 'noise' in the data may disappear, at least for some analyses, should be treated more as an instrument to help us to present a range of indications of what are important conditions for the development of urban economies, rather than treating this as a perfect representation of the wide variety of situations and conditions that may exist in reality.

The information we obtained from managers and (self-employed) entrepreneurs applied to the same sectors, but was collected through an average of 25 semi-structured face-to-face interviews per urban region (reports 6.1–6.13). A similar strategy was applied to collect information from transnational migrants and a similar number of responses formed

---

[3] http://acre.socsci.uva.nl/results/reports.html

the basis for our comparative analyses (reports 7.1–7.13). We also used statistical material, as well as other written sources to get a better understanding of the various pathways affecting each region. For the policy section in this volume, we collected a range of policy documents at various spatial scales and combined the information in these documents with interviews with key informants.

The approach we have adopted enables us to engage with the contemporary debate but we do not attempt to address all aspects of it. While we refer at various points to the impacts of the development of creative and knowledge industry our focus is more on what attracts key groups to cities and on what common and distinctive factors are associated with different cities. The combination of the theoretical approaches and the opinions and behaviours of three categories of actors provides important insights that may be used as input for urban policies aimed at future urban economic developments. However, in advance of that understanding, policies have been developed in the past and policies are currently being developed. It is important to refer both to general policies which affect urban economic outcomes and to sector and other policies for economic development. This is not a simple task, since the policy landscape itself has become highly complex, not only because of the range of policies and professions that impact on urban economic development, but also because policy making in this field is multi-scalar and multi-actor. There is new governance that goes beyond the impact of classic government; but there are also new geographic scales that may be important, from the very local neighbourhood scale, via the city, to the urban region, the state and the higher levels, both governmental (e.g. the EU) and other international organisations (IMF, World Bank, OECD).

Regions and sources

This volume has been developed on the basis of a large research and policy project investigating the impact on the competitiveness of EU metropolitan regions of developing 'creative industries' and 'knowledge intensive industries'. The central research focus has been on the conditions that drive the development and questions that are very close to those that guide the contributions in this volume. This volume refers to the results of research on economic developments, experiences and strategies in 13 metropolitan regions across Europe. The metropolitan regions involved are those of: Amsterdam, Barcelona, Birmingham, Budapest, Dublin, Helsinki, Leipzig, Milan, Munich, Poznan, Riga, Sofia and Toulouse (Figure 1.1).

This includes cities with different histories and roles – capital cities and second cities, cities with different economies, cities with industrial and port-based histories, but also cities with other profiles; and cities with different

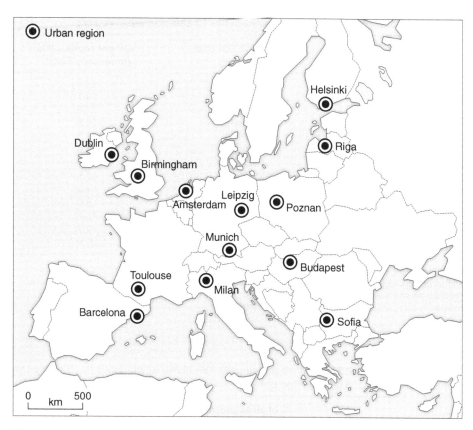

Figure 1.1 Thirteen urban regions included in the international comparative research programme ACRE.

cultural, political and welfare state traditions. This includes a much wider set of cases than is commonly addressed in debates about creative and knowledge-intensive industry within economic development and competitiveness policies. Through this we hope it will move the debate forward and provide a richer set of examples and tests for debate than exists at present.

The evidence discussed in this book refers to cities and their regions that are not leading in the European urban hierarchy and do not belong to the first range global cities. While the first range global cities (including London and Paris) are clearly able to demonstrate successful development of creative and knowledge-intensive industry, the questions we are addressing relate to whether other, 'more ordinary' cities are also able to achieve such development. We discuss urban regions from all over Europe and include eight west European metropolitan regions and five post-socialist cities in central and eastern Europe. Five of the thirteen urban regions are in southern Europe. The selected urban regions vary in size of population (from half a million in Leipzig to 4.2 million in Milan) and in the level of GDP per capita (from 2.7 to 54.0 thousands Euro) (Table 1.1).

Table 1.1   Population and GDP per capita in the 13 selected urban regions.

	Population 2003–2006 (thousands)	GDP per capita, 2005 (thousands Euro)
Amsterdam	1,100 (2005)	49.8
Barcelona	3,900 (2001)	24.7
Birmingham	2,284 (2001)	27.8
Budapest	2,100 (2005)	18.8
Dublin	1,230 (2006)	52.3
Helsinki	1,100 (2000)	34.0
Leipzig	570 (2001)	24.1
Milan	4,200 (2001)	37.5
Munich	1,675 (2001)	54.0
Poznan	856 (2005)	6.0
Riga	750 (2005)	10.2
Sofia	1,050 (2001)	2.7
Toulouse	1,133 (2005)	26.9

Source for population figures: Demographia World Urban Areas: Population & Density. 4th Comprehensive Edition: revised. August 2008. http://www.demographia.com/db-gdp-metro.pdf (for Poznan and Toulouse figures from national and local Statistical Offices); *Source for GDP figures*: Eurostat, NUTS 3 level; supplemented/ updated by data from national and regional statistical offices.

Table 1.2   Employment in creative and knowledge-intensive industries in 13 European metropolitan regions; data collected between 2000* and 2006.

City regions	% of all employment accounted for by		
	Creative industries	Knowledge-intensive industries	Creative and knowledge-intensive industries
Amsterdam	8	18	26
Barcelona	12	10	22
Dublin	11	10	21
Munich	8	21	29
Helsinki	13	18	31
Budapest	13	16	29
Milan	14	17	31
Riga	6	23	29
Sofia	8	19	27
Leipzig	9	16	25
Toulouse	6	16	22
Poznan	7	11	18
Birmingham	6	19	25

Source: ACRE reports 2.1–2.13 (http://acre.socsci.uva.nl/results/reports.html).
* In the case of Toulouse the figures are for 1999.

They also vary in terms of the actual employment in creative and knowledge-intensive industries. Table 1.2 shows that all of the cities we are focusing on have developed significant employment in these sectors – from 18 per cent in Poznan to 31 per cent in Helsinki – but that some cities are more

Table 1.3 Differences in housing and housing costs: Percentage of households in owner occupied and social housing, prices of houses and apartments and average living area.

	Year	% owner occupiers	% social renters	Year	Average house price (per m²) (€)	Year	Average living area m² per person
Amsterdam	2004	18	50	2004	2,044	2004	34
Milan	2001	59		2004		2001	38
Birmingham	2004	75	28	2004	2,261		
Helsinki	2004	45	23	2001	1,943	2004	34
Poznan	2001	8	10	2001	430	2004	24
Budapest	2001	84	9	2004	811	2001	21
Riga	2001	50		2004	896	2004	15
Toulouse	2001	39	14			2001	38
Barcelona	2001	68		2001	2,500	2001	32
Dublin	2001	62	11				
Leipzig	2001	10	4	2004	1,670	2001	36
Munich	2001	22	7	2004	4,530	2001	40
Sofia	2001	81				2001	15

Source: Urban Audit.

dependant on creative and knowledge-intensive industries than others. Helsinki, Milan, Munich, Budapest and Riga have particularly high shares of employment in these sectors. The distinctive nature of the economies emerging is indicated by the skewness between 'creative' and 'knowledge based'. Milan, Budapest, Barcelona and Dublin have higher shares of employment in creative industries while Riga, Munich, Birmingham, Sofia and Amsterdam are more knowledge based. Helsinki in strong in both sectors.

However, these cities and urban regions differ from each other in many other respects as well. In the current debates on the importance of 'soft' conditions for urban economic development it would, for example, be interesting to see how these territories differ from each other in terms of essential housing parameters. There are no obvious and reputable sources to consider the profile of cities in terms of these kinds of 'soft' conditions and one contribution of the research reported in this book is to fill this gap in evidence. Nevertheless some sense of the differences likely to apply in this area is indicated by data on housing tenure, housing costs and average consumption of housing space (Table 1.3).

These data indicate the complexity of the housing offer associated with different cities. The cities in central and eastern Europe have the smallest and the least-expensive housing and to some extent the pattern mirrors differences in GDP. However tenure differences reflect different histories of state intervention and privatisation and the relationships between housing provision variables, and between these variables and others, are not simple or linear. We do not have at one extreme a set of affluent, mature cities and at the other cities that are relatively new in responding to the demands of a competitive global economy. Nor do we have a simple continuum of city types at different stages of development. Rather we have cities with different economic and housing structures and strengths and – as we will see in greater detail later in this volume – also with different assets, histories and legacies and different governance and organisational arrangements and policy traditions. Each of these different dimensions has the potential to affect the opportunity, approach and pattern of economic development and especially the development of creative and knowledge-based economic activity. In short, there is much structural variety of the urban regions in Europe. The focus on these cities in the rest of this book highlights the diversity in Europe. It also enables discussion of the different strands of theory set out in Chapter 2.

In this book, we present the results of research by referring to a limited number of urban regions in each chapter and comparing aspects of the urban economic development in these regions. The research teams are specialised in the fields we cover and based in 13 European scientific institutions. They were brought together to rigorously evaluate, reformulate and empirically test assumptions about European urban regions and their potential for attracting creative industries and knowledge-intensive industries.

Pathways, actors and policies

The considerations set out in this introduction have informed the structure adopted for this volume. The introduction and a wider elaboration on the literature in Chapter 2, together form Part I. Four different sections follow this. In Part II (Pathways) we concentrate on the development paths of urban regions. The basis for this is an analysis of available statistical data over time and analysis of the conditions that have played a significant role in developing the regions. This section covers some of the typical paths cities have followed or are still following. The chapters deal with robust comparisons between the cities and identify commonalities between them. However, it is also evident that key events, political and economic 'ruptures' and other factors have created very special trajectories and distinctive pathways. In this section, the real character and the special assets of each city are stressed while highlighting what is most characteristic and distinctive about the paths that the city and its region have followed over time and how this shapes the potential for development of knowledge-based and creative industry for the urban region's position in terms of urban economic potential today. There are clear differences in the type of pathway followed and this has implications for policy development in the creative and knowledge sectors.

In Part III (Actors) we address the importance of key actors or target groups in the development of creative knowledge regions. Following the directions indicated by the literature, we focus particularly on three groups: managers of creative and knowledge-intensive firms, transnational migrants who are working in creative and knowledge-based industry and employees with higher educational qualifications. The aim is to understand the drivers behind the decisions made by them and through this to contribute to the discussion of recruitment and retention within strategies for the development of knowledge-intensive and creative industry.

The chapters are based on answers to questions about the extent to which these actor categories are satisfied with their living and working environment; the reasons for moving to their current region of residence; the extent to which their expectations of living and working in this region (based on the regional image in the outside world) have been justified; how long they are planning to stay in the region and, when planning to move, the main reasons for this decision. We assess the relative importance of the location factors that have played a role in the decision-making process and include 'classic' factors, such as accessibility, job availability and 'tax-climate', the importance of clustering opportunities, the role of networks and the presence of 'soft' factors, such as the quality of space and atmosphere of the city and region.

In Part IV (Policies) the focus is on policy. Whilst there is a wide variety of urban economic realities, there is an even wider variety of intervention strategies. Reference is made to current policy, and visions of local and regional governments in different cities and this is used within a common framework to complete a review of the approaches adopted. The central contribution of this section is to address the question: 'What do the policy makers see as the most relevant strengths and weaknesses of their metropolitan regions with respect to international competitiveness?' 'To what extent do local and regional governments in the case study regions aim to build on existing regional strengths, and to what extent do they look for new strengths with regard to economic specialisations?' 'To what extent are the economic development strategies and visions embedded in broader urban development strategies and visions?' 'Are economic development policies connected to regional spatial development policies, housing policies and/or policies to attract and cater for a "talent pool"?' 'What is the role of "hard" location factors? Is there sufficient opportunity for "clustering", are there enough facilities that enable networking, and how about the state of the "soft" location factors in the metropolitan economic development strategies?' 'Do metropolitan economic development strategies specifically address the conditions for attracting a skilled international labour force?' 'To what extent can we speak of an integrated regional strategy, and on what geographic and administrative level?'

Finally, in Part V (Synthesis) we highlight the crucial findings that have been elaborated upon in this book and set out the implications arising from this.

References

Bourdieu, P. (1984) *Distinction. A social critique of the judgement of taste.* London: Routledge.

Buck, N., I. Gordon, A. Harding and I. Turok (eds) (2005) *Changing cities: Rethinking competitiveness, cohesion and governance.* New York: Palgrave Macmillan.

Clark, T.N., R. Lloyd, K.K. Wong and P. Jain (2002) Amenities drive urban growth. *Journal of Urban Affairs*, 24: 493–515.

Florida, R. (2002) *The rise of the creative class and how it's transforming work, leisure, community and everyday life.* New York: Basic Books.

Florida, R. (2005) *The flight of the creative class. The new global competition for talent.* New York: Harper Business.

Gibson, C. and L. Kong (2005) Cultural economy: A critical review. *Progress in Human Geography*, 29 (5): 541–561.

Hall, P. (1998) *Cities in civilization.* London: Weidenfeld & Nicolson.

Hall, P. (2004) Creativity, culture, knowledge and the city. *Built Environment*, 30 (3): 256–258.

Kloosterman, R.C. (2004) Recent employment trends in the cultural industries in Amsterdam, Rotterdam, The Hague and Utrecht: A first exploration. *Tijdschrift voor Economische en Sociale Geografie*, 95 (2): 243–252.

Landry, C. (2000) *The creative city: A toolkit for urban innovators.* London: Earthscan.

Markusen, A. (2006) Urban development and the politics of a creative class: Evidence from the study of artists. *Environment and Planning A*, 38 (10): 1921–1940.

Peck, J. (2005) Struggling with the creative class. *International Journal of Urban and Regional Research*, 29 (4): 740–770.

Pratt, A.C. (1997) The cultural industries production system: A case study of employment change in Britain, 1984–91. *Environment and Planning A*, 29: 1953–1974.

Scott, A.J. (2006) Creative cities: Conceptual issues and policy questions. *Journal of Urban Affairs*, 28 (1): 1–17.

Simmie, J. (2005) Innovation and space: A critical review of the literature. *Regional Studies*, 39 (6): 789–804.

Storper, M. and M. Manville (2006) Behaviour, preferences and cities: Urban theory and urban resurgence. *Urban Studies*, 43 (8): 1247–1274.

2

The Idea of the Creative or Knowledge-Based City

Sako Musterd and Alan Murie

Essential conditions for competitive cities

The main focus of this book is on the conditions that are required for the settlement and development of creative industries and knowledge-intensive industries in metropolitan regions: that is, industries that are regarded to be crucial for future urban economic development. What is it that attracts firms and, more particularly, those who are employed in them, to certain locations and thus subsequently makes cities competitive? These are old yet also current questions. While they have only partly been answered in the past they also require new answers that take account of the major societal changes experienced over time. These changes include structural transformations in the economy, globalisation processes and the 're-invention' of local qualities.

Phelps and Ozawa (2003) have highlighted the main shifts in agglomeration factors that occurred during the major economic restructuring associated with the post-industrial era. They refer to changing geographic scale (cities now function as urban regions with multiple cores that relate to each other in a complementary form and less as mono-centric towns-with-suburbs), changes in economic specialisation (from manufacturing to services) and in the mode of production and the division of labour. The latter has major implications for the labour skills that are generally required, but also has major effects on the composition of the labour force within firms and on relations between firms, within and between sectors and within and between cities and regions.

The shift in geographic scale and its implications have also been highlighted by Alan Scott (2006) when he referred to the effects of globalisation processes.

Globalisation has allowed many firms and cities to extend their reach well beyond immediate and national boundaries. Scott argues that cities with strong creative sectors – especially firms in high technology production, business and financial services, media and cultural-products industries and neo-artisanal manufacturing – profit most from these processes. He relates the fortunes of cities to expanding markets, which increase output opportunities and allow for deeper and wider divisions of labour at the point of production. This stimulates trends towards further and more intensified urban agglomeration, because of the external economies of scale and scope that are connected with these processes. Therefore, globalisation goes hand in hand with the increasing importance of metropolitan regions. He also identified that many of the most dynamic firms participate in international networks and partnerships (joint ventures, strategic alliances, co-productions). By bringing diverse talent together – using the opportunities globalisation is offering – these firms may be able to produce new competitive products. However, Scott also indicates a process that operates in the opposite direction. Because of better connections across the globe, it has become easier to use outsourcing as a way of achieving reductions in production costs; certain standardised activities can easily be produced in sub-centres, wherever they are located (Henderson and Scott, 1987).

Krätke (2003) studied globalisation processes in relation to the production and distribution of cultural goods, referring in particular to the media industry. Increasingly, media has become a global business, in which multinational conglomerates have branches all over the world. However, they show a strong tendency to cluster their headquarters and main production facilities in a highly selective group of 'global media cities', so these firms did not become footloose. Krätke shows that the top of the global media cities hierarchy is, at this stage, exclusively North American and European; global, continental, national, regional and local scales obviously demonstrate a complex interplay in producing the global and local media landscapes.

The local is also prominently present in the work of Malecki (2000). He concluded that knowledge, rooted in regional and local cultures, is fundamental to understanding both the agglomeration and clustering of economic activity and the ability of cities and regions to increase their competitiveness. Globalisation and the transportation and telecommunication revolutions did not reduce the importance of the geographic location. In fact, local qualities seem to have become more important instead of less. The local context offers opportunities to distinguish themselves from others. Better communication across the globe implies that the connectedness and accessibility factors by which cities distinguish themselves from others, lose significance. These factors are still important, but many cities have been able to acquire these assets. It is exactly this process that seems to have increased the importance of path dependent networks and local qualities. These provide essential conditions for attracting new economic activities.

The local qualities can take many forms, but many authors believe that places that succeed in connecting the local 'tacit knowledge' and 'buzz', with more widely available 'codified knowledge' via global 'pipelines' and 'nodes', may offer the most innovative and economically successful local environments (Lambooy, 2002; Simmie et al., 2002; Bathelt et al., 2004; Helbrecht, 2004; Storper and Venables, 2004; Simmie, 2005).

Economic restructuring, globalisation and localisation processes tend to be dynamic and complicated. They have major effects on many urban regions and their activities. The complexity and dynamic character of the transformations are food for thought and it is not a surprise that debates on conditions for economic development do not end in consensus about what would be the best or most robust theory. On the contrary, the turbulence seems to feed the development of competing theories about how economic sectors would best be nurtured and about what would help to develop them further.

All theories concerned with the conditions for economic development are multidimensional and multi-scalar and highly affected by the processes referred to. They can also be ordered or classified in various ways and be developed from various perspectives. In this book – at least initially – we have organised the theoretical discussion that frames the chapters to follow into the four fields briefly referred to in Chapter 1. These include a field of theory in which so-called 'hard' or 'classic' conditions are central; a field of theory in which the clustering of firms is the main focus; a field of theory in which 'networks' are put central; and a field of theory in which so-called 'soft' conditions come first. In all of them processes of economic transformation, globalisation and localisation may play a role. Moreover, in all of these fields of theory the attention may go to the firms that apparently settle somewhere or that decide to stay at a certain location; but the attention may also go to the actors who are involved. These actors may be the decision-makers who will finally decide to locate the firm in a certain place or who will make the relocation decision, but crucial actors may also be the employees who cannot be missed because they are the key to the production of goods and services. Highly skilled and specialised employees may be particularly important because they are more 'scarce' than the not-so-highly skilled. Consequently, decision-makers have to take into account the needs and demands of these crucial employees. In a globalising world, the connections between various parts of the globe will also increase with greater exchange of knowledge and skills as a result. That implies that the behaviour and considerations of transnational migrants become more important and consequently this category of actors should also have a more prominent position in revised theories (Mahroum, 2001).

Although this chapter refers in turn to the four fields of theory, and although attention is given to the three categories of actors that are crucial – managers, transnational migrants and highly skilled employees – it is still not an easy thing to cover all the potential factors that impact on any decision about where to participate in economic activity from and where to participate in producing and delivering products or services. Since all actors are embedded in multiple networks of relations with others who influence the decision-making process and the decisions themselves, there is in principle a multitude of factors that simultaneously and interactively have a critical influence on the final decision. The complexity also forces us to pay attention to the inter-play between 'demand' and 'supply'. The characteristics and relations of individuals who are involved in the economic activities we consider also have an impact on the characteristics of the firms, locations and places in multiple networks of institutional and economic relations. In order to gain a comprehensive understanding of what creates competitive cities, we should avoid reading any categorisation in a rigid way. We should remain open to other categorisations, which may, in the end, result in a new focus or even a new theory for competitive cities.

'Hard' conditions theory

The most well-known theoretical approach focuses on conditions that we call 'hard' conditions. We also call this field of theoretical thought: 'classic' location theory. In that theory, key factors include the availability of capital and of a labour force with the requisite skills, an institutional context with the right set of regulations and sufficiently attractive tax regimes, the right infrastructure and good accessibility, but also availability and affordability of (office) spaces. Subsidies and/or tax abatements in less developed regions (e.g. the EU Regional Funds and the German regeneration programme for the former GDR) can also be included in these 'hard' location factors and they have frequently been shown to make a difference in company relo-cation decisions. In more concrete terms, this is about nearness to global financial centres, the presence of a major international airport, telecom-munication services and other service suppliers and clients, as well as the availability of an international labour pool (Sassen, 1991, 2002; Derudder et al., 2003; Scott, 2003; Taylor, 2004).

Development strategies that adopt a theoretical view in which these factors are central, tend to improving infrastructure including transport and other connections (e.g. this was typically one of the big investments in eastern European countries that entered or intend to enter the European Union), and business parks. These business parks often have a mono-functional feel and some express doubts about longer-term sustainability because the development of these parks would typically reflect outmoded Fordist types of production and not fit anymore in Post-Fordist production regimes. Clark et al. (2002), for example, argued that the post-industrial trends and globalisation result in growing importance of culture. They argue that cultural activities are increasingly crucial to urban economic vitality. Citizens in the post-industrial city would treat their own location as if they were tourists.

Therefore, one may wonder whether continuing with the creation of business parks is a good strategy, especially for creative industry development that is associated with specific urban environments. However, even those activities that begin small, distinctively, flexibly and locally rooted may grow and generate land/property appreciation and speculation that changes the initial character and distinctiveness; moreover, processes of gentrification and related urban development pressures can displace or exclude firms, community amenities and certain residents. In addition, not all creative industries or creativity in general requires highly urbanised and mixed centres – numerous examples can be given of innovative developments in more homogeneous, less urban environments and especially when firms expand, other 'hard' factors may become more important.

In the 'hard' conditions literature, several authors pay attention to the importance of educational facilities, more particularly high quality public schools and universities. The presence of these facilities ensures the availability of highly skilled labour and attracts firms to these places. Glaeser and Saiz (2003) found that 'for more than a century, educated cities have grown more quickly than comparable cities with less human capital'. The findings resulted from an analysis in which they controlled for a range of other variables. They also found that 'skilled cities are growing because they are becoming more economically productive (relative to less skilled cities), not because these cities are becoming more attractive places to live'. However, the presence of good schools and universities typically fits all theoretical perspectives. It may be presented as a crucial 'hard' economic condition, but it may also be presented as a factor that is essential for the attraction of talented young people, and thus be labelled as an essential soft condition. Moreover, those who defend network theories and cluster theories also connect educational facilities with other cluster characteristics.

Even though other factors may have gained in importance, we do not intend to suggest that 'hard' conditions have become irrelevant today. On the contrary, today's cities and urban regions should all meet certain 'classic' location conditions. They seem to be necessary conditions, albeit not sufficient conditions. Larger cities and regions are generally able to offer essential 'hard' conditions. However, there still are differences between the regional (tele) communication networks and other regional infrastructures such as road systems, railway connections and accessibility through water and the air. Availability of capital, qualified labour and the wider institutional settings are still highly relevant and thus it is crucial to consider that these are not evenly distributed. Tax policies, rent levels, labour costs and legislation regarding labour and wages remain essential factors. These offer different opportunities to urban regions (Sassen, 1991, 2002; Derudder et al., 2003; Taylor, 2004). These differences will result in unequal positions in economic competition. This may be especially relevant to the internal differentiation between European cities.

Due to the evolution of Europe after World War II, cities in western Europe are likely to have a very good position in terms of 'classic' conditions. Over the past 60 years western Europe has proven to be able to build a more varied infrastructure and firmer connections to the rest of the world. In general, there is a suggestion that east and central Europe have weaker positions in terms of 'hard' conditions for economic development in new creative industries and knowledge-intensive industries. However, that conclusion should not be arrived at too quickly. There are a few counterbalancing factors. First of all, some of the cities in east-central Europe may regain their former central geographical position. Cities like Budapest come closer to the centre of gravity of Europe and its potential position as a spider in the web may change the status of the region. Second, eastern European states have been able to create conditions in which a very large share of the population attained a high level of education. This might facilitate the transformation towards knowledge societies. Third and more generally, many of the 'hard' conditions may be especially important for larger firms but less important for smaller firms and newly established start-ups. The fact that hard conditions overall may be less developed in some contexts, therefore does not have to imply that economic development of new activities will not be possible in these contexts (Dövényi and Kovács, 2006; Stanilov, 2007).

Cluster theory

Economic cluster theory again overlaps with the other theoretical fields. The concept of agglomeration economies plays a major role in cluster theory. A key element in this theory is the fact that activities are assumed to cluster because they have linkages to each other, use the same public and private services and institutions and are connected to the same environment, while profiting from each other's presence. Together they create a cluster image. The development of clusters gets special salience in debates on pathways urban regions have followed over time. This relates to path dependence debates.

Wu (2005) referred to specific creative clusters. These were associated with high quality universities, commercial linkages, availability of venture capital, support by public policies and good quality services and infrastructure and with quality of place.

Porter defines clusters as 'geographic concentrations of interconnected companies and institutions in a particular field. Clusters encompass an array of linked industries and other entities important to competition' (Porter, 1998, p. 78). Among these 'other entities', Porter mentions suppliers of specialised inputs and infrastructure, customers, manufacturers of complementary products, companies related by skills, technology or common inputs, governmental and knowledge institutions, and trade associations. Porter's cluster concept rapidly became dominant in academic and policy discussions about urban, regional and national competitiveness. Encouraged by success stories like the knowledge-intensive ICT cluster in Silicon Valley (Saxenian, 1994), the Cambridge region (Keeble et al., 1999) or the Third Italy (Bathelt, 1998), many cities, regions and countries built on this theory to develop cluster policies.

The cluster concept is of high value, but should not be seen in isolation. With Turok (2004), we share the view that city-regions need to be understood as part of wider economic systems and external business connections. The efficiency of 'hard' conditions such as communications and transport links should be taken into account, as well as wider national and international policies and frameworks. We would like to add that the way these clusters developed should also be considered. Concepts like 'path dependency' and 'embeddedness' of firms and people underline the importance of historically grown local conditions (Storper, 1992; Kloosterman and Lambregts, 2001; Musterd, 2004). Path dependence applies to the development of economic organisation and clusters, but also to the impacts of political and social and other institutional and organisational structures. These often have their origins in the past and once structured they play a crucial role in the future development of certain activities and territories. The presence and functioning of place-bound formal and informal institutions is considered to be very important for development perspectives. Again, (old) universities and other institutions of learning are particularly relevant historical drivers behind ongoing and future developments. Path dependency encompasses the institutional and organisational change of local, regional and national political–economic systems. The dependence on developments in history implies, for example, that privatisation and institutional change in former state-socialist countries does not necessarily result in the establishment of a west European type of market economy or social and cultural milieu (Harloe, 1996). Some urban regions have to 're-invent' themselves to a considerable extent. This may be especially true for those that until recently specialised in manufacturing and were cut off from global restructuring. The notion of 'embeddedness' was initially used by Polanyi (1944) to designate the fact that in traditional societies, commercial trade depended upon social relations. However, the concept is still alive. In a recent study, Taylor (2005, p. 70) referred to embeddedness as: 'the incorporation of firms into place-based networks involving trust, reciprocity, loyalty, collaboration, co-operation and a whole raft of untraded interdependencies'.

One of the problems with economic cluster theory is that clusters may be identified at virtually all geographic scales. The question then is: to what extent can we really speak of 'geographic concentrations'? Another question is to what extent clusters can be created by governments or through deliberate partnerships? The most well-known clusters, such as Silicon Valley seem to have emerged because there were innovative firms and individuals, fortunate events or even coincidences (Martin and Sunley, 2003; Cumbers and MacKinnon, 2004; Boschma and Kloosterman, 2005).

Some additional caution may be appropriate in relation to the issue of scale. In urban geography textbooks, smaller areas are very often designated as having a specific functional structure. In many urban regions, highly complex bundles of economic and social activities can be found at a small scale. Examples in the creative industries include media-clusters, jewellery quarters, arts conglomerates and entertainment clusters. Many of these can be found in rather small areas, in specific parts of cities or urban regions where special features can be found; and their economic relations may be restricted to a small part of town. However, these new economic activities are often rather labour intensive (Scott, 2006, p. 6) and this implies that a large supply of labour may be required. Consequently, these clusters cannot exist without being embedded in larger cities or urban regions with a wide variety of professions and skills.

Cluster theory has become prominent in many national, regional and urban development strategies and will probably remain so in the coming decades. Currently, clusters related to creative and knowledge-intensive activities are among the 'most wanted' targets of cities, regions and countries in the advanced capitalist world. Cities and regions trying to develop, facilitate or promote concentrations of creative, innovative and/or knowledge-intensive industries in order to become more competitive have attracted considerable interest. 'Cluster policy' has become one of the most common instruments to transform an urban or regional economy into a creative and knowledge-intensive economy. Different concepts of 'cluster' are evident in the literature. These are the creative cluster or quarter as a local and well-defined physical entity and space where industries locate in one building or neighbourhood (e.g. the Custard Factory in Birmingham, the Westergasfabriek in Amsterdam or Manchester's Northern Quarter – see Mommaas, 2004); and the cluster as expressed by Porter, which is an industrial sector definition usually wider in space (Wu, 2005).

Personal networks

Hard conditions, in the form of enabling connections, and clustering processes, which are characterised by relations between partners and firms, already reveal that the division between the fields of theory we present is a relative one. Many debates about classic location factors and about cluster theory might also be positioned under a heading: network theory. In this volume, we also explicitly pay attention to the role of networks. Inspired by the work of Grabher (2002, 2004) and Turok (2004), we pay attention to the impact of personal ties, local relations and organisational affiliations. In some contexts these relations and networks are referred to under concepts such as 'individual trajectories'. The application of these concepts seems most functional when trying to understand what drives various types of actors in deciding where to settle and where to stay. This introduces a criterion for differentiation on the basis of the origin and history of individuals' personal relationships. Geographical relationships that receive special attention are those with the place of family, the place of birth, the place of study, including the university milieu, and the proximity to friends. These relate to path dependence, but also to the idea that embeddedness is a crucial concept that drives various actors. In various chapters, we refer to these personal networks and individuals' trajectories and gauge their potential relevance as conditions for economic development.

Clearly, the cluster concept is associated with network theory. As early as the end of the 1970s Italian economists (Beccatini, 1979) and French sociologists (Ganne, 1983; Raveyre and Saglio, 1984) showed that small- and medium-sized enterprises specialising in the same industry were organising in a way which involved both competition and cooperation. These particular instances were based on social relations and shared conventions; personal relations and clusters went hand in hand. Later on also clusters with a less personalised character have been defined and developed.

'Soft' conditions theory

The 'soft' conditions field of theory asserts the importance of specific urban amenities that create an environment that attracts people who are key to the most promising economic activities for the economic development of the urban region. The use of the concept 'soft' is related to the fact that it is very difficult to find adequate operational and objective definitions for the concepts that are collected under this umbrella. The soft conditions include urban 'amenities', such as the quality of life, urban atmospheres, housing market situations, levels of tolerance, openness and the diversity of the population. Helbrecht (2004) talked about the 'look and feel' of a city. The vagueness and subjective nature of these terms provides a lack of clarity but also offers flexibility and thus major opportunities for politicians and city managers. They may also favour these terms because the idea that urban amenities are good for the urban economy provides the opportunity to connect (physical) urban development agendas and social agendas with economic agendas.

The idea that investment in soft conditions is a panacea for urban economic problems has become the 'New Conventional Wisdom' (Gordon and Turok, 2005) in circles that aim at strengthening the urban economic base.

The debate about 'soft' conditions has increasingly become dominated by Richard Florida (2002, 2006). He used the term 'creative class' to refer to people whose presence is absolutely crucial for economic development. He refers to people with original ideas of all sorts, not just technical geniuses inventing products, but also people developing concepts and images. According to Florida (2002, p. 8): 'The creative class is comprised of a 'super creative core', which consists of a new class of scientists and engineers, university professors, poets, actors, novelists, entertainers, artists, architects and designers, cultural worthies, think-tank researchers, analysts and opinion formers, whose economic function is to create new ideas, new technology, and/or new creative content'. Beyond this core group, the creative class also includes a wider circle of talent working in knowledge-intensive industries. The latter industries include high-technology sectors, financial sector and juridical services. Those who are employed in these sectors are often engaged in complex problem solving that involves a great deal of independent judgement and creativity and requires high levels of education or human capital. The creative class is seen as vital for economic development and urban and regional success. Florida argued that economic growth is powered by creative people, or 'talent'. In his view it is, consequently, vital to create the conditions they require. Florida has moved away from emphasising the role played by the economic activities themselves and argues that 'talent' prefers places that are culturally diverse and open to new ideas: in short places that are 'tolerant'. When this is combined with a concentration of 'cultural capital' wedded to new products ('technology'), the ideal conditions have been created. The three T's (talent, tolerance, technology) together stimulate 'business formation, job generation and economic growth'. Referring to Jane Jacobs (1961, 1970) as one of his main inspirations, Florida claims that creative and talented people prefer to live in cities with diverse populations and a tolerant atmosphere. In more recent work, Florida (2006) added that 'talent is not a stock, it is flow'. Talent can move from one place to another. Cities might try to attract talented and creative people but they could also try to invest in 'growing' them. The latter requires a tolerant climate. 'To create a growth region, you need the kind of place that people want to come to and can easily get to, where they can lead the lives they want and express themselves freely' (p. 26).

As in the work on the character of global cities (Sassen, 2002) and the studies on world city networks (Taylor, 2004), the attraction of a 'talent pool' through (inter) national migration plays a prominent role in Florida's creative class concept. The most important target groups for 'creative knowledge city' strategies are, according to Florida: higher educated graduates and employees in knowledge-intensive and creative industries, managers of creative and knowledge-intensive companies, and trans-national migrants.

Florida was neither the only one nor the first to come up with these ideas. Scott (2006), for example, refers to Gouldner (1979) who wrote about 'the rise of the new class' almost 30 years ago. He referred to the upper employment strata and a 'class' that combined highly educated and technology-driven people. In recent years, Charles Landry (2000) also asked for more attention to be given to the environment. He stressed the institutional and economic context, while Florida focused on the physical structures and public spaces where people can meet, including bars, cafes and restaurants. Both, however, regard public and semi-public spaces as relevant for a city to attract talented people.

Several other authors followed in the footsteps of Florida and provided similar types of 'recipes' for building a creative city. Montgomery (2005) for example concluded that if cities want to be successful in the future, they will need to promote artistic, design and technological skills, back local talent, grow the creative industries, offer a good cultural and artistic life and organise services such as education to support all of this. He also stresses that 'the key figures in all of this are the visionary political leaders and the artists, investors and entrepreneurs, the former creating the conditions for the latter to invest and prosper' (p. 343). Yigitcanlar et al. (2007) investigated the urban orientation of the 'ideal knowledge worker' and concluded that quality of life and place, urban diversity and social equity are most important to them.

Difficult to measure concepts, such as 'urban atmospheres' or 'social climates', but also slightly less vague concepts, such as the quality of the housing stock and neighbourhood and the functioning of the housing market are essential dimensions in the discussion of 'soft' conditions theory. It may or may not be true that potential talent will opt for another city – perhaps even another country – if an initially preferred city does not offer the right combination of conditions. If the housing market does not offer what is asked for, talented people may move elsewhere. So far, there is little work that has directly addressed what housing factors are important here. Reference could be made to price and affordability, dwelling size and mix or to innovation in style and design or to neighbourhood character. Issues related to the housing market have been discussed in relation to the city of Amsterdam. Musterd (2004) and Bontje and Musterd (2005) found that a combination of long waiting lists and rapidly rising house prices [which hardly dropped even during the financial crisis around 2009], especially in the inner city, resulted in very little effective choice available to young starters on the housing market, even if they are highly skilled. If residential or location decision-making processes by creative talent are becoming much more important and if, consequently, the location preferences of managers of companies and of their employees become key factors, this would require a radical change in local and regional economic development strategies. Such a shift would also have major implications for the ambition to increase the EU's competitiveness as a knowledge-based economy.

Florida's ideas have met with increasing criticism, partly because of his theoretical assumptions, but especially because of the weak empirical basis for his arguments. This is also due to the application of imprecise and ill-defined operational concepts in empirical research, if applied at all. As argued by several geographers and economists (Sawicky, 2003; Musterd and Ostendorf, 2004; Glaeser, 2004; Hall, 2004; Peck, 2005; Storper and Manville, 2006; Scott, 2006; Hansen and Niedomysl, 2009), the existing research evidence is far from convincing and other theory cannot be set aside. Storper and Manville (2006) noted that it is not that simple to make a city 'cool' and that there is a 'larger difficulty of developing its 'amenities'. 'Amenity' can mean many things (...). One person's amenity is often the next person's inconvenience' (p. 1252). They then expressed their preference arguing that 'the notion that skills have driven growth, and that skilled workers locate according to some set of exogenously determined preferences and therefore determine the geography of growth, is less convincing than a theory that the preferences of firms – i.e. agglomeration economies – give rise to growth' (2006, p. 1254).

Although there are impressive examples of growth of the share of creative industries in cities such as Milan (Amadasi and Salvemini, 2005; Salvemini et al., 2005), there is as yet insufficient evidence to argue that the rise of the 'creative class' and the 'creative and knowledge-intensive industries' is a long-term trend. In fact, the collapse of the financial sector may be illustrative of the potential 'hype' character of the 'soft' conditions theory. Some of the products created by 'creative talent' in the financial sector, turned out to be unsustainable.

This is not to say that there would be no place for creativity in theories of urban economic development. With all the criticism on Florida's writings, we should avoid throwing the baby out with the bath water. From a historical point of view, we know that the world's great cities throughout history have always been centres of creativity and innovation (Hall, 1998; Simmie, 2005), but we also know that not all cities could be labelled like that. Hall (2004) rightly stated that creative cities or regions can hardly be created 'out of thin air'. His criticism especially relates to Florida's suggestion that urban transformation can be realised almost 'overnight', for instance by scattering the notions of tolerance, openness and diversity over a city. He argues '...building innovative or creative cities was a long and slow, sometimes agonizingly slow process, and ... the outcome could by no means be guaranteed or ordained in advance' (Hall, 2004, p. 257). He notes that creating the necessary preconditions can be very time consuming.

Although things will not change overnight, the logic of path dependence and societal changes is that cities adapt to changing circumstances. It is true that the chances of a city or region specialising in creative and innovative activities and attracting the talent needed are considerably larger where there is a long tradition of creativity and innovation, but it is not impossible, neither unwise for many cities to continue changing their profile accordingly. Even though changes are slow and cities will be differently constrained by their histories, they adapt to new circumstances and new opportunities. However, the adaptation process should be informed by more knowledge about why there is spatial selectivity in the settlement behaviour of creative and knowledge-intensive industries. At least part of the production seems to be connected to specific urban contexts at various scales (Lash and Urry, 1994; Zukin, 1995; Kloosterman, 2004; Musterd, 2006). To us it makes sense to investigate to what extent the location decisions of the various actors are related to local attributes, such as distinctiveness and authenticity, to what extent this is helped by small scale and fine-grained development; it also makes sense to investigate how important specific urban atmospheres and urban qualities are and how these fit the lifestyles of young high skilled people; and it makes sense to further investigate whether diversity of population that refers to ethnicity, cultural preferences, and a range of urban lifestyles, really is becoming an essential asset for cities and urban regions.

Three parts

We will start the empirical sections of this book with a set of contributions in which questions related to path dependency and legacies of embeddedness will be central and in which we deal with very different contexts. This will show that 'stable' development paths in some cities contrast with very dynamic changes in other cities; some cities show that they were able to re-invent themselves, which means that a tremendous transformation has shaped the new form and function of the urban region under consideration. The East–West distinction receives special attention, which allows us to highlight the impact of major institutional changes and new developments.

A second set of contributions considers how various actors think about a variety of urban conditions. Managers and transnational migrants, young and high-skilled, poor and rich, may all have their own agendas and own requirements about where they intend to settle and stay. What is relevant to these actors? We intend to reveal to what extent they have similar or dissimilar ambitions and demands and to what extent these differ in varying contexts.

The final issue we address relates to policy. Although there seems to be a 'New Conventional Wisdom' as far as policy responses aimed at urban economic competitiveness are concerned, a wide variety of interventions exists. Policies may be general or sector specific; they may be new or old; they can build on existing strength or focus on new development; they can be focused on individuals or on firms. In this set of contributions, we investigate what the typical strategies are and again how these strategies vary between urban regions and wider contexts.

References

Amadasi, G. and S. Salvemini (eds) (2005) *La città creativa. Una nuova geografia di Milano*. Milano: EGEA.

Bathelt, H. (1998) Regional growth through networking: A critical reassessment of the 'Third Italy' phenomenon. *Die Erde*, 129 (3): 247–271.

Bathelt, H., A. Malmberg and P. Maskell (2004) Clusters and knowledge: Local buzz, global pipelines and the process of knowledge creation. *Progress in Human Geography*, 28 (1): 31–56.

Beccatini, G. (1979) Dal settore industriale al distretto industriale: Alcune considerazioni sull unita de indagine dell economia industriale. *Rivista di Economia e Politica Industriale*, 1: 35–48.

Bontje, M. and S. Musterd (2005) What kind of a place do the creative knowledge workers live in? In: E. Verhagen and S. Franke (eds), *Creativity and the city. How the creative economy is changing the city*, pp. 166–175. Rotterdam: nai Publishers.

Boschma, R.A. and R.C. Kloosterman (2005) Further learning from clusters. In: R.A. Boschma and R.C. Kloosterman (eds) *Learning from clusters: A critical assessment from an economic-geographical perspective*, pp. 391–405. Berlin: Springer Verlag (geojournal Library, Vol. 80).

Clark, T.N., R. Lloyd, K.K. Wong and P. Jain (2002) Amenities drive urban growth. *Journal of Urban Affairs*, 24 (5): 493–515.

Cumbers, A. and D. Mackinnon (2004) Introduction: Clusters in urban and regional development. *Urban Studies*, 41 (5/6): 959–969.

Derudder, B., P.J. Taylor, F. Witlox and G. Catalano (2003) Hierarchical tendencies and regional patterns in the world city network: A global analysis of 234 cities. *Regional Studies*, 37 (9): 875–886.

Dövényi, Z. and Z. Kovács (2006) Budapest: Post-socialist metropolitan periphery between 'catching up' and individual development path. *European Spatial Research and policy*, 13 (2): 23–41.

Florida, R. (2002) *The rise of the creative class and how it's transforming work, leisure, community and everyday life*. New York: Basic Books.

Florida, R. (2006) The flight of the creative class. *Liberal Education*, 92 (3): 22–29.

Ganne, B. (1983) *Gens du cuir, gens du papier, transformations d'Annonay depuis les années 1920*. Paris: Centre national de la recherche scientifique.

Glaeser, E.L. and A. Saiz (2003) *The rise of the skilled city*. HIER (Harvard Institute of Economic Research). http://www.economics.harvard.edu/pub/hier/2003/HIER2025.pdf (accessed 6 March 2009).

Glaeser, E.L. (2004) *Review of Richard Florida's 'The rise of the creative class'*. http://post.economics.harvard.edu/faculty/glaeser/papers/Review_Florida.pdf (accessed 21 March 2005).

Gordon, I. and I. Turok (2005) Moving beyond the conventional wisdom. In: N. Buck, I Gordon, A. Harding and I. Turok (eds), *Changing cities*, pp. 265–282. New York: Palgrave Macmillan.

Gouldner, A. (1979) *The future of intellectuals and the rise of the new class*. New York: Seabury.

Grabher, G. (2002) Cool projects, boring institutions: Temporary collaboration. Social context. *Regional Studies*, 36 (3): 205–214.

Grabher, G. (2004) Learning in projects, remembering in networks? Communality, sociality, and connectivity in project ecologies. *European Urban and Regional Studies*, 11 (2): 103–123.

Hall, P. (1998) *Cities in civilization*. London: Weidenfeld and Nicholson.

Hall, P. (2004) Creativity, culture, knowledge and the city. *Built Environment*, 30 (3): 256–258.

Hansen, H.K. and T. Niedomysl (2009) Migration of the creative class: Evidence form Sweden. *Journal of Economic Geography*, 9 (2): 191–206.

Harloe, M. (1996) Cities in transition. In: G. Andrusz, M. Harloe and I. Szelényi (eds), *Cities after socialism*, pp. 1–29. Oxford: Blackwell.

Helbrecht, I. (2004) Bare geographies in knowledge societies – Creative cities as text and piece of art: Two eyes, one vision. *Built Environment*, 30 (3): 194–203.

Henderson, J.W. and A.J. Scott (1987) The growth and internationalisation of the American semiconductor industry: Labour processes and the changing spatial organisation of production. In: M.J. Breheny and R. Mcquaid (eds), *The development of high technology industries: An international survey*, pp. 37–79. London: Croom Helm.

Jacobs, J. (1961) *The death and life of great American cities*. New York: Random House.

Jacobs, J. (1970) *The economy of cities*. London: Jonathan Cape.

Keeble, D., C. Lawson, B. Moore and F. Wilkinson (1999) Collective learning processes, networking and 'institutional thickness' in the Cambridge region. *Regional Studies*, 33 (4): 319–331.

Kloosterman, R.C. (2004) Recent employment trends in the cultural industries in Amsterdam, Rotterdam, The Hague and Utrecht: A first exploration. *Tijdschrift voor Economische en Sociale Geografie*, 95 (2): 243–252.

Kloosterman, R.C. and B. Lambregts (2001) Clustering of economic activities in polycentric urban regions: The case of the Randstad. *Urban Studies*, 38 (4): 713–728.

Krätke, S. (2003) Global media cities in a world-wide urban network. *European Planning Studies*, 11 (6): 605–628.

Lambooy, J. (2002) Knowledge and urban economic development. *Urban Studies*, 39 (5/6): 1019–1035.

Landry, C (2000) *The creative city: A toolkit for urban innovators*. London: Earthscan.

Lash, S. and J. Urry (1994) *Economies of signs and space*. London: Sage.

Mahroum, S. (2001) Europe and the immigration of high skilled labour. *International Migration*, 39 (5): 27–43.

Malecki, E.J. (2000) Knowledge and regional competitiveness. *Erdkunde*, 54 (4): 334–351.

Martin, R. and P. Sunley (2003) Deconstructing clusters: Chaotic concept or policy panacea? *Journal of Economic Geography*, 3 (1): 5–36.

Mommaas, H. (2004) Cultural clusters and the post-industrial city: Towards the remapping of urban cultural policy. *Urban Studies*, 41 (3): 507–532.

Montgomery, J. (2005) Beware 'the Creative Class' creativity and wealth creation revisited. *Local Economy*, 20 (4): 337–343.

Musterd, S. and W. Ostendorf (2004) Creative cultural knowledge cities: Perspectives and planning strategies. *Built Environment*, 30 (3): 189–193.

Musterd, S. (2004) Amsterdam as a creative cultural knowledge city: Some conditions. *Built Environment*, 30 (3): 225–234.

Musterd, S. (2006) Segregation, urban space and the resurgent city. *Urban Studies*, 43 (8), 1325–1340.

Peck, J. (2005) Struggling with the creative class. *International Journal of Urban and Regional Research*, 29 (4): 740–770.

Phelps, N.A. and T. Ozawa (2003) Contrasts in agglomeration: Proto-industrial, industrial and post-industrial forms compared. *Progress in Human Geography*, 27 (5): 583–604.

Polanyi, K. (1944) *The great transformation*. New York: Rinehart and Co.

Porter, M.E. (1998) Clusters and the new economics of competition. *Harvard Business Review*, 76 (6): 77–91.

Raveyre, M.F. and J. Saglio (1984) Les systèmes industriels localisés: Eléments pour une analyse sociologique des ensembles de P.M.E. industriels. *Sociologie Du Travail*, 2: 157–175.

Salvemini, S., , R. Cappetta, A. Carlone, B. Manzoni and M. Sommaruga (2005) *La specificità della classe creativa a Milano: Sfruttare i punti di forza della città per supportare i creativi* [The specificity of the creative class in Milan: Exploiting strength of the city in order to support creative workers]. Research of the Bocconi University for the Chamber of Commerce of Milan.

Sassen, S. (1991) *The global city: New York, London, Tokyo.* Princeton, N.J.: Princeton University Press.

Sassen, S. (2002) *Global networks, linked cities.* New York: Routledge.

Sawicky, D. (2003) Review of R. Florida, The rise of the creative class and how it's transforming work, leisure, community and everyday life. *APA Journal,* 69 (1): 90–91.

Saxenian, A.L. (1994) *Regional advantage: Culture and competition in Silicon Valley and Route 128.* Cambridge, MA: Harvard University Press.

Scott, A.J. (ed.) (2003) *Global city-regions: Trends, theory, policy.* Oxford: Oxford University Press.

Scott, A.J. (2006) Creative cities: Conceptual issues and policy questions. *Journal of Urban Affairs,* 28 (1): 1–17.

Simmie, J. (2005) Innovation and space: A critical review of the literature. *Regional Studies,* 39 (6): 789–804.

Simmie, J., J. Sennett, P. Wood and D. Hart (2002) Innovation in Europe: A tale of networks, knowledge and trade in five cities. *Regional Studies,* 36 (1): 47–64.

Stanilov, K. (ed.) (2007) *The post-socialist city. Urban form and space transformations in Central and Eastern Europe after socialism.* Geojournal Library. Heidelberg: Springer.

Storper, M. (1992) The limits to globalization: Technology districts and international trade. *Economic Geography,* 68 (1): 60–93.

Storper, M. and A.J. Venables (2004) Buzz: Face-to-face contact and the urban economy. *Journal of Economic Geography,* 4 (4): 351–370.

Storper, M. and M. Manville (2006) Behaviour, preferences and cities: Urban theory and urban resurgence. *Urban Studies,* 43 (8): 1247–1274.

Taylor, M. (2005) Embedded local growth: A theory taken too far? In: R.A. Boschma and R.C. Kloosterman (eds), *Learning from clusters: A critical assessment from an economic-geographical perspective,* pp. 69–88. Berlin: Springer Verlag (geojournal Library, Vol. 80).

Taylor, P. (2004) *World city network: A global urban analysis.* London: Routledge.

Turok, I. (2004) Cities, regions and competitiveness. *Regional Studies,* 38 (9): 1069–1083.

Yigitcanlar, T., S. Baum and S. Horton (2007) Attracting and retaining knowledge workers in knowledge cities. *Journal of Knowledge Management,* 11 (5): 6–17.

Wu, W. (2005) *Dynamic cities and creative clusters.* World Bank Policy Research Working Paper 3509, February.

Zukin, S. (1995) *The cultures of cities.* Oxford: Blackwell.

Part II

Pathways

Amsterdam – Old gasworks converted to creative industry complex. Photo by Marco Bontje.

Leipzig – Inner city recovery. Photo by Bastian Lange.

3

Pathways in Europe

Denis Eckert, Alan Murie and Sako Musterd

Path dependency

This book is concerned with the development of the creative knowledge economy in European cities and focuses on contemporary processes and policies. However, it is essential that we develop an understanding of how current patterns and processes are influenced by past events and legacies. In seeking to understand the most contemporary processes, it is possible to regard the past development and structure cities as having no influence on the present – as an irrelevant curiosity, or a frozen, dead object which acts as a more or less neutral factor in shaping the economy of the contemporary city. In this perspective, contemporary processes and dynamics (including those associated with globalisation) operate in an almost independent manner, and what went before has little or no influence on the outcomes in any particular city. In contrast to this view, the temporal dimension of urban transformation processes is now widely acknowledged – historical factors affect the ways in which urban economies undergo transformation.

The issue of 'path dependency' is widely posed in the social sciences (Sewell, 1996), and the 'development pathways' of cities are important if we are to explain different trajectories and contemporary mutations (see Boschma and Martin, 2007). The neglect of distinctive legacies associated with different development paths is particularly risky on a continent that is characterised by a rich and complex urban history. European cities have experienced and adjusted to different forms of economic organisation – the early development of trade, the beginnings of industrialisation and changes in industrial and financial processes. They have also faced a history where geopolitical fluctuations have deeply influenced development trajectories. The evolution of the 13 cities considered in this book attest this fact. It is particularly difficult, even in analysing their most recent evolution, not to link the current processes with this turbulent historical context.

The importance of the historical background can be addressed at different levels. Initially, the nature of European cities links to global patterns and the evolution of the world system (see Wallerstein, 1974). The geopolitical and economic division within Europe, after 1945, was an important part of this, as was subsequent change. The development and then the disappearance of a collectivised economic system, and the division and reunification of Germany, are only the most visible events of the complex evolution of the European continent that have impacted on cities and urban systems. The impact is most apparent when reflecting on the development of central and eastern European cities that faced the same necessity to reconstruct their economies and development strategies after 1989–1991. The geoeconomic position of these cities in a progressively reunified continent with a 'back to Europe' context, in which European space forms as a more and more consistent ensemble and is submitted to the same strengths and centrality gradients, influences their development conditions (Didelon et al., 2008).

Beyond this recognition of European cities within the general history of the continent, it is essential to drop down a level and to also take into account the particular evolutions experienced by each city and consider, one by one, how these affect contemporary urban change. The work reported in this book refers to a wide range of cities and reflects a variety of evolutions: cities that were integrated into an international market economy at an early stage (Amsterdam, Milan), some that were among the key metropolises of the industrial revolution (Birmingham, Barcelona, Leipzig), others for which the economic take-off and the internationalisation of trade are much more recent, whether it dates back from the middle of the twentieth century (Munich, Toulouse), or from even more recently (Helsinki, Dublin). For some cities, the role as capital city and centrality within national spaces is critical and this applies to cities with long established political functions (such as that of Budapest within the Austro-Hungarian Empire) as well as to capitals that are more recent and more or less important.

Once the significance of the distinctive history of cities is acknowledged, it becomes important to refer to trajectories and to specific events that have affected development paths. How, with their very different backgrounds, do cities develop their competitive positions in relation to the change towards a creative knowledge economy? Have the particularities of their evolution affected the nature of the role they play in the 'new urban economy' and their current competitiveness? Or is there a 'blank page' that contemporary actors work on, unaffected by legacies from the past? At the beginning of the 1990s, the strategic change promoted in Helsinki by actors responding to the serious economic crisis that affected Finland resulted in a reorientation of the economy of the city and to a rapid internationalisation of its productive model. How far does this 'unconstrained' model apply to cities and do they reinvent themselves without constraints? Or is it more normal for current actors to be able to make a real impact on the development of the city (as the ambitious urban regeneration policy in Birmingham shows) but with legacies from the past also acting as important influences?

These questions are addressed through the studies of individual cities reported throughout this book. Without denying the importance of breaks and recent changes in political systems and policies, the studies of individual cities highlight the importance of longer development paths. The nature and shape of city economies do not necessarily result from policies and the most recent choices. Key decisions, developments and innovations in the past (the development of the scientific potential of Munich or Toulouse from the nineteenth century onwards) are often the essential factors explaining the current evolution towards the knowledge economy. The cities demonstrate the importance of long established policies and structures and often a strong inertia (Hall, 2004). This does not mean, however, that there is no space for contemporary political action or for contemporary decisions or policies to have an impact.

Major and brutal changes can be a powerful spur to the 'reinvention' of the city. In a context of radical economic crisis (as in Birmingham in the 1970s, where the industrial base of the city was seriously undermined), it was essential to rethink the economic model. In Poznan, Leipzig, Sofia or Riga, faced with the end of the communist model, it was equally important to find a new approach and the end of the Franco regime in Spain gave Barcelona a new ability to rethink the future of their city. However, specific 'success' stories can result from less concerted actions that nevertheless deeply modify the local economic system – as in the case of Toulouse. Nobody actually decided to transform this city into a high-tech metropolis, where research and industry fertilise each other. It is the conjuncture of various factors and decisions operating over different timescales that explain this development. For Munich, the division of Germany and the decline of Berlin after 1945 acted as major influences in increasing the strength of the local industrial and scientific system – a process that was made possible by local political action operating in this context – but was not determined by the context.

A last good reason for attaching importance to the development pathways of cities in considering the contemporary creative city relates to the qualifications and creativity of individuals – to their skills and talents. These competences and talents are decisive for the development of the new economy but result for a wide part from the capacity of the cities to build themselves as intellectual, cultural and educational poles: they are historical constructs often built up over a long period and evident in institutional and organisational arrangements. These arrangements may remain settled for political reasons and may be closely linked to the dominant orientations of the local economy but form an asset that can be reinvested in and enable further evolution of the economy.

All of these examples testify to the need to understand the trajectories of cities. Do starting points have no effect on outcomes? Are some types of pathway more favourable than others for the evolution towards the model of the creative knowledge city? How do past legacies and pathways determine the distinctive nature of the creative and knowledge-based economic activity that is emerging in different European cities?

Initial expectations and comparisons

At the outset, we can formulate what the expectations of the performance of different cities would be in relation to deep structural conditions (former pathways) and contemporary location factors (recent pathways) (also Musterd and Gritsai, 2009). A series of hypotheses relate to the view that deep structural conditions are key determinants of the development of city economies:

- Cities known as national or international political and economic decision-making centres have a better chance for innovative restructuring (in our case, for creative and knowledge-based industries) than cities without a pronounced decision-making function. This results in potential favourite positions for 9 out of 13 urban regions we dealt with (Table 3.1): national capitals (Amsterdam, Budapest, Helsinki, Dublin, Sofia and Riga) or cities with partial capital city functions (Munich, Milan and Barcelona).
- Cities, internationally known as historical–cultural and educational centres, especially those with a preserved urban core, are supposed to be more attractive for creative industries. Therefore, they have advantage as potential creative cities. These are cities with traditionally rich cultural life (Amsterdam, Budapest, Munich, Dublin, Riga, Milan and Barcelona).
- Cities specialised in high-skilled activity, engineering and high-tech activity, as well as cities with an early service profile, where industry has never been a dominating sector, have a better starting point for creative and knowledge-based industries than those which still have remnants of heavy industry. This group includes the well-known high-tech centres such as Munich, Toulouse and Helsinki, as well as the multifunctional, mostly service-oriented centres such as Amsterdam, Barcelona, Dublin and Poznan.

The cities can also be compared in terms of international rankings that relate to more contemporary conditions that say something about recent pathways. Table 3.2 presents data from the annual European Cities Monitor 2007, based on the opinions of 500 (large) European firms (Cushman and Wakefield). Next to the overall ranking (position in top 30), Table 3.2 presents scores on the most important factors, according to that monitor: availability

Table 3.1   Strong urban economic profile based on deep structural conditions (grey bars: relatively good position).*

Urban region	Known as established international political and economic decision-making centre	Internationally known as strong historical centre for education, government and commerce	Known as strong high-tech centre or early service centre where manufacturing industry was never dominant
Amsterdam			
Barcelona			
Dublin			
Munich			
Helsinki			
Budapest			
Milan			
Riga			
Sofia			
Leipzig			
Toulouse			
Poznan			
Birmingham			

Source: ACRE reports 2.1–2.13 (http://acre.socsci.uva.nl/results/reports.html).
* The evaluation of deep structural conditions was made by the experts of the ACRE local research teams; the emphasis was made on a relative position of a certain urban region within the whole group of selected areas.

Table 3.2   Strong urban economic profile based on contemporary conditions 2007 (overall score and four most important factors).

Urban region	Position in top 30 (rankings within the selected cities)	Easiest access to markets	Best qualified staff	Best external transport links	Best quality telecommunications
Amsterdam	1	1	2	1	2
Barcelona	1	4	5	3	6
Dublin	4	6	6	6	5
Munich	2	3	1	2	1
Helsinki	7	8	7	–	3
Budapest	6	7	8	–	–
Milan	3	2	3	5	7
Riga	–	–	–	–	–
Sofia	–	–	–	–	–
Leipzig	–	–	–	–	–
Toulouse	–	–	–	–	–
Poznan	–	–	–	–	–
Birmingham	5	7	4	4	4

Source: European Cities Monitor 2007.

of qualified staff, access to markets, quality of telecommunications and transport links. Amsterdam and Munich seem to have the best scores on these most important factors. The reason why Barcelona has a high overall score is mainly because Barcelona has a very attractive tax climate and offers high-quality and low-priced office space. Cities including Toulouse and the eastern European cities, Sofia, Poznan and Riga, do not reach high scores in this ranking. In terms of access to markets and external transport links Amsterdam stands out. This is related to the city's position in air traffic. After London, Paris and Frankfurt, Amsterdam has the most extensive international hub function in European and worldwide air traffic and these four 'hubs' clearly distinguish themselves from the rest. However, most of the eastern European cities have constructed new terminals and new airports recently (Sofia, Riga, Budapest), and this may bring them into positions that are comparable to many large western European cities. The eastern European cities may also quickly catch up in terms of quality of staff – the high level of education in eastern European states suggests this – although out-migration of highly educated people also undermines it. Strongly industrialised cities in eastern and western Europe, including Birmingham and Barcelona, are challenged to re-train their former industrial workforce and to provide new opportunities for migrant labour.

Based on these more contemporary attributes, it appears that opportunities are best for Amsterdam and Munich, followed by a group consisting of Barcelona, Milan, Dublin, Birmingham, Budapest, Helsinki and Toulouse. Leipzig seems to lead the other eastern European cities.

The chapters to come

What determines the capacity of cities to reinvent themselves and to turn towards the creative knowledge economy? The pragmatic answer is that each city shows a singular evolution but, at the same time, tendencies can be gathered into families. Any gathering is obviously arbitrary, since the idea of 'development pathway' itself aims at taking particular histories in their complexity; and it would be very risky to consider the groupings we have made as the only possible ones. In the following four chapters we have grouped cities in order to give prominence to the most important dimensions and differences in the pathways of the cities we discuss. In Amsterdam, Munich and Milan, the recent economic developments towards creative knowledge can be seen as deeply embedded in a rather linear process. Despite obvious differences in the evolution, structure and initial orientation of their economies, the role played over two centuries by culture in their life was conducive to an extremely fast 'creative and knowledge turn', having posed the basis for quick economic change in the post-industrial era. Their geographical position in the central part of the most developed and urbanised region of the European Union (EU) explains a lot of their recent economic performance, and this is also an important argument for grouping these cities in a single chapter.

The cases of Birmingham, Barcelona and Dublin pose the question of the influence of critical decisions that were taken in a much more recent past when compared with the long cumulative processes that led to the recent development of Milan, Munich or Amsterdam. For different reasons, each of these three cities had to 'reinvent itself': Birmingham facing a deep industrial crisis after the disastrous 1970s; Barcelona trying to build a structured development strategy after the Franco regime disappeared, on the basis of new political rights and the 'autonomies' within Spain; and Dublin, a long established capital city and cultural and educational centre at last developing, on the basis of political decisions of the Central State, a pro-business policy (in the context of integration in the EU market) which led to the speedy development of various service activities of high level.

Major institutional change was of critical importance for all cities that were for about 40 years a part of Socialist Europe. The forced transformation of their economies in the late 1940s destroyed much of their previous ties and networks (Riga, Budapest, Poznan), led to rather artificial industrialisation (Sofia) and, in the case of Leipzig entrepreneurs, destroyed the leading position they had built up in some German economic sectors. Could these breaks to 'normal' evolution be compensated in the aftermath of the fall of communist regimes? The 'return to Europe' *de facto* revived much of the geographical assets of Poznan or Budapest; Riga benefitted again from its position in the Baltic region; Sofia, as the major economic, scientific and cultural centre in Bulgaria, was a leader in its changing economy and could adapt quickly to new conditions – much of the evolution and transformation of the Bulgarian capital is due to the free functioning of the economy and the initiatives of entrepreneurs. In the meantime, Leipzig faced a difficult situation, both demographically and economically, and could not regain its previous economic orientation, despite heavy investments by the Federal State. In such a case, it was of critical importance to define an elaborate strategy aiming at establishing a new economic base and using new ideas and concepts, such as the promotion of the creative knowledge economy.

The last chapter of this section refers to Helsinki and Toulouse. One would not spontaneously compare the Finnish capital with the fourth French city. However, both cities experienced a late industrial development from economies that were for a long time linked to traditional sectors. Surprisingly, their development model changed quite quickly towards a knowledge economy and in both cases strategic decisions by government played a critical role. Their industrial activity now relies on global markets (ICT in Helsinki, Automatics, Space and Aeronautics in Toulouse) and on the presence of a highly skilled workforce. This last factor reminds us again of the importance of long-term processes. Whatever groupings of cities are used the explanation for the particular nature of the creative and knowledge-based sectors that have emerged in cities is affected by a longer history – in all cases local characteristics that were the outcomes of previous patterns of development are identifiable influences. The new economy reflects legacies that themselves could have been shaped by various classical or other influences on economic development or could have been driven by early development policies – long before the idea itself of the 'creative knowledge economy' was formulated.

References

Boschma, R.A. and R. Martin (2007) Editorial: Constructing an evolutionary economic geography. *Journal of Economic Geography*, 7 (5): 537–548.

Didelon, C., C. Grasland and Y. Richard (eds) (2008) *Atlas de l'Europe dans le monde*. Paris: La Documentation française, 264 p.

European Cities Monitor 2007. London: Cushman and Wakefield.

Hall, P. (2004) Creativity, culture, knowledge and the city. *Built Environment*, 30 (3): 256–258.

Musterd, S. and O. Gritsai (2009) Creative and knowledge cities: Development paths and policies from a European perspective. *Built Environment*, 35 (2): 165–180.

Sewell, W.H. (1996) Three temporalities: Towards an eventful sociology. In: T. McDonald (ed.), *The historic turn in human sciences*, pp. 245–280. Ann Arbor: The University of Michigan Press.

Wallerstein, I. (1974) *The modern world-system*, vol. 1. New York: Academic Press.

4

Stable Trajectories Towards the Creative Knowledge City? Amsterdam, Munich and Milan

Anne von Streit, Marco Bontje and Elena dell'Agnese

Introduction

Munich, Milan and Amsterdam are leading regions for the creative knowledge economy in Europe. As was suggested in Chapter 3, they are cities that might be expected to become creative knowledge cities. In contrast to the other cities discussed in Chapters 5–7, they neither experienced major political and economic 'ruptures' nor did they have to 'reinvent' themselves completely. Their common and most characteristic feature is their rather stable development which is more characterised by incremental than radical change. We argue that this stability is one explanation for the current success of these regions in the creative knowledge industries. By stability we mean, first, that the cities never had to break completely with their past and, second, that they were constantly able to respond to economic change. They seemed to have kept the right balance between stability and inertia. We contend that five factors have played a major role in this respect.

First, the three cities have a long tradition as centres of power, culture and trade and they are national and international economic decision-making centres. Second, Milan, Munich and Amsterdam are associated with small firm development and show a long-run regional diversity. Third, concerning their economic base, heavy manufacturing has never been a dominating sector in Amsterdam and Munich and it has only played a relevant role in Milan for a short period of time. Fourth, the three cities share a good location as nodes of relevant communication networks, which have played a meaningful role in their development. Fifth and finally, all three cities are internationally known as historical–cultural centres with a preserved urban core.

We will mostly use a historical perspective to analyse the conditions that appear to have played a significant role in developing the regions as they are. We understand path dependency in the way that the economic landscape inherits the legacy of its own past industrial and institutional development and that this history can exert a major influence in conditioning its future development and evolution (Martin and Sunley, 2006). At the same time not only history matters but also place matters; many basic mechanisms that make for path dependence have a local dimension in their form and operation. Consequently, path dependence can be seen as a process that is locally contingent and locally emergent and to a large extent place dependent.

Although a path dependency perspective often explains the different potential of cities or urban regions, most analysis hardly goes beyond the description of historical processes. To become more analytical we want to focus on several concrete dimensions: the economic dimension, the socio-demographic dimension, the institutional dimension as well as events and people who had a significant impact on regional development.

The first part of this chapter is concerned with the economic base and the creative knowledge economy of the three cities. The second and main part involves a comparison of the types of development paths the three cities have followed over their history and this is followed by a synthesis and conclusion.

The economic base and the creative knowledge economy

The economic base of an urban agglomeration is decisive for its transition into a creative knowledge city. In economic terms, the city regions of Munich, Milan and Amsterdam belong to the most profitable and most advanced regions in Europe. Their economic strength is reflected in their relatively high gross domestic product (GDP) per capita (see Chapter 1, Figure 1.1) and in their low unemployment rates (Table 4.1). Nevertheless, they have remarkably different economic profiles.

The Munich region occupies a leading economic position in Europe with both purchasing power and GDP per capita among the highest of the continent. Today almost one-third of the whole GDP of Bavaria is generated in the Munich region. In 2007 this was almost €50,000 per capita and Munich had the lowest unemployment rate of all German metropolitan regions.

There are 1.56 million employees in the region of Munich and compared with Milan it has more employees in the tertiary sector: three-quarters of all employees who make social insurance contributions were working in

Table 4.1 Basic economic indicators of the three metropolitan areas/city regions.

	Amsterdam	Milan	Munich
Unemployment rate	6.1% (2006)	3.9% (2008)	5.7% (2007)
Employment in services	85% (2005)	60.2% (2008)	74.5% (2007)
Employment in manufacturing	14% (2005)	34% (2008)	25% (2007)

Source: Planungsverband Äußerer Wirtschaftsraum München, 2008; Statistisches Landesamt Bayern, 2009; Dienst Onderzoek en Statistiek, 2008; Istituto Tagliacarne, 2007; Assolombarda, 2009.

services and one-quarter in manufacturing. A disproportionate number of employees work in knowledge-intensive business to business services, such as consultancy and planning – and these activities generated most new jobs in recent years. Nevertheless, manufacturing continues to account for almost a quarter of jobs in the Munich region (LH München, 2009). These jobs are, however, mostly in high-technology industries which are R&D intensive (Sternberg and Tamásy, 1999).

About 28.5 per cent of all employees in the Munich region work in the creative knowledge sector that is the focus of this book. In the city of Munich their proportion is 32 per cent and in Bavaria as a whole 18 per cent (Table 4.2).

Only around a quarter of the 305,000 creative knowledge workers are employed in the creative industries, most of them in computer games/ software and electronic publishing as well as publishing. Around 17,000 employees are employed in the audiovisual media branch in the region of Munich. Media has developed into one of the most important sectors of the Munich economy in the last two decades (Biehler et al., 2003). The media industry is mainly made up of small and medium-sized companies, with about 30 large-scale enterprises. In terms of their influence and turnover, these large-scale enterprises can be regarded as 'global players'. Concerning the spatial concentration of the media industry, the media enterprises are almost entirely concentrated in the city of Munich and in the northern, eastern and southern parts of the adjacent Munich county administrative district (*Landkreis München*).

In the Munich region more than 220,000 people work in the knowledge sector. The two biggest categories within the knowledge sector are finance and law and other business services (Table 4.2). After Frankfurt, Munich is Germany's second most important banking centre, the number one place for insurance companies, and also a top location for asset management firms, funds, leasing companies and venture capital firms. The Munich region is also the leading centre for ICT in Germany. In contrast to Amsterdam, the banking and insurance sectors are very much concentrated in the city of Munich, whereas ICT is also found in the wider region.

Table 4.2 Creative and knowledge-intensive industries in city and region of Amsterdam, Milan and Munich.

Sector	City Amsterdam 2005		Amsterdam Region 2005		Province of Milan (metropolitan area) 2001		City Munich 2004		Munich Region 2004	
	N	% workforce	N	% workforce	N	% workforce	N	% workforce	N	% workforce
All sectors	406,139	100	980,372	100	1,790,092	100	663,961	100	1,069,510	100
Creative industries	37,476	9.2	83,701	8.5	250,896	14.0	51,845	8.81	81,875	7.66
ICT	11,100	2.7	28,181	2.7	88,863	5.0	31,352	4.72	47,375	4.43
Financial services	38,683	9.5	54,828	5.6	89,494	5.0	59,866	9.02	76,064	7.11
Law and other business services	36,850	9.1	72,939	7.4	108,707	6.1	56,529	8.51	72,551	6.78
R&D and higher education	11,211	2.8	14,199	1.4	16,009	0.9	14,904	2.24	26,708	2.50
TOTAL creative knowledge	136,362	33.6	275,152	28.1	553,996	30.9	214,496	32.31	304,573	28.48

Source: Bundesagentur für Arbeit, 2004; Istat, 2001; LISA, 2005.

Although around 60 per cent of all jobs in the creative knowledge sectors are still located in the city of Munich, a more recent trend is that knowledge-intensive enterprises as well as headquarters locate themselves in suburbia – especially in the north-eastern part of the Munich region, on the so-called airport axis, where the construction of the new airport in 1992 triggered a dynamic economic development in the north of Munich (Haas and Wallisch, 2008).

In a study of wealth generation among European cities, conducted by *Barclays Private Clients* (2002), Metropolitan Milan (with an estimated 2001 GDP of $110 billion) ranked third among European cities, after London and Paris. That level of economic performance is confirmed at the national level. Metropolitan Milan has long been considered the richest and economically best developed area in the whole of Italy. According to the OECD Territorial Report (2006, p. 22), 'Milan has historically been a leading city (...). On the national scale, Milan is the most densely populated agglomeration and the economic capital of Italy (...). On the regional scale, Milan has driven the growth of Northern Italy and particularly of the Region of Lombardy (...)'. As far as per capita income is concerned, the metropolitan area of Milan[1] is the wealthiest area in Italy, with a per capita annual income of around €30,000, against an average value for Lombardy of €27,000 and a national mean of €20,000 (OECD, 2006, p. 22). According to the aforementioned Barclays report, however, Milan, notwithstanding its third position among the top 10 European cities in total GDP (Munich ranks eighth), is not even included in the top 10 European cities in GDP per capita (while Munich here ranks fourth; Amsterdam did not reach the top 10 of both lists). Employees in the metropolitan area of Milan are 1,880,000 (Assolombarda, 2009). Most of them are at the moment employed in the service sector, while the percentage of employees involved in the industrial sector is constantly decreasing (Table 4.1).

The economic performance is based on a complex and differentiated variety of activities especially in the creative knowledge economy. According to Istat (2001), creative companies – that is those whose main product is creativity – account for 31 per cent of the economic system of the metropolitan area of Milan in terms of the number of people employed. Milan is the undisputed leader in Italy in the financial sector. Some of the most important Italian and foreign banks, financial holdings and insurance companies are located there, together with the headquarters of major companies and the Milan Stock Exchange (Italy's gateway to the international capital market). Milan is famous for sectors such as design and fashion; of about 2400 studios or small firms working in the field of design in Italy,

---

[1] The OECD Territorial Report (2006) refers to the former Province of Milan, now split in the two Provinces of Milan and of Monza-Brianza.

about 500 are located in the metropolitan area of Milan, together with more than 50 public and private training centres and schools (Province of Milan, 2008). In fashion, metropolitan Milan hosts brands which are famous all over the world, and a myriad of small enterprises, more than 800 showrooms and some specialist trade fairs. The metropolitan area of Milan is a major centre for media production and advertising and is considered to be the Italian capital of the publishing industry. Milan is also a leader of the biotech industry in Italy, with research centres, scientific and technological parks and medical research laboratories (Province of Milan, 2008).

The Amsterdam Metropolitan Area is currently the most advanced regional economy of the Netherlands. After a serious crisis in the late 1970s and early 1980s, and a brief stagnation between 2000 and 2004, the city region is again among the fastest growing parts of the country in terms of employment growth. The city of Amsterdam still represents the main employment concentration in the city region with about 400,000 jobs, while the city-regional total is close to 1 million. However, since the 1990s, a deconcentration trend has been evident both within the city and at the city-regional level. Within Amsterdam, several office concentrations have emerged at the city edge along the ring road. Outside the city, Schiphol Airport in particular has become a major employment concentration, with almost 60,000 jobs.

The city-regional economy shows major specialisations in the creative knowledge sectors, including the financial sector, commercial services (next to finance also law, accountancy and consultancy), ICT and creative industries.

As Table 4.2 shows, the creative and knowledge-intensive sectors are prominently present in the Amsterdam Metropolitan Area. The city of Amsterdam is the dominant centre of both creative and knowledge-intensive industries within the region. Nevertheless, some important sub-centres should also be mentioned. First, Hilversum has a strong position in media and entertainment. The Dutch public broadcasting system has its roots in Hilversum and still most of the public broadcasting organisations and affiliated facilities and companies are in Hilversum. A division of labour has gradually emerged since the 1990s, in which Hilversum is home to large-scale media companies, while Amsterdam is the preferred location of smaller companies, freelancers and self-employed. This is combined with a specialisation of Hilversum in TV content production (shows, news, series, TV films, etc.) and Amsterdam in the production of commercials (Van der Groep, 2006). Next to this specialised sub-centre, we should mention Haarlem and Almere as important sub-centres in the creative knowledge economy in a more general sense. Within the city of Amsterdam itself, we see a spatial division between creative and knowledge-intensive industries, with creative companies being more concentrated in the inner city, while knowledge-intensive industries have their main concentrations at the city edge at infrastructural nodes.

In comparison, the three city regions can be considered to be among the leading European regions for creative and knowledge-intensive industries. However, they show specialisations in certain sectors (Table 4.2). Whereas the quota of those who are employed in the creative industries in Milan is almost twice as high as in Amsterdam and Munich, the latter two cities show high percentages of employees in the knowledge-intensive industries. The percentage of people employed in R&D is twice as high in Munich as in Milan and Amsterdam.[2] The Amsterdam region has the most service-oriented economy when compared with Milan and Munich. The industrial past of Milan is reflected in continuing high shares of manufacturing. Munich also still has a considerable share of manufacturing but with a specialisation in high-tech industries. Whereas Amsterdam and Munich have a broad specialisation in the creative knowledge economy, Milan is much more specialised in the creative industries. These considerable differences in current economic profile can – at least in part – be explained by common as well as distinctive elements in their development paths.

Development path: roots and current conditions of the creative knowledge economy

We apply the concept of path dependency not only to the development of certain sectors and clusters but also to look at the impacts of political, social and other institutional and organisational structures. Institutions are place-specific and like the economy they tend to inherit the legacy of their past (Martin and Sunley, 2006). Therefore, the role of formal and informal institutions is extremely important for the understanding of relevant forms of entrepreneurial and corporate practices in the field of production, communication and learning – all important conditions for the development of creative and knowledge-intensive industry. Path dependency studies in economic geography also point towards the significance of (unintended or intended) events and the roles of individuals for path creation and reproduction of clusters. It is also important to consider whether the city structure and built environment fit the actual requirements of the work-

---

[2] When comparing the data of the three city regions, it must be taken into account that the data for Munich contains only employees subject to social security contributions – civil servants as well as self-employed are not included. The absolute numbers of people employed in the creative sectors where freelancers are very common are therefore underestimated.

force in the creative knowledge economy. These issues are considered for each city followed by a comparative discussion.

The development path of Munich

Munich's position as an established centre of the knowledge-intensive industry as well as knowledge-intensive services (Krätke, 2007) is the result of relatively recent developments mostly since the 1960s. Before World War II, the city had some light industries and was a regional capital for its mainly agricultural hinterland. Nevertheless, important foundations for Munich's positive economic development after the World War II were laid long before the twentieth century. Munich has been a capital city and administrative centre since the fifteenth century. Being the residence of the Bavarian king and the royal family, the city's economic and cultural development profited from high investment in the arts, architecture and sciences, especially in the nineteenth century. Munich's central function for the whole of Bavaria enhanced theatres, orchestras, museums and other cultural institutions, a broad range of training facilities as well as the cityscape.

Munich's current strength in the knowledge industries and services can be attributed to the existence of numerous clusters classified under high-tech and knowledge-intensive industries (including automotive, ICT, biotechnology, aerospace), the knowledge-intensive service sector (including finance and insurance) and the creative sector (including media). They form the innovative growth poles of the region. According to Sternberg and Tamásy (1999, p. 370), the Munich region 'represents a regional – sectoral, high-technology cluster in the positive regional economic sense: the region and individual firms profit from synergy effects arising from the close networking of R&D-intensive industries. This is the result of highly flexible production and specialisation'. Studies have shown that the clusters not only comprise links among enterprises in the respective sectors but also embrace links to the numerous research and educational institutions in the Munich area, by the networks of SMEs and large enterprises, as well as links to commercialisation protagonists (for the example of microelectronics see Stenke (2002, 2008); for the media sector see Biehler et al., 2003 or Mossig, 2004; for biotechnology see Ossenbrügge and Zeller, 2002).

Which preconditions can be identified for Munich's industrial trajectories? Although it is always difficult to identify causal and preconditioning factors, important legacies of the high-tech and creative industries can be traced back to the nineteenth century when Bavaria was enlarged to become the third state of central Europe after Prussia and Austria under the Napoleonic 'New Order'. With the explicit aim of making Munich a European cultural and scientific centre, the Bavarian kings attracted artists and scientists to the city. The favourable influence of the Bavarian king's patronage of the arts and the sciences as well as Munich's lack of raw materials created the conditions for the development of quality industries and higher value-added production which capitalised on the new technologies and inventions. This tradition of science-oriented industry promoted the establishment of businesses in the field of precision instruments and photographic material (some of them still exist today like ARRI or Rodenstock) as well as the development of special skills in this field and laid the foundation for the city's tradition as a centre of research and the applied science. The relocation of the university to Munich and the founding of the Technical University in the late nineteenth century further stimulated intensive interaction of research and industrial production in the region.

Coming to the more recent past, several factors have influenced the regeneration of the region of Munich after the World War II: the relocation of headquarters, the continuous inflow of qualified workers as well as technology policy measures of the federal and state governments.

The transfer of the Siemens administration and production from Berlin to Munich in 1948 for reasons of military policy and the fear of dismantling after World War II is regarded as the most important entrepreneurial impulse for the development of Munich as a high-tech centre (Castells and Hall, 1994; Sternberg, 1995). First, this relocation created an important nucleus for the allocation of other German and international companies (Häußermann and Siebel, 1987) and, second, it created the path for the microelectronic industry to become the lead industry in the region in the following decades (Sternberg and Tamásy, 1999). Thus, it can be argued that the transfer of Siemens to Munich initiated a new industrial path but only because the Munich region already possessed the absorption capabilities and competences of the industrial base. Major assets were the well-developed scientific sector and universities, the tradition of precision engineering and the lack of older heavy industrial legacy. Furthermore, the number of companies in consumer and investment goods industries was high, and the service sector, which comprised public administration, arts and sciences, the media and financial system, was already well developed in the post-war period (Biehler et al., 1994). The development which followed can be described in terms of circular and cumulative causation. Siemens is a supplier but also an important customer for microelectronic companies. Thus, Siemens as well as other microelectronic companies in the Munich region profit from localisation economies. Another important factor for the development of the strong cluster in microelectronics is the high demand for the products of the electro-technical industry in the region: the federal, state and local authorities, the insurance and banking sector, the automotive and aerospace sector as well as the media companies are major purchasers of the hard- and software products and services (Stenke, 2002). The microelectronics cluster has intensive connections to other modern clusters and that strengthens their innovative potential (Biehler et al., 2003). Although the Munich region experienced a loss of jobs in manufacturing especially in the automotive sector as well as in microelectronics in the 1990s, this loss was more than compensated by a rise of white collar work (management, R&D) in the respective industries. Furthermore, the economic structure became more diversified in the last two decades. This led to a growth in those sectors which show strong connections to microelectronics like the IT sector, software, media and new media. Thus, until now the region of Munich has been capable of responding to change and developing new technological fields and sectors in the knowledge economy on the basis of its traditional industrial structure (Stenke, 2002). The broad specialisation of the Munich region in the knowledge-intensive sectors might be another major asset to promote constant innovation and economic reconfiguration because '(T)he more economically diverse is a region, (...), the more likely it is to contain multiple instances of path dependence' (Martin and Sunley, 2006, p. 412). Compared with other German regions, Munich has one of the highest levels of new firm creation. The diversity of the knowledge-intensive economies offers a wide scope for the creation of new markets (Martin and Sunley, 2006) and the concentration of R&D activities in firms and research institutions lead to spill-over effects (Stenke, 2002). Cultural elements like the high level of entrepreneurial spirit as well as the availability of capital for start-ups in the Munich region also play a major role (Tamásy, 2006).

The dynamic development of the high-tech industries in the south of Germany is also the result of technology policy measures of the federal and state governments (Häußermann and Siebel, 1987). In technology policy, decisions were in favour of the region of Munich in the 1950s and 1960s. Several federal research and development institutions, which were founded at the time, belonged to the field of nuclear and/or armaments research and owed their allocation in Munich indirectly to the influence of the temporary conservative Minister of Defence (1955–1956) and Prime Minister of Bavaria (1978–1988) Franz Josef Strauß (Sternberg, 1995). This is how the development of Munich to a centre of modern high technology – to a 'Municon Valley' – owes its economic success after the mid-1980s in the end to a large extend to technology and defence policy (Castells and Hall, 1994). Nowadays, the Munich region is still very well served by fully or partially state-funded research facilities (BMBF, 2008). Up to the present time, the state of Bavaria and the City of Munich deploy an impressive variety of policies directed at improving entrepreneurship, commercialising knowledge and creating networks of innovation.

One important factor for the knowledge-intensive industries is the comprehensive range of qualified staff and a creative labour pool. Due to the immigration of approximately 150,000, partly highly qualified, ethnic German repatriates and refugees after the World War II, enterprises in Munich could rely on an ample and qualified labour pool (Fritsche and Kreipl, 2003). Furthermore, due to the north-south and later east-west disparities in Germany, Munich constantly profited from highly qualified German migrants up to the present time.

Nowadays, the educational level of the population in Munich is very high compared with other German cities. The city has a large number of knowledge institutions – universities as well as public and semi-public research establishments – and more than 20 per cent of the working population has a university degree (Institut der deutschen Wirtschaft, 2008). The universities with more than 90,000 students and 10,000 academic employees contribute largely to the supply of skilled workers. This broad knowledge base results in the ability of actors in a region to apply new knowledge. An analysis of patent registrations suggests that the region of Munich is one of the most innovative regions in Germany. With 1508 patent registrations per million inhabitants, Munich ranks second in Germany after Stuttgart with 1790 in 2006 (Greif, 2006).

Apart from the good labour market, soft location factors such as arts, culture and landscape (Biehler et al., 1994) also play a role in attracting talent to Munich. The historical cityscape can also be regarded as a soft location factor: Large parts of Munich were destroyed during World War II. After 1945, the City Council of Munich decided in favour of a tradition-oriented reconstruction which preserved its pre-war street layout and aimed at the reconstruction of the historical city centre. Furthermore, unlike other German cities, the cityscape of Munich had not been altered greatly by the industrial development before the destruction in the war. The so-called Munich way combined the rebuilding and preservation of traditional structures with future-oriented planning. The result decisively contributed towards the restoration and preservation of the historical cityscape. One important event for the development of the city as well as the image of Munich was the Olympic Games in 1972. In the course of the Games, ambitious infrastructure projects were accomplished in a short period of time: the first metro stations were opened, a regional railway network was developed and the so-called Middle Ring Road (*Mittlerer Ring*), a circular motorway around the inner city, was opened. Nowadays, the public transport system and bicycle lanes contribute to Munich's image of being a human scale city with a high quality of life.

In the 1980s and 1990s, the nineteenth century districts in particular became the targets of urban renewal strategies. Artists and other members of the cultural industries profited from the renewal strategies as those quarters became the preferred places to work and live for these groups; and they were important actors in the gentrification process. Up to the present several sub-sectors of the cultural industries like designers, film production, architects, publishers and new media firms are concentrated in those inner city districts. Due to gentrification processes in the inner city and as there are almost no industrial wastelands from former periods to be found within the city limits, Munich has a lack of sites available for artistic experimentation and less profitable businesses in the creative industries. Thus, the high rent levels and high cost of living which are a direct consequence of the economic success of the city in the knowledge-intensive industries pose major problems for less affluent professional groups.

The development path of Milan

Milan is, 'of course, famous for its fashion houses, with names such as Armani, Versace and Valentino' (TimesOnLine, 2009). We could add that Milan is also famous for its soccer teams, the theatre La Scala and the international furniture design fair called *Salone del Mobile*, which attracts more than 300,000 visitors every year. But the city is not only fashion, soccer and design; it is home to advertising agencies, publishers and a large number of telecommunication companies, including the media empire of the Mediaset group and a big cluster of smaller firms in the same sector. It hosts seven universities and many other research establishments. Moreover, the city past as manufacturing centre, hosting companies such as Alfa Romeo and Pirelli, but also industries producing chemicals, machinery, pharmaceuticals and plastics, has left a tradition in R&D activities that can partly explain the role of Milan as 'the pillar of Italy in high-tech-knowledge intensive activities, both in manufacturing and service sectors' (OECD, 2006, p. 32).

Milan has long tradition as a historic city and centre of education and learning, innovation and entrepreneurship. Indeed, Milan has been a prosperous city and a cultural centre for many centuries. As applies to Amsterdam and Munich, the city enjoys a strategic location at the crossing point of European trade routes; perhaps, the first stone of its success consists in being a node (Bassetti, 2005), the crossing point between the transalpine axis of communication and the road network developed along one of the most important crossroads in the history of Europe, the isthmus connecting Genoa to Venice (Gottmann, 1978). Since the Roman times when Milan was called Mediolanum ('the one that is in between'), this favourable location, between the Alps and the prosperous plains of the Po, has propelled the development of the city.

In the late Middle Ages, when the city had gained its political independence, its location at the intersection of several major transportation routes was again a start-up for success. Together with other independent cities of Northern Italy, such as Florence and Venice, Milan developed an intense commercial network connecting Asia, the Mediterranean and northern Europe. Merchants traded not only spices, dyes and silks but also cloth, silver and armour. The richest ones acted sometimes as bankers, making capital available to be spent for other enterprises. The abundance of money created a market for luxury goods. In this way, new stones were placed along the development path of Milan not only as a centre for trade and financial activities but also as a place renowned for fashion. In those years, wool manufacture and silk production established themselves as the most important sector of the regional economy, setting a tradition of skilled artisans, with an expertise in the making of luxury products and textiles, that was going to last.

If the basis of the future development of Milan as a fashion capital can be seen in the traditions of the local textile industry, the role of Milan as a cultural city has its foundations in the Renaissance, when Milan hosted one of the most glittering courts of the time. By then, together with the Dukes' patronage, private capital accumulated by the landed aristocracy and the local merchants supported political and cultural achievements, and attracted artists such as Leonardo da Vinci. At the end of the fifteenth century, 'the city in between' had already acquired a class of merchants and bankers, capable of handling money, and a number of architects, artists and intellectuals, capable of spending it. Again, the tradition was sustained, notwithstanding a long period of political and economic stagnation in the seventeenth century, marked by the Spanish domination, climate deterioration ('the Little Ice Age') and the plague. Only in the eighteenth century, because of the subsidies offered by the new rulers, the Austrians, new textile industries started developing in the city, and in the vast hinterland around it. By then, the region's agriculture was also modernised, with a massive conversion to corn and rice cultivation providing new staples to the rising population. Again, the role of the merchants and landowners was relevant, not only from an economic point of view but also from a cultural one. At the end of the century (1778) La Scala was opened, the Opera House bound to become one of the most celebrated theatres in the world, and more than 40 newspapers were published in the city (while Rome, Venice and Naples published only 10 each), making Milan 'the press capital of Italy' (Hibberd, 2008). In the nineteenth century, because of the large class of well-to-do business and professional people living in the city (and consuming culture), Milan was already a thriving cultural market. Musicians flocked to La Scala from all over Europe, printers, publishers and writers moved to Milan from the rest of Italy, political journalism flourished. Alessandro Manzoni, who lived in Milan and published *The Betrothed* in 1827, was one of the first Italian writers actually gaining money from their work. In 1876, the *Corriere della Sera* was founded in Milan, the newspaper that was going to rule the Italian mediascape throughout the twentieth century; in the same period, publishing firms such as Hoepli, Treves and Ricordi, and later Mondadori e Rizzoli, based their headquarters in Milan. By the turn of the century, the development path of the city towards its future role of media capital had been laid down, stone by stone.

In the twentieth century, the presence of some of the most important Italian publishers (at the beginning of the 1950s, 200 of 400 Italian publishing enterprises were located in Milan) helped the city in establishing its leadership in the media sector. The turning point in the history of Milan as media city must be set in the 1970s, when State control over the Italian broadcasting system was broken by the appearance of the first commercial radios and TVs. A grass-root phenomenon, private radios and TVs were, at the beginning, small private enterprises, mushrooming along the entire peninsula. Soon, many of them started networking, turning their local audiences into national ones, and the big publishing groups located in Milan started buying them. In a few years, the first nationwide TV network, Canale 5, bought also its main competitors, Italia 1 (1982), and Rete 4 (in 1984), establishing a Milan-based company, called Fininvest (now Mediaset), which first gained control over most of the national system of commercial TVs (Ortoleva, 1996) and later became one of the global media giants.

Other developments of Milan as an intensive knowledge and creative economy centre can partly be linked to the city's economic past. For instance, the massive industrial development experienced by Milan in the first half of the twentieth century also promoted R&D activities. At the same time, the growth of a vast industrial sector in the suburbs of the city, the concentration of banks and financial institutions in the city centre, the rise of a commercial sector and the opening of the Fiera, put Milan in a privileged position in Italy. The economic weight of Milan reinforced the emblematic image of the city as the moral capital of Italy, which started from the Expositions of 1881 and 1906. In 1923, the Triennale was set up, a design museum and events venue hosting exhibitions to highlight contemporary Italian design and emphasising the relationship between art and industry. The rising importance of Triennale gave local designers a stage. In the 1950s Milan was one of the most flourishing centres for design worldwide (Foot, 2001), and also the favourite city for advanced industrial sectors and for design-based production, a specialisation supported by the presence of high-level design schools. Within the fashion system, the predominance of Milan over other Italian cities was settled by the 1970s and these years saw the debut of Giorgio Armani who showed in Milan. The sector had an absolute success, due to its geographical position and its strong links with foreign markets, but also, most importantly, the proximity, both geographically and for the established commerce, to the long tradition of silk production, wool and cotton weavers in Lombardy. The rise of many industrial design companies, the success of the Triennale and the image of the city as a good base for design and innovation, have made Milan the place-to-be for the design of clothes, too. Moreover, private infrastructures allowed for the provision of services essential to the fashion industry and less available in other Italian cities: from photographers to drivers, to studios and model agencies. Thanks to its long established history as 'the journalistic capital of the peninsula', Milan is also the centre for the fashion publishing industry, and for the advertisement industry.

Finally, Milan has recently developed a biotechnology cluster. Following an OECD report (2006), Italy ranks fifth in EU-15 (plus Switzerland) in terms of the number of biotechnology organisations. It has been calculated that Lombardy alone concentrates 63 per cent of Italian biotechnology firms, which are mainly located within the metropolitan area of Milan.

If the fashion industry shows a clear connection with the local tradition in the textile industry, and the media production is openly dependent on the long established supremacy of Milan in the publishing industry, the biotechnology sector may appear as less connected with the city's past. But this is not true: indeed, major pharmaceutical multinational groups used to establish their research centres in Milan to take advantage of its historic specialisation in pharmaceuticals. When these multinational groups relocated their activities out of Milan during the early 1990s, the Italian government incited them to allow the small firms that used to be their suppliers to continue using the registered patents and to carry on with research. The government also provided financial aid to support the survival of small firms. Moreover, the universities located in the city have generated highly skilled researchers and workers. Some of these initiatives have been successful in creating university spin-off firms. Eventually, the local health care sector provides the downstream market for the cluster. So, factors that can be identified as important for Milan's development path include:

- Position in relation to transport and communication in Europe, infra-structure and natural resources.
- Design and manufacturing traditions and the development of clusters particularly related to the textile and fashion industry, furniture and design.
- A long tradition as a centre for literary and artistic innovation including commercial broadcasting.

Unfortunately, these forces of attraction seem to be slowing down. At the national scale, Milan is becoming more and more economically inaccessible (increasing housing prices and cost of living) and environmentally problematic (high level of pollution). But also the competitiveness of Milan metropolitan area is losing ground compared with other European cities. This leads us to question if Milan is still attractive to creative groups and knowledge-intensive activities, or if the city is going to lose its historical drive, due to global competition and the shortfall of innovation capacity?

The development path of Amsterdam

The main strengths of the Amsterdam Metropolitan Area as a creative knowledge region are in finance and related business services, media, advertising, higher education, art and art trade. The development path of Amsterdam is rather curious: the city region took its most decisive steps towards the status of 'world city *avant la lettre*' in the late sixteenth and early seventeenth centuries; then slowly faded away and stagnated in the eighteenth and early nineteenth centuries; and revitalised in the second half of the nineteenth century. The emergence and subsequent ups and downs of most of the economic sectors just mentioned can clearly be linked to the overall ups and downs of the city region.

The Amsterdam city region, and especially Amsterdam as its dominant centre, enjoyed its best years during the Dutch 'Golden Age', roughly covering the first half of the seventeenth century. The fast accumulation of wealth and economic power in this era was mainly linked to colonial trade. The Dutch Republic emerged as a world power with resource-rich colonies in Southeast Asia and the Caribbean. By that time Amsterdam had already become the largest city of the Dutch Republic (Roegholt, 1997), and it grew into a 'world city' as the country's main hub of colonial trade. The Dutch cleverly linked the exploitation of their colonies to the introduction of several innovations in finance and trade. The East Indies Company (VOC, founded 1602) claimed a monopoly on European trade with Asia. In retrospect it can be seen as the world's first multinational and the first company with shareholders. In 1621, the West Indies Company (WIC) was established to perform a similar role in Dutch trade with the Americas and the west coast of Africa. Amsterdam was home to the headquarters of both VOC and WIC and to the largest part of their fleet. It was also the centre of the Dutch financial, insurance and legal service sector. Other innovative institutions were the Stock Exchange (1611), the Money Exchange (1609) and the introduction of giro bank transfers (Van Stipriaan, 2006).

Next to colonial trade and economic innovation, a third important growth impetus came from migrants. The Dutch 'Golden Age' coincided with the war against Spain. In 1578, Amsterdam joined the camp of Dutch resistance against Spanish rule. Soon afterwards the city would profit from this switch of sides. The Flemish city of Antwerp, a direct competitor of Amsterdam, was conquered by the Spanish. Antwerp's harbour was then blocked by the Dutch, and the combination of economic demise and religious oppression encouraged many to migrate to cities in the liberated northern Netherlands like Amsterdam and Haarlem. These migrants included rich merchants, experienced money traders, skilled textile workers and talented artists (Mak, 2005). Examples of sectors that took off with significant migrant influence were the textile industry, diamond manufacturing and trade, and an early version of what we would now call creative industries, especially in visual arts, in cities like Amsterdam and Haarlem. The city became a favourite living and working place for artists, especially painters, and scientists. While many artists only reached world fame (long) after their death and most were not rich, they generally combined artistic work with portrait assignments for the Amsterdam merchant elite. So rather than 'l'art pour l'art', we could consider the painters in Amsterdam, Haarlem and other Dutch cities as part of a cultural industry (Kloosterman, 2004). Science was also strongly related to the Amsterdam merchant and bourgeois elite. The *Athenaeum Illustre* was founded in 1632 by the Amsterdam city government, in which the richest and most influential families of the city (most often traders rather than noblemen) were represented. This institution would eventually become the University of Amsterdam.

The interrelatedness of the emergence of Amsterdam as a centre of trade and finance on the one hand, and the creative industries and higher education on the other, is clear: the artists and art producers earned their living with assignments for the traders and merchants, who also were the main sponsors of academic education. We should not forget to mention a fourth important explanatory factor of Amsterdam's economic success: the strong local autonomy and tolerant local regime. The relatively loose reign of the Dutch 'regent' combined with the importance of international trade and the relatively unproblematic influx of migrants has granted Amsterdam a reputation as a haven of liberalism and tolerance (Olsen, 2000; Mak, 2005). The civic elite of Amsterdam could largely decide about its own local affairs, and also largely determined the physical and economic development of Amsterdam's hinterland.

The Dutch Golden Age faded out towards the end of the seventeenth century. The Dutch Republic rapidly lost international status, and Amsterdam and its hinterland somehow lost their innovative edge. Roughly between 1750 and 1850, we could almost speak of a 'lock-in' situation. The city region and especially its core city Amsterdam almost became an open air museum in various respects. The lack of economic innovation combined with a lack of political innovation, continuous local and national power struggles, the problematic sea access of Amsterdam's harbour, and a lack of hinterland compared to rivals like London and Hamburg (Mak, 2005). Towards the end of the nineteenth century, however, Amsterdam and its region managed to return to a growth path. The main reason of new growth and prosperity was again colonial trade. Amsterdam's sea access was dramatically improved and the sea route to the East Indies was shortened significantly. The exploitation of the colonies was intensified. Connected to this Amsterdam strengthened its specialisation in commercial services like finance, insurance, legal services and logistics (Wagenaar, 2003). The founding of a second university, the Free University, was an important addition to Amsterdam's strength as a centre of knowledge. Important cultural institutions were added in these decades too: Rijksmuseum (the podium for the Dutch 'masters' of the 'Golden Age'), Stedelijk Museum (for the modern arts) and Concertgebouw (concert hall for classical music). A striking parallel with the 'Golden Age' is that again, trade, arts and creative industries and higher education flourished in mutual interrelatedness. Another parallel is a rather liberal and tolerant local policy regime enabling market-driven development and citizen initiatives.

Amsterdam reached its maximum population size around 1960 with almost 900,000 inhabitants. Between the early 1960s and mid-1980s, however, mass suburbanisation reduced Amsterdam's population size with more than 250,000. Suburbanisation and the Dutch new town policy transformed the Amsterdam Metropolitan Area into a polycentric urban area with several sub-centres (Musterd et al., 2006). The 1970s and early 1980s were a difficult time for the Amsterdam Metropolitan Area, and most of all for its core city. Amsterdam was a problematic city characterised by mass unemployment, large parts of the city in a bad state of maintenance (especially the nineteenth-century neighbourhoods), and frequent violent confrontations of police and government with civic resistance groups. The local planners in the 1960s and 1970s wanted to modernise Amsterdam with a new CBD, highways across the city centre and a subway network between city centre and outer areas. Mass citizen protest against the demolition of inner city neighbourhoods contributed to a radical turn in urban renewal policy: demolition and large-scale new construction were replaced by renovation and small-scale new building fitting better in the surrounding built environment. This civic resistance movement and the subsequent squatter movement in the 1980s have contributed significantly to the preservation of Amsterdam's historic city centre, and therewith probably also to its spectacular recovery in the 1980s and 1990s (Terhorst and Van de Ven, 2003). Next to the results of urban renewal, this recovery was also encouraged through the re-development of former manufacturing and harbour sites. The inner city, the nineteenth-century neighbourhoods and the re-developed former harbour area have become the favourite working environment for Amsterdam's creative industries in the 1990s and this concentration is still present today.

Next to the historic city centre, the most important city-regional growth engines in recent years are Schiphol Airport and the South Axis. Offering employment to almost 60,000 people, one of the largest shopping centres of the city region and several hotel and conference facilities, Schiphol has grown from an airport into an airport city (Van Wijk, 2007). The South Axis along the A10 ring road is destined to become Amsterdam's new CBD. Amsterdam has formed a public–private partnership with the national government, multinational banks, the Free University, the Dutch Railways and other private partners to turn the South Axis into a commercial centre of international importance (Majoor, 2008). Additional new sub-centres of the Amsterdam Metropolitan Area have emerged at other multimodal traffic nodes. Moreover, Almere is growing fast from a new town with mainly suburban traits towards a complete city, offering almost 60,000 jobs and an increasing array of urban retail, cultural and leisure facilities.

An important recent change in the institutional dimension is the improvement in regional co-operation. Until very recently, Amsterdam and its neighbours were mainly competing and hardly co-operating for inhabitants, companies and infrastructure. While attempts to formalise city-regional co-operation largely failed in the 1990s, the informal meeting and negotiation platform Amsterdam Metropolitan Area seems to have contributed to a breakthrough in the early twenty-first century. At the same time, the strong influence of the 'Schiphol growth coalition' pushing growth of the airport forward continuously creates tensions putting the city region's sustainable development at stake. Looking at the socio-demographic dimension of path dependency, two striking recent parallel developments are the growing socio-economic differentiation between parts of the city of Amsterdam and the declining socio-economic differentiation between Amsterdam and the rest of the city region. The traditional dichotomy between richer suburbs and poorer city no longer holds, but at the same time, tendencies towards polarisation between the core city's richest and poorest parts have become apparent. Still, Amsterdam is a city where socio-economic differentiation is relatively modest compared with most other leading creative knowledge centres in Europe.

Development paths: a synthesis and conclusion

Tables 4.3–4.5 summarise the key dimensions of the pathways followed by each of the three cities and their urban regions.

Although each of the cities has a unique character, some common elements in their respective histories can also be discovered. The three urban regions are all characterised by a long but more or less stable development. There were periods of growth and active development and there were periods of decline or stagnation; however, these periods were not the same for each of the cities. In the longer run, these cities have been able to build upon the past and to reorganise themselves and re-position themselves in

Table 4.3 Dimensions of path-dependent development of the Munich region.

Dimension	
Economic	Long tradition as a political and cultural centre
	Encouragement of scientists and artists by the Bavarian kings in the nineteenth century
	Tradition of precision engineering
	Well connected globally, especially by air
Events, decisions	Relocation of headquarters to the Munich region after World War II
	Technology policy measures in the twentieth century
	Construction of the new airport in 1992 in the north of Munich
Built environment	Tradition-oriented reconstruction after World War II
	Historical cityscape
	Infrastructure projects in the course of the Olympic Games (1972)
	Gentrification and urban renewal strategies in nineteenth century areas (1980s and 1990s)
Institutions	Entrepreneurial spirit
	Broad knowledge base: universities, research institutions
	Growth coalition between Bavarian State government and city government: modernisation and investment policy
Socio-demographic	Constant influx of qualified and skilled workers

Table 4.4 Dimensions of path-dependent development of the metropolitan area of Milan.

Dimension	
Economic	Strategic position in Europe Long tradition as centre of trade, finance and culture Long tradition in the manufacture of textile and of luxury goods (fifteenth century) Encouragement of scientists and artists by the Sforza dukes in the fifteenth century Economic innovations: banking (early fifteenth century) Heavy industries in the first half of the twentieth century and massive deindustrialisation in the 1980s and 1990s
Events, decisions	The opening of La Scala 1778 The Expositions of 1881 and 1906, the opening of the 'Fiera campionaria' in 1920, and of the new pole in 2005 The Triennale, 1923 The founding of Fininvest (now Mediaset) by, 1978
Built environment	Tradition oriented Historical cityscape Gentrification of nineteenth century areas (1980s and 1990s) New advanced tertiary functions for heavy industries areas of Bovisa and Bicocca (1990s–present)
Institutions	Trading and entrepreneurial spirit Bourgeois elite Universities
Socio-demographic	Constant influx of qualified and skilled workers

a way that allowed them to join others in a new era of social and economic development. It is also clear that all have gathered wealth somewhere in the past and were important power centres, well connected with wider networks. All are characterised by important financial institutions and all have a history as being an important cultural centre. Historical core cities and entrepreneurial spirits, as well as the early presence of universities, were also 'returning' elements in the descriptions of the selected pathways. Key developments and events of a more unique character could also be shown in each of the pathways and some of these may actually have triggered long-term periods of affluence. All of the cities dealt with have also been able to establish multidimensionality, or in other words multiple layers of development, which could be re-capitalised on in later periods. This includes the presence and maintenance (or re-development) of historical cityscapes and gentrification of nineteenth century areas in the cities in particular.

The comparison has shown that all three city regions have been capable of responding to change and to develop new technological fields and sectors on the basis of their traditional skills and economic structure. Nevertheless, the cities differ in respect to their historical industrial development: whereas Amsterdam and Munich were more or less bypassed by earlier phases of

Table 4.5 Dimensions of path-dependent development of the Amsterdam metropolitan area.

Dimension	
Economic	Colonial trade (seventeenth to mid-twentieth centuries)
	Economic innovations: stock market, multinational company, money exchange (early seventeenth century)
	Long tradition as centre of culture and finance
	Well connected globally, especially by air
Events, decisions	War with/liberation from Spanish empire (sixteenth/seventeenth century)
	Extension Schiphol Airport 1967
	Changes to urban renewal strategy 1970s
Built environment	Canals (sixteenth century)
	'City as monument' instead of monumental buildings
	Gentrification Jordaan (1970s/1980s) and nineteenth century areas (1990s)
	Re-development old harbour (1980s–present)
	New functions for warehouses, manufacturing and energy complexes (1980s–present)
Institutions	Trading and entrepreneurial spirit (since founding of Amsterdam)
	Reputation of tolerance since late nineteenth century
	Bourgeois elite more influential than monarchy (Dutch Republic and after)
	Colonial trading companies: East Indies Company, West Indies Company (seventeenth/eighteenth century)
	National strategic planning policies: new towns (1960s–1980s), VINEX (1990s)
	Regional governance problematic until recently
	Influence of the 'Schiphol growth coalition' (since 1980s)
Socio-demographic	History as immigrant city (since late sixteenth century)
	Recent migration waves: former colonies, Mediterranean, refugees
	Suburbanisation 1960s–1980s, parallel growth of suburbs cities since late 1980s
	Growing socio-economic differentiation within city of Amsterdam
	Declining socio-economic differentiation between core city and city region

the Industrial Revolution, Milan coped with massive deindustrialisation in the 1980s. Amsterdam developed an early service profile and Munich specialised in engineering and high-technology activity as well as service activities. Milan, after being for centuries a centre of trade and cultural economy, in the first part of the twentieth century turned into a heavy manufacturing city, only to focus again on trade and cultural economy activities in recent decades. The historic development of the three city regions is also reflected in the process of structural change towards the creative knowledge economy.

Remarkably, the 'Golden Ages' of the three cities have been in different centuries. Munich was largely unimportant compared with other free cities in the Middle Ages. Milan, which had already been a relevant centre of the Roman Empire, experienced a new economic, cultural and political upturn in the fifteenth century. Amsterdam became an almost 'global' centre in the seventeenth century, whereas Munich's upturn did not start before the nineteenth century. However, in Munich the foundations laid in the nineteenth century were favourable for the specialisation of the city's economy into high-tech industries as well as media. Similarly the long tradition in trading and banking, and also in the production and consumption of luxury goods, has left their marks in the features of contemporary Milan and Amsterdam.

Common characteristics of the three cities are their geographical position in the European core economic area as well as that they have been economic and cultural centres for centuries. The latter has had a decisive impact on their creative economies. Help from the state or government has also been fundamental at least in the case of Milan and Munich. Nowadays, it is the capacity to produce innovation that enables the three cities to keep their role as centres of the creative knowledge economy.

References

Assolombarda (2009) *Andamento del mercato del lavoro. Rapporti e sintesi.* http://www. assolombarda.it/fs/2009624152942_185.pdf (accessed 5 July 2008).

Barclays Private Clients (2002) *May 2002 report.* htttp://news.bbc.co.uk/2/hi/business/ 1978788.stm

Bassetti, P. (2005) *Milano, nodo della rete globale.* Milan: Bruno Mondadori.

Biehler, H., K. Brake and E. Ramschütz (1994) *Standort München. Sozioökonomische und räumliche Strukturen der Neo-Industrialisierung.* München: IMU-Institut.

Biehler, H., J. Genosko, M. Sargl and D. Sträter (2003) *Standort München. Medienwirtschaft und Fahrzeugbau.* Marburg: Schüren Verlag.

BMBF (2008) *Bundesministerium für Bildung und Forschung. Forschung in Deutschland – Forschungslandkarten.* http://www.bmbf.de/de/5355.php (accessed 1 December 2008).

Castells, M. and P. Hall (1994) *Technopoles of the world – The making of 21st century industrial complexes.* London, New York: Routledge.

Dienst Onderzoek en Statistiek (2008) *Amsterdam in cijfers 2008.* Amsterdam: Gemeente Amsterdam, Dienst Onderzoek en Statistiek.

Foot, J. (2001) *Milan since the miracle. City, culture, identity.* Oxford: Berg.

Fritsche, A. and A. Kreipl (2003) Industriestadt München – Eine Nachkriegskarriere. In: G. Heinritz, C.-C. Wiegandt and D. Wiktorin (eds), *Der München atlas,* pp. 160–161. Italien: Emons.

Gottmann, J. (1978) Verso una megalopoli della pianura. padana? In: C. Muscarà (ed.), *Megalopoli mediterranea.* Milano: Franco Angeli.

Greif, S. (ed.) (2006) *Patentatlas Deutschland. Regionaldaten der Erfindertätigkeit.* München: Deutsches Patent-und Markenamt.

van der Groep, R. (2006) *Global change and local challenges towards flexibility in the audiovisual industry: The Dutch case.* Paper presented at the DRUID-DIME Winter PhD Conference, Skoerping, Denmark, 15–17 January 2006.

Haas, H.-D. and M. Wallisch (2008) Wandel des Münchner Flughafens zur 'Airport City'. *Geographische Rundschau,* 60 (10): 32–38.

Häußermann, H. and W. Siebel (1987) *Neue Urbanität.* Frankfurt/Main: Suhrkamp Verlag.

Hibberd, M. (2008) *The media in Italy.* Maidenhead: Open University Press, McGraw-Hill.

Institut der deutschen Wirtschaft (2008) *Deutsche Großstädte im Vergleich. Untersuchung für das Jahr 2007 und den Zeitraum von 2002 bis 2007.* Köln: Institut der deutschen Wirtschaft.

Istat (2001) *Censimento dell'industria e dei servizi 2001.* Milan: Istat.

Istituto Tagliacarne (2007) http://cidel.tagliacarne.it/

Kloosterman, R.C. (2004) Recent employment trends in the cultural industries in Amsterdam, Rotterdam, The Hague and Utrecht: A first exploration. *Tijdschrift voor Economische en Sociale Geografie,* 95 (2): 243–252.

Krätke, S. (2007) Metropolisation of the European economic territory as a consequence of increasing specialisation of urban agglomerations in the knowledge economy. *European Planning Studies,* 15 (1): 1–27.

LH München (2009) *Jahreswirtschaftsbericht 2008.* München: Landeshauptstadt München, Referat für Arbeit und Wirtschaft.

LISA (2005) *Regiomonitor 2005 (database).* Tilburg: LISA.

Majoor, S. (2008) *Disconnected innovations, new urbanity in large-scale development projects: Zuidas Amsterdam, Ørestad Copenhagen and Forum Barcelona.* Delft: Eburon.

Mak, G. (2005) *Een kleine geschiedenis van Amsterdam* (2nd revised edition). Amsterdam, Antwerpen: Atlas.

Martin, R. and P. Sunley (2006) Path dependence and regional economic evolution. *Journal of Economic Geography,* 6 (4): 395–437.

Mossig, I. (2004) Steuerung lokalisierter Projektnetzwerke am Beispiel der Produktion von TV Sendungen in den Medienclustern München und Köln. *Erdkunde,* 58 (3): 252–268.

Musterd, S., M. Bontje and W. Ostendorf (2006) The changing role of old and new urban centers: The case of the Amsterdam region. *Urban Geography,* 27 (4): 360–387.

OECD (2006) *Territorial reviews. Milan, Italy.* Paris: OECD Publications.

Olsen, D. (2000) Urbanity, modernity and liberty. Amsterdam in the seventeenth century. In: L. Deben, W. Heinemeijer and D. van der Vaart (eds), *Understanding Amsterdam. Essays on economic vitality, city life and urban form* (2nd edition), pp. 229–248. Amsterdam: Het Spinhuis.

Ortoleva, P. (1996) A geography of the media since 1945. In: D. Forgacs and R. Lumley (eds), *Italian cultural studies.* Oxford: Oxford University Press.

Ossenbrügge, J. and C. Zeller (2002) The biotech region Munich and the spatial organization of its innovation networks. In: L. Schätzl (ed.), *Technological change and regional development in Europe,* pp. 233–249. Heidelberg: Springer.

Planungsverband Äußerer Wirtschaftsraum München (2008) *Region München 2008. Ausführliche Datengrundlagen.* München: Planungsverband.

Province of Milan, Greater Milan (2008) *Dynamics and excellence in metropolitan Milan.* www.provincia.milano.it/economia

Roegholt, R. (1997) *Amsterdam, a short history.* The Hague: Sdu Uitgevers.

Statistisches Landesamt Bayern (2009) http://www.statistik.bayern.de/daten/intermaptiv/archiv/home.asp?UT=vgr-bip.csv&SP=2

Stenke, G. (2002) *Großunternehmen und innovative Milieus – Das Beispiel Siemens/München.* Köln: Selbstverlag im Wirtschafts-und Sozialgeographischen Institut der Universität zu Köln.

Stenke, G. (2008) Innovationsregion München. Das Geheimnis ihres Erfolges. *Geographische Rundschau,* 60 (10): 24–30.

Sternberg, R. (1995) *Technologiepolitik und high-tech-regionen – Ein internationaler Vergleich.* Berlin: Lit Verlag.

Sternberg, R. and C. Tamásy (1999) Munich as Germany's No. 1 high technology region: Empirical evidence, theoretical explanations and the role of small firm/large firm relationships. *Regional Studies,* 33 (4): 367–377.

van Stipriaan, R. (2006) Amsterdamse branie. De geest van Andries Bicker. In: M. Hageman, N. Huizinga, J. Krom, D.J. Rouwenhorst, B. Speet and E. Wouthuysen (eds), *De 25 dagen van Amsterdam,* pp. 5–23. Zwolle: Waanders.

Tamásy, C. (2006) Region München: Was ist das Geheimnis der Gründungsaktivität? In: R. Sternberg (ed.), *Deutsche Gründungsregionen,* pp. 25–49. Berlin: Lit Verlag.

Terhorst, P. and J. van de Ven (2003) The restructuring of Amsterdam's historic city centre. In: S. Musterd and W. Salet (eds), *Amsterdam human capital*, pp. 85–101. Amsterdam: Amsterdam University Press.

TimesOnLine (2009), *Business city guide.* http://www.bcglocations.com/italy/milan/milan_intro.html

Wagenaar, M. (2003) Between civic pride and mass society. Amsterdam in retrospect. In: S. Musterd and W. Salet (eds), *Amsterdam human capital*, pp. 49–66. Amsterdam: Amsterdam University Press.

van Wijk, M. (2007) *Airports as cityports in the city-region. Spatial-economic and institutional positions and institutional learning in Randstad-Schiphol (AMS), Frankfurt Rhein-Main (FRAU), Tokyo-Haneda (HND) and Narita (NRT).* Utrecht: KNAG/Faculteit Geowetenschappen Universiteit Utrecht (Netherlands Geographical Studies No. 353).

5

Reinventing the City: Barcelona, Birmingham and Dublin

Veronica Crossa, Montserrat Pareja-Eastaway and Austin Barber

Introduction

In the last two decades, the management, organisation and governance of cities have undergone important transformations (Hall, 1999). Cities are also facing harsh competition for investment as a result of the hypermobility of capital, the shifting geography of production, and the growth of low-cost, emerging industrial cities, particularly in India, China and Brazil. The determinants of urban competitiveness are complex and dynamic, and include aspects such as availability of highly skilled workers and an attractive fiscal context. As a recent OECD (2006) report on competitive cities argued, it is difficult to disentangle cause and effect in terms of whether economic growth causes urbanisation or whether dynamic urban areas generate economic growth. Indeed, the determinants of city competitiveness are intricate. A central component of urban competitiveness is that cities have had to change themselves from areas of industrial production to cities of mass consumption and services.

One theme emerging within this book is that there are resources and actions that enable cities to make a successful transition and retain competitiveness in a changing global context. Taking the steps that are needed may be easier where certain resources are embedded within the city (e.g. those associated with capital cities and universities) and more difficult where there are legacies in the built environment that are a barrier to adjustment for new activities (e.g. poor infrastructure and dereliction, and contamination associated with previous industrial activity). But in either case, the actions taken by various stakeholders and especially important are the public policy interventions taken by government at different levels.

The three cities considered in this chapter – Barcelona, Birmingham and Dublin – have very different economic, political and social histories, but none has had in the past a strong image as a historical cultural centre comparable with, say, Milan, Munich or Amsterdam. The underlying questions guiding this chapter relate to the process of urban reinvention and the role of public policy within it. Barcelona, Birmingham and Dublin have all attracted attention as cities that have expressly set out to transform their economies, to modernise themselves and to increase their competitiveness and affluence. This chapter considers the background to these more recent changes and discusses key elements in the approach they have adopted to reinventing the city.

Historical context

This work draws on the theoretical insights and assumptions in the literature on path dependency, particularly to the understanding that a city's current economic development path is shaped by its historical conditions associated with economic and social change. The cities explored in this chapter have experienced distinctive historical pathways which help to understand the variation in the current state of affairs of creative and knowledge-intensive industries in different European cities. Both Barcelona and Birmingham share a similar historical characteristic as non-capital cities striving to compete with the centre of political and economic power, Madrid and London, respectively. Dublin, however, has a history of urban primacy in Ireland. Since independence from the UK in the early 1920s, Dublin has stood as the economic, political, social and cultural centre of the country. More importantly perhaps, Barcelona and Birmingham, as opposed to Dublin, have a rich history of industrial development which commenced in the case of Birmingham at the start of the industrial revolution. With industrial growth both cities expanded to absorb adjacent settlements. Simultaneously, population massively increased as a strong demand for workforce was expressed in each city. In the case of Barcelona, the city absorbed many existing towns and villages at the start of the nineteenth century. Simultaneously, the process of industrialisation determined the location of the textiles and engineering factories in this periphery; it was the beginning of the industrial historical tradition of the area. Nowadays, many of these activities have been moved to other centres of the metropolitan area. From then on, Barcelona became an important political, economic and cultural centre in the country. After the immediate period which followed the Civil War (1936–1939), Barcelona and its surroundings experienced a second industrial revolution which attracted many migrants from the rest of Spain until the end of the 1960s. These families, low income and with poor levels of education, located in the periphery of the city, near the industrial fabric and delimiting borders of the city by large housing estates built in a short period of time to give shelter to the newcomers.

While Barcelona's workforce during the nineteenth and twentieth centuries was mainly low skilled, Birmingham's industrial structure was based predominantly on small firms and highly skilled labour. It was associated with inventiveness and innovation and an enormous variety of new products that attracted an international customer base. During the Industrial Revolution, the West Midlands became the pre-eminent manufacturing region of the UK, with a particular focus on metal working. Its geographical location in the middle of the country became an asset as the canal and later rail networks developed around it and brought it to the centre of the national and international economy. It expanded in size to overtake other cities including Bristol, Liverpool and Manchester as the largest city in the UK after London. In the first half of the twentieth century, Birmingham was well placed to benefit from the expansion of consumer-goods industries. Although the rate of population increase slowed in this period, continued industrial expansion and new job opportunities in the Birmingham area encouraged further inward migration, including an influx of workers from the declining heavy industrial areas of Britain.

Unlike Barcelona and Birmingham, Dublin has never been an industrial city. This is primarily because of the traditional importance of agriculture to the national economy and the dominance, until recent decades, of a rural lifestyle ideal. Even in the nineteenth century when many other cities were at the height of their industrial power, the city of Dublin had only two small industrial zones which included the Guinness Brewery. Small industries developed in Dublin, generally as a spin-off of port activity, and included fertiliser factories, chemical works as well as a number of gas-works. Although it has not had a strong history of industrialisation, the city has been established as an important political and economic centre since at least the eleventh century. This role grew in importance over time and Dublin as an established university city and centre of public administration, and government had a long established and significant status among cities in the British Isles.

The trajectory of industrial development

The three cities considered in this chapter have different industrial histories and economic trajectories, and these are summarised in the following sections.

Barcelona

The development of Barcelona has been historically determined by the strategic geographical and political position of the city. Its situation on the coast and its significant harbour meant that Barcelona developed a strong trading role in medieval times, rivalling Italian cities. Its historic role as the capital of Catalonia was, however, diminished by the unification of Spain and it was neither able to maintain its economic influence in the Mediterranean nor benefit from the development of transatlantic trade. Until the beginning of the eighteenth century, the city was in permanent recession. Its trading tradition however supported a solid bourgeoisie and this provided the base for the development of a new textile industry and economic boom in the nineteenth century. The demands of the Catalan bourgeoisie were part of wider cultural movement associated with Catalan nationalism and the recovery of Catalan culture and the enlargement of Barcelona and destruction of the city walls that restricted such enlargement were important parts of their demands. In spite of the reluctance of central government, the demolition of the city walls commenced in 1854 and this was followed by a period of planned expansion for an industrial era with housing, industrial districts and transport including the first railway line in Spain in 1848.

Although political developments meant that it suffered a historical delay in terms of economic transformation, Barcelona and its surrounding region became the main industrial region of Spain. It embraced modern and diverse industrial activity and at the same time managed to consolidate the cultural recovery of Catalonia. A resurgent literature arts and architecture symbolised this change and the distinctive architecture of Gaudi and others are the visible products of this period. The drive of the city and the Catalan bourgeoisie were also evident in two exhibitions in 1888 and 1929 and these further consolidated the growth of the city. The Spanish Civil War and the Franco regime changed the pattern of development and a period of stagnation gave way to economic growth in the 1950s. From this period onwards, the city attracted considerable migration from elsewhere in Spain and housing this population accelerated the growth of the city but without adequate infrastructure and with sub-standard housing.

This history left Barcelona an industrial city, one of the biggest industrial agglomerations of Spain and an essential agent for the Spanish economy in the European context. Barcelona's regional industrial structure is based on its polycentric nature, with a diversified economy overall but with specialised centres in the medium and small cities surrounding Barcelona (Trullén and Boix, 2003). The city of Barcelona represents the hard core of the region, where the creative and knowledge economy plays a leading role, and many other smaller sub-centres like Terrasa, Sabadell o Molins de Rei, are important for the industrial GDP of the region (Figure 5.1).

The diversified industrial fabric of the Barcelona Metropolitan Region (BMR) economy has been the basis for the development and transformation of traditional sectors into creative and knowledge areas of growth. However, the productive model of the region, as in the rest of Spain, was

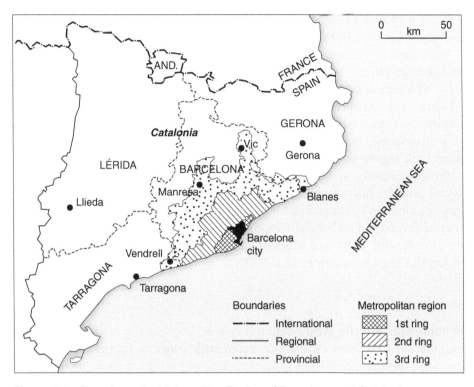

Figure 5.1 Barcelona, the Metropolitan Region of Barcelona and Catalonia.

based on low productivity levels together with poor innovation investments. The construction sector has played a key role in the more recent GDP
growth rate of the country and the region. In fact, while the whole GDP of the
region grew 3 per cent in 2005, agriculture and industry showed a declining growth rate (−2 per cent and −0.5 per cent, respectively), construction
increased by 5.2 per cent and the service sector by 4.1 per cent (Oliver,
2006). Analysis of the BMR shows the stagnation of traditional activities
such as textiles or machinery and technical equipment although their
absolute contribution to GDP remains important. The two main activities
that contribute almost half of the tertiary GDP are services related to public
administration (21.2 per cent) and services to enterprises and real state agencies (26.7 per cent). Until the economic crisis arrived in 2007, the creation
of labour opportunities was mainly in activities which did not require high
qualifications and offered low wages.

Data for the whole province of Barcelona reveal that 63 per cent of total
jobs are in tertiary activities. Since 2003, roughly 3 per cent of total industrial sector jobs have disappeared. The sub-sectors that lost a higher number
of jobs were textiles and electronics. Workers in textile industries decreased
9 per cent in 2004 and 11 per cent in 2005, and the electronics sector lost
5 per cent of jobs every year. In contrast to that, all sub-sectors in services

experienced considerable growth with outstanding increases in transport
and communication, housing related services and services to enterprises.

The region is still one of the main providers of low-technology manufactures
and far from other OECD countries in the provision of dense-knowledge-based
jobs. The region continues to have poor education levels: only 13 per cent
of adults have a degree whereas more than 60 per cent have completed only
compulsory education (IDESCAT, 2006). Consequently, there is a deficit
of skilled labour in Spain, particularly in the BMR. The economic growth of
Barcelona region is sustained to great extent by non-industrial economic
activities, mainly services and construction activities. The construction
sector and the housing market are of huge importance in recent economic
development in Spain and particularly in the BMR. Indeed, Barcelona's history of diversified rather than specialised industry makes it a fertile ground
for the development and strengthening of creative and knowledge-based
industries (Pareja-Eastaway et al., 2007).

Birmingham

Birmingham and the West Midlands rose to become the UK's pre-eminent
manufacturing region during the nineteenth century. Its industrialisation
predated Barcelona's and by 1841 the share of employment in manufacturing (47 per cent of total) was already much higher than that in the UK as
a whole. It was not a city dominated by a few employers or by heavy or
extractive industry (coal, steel and shipbuilding are associated with other
cities) or of the large mill and factory production associated with textiles
further north in England or casual labour associated with the docks in
other cities. Rather Birmingham and the adjacent Black Country were associated mainly with smaller workshop-based activity – a city of thousand
trades and thousands of businesses. The historic industrial structure of
Birmingham was unique in the UK context as it was based on small firms
with highly skilled workers. The city maintained a tradition of individual
craftsmen and artisans, working independently or semi-independently in
small, often family owned and run workshops. The city developed specialisms
in four 'staple' trades – guns, jewellery, buttons and brass products – which
became concentrated into quarters in the inner city. However, the diversity
of industrial output included tools of all description, including light cast-
ings, fenders and grates, coin and medal making, toys, pens, blades, pins,
nails, screws, bolts, buttons and bedsteads.

In the first half of the twentieth century, Birmingham was well placed to
benefit from the expansion of consumer-goods industries and the emergence
of the automotive sector. However, the period from the World War I through
the 1920s and 1930s saw the complexion of Birmingham's industrial base
change towards more standardised factory production on a much greater
scale, and a concentration of ownership in a smaller number of companies

that were increasingly based outside of the region and even in the UK. The post-war era of the 1950s and 1960s constituted a final boom period for Birmingham's industrial base. The West Midlands region was the centre of national production in the motor vehicle and electrical equipment industries which were both major growth sectors in the UK following the war. Employment became increasingly concentrated in the motor vehicle and parts production sectors, and by the end of the 1960s Birmingham and the West Midlands had the second largest concentration of automotive sector employment in Europe, after Paris.

However the increasing reliance on a few key industries with suppliers and sub-contractors dependent on a small number of large firms, left Birmingham extremely vulnerable to structural economic changes and growing international competition from the mid-1960s onwards. These wider economic processes precipitated a rapid contraction of the manufacturing sectors, particularly automotive and related fields, from the late 1960s through the 1970s and into the 1980s. The implosion of major employers had a knock-on effect on component suppliers and related industries as well as parts of the service sector (notably transport and communications, hotels and catering) which depended on manufacturing firms for their business. This industrial decline left a legacy of dereliction, high rates of long-term unemployment, deprivation and environmental degradation, particularly in inner city areas. All of this discouraged new inward investment and diversification of the economy.

In response to the economic crises arising from rapid de-industrialisation, Birmingham policy makers embarked on an ambitious programme to develop new economic foundations for the city. In particular, initiatives were launched to grow the business tourism and related leisure sectors, and financial and professional services, with a spatial emphasis on the central districts of the city (see following section). This began to bear fruit in the 1990s as professional and business services grew significantly and drove a net increase in employment from 1993 onwards. The city has strengthened its role as a regional capital in this respect. Despite these changes, Birmingham continues to be characterised by an over-reliance on lower growth sectors, with high representation in particular manufacturing sub-sectors related to automotive and metal products. Manufacturing still accounts for a higher proportion of employment than in the country as a whole, and the city has a weak presence in high technology growth sectors such as computer manufacture, other electronics and pharmaceuticals. While overall employment has grown substantially since the mid-1990s, it remains well below the levels of the early 1970s, and long-term unemployment and social deprivation have become more deeply entrenched despite the revival of the city's economic fortunes more generally. Birmingham's increased exposure to low-value sectors and the shrinkage of its entrepreneurial based left a difficult foundation from which to nurture the growth of creative and knowledge-intensive industries in the late twentieth century.

Dublin

Dublin was never an industrial city to the extent of Barcelona or Birmingham. Ireland's predominantly rural economy and Dublin's role as the capital city diversified its economic and employment base. Nevertheless, within Ireland, Dublin had a key role in the reorientation of the Irish economy especially after Ireland became an European Union (EU) member state.

Historically, the Irish economy was largely agricultural and the industrial revolution had relatively little direct impact on Dublin. Dublin's manufacturing sector developed to a limited extent during the nineteenth and beginning of the twentieth century. The most important industrial activities in terms of occupational structure in Dublin were in the production of food, drink and tobacco, with more than 7 per cent of the workforce located in Dublin by the mid-twentieth century. In the mid-1950s, the Undeveloped Areas Act was introduced which sought to industrialise a predominantly rural society and reduce levels of unemployment by attracting branch-plant manufacturing activities. This spatially selective strategy of economic development favoured industrial development outside the capital and this facilitated Dublin's focus on services, and particularly professional services. The city was thus well positioned to take advantage of the impacts of global economic restructuring and the rising international importance of the tertiary sector without having to deal with the legacy of industrial activities.

Global economic restructuring in the late 1970s and 1980s had undeniable effects on Ireland's recently developed branch-plant economy characterised by low-skilled, low-wage labour located predominantly in rural areas. Unemployment in Ireland reached 17 per cent in 1986, whilst emigration peaked at 40,000 in 1989 (Burnham, 2003). Dublin was also hit by the recession and in a period of less than 10 years the city's subregion lost more than 30,000 industrial jobs, affecting almost every branch of the manufacturing sector (MacLaran, 1993). Dublin's share of national employment in manufacturing decreased from 37.3 per cent in 1971 to 27 per cent by 1989 (MacLaran, 1993). Between 1981 and 1987, unemployment in Dublin increased from 36,500 to 82,000, giving rise to the highest rate of unemployment in the country (MacLaran, 1993).

The downward trends experienced during the 1980s were rapidly transformed in the early 1990s as new attempts were made to reorient Ireland's economy towards new high-tech, knowledge-based sectors, particularly information technology, biotechnology and financial services sectors. Rapid economic change resulted in rapid population growth especially in the Dublin region (Figure 5.2).

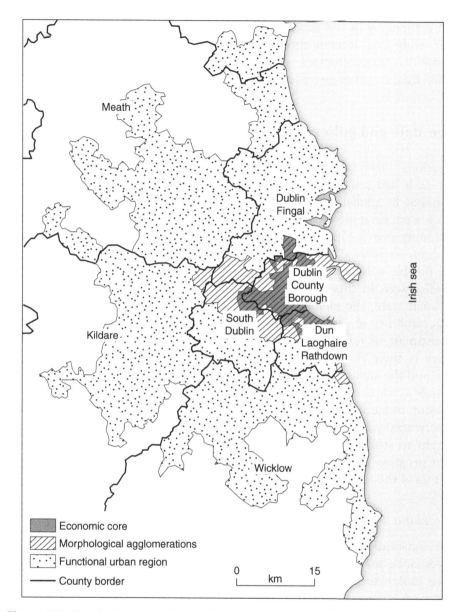

Figure 5.2 Population change in the Greater Dublin Area, 2002–2006.
Source: Williams (2006).

In the case of Dublin, successful attempts were made to shift and strengthen investment in service activities. This shift was achieved by a number of factors including the creation of an International Financial Service Centre (IFSC) which encouraged new investment facilitated by low tax rates. Furthermore, Dublin's concentration of high-skilled labour placed the city in a more competitive position relative to other areas in the country. Hence, Ireland's economic development strategies shifted from the promotion of self-sufficiency in the pre-1950 period to a more outward-looking agenda that embraced foreign direct investment and promoted international competitiveness, changes which have been largely driven and shaped by differential levels of government involvement.

The state and policy intervention

Barcelona, Birmingham and Dublin had very different industrial structures, but each had low productivity manufacturing sectors that were severely damaged by global economic restructuring during the 1970s and 1980s. They were each affected by a number of complex and interrelated shifts, including greater capital mobility and flexibility (Harvey, 1985, 1989), shifts in the international geography of production (Scott, 1988, 1998), growth in the flexible service economy (Sassen, 2000) and a 'rescaling' of state territorial power. In this context and with the decreasing fiscal power of the national state, the changing order of economic competition and the new hypermobility of capital, each of the cities sought new ways of attracting investment to remain competitive. One common feature of these three cities is their emergence as models of successful economic transformation and the significant role of the state in achieving substantial economic change – whether its role has been an interventionist one or one of submission to facilitate the wishes of the private sector. Each city-region has experienced particular types of state and policy interventions which have sought to stimulate the rise of creative industry. Each city made significant progress in diversifying its economy and replacing jobs lost to key sectors of their economies.

Barcelona

The consolidation of democracy in Spain meant a new paradigm of urban governance for the BMR. In 1979, the first democratic municipal elections took place. In the BMR, the socialist and communist parties became the most relevant political forces, with the area called the 'red belt' of Barcelona. Ideological proximity generated synergies amongst the different city councils. The newly elected local governments had to address the significant social problems inherited from the Franco regime. To face this challenge, the city council constructed a governance model based on collaboration with civil society associations and taking into consideration the interests of different economic and social actors. The city council was decentralised, whereas advisory councils on welfare and other issues were created. From 1980 onwards, democratic city councils started working on a huge list of urban interventions designed to improve the quality of life at neighbourhood level. The objective was the decentralisation of Barcelona through the creation of new nodes where different activities would emerge. Cultural and health facilities were created in deprived neighbourhoods with the collaboration of neighbourhood associations.

Coordination between different areas of responsibility within the councils was badly needed, but coordination and collaboration was also needed between the different municipalities. In 1974, the Consortium of the Barcelona Metropolitan Area was created with this aim. During the first half of the 1980s, that institution continued and expanded its functions. It included the city of Barcelona and the cities of the first ring. Through this institution, public services – including water, public transport and waste – were managed and coordinated. The Consortium of the Barcelona Metropolitan Area was dissolved in 1984, however, as it was seen as a major threat to the Autonomous Community government, led by a nationalist conservative party.

The process of consolidation of an autonomous governance system for the city of Barcelona and the metropolitan region must be understood in the context of urban transformation in the 1980s. During the second half of the 1980s, Barcelona and its metropolitan region undertook this strategy, but it was determined by the development path of the city. There is no doubt that associational life and the desire for participation in the whole society was a key factor in the success of Barcelona in enabling the city to address the global scene (McNeill, 1999). Moreover, the need for provision of basic resources created a welfare-provision framework within which the local strategies of Barcelona developed. A key feature of the Barcelona experience was the success of these local strategies and this has been taken as a model for many European cities since.

The year 1986 represented a turning point for BMR for two reasons. First, the city was nominated to organise the 1992 Olympic Games, what meant an opportunity for the scaling to a global city-region. Second, in that year Spain was admitted as a member state of the EU. These two combined developments generated an unprecedented economic and territorial change. The organisation of the Olympic Games benefited from the associative and participatory life of the city and also from the relative economic boom of these years.

The organisation of the Games was based on public sector leadership and the political and collective consensus around the project. In that sense, the organisation was based on partnership between public and private sectors and the active participation of citizens. That configuration of governance was a success and was considered a model to follow by many cities. Nevertheless we must stress the relevance of the specific circumstances of Barcelona, not only of the context of participation but also of the leadership by the mayor, Pasqual Maragall, and the role of political and economic elites. In terms of urban outcomes, the Olympics meant the development of the coastal area and the construction of the ring road – *Les Rondes* – around the city. Also 'monumentalising the periphery' (the term adopted by Oriol Bohigas who was responsible for Barcelona's urban planning at the time) was an attempt to solve the historical problems of the peripheral neighbourhoods of the city that had been chaotically planned in the 1960s. Design and architecture were used to redraw and redesign these areas.

In Barcelona the tradition of using large events is to promote the city and solve existing problems of infrastructure or transport dates from the nineteenth century with the organisation of the first Universal Exhibition. The celebration of the Olympics had an additional feature – the relatively new democratic context in which it took place. The political elites were forced to create consensus and gain support across the social fabric, to present the city in a way that resonated with the global context and as relevant to actors at a global sale. In that sense the Olympics created the framework for the city to be pioneering in policy planning taking into consideration the wide array of interests of the different actors of the city.

The leadership role played by local authorities emerges as the critical determinant in the transformation of the city-region since the beginning of the 1980s. In particular, the municipality of Barcelona developed the strategic plan for the metropolitan region as long-term guidance for the whole area. The wide range of projects developed in the BMR went from the historic lack of infrastructures to the stimuli to knowledge and research.

The competitiveness of the Metropolitan Region of Barcelona has been reoriented towards the service sector; in particular the creative and knowledge-based services are increasingly understood as the basis for growth in innovation and talent. Many policies and institutions are engaged in the promotion of Barcelona as a creative city in which the cultural sector plays a key role. This change of model, moving from traditional activities such as the real estate or mass tourism towards innovative and creative activities, requires a change in the attitude of public entities and of all those who could be involved.

Creative industries are mainly linked to cultural aspects in Barcelona. The city of Barcelona has knowledge-intensive sectors and culture as main targets of economic specialisation. Certainly, the rise of the creative industry at the BMR is due to the degree of involvement and support of public authorities. However, there is a long tradition of creative industries linked to the cultural sector such as publishing, advertising, architecture and design. All of the industries identified as forming the cultural sector are represented among the creative industries in the BMR (Pareja-Eastaway et al., 2007) and culture and creativity are key aspects of the city-region transformation. The transformation of traditional industrial sectors towards knowledge-based ones is a key factor for success at the BMR and the significance of existing expertise is most evident in the fashion sector which benefits from the textile tradition in the region.

In terms of employment, each of the industries within the creative sector (see Chapter 1) separately represents more than 4 per cent of the total employment in Barcelona. In 2001, the activities included under the information and communication technology (ICT) label accounted for 4.45 per cent of GDP in the province of Barcelona. As in many other regions, creative industries have an important percentage of micro companies, freelances and small enterprises (1–3 workers) which provide of flexibility and mechanisms of adaptation to a changing competitive environment.

Birmingham

For most of Birmingham's recent history, the role of the national and local state in supporting the city's economic growth has been indirect in nature. In the nineteenth century, Birmingham under the leadership of Joseph Chamberlain was regarded as the 'best governed city in the world'. Its most striking municipal initiatives were concerned with raising living conditions in the city (municipal water and gas services) and improving the city centre environment rather than the economy per se. However, this municipal enterprise and, for example, the actions of civic leaders in establishing a new independent university in the city were recognised as contributing to the city's continued development more widely.

In the first half of the twentieth century and in the two decades following the World War II, Birmingham's economic boom occurred largely independent of any direct local policy influence. National planning policy in the post-war era, involving slum clearance programmes and dispersal of populations out of urban cores, contributed to the decentralisation of population and employment described above. The city council was highly active in the reshaping of the city from the 1950s through the 1970s in two respects: the substantial programmes of council house building, including many new inner city estates in areas where slum clearance had occurred, and a dramatic rebuilding of the city centre in a manner that gave prominence to road infrastructure and automotive mobility. Both of these contributed to the poor environment that became the focus of regeneration efforts in subsequent decades. For the most part, however, local authority activity in this period was concerned with provision of public services and direct support for economic ambitions (e.g. the provision of premises for small businesses displaced through redevelopment) took second place.

The turning point with regard to policy intervention came in the mid-1980s. The economic changes of the mid-1970s onwards had created a crisis in industry and manufacturing with rising unemployment. Birmingham was facing an urgent need to respond to the deepening economic crisis, but the UK government had significantly curtailed local government autonomy and financial powers. In this context, Birmingham emerged as a pioneer in Europe of what has been termed the shift to urban entrepreneurialism. The city council, in partnership with private sector interests such as the Chamber of Commerce, embarked on a proactive strategy to rebuild the city economy and its physical environment largely independent of any support from central government. This endeavour was rooted in Birmingham's long history of pragmatism in political affairs, a bipartisan approach to such economic challenges and effective working between public and private sectors, long before this became the norm in most European cities.

The core of Birmingham's approach was to create the conditions for new economic functions, particularly in business tourism, related aspects of the visitor economy and financial and professional services. The first step had been the construction of the National Exhibition Centre on the eastern fringes of the city in 1976 and this was subsequently expanded several times to become one of the ten largest such facilities in Europe. In the 1980s, the city sought to build upon this success with a renewed focus on the city centre in two respects: the development of several mainly public sector-funded flagship projects and a new planning framework to dramatically enhance the environment in central areas. The flagship projects, opened between 1991 and 1993, included the International Convention Centre and Symphony Hall, Hyatt Hotel and National Indoor Arena. Their construction was accompanied by a programme of improvements to the public realm nearby including extensive pedestrianisation, upgrading of the extensive canal environment to make this a celebrated (rather than hidden) feature of the city and creation of new public squares. Through the late 1990s and into 2000s, this initial investment spawned significant spin-off private investment including the growth of a significant city centre housing market, initially using canal side locations, attracting a young professional residential base into the heart of the city.

This proactive policy approach provided Birmingham with an important platform for diversifying the economy and growing new sectors, but it still masked serious problems concerning the underlying structure of the economy and deeply entrenched multiple deprivation. This deprivation was particularly pronounced in parts of the inner city and among some BME communities, which failed to benefit significantly from the positive achievements of the policy interventions since the 1980s. Overall, Birmingham's main policy interventions were more attuned to attracting tourism and major corporate investments rather than nurturing of a small business base or the development of new economic districts. The continuing importance of small businesses may be more attributable to the long established tradition and the business culture of the city than to promotion through public policy. Nevertheless there was an indirect impact of public policy on the economy, as the policies did gradually improve the image of the city and especially Birmingham's profile as a place for young people to live, work and study.

The creative and knowledge-based industries have emerged as a strong and vital economic driver for Birmingham since the 1990s as it has diversified away from its longstanding dependence on manufacturing. The creative industries in Birmingham constitute a growing, diverse set of economic activities that exhibit some distinctive characteristics. In general terms, however, creative firms are still somewhat underrepresented in Birmingham – they represent 10 per cent compared with 12 per cent nationally. In line with national trends, Birmingham's creative firms are small – 89 per cent have less than 10 employees – and it is estimated that freelancers comprise about one-fifth of all creative businesses, and are particularly prominent in the music and performing arts sub-sector.

In terms of employment, creative firms accounted for over 28,000 jobs in Birmingham in 2004. This 5.7 per cent proportion of the overall city employment is slightly below the comparable figure at a national level. The most important sub-sectors for employment are software, arts and antiques, and architecture/engineering, which taken together account for nearly three-quarters of all jobs.

Importantly, however, the expansion in Birmingham's creative industry employment has outpaced the national growth rate in recent years. The growth of 41 per cent between 1998 and 2005 (against 28.4 per cent nationally) has been driven by rapid expansion of the architecture sector, linked in part to the city's development and regeneration momentum during this period. Some 92 per cent of creative firms were started in Birmingham, illustrating that this sector very much emerges from the local environment.

In spatial terms, some sectors such as software are relatively dispersed, but there are concentrations of creative jobs in two historic districts on the fringe of the city centre – the Jewellery Quarter and Digbeth in Eastside (see Figure 5.3). These have emerged organically for a range of reasons – historical factors, the benefits of a central location for staff recruitment and access; proximity to customers; the availability of inexpensive, suitable property/premises; the social and creative milieu and intangible ecology in these districts. Spatial policy has had little effect on this process and there remains a view in the city that more proactive planning could strengthen these clusters significantly.

Birmingham's strength in other knowledge-intensive sectors is highly varied. The city generally has a low presence in high-tech industries and services such as computers, electronics, pharmaceuticals and computer services. Medical and precision instruments were a major exception, reflecting the role played by major medical centres and teaching/research clusters in Birmingham. Financial and professional services have grown markedly in the past 15 years and exceed national employment ratios. This expansion has been closely linked to the city's spatial policy interventions and its regeneration strategy since the 1980s, with the majority of employment growth clustered in the expanding, modernised city centre.

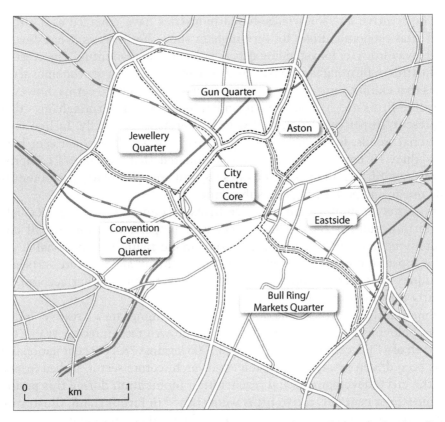

Figure 5.3 Birmingham city centre quarters: creative industry clusters in the Jewellery Quarter and Eastside (Digbeth).

Higher education research is another important strength, reflecting the presence of three major universities and several other institutions. However, R&D outside higher education institutions is weak. This is linked to the low presence in high technology industries noted above, and reflects the changing nature of Birmingham's industrial base through much of the twentieth century.

Dublin

Dublin's economic development path has been strongly influenced by government policy. The free trade approach prior to and immediately after independence, followed by the development of protectionism and self-sufficiency and, subsequently, active policies to modernise the economy are examples of the ways in which the state has played a critical role in driving development and has been the most active agent or enabler of change in Ireland. During the post-independence period, and until 1960, the new independent government's policies were explicitly targeted at improving the agricultural-production conditions of the country. The government's economic policies maintained a free trade and 'hands-off' approach, adhering to the same model that the British imposed prior to independence. This economic objective had an underlying political agenda. The government of the new state's insistence on supporting an agricultural economy was partly a way of marking a difference between Ireland and the UK, as the latter had a much stronger industrial economy. The idea of a rural, Catholic Ireland was central to the post-independence discourse and was embraced by many of the new political figures in the country. Hence, unlike other European countries, Ireland bypassed the Industrial Revolution. In a predominantly rural-based economy, Dublin's role was not as salient as it is today, with less than 20 per cent of the labour force located in Dublin in the early 1940s. The government's approach to supporting an agricultural economy was through the development of an export market economy.

The economic decline of the independent state led to the reorientation of government policy away from free trade towards protectionism. New protectionist policies were based on notions of economic nationalism and ideologically committed to a policy of greater self-sufficiency (O'Hagan, 1991). The main instruments used to achieve self-sufficiency were high tariff barriers and the introduction of a wide range of quotas and import licences to assist indigenous industries develop and prosper (MacLaran, 1993). Ireland's economic development strategies focused largely on industrialising a predominantly rural society and reducing levels of unemployment by attracting branch-plant manufacturing activities that required low-skilled labour. Ireland's economic policy became increasingly outward oriented. The government offered a wide array of incentives for attracting inward investment, including low corporation tax rates and remission of local authority rates. By the end of the 1960s, Ireland had rapidly changed from a predominantly agricultural to an industrial-based economy (Sweeney, 1999). Service sector employment in the Dublin sub-region grew by more than 120 per cent from 1971 to 2002 (Williams and Redmond, 2006). Since the beginning of the 1990s important changes occurred in the Irish economy, which have had a great impact on Dublin's functional role relative to both the domestic economy and the international division of labour (Breathnach, 2000).

Dublin has become a model for economic development for many other countries, particularly to the newer EU states. While this success is undeniable, it must be recognised that it has been built on many decades of an interventionist government facilitating, managing, and in many cases directing economic growth. Ireland's economic strategy has focused on creating an attractive financial environment for investment, primarily through relatively low corporate tax rates and the provision of generous incentives to certain industries in particular locations – the traditional 'hard' location factors. In terms of people employed, the three most important branches of the creative sector in Ireland are architecture, the ICT and the financial sector. For many years, the ICT companies have enjoyed success in Ireland and have helped place Ireland on the international map as a key location for investment across the ICT value chain. In the 1980s, young, fast-growing companies such as Lotus, Microsoft, Symantec and Oracle established manufacturing and localisation centres in Ireland to supply the European, Middle East and African markets. This initial growth later became the catalyst for the emergence of a world-class sub-supply and vendor industry in Ireland. In addition to the first wave of investments from Intel, SAP, Sun, Novell, and Dell, Ireland's existing Foreign Direct Investment – such as Microsoft, IBM, Accenture, Ericsson, Motorola, Apple and EDS – began to expand their operations during the 1990s. In the 10 years from 1991 to 2001, Ireland's software industry experienced extraordinary levels of growth such that today it is the largest exporter of software in the world. Eight of the top 10 software suppliers in the world have operations in Ireland and it continues to be a leading European location for technology companies as demonstrated by recent investments such as Siebel, SAP, Net IQ, Google and Adobe. These newer investments tend to be more strategic in nature and many have European or global mandates for product development, high level pan-European technical support, revenue accounting and financial shared services. Seven of the world's top 10 ICT companies have a substantial base in Ireland and overseas companies, such as IBM, Intel, Hewlett Packard, Dell and Microsoft, employ 45,000 people in Ireland.

Highly skilled workers in the financial sector also constitute a key component of the creative and knowledge-intensive. The Irish state has purposively sought to develop its financial services sector which now contributes up to one-third of the country's service sector exports (Hardiman, 2007). A central element in Ireland's strategy has been the formation and maintenance of a tax incentive zone within inner city Dublin, the IFSC. Established in 1987 with EU approval as a means of regenerating part of the derelict docklands zone, firms locating in the IFSC were subject to a very low corporation tax rate of 10 per cent until the end of 2005. The IFSC has played a major role in helping to regenerate parts of inner city Dublin. Institutionally, the Docklands Authority is involved in helping developments in the IFSC to spill over into the entire docklands area, and a significant legal quarter supportive of the financial services sector has been established in this part of the inner city. The success of the IFSC project, as a key driver of the knowledge-intensive sector, is evident in the fact that for the first time in 2005, the funds industry in Ireland broke through €1 trillion (1000 billion) mark, of which some €633 billion represented funds domiciled in Ireland. More than 430 international operations are approved to trade in the IFSC, while a further 700 managed entities carry on business under the IFSC programme. In 2005, 1485 net new jobs were created in

Ireland's international financial services (IFS) sector, most of it based in the Greater Dublin region. According to *Finance Dublin Yearbook 2006*, total employment in the three core sectors of banking, funds and insurance at the end of December 2005 was 19,095, a growth of 8.4 per cent from the same date a year earlier (Moore, 2008). The credit crunch has impacted on this sector since and severely affected Dublin's economy.

Ireland's emphasis on stimulating a creative and knowledge-intensive economy has had tremendously positive impacts on the economic success of the country and, more importantly, on the growth of the Greater Dublin Area. This success has been built on many decades of interventionist government policies, facilitating, managing and in many cases directing the economic growth of the country and city-region. Dublin's development path can therefore be characterised as having emerged from a relatively weak industrial base with the aid of significant pro-market government intervention to a situation where currently the development and promotion of a knowledge-intensive and creative city has become a central aspect of the national economic imperative.

The challenge of soft factors

Each of the three cities under discussion has changed their economic structure, but the emphasis in much contemporary discussion of urban competitiveness also refers to the image of the city and the importance of lifestyle and cultural diversity. In this context it is important to consider how far each of these cities' strategies has addressed the need to make them more attractive as places to live and work in.

Barcelona

Barcelona emerged in the post-Olympic period as a well-known city in international forums and with an improved infrastructure and increased tourism. Its earlier architectural and other cultural legacies had become better known and celebrated, and the active partnership between the private and the public sector represented an important organisational legacy. Key private partners emerged and together with the public sector continued to be engaged in the promotion of the Barcelona 'brand'. This promotion aims to benefit from the strong international reputation after 1992 and to promote certain sectors which are considered of high priority in the international competitive arena. The food and the design sector and universities are examples where partnerships have been developed.

Priorities about which sectors to promote have changed from the university or tourism to cultural industries and information technologies.

Certainly Barcelona profits from the attractiveness of the city, and projects the image of the city as an ideal place for business, to stimulate successful projects, disseminate the results and attract Spanish capital investment into large enterprises. However, once the Barcelona image and the attributes attached to the Barcelona brand are known internationally, the support of the public administration is needed to achieve further improvement of the basis for the creative knowledge city (universities, research centres, and of the transmission and dissemination of information). In spite of the high level of quality of life offered by the city, the seven public universities, the amount of technological and research centres and so on, it remains unclear who takes the leading role given the numbers of organisations (universities, ministries, governments) involved.

According to data compiled by the Strategic Metropolitan Plan of Barcelona, the region still has poor levels of R&D and public investment in this field in order to improve innovation patterns is urgently needed – focused on the creation of new innovative enterprises, transferability of technology and particularly on education. The creation of laboratories for innovation and creativity should be stimulated from the public sector without forgetting the existing network of social initiatives. Programmes oriented to promote innovation in small and medium enterprises are needed as the problem is less the absence of infrastructure and more the lack of knowledge to use it.

In terms of new infrastructures and upgrading the existing infrastructures, Barcelona and its metropolitan region face new challenges. First of all, telecommunication infrastructures have to be improved. Poor technological infrastructures produce poor results in innovation and ICT (Vives and Torrens, 2004). The construction of new infrastructures and the better management of existing infrastructures are priorities for the generation of economic growth in the BMR. Air and rail networks are far from optimal with. Barcelona airport is the ninth largest European airport as far as numbers of passengers is concerned and the lack of intercontinental flights poses a handicap for activities that fall within the knowledge economy. This raises questions about the wider system of management of airports in Spain. The delay in the construction of the high-speed train (AVE), particularly its arrival in Barcelona and the connection to France, is another deficit in the infrastructure of the region. The situation will be improved by the enlargement of the airport where a new runway and a new terminal are under construction. New infrastructure in the port of Barcelona will also allow it to become the first European port in annual numbers of cruises.

One attempt to create the environmental conditions for the cluster location of highly innovative and creative enterprises is 'Barcelona, city of knowledge' and the projects within it – including the 22@ project in Poblenou (Barber and Pareja-Eastaway, 2010). This larger project is not merely a planning initiative but signalled a new form of understanding the city (Oliva, 2003); its main objective is to transform Barcelona into a leading knowledge society, in particular by encouraging new-generation activities related to and requiring education, creativity and innovation. This larger project started in 1998 with major urban redevelopment and currently with the attraction of firms to five existing clusters (biomed, energy, design, media and ICT). It is of outstanding importance, especially taking into account that the only economic growth and employment creation is in these types of activities.

Birmingham

By the 1980s, Birmingham's industrial legacy and its social and environmental implications left the city with a poor image and weak conditions for the growth of many modern economic sectors. The city made some significant inroads into this through the ambitious regeneration activities of the 1980s and 1990s. It achieved some success in developing a new tourism economy for the city, including expanded leisure, cultural and retail amenities, and it did much to enhance the overall environment and public realm in the heart of the city.

These changes provided a much improved context for the growth of creative and knowledge-intensive industries in Birmingham over the past 15 years. However, there remain significant limitations in this respect, both in practice and in perception. There are enduring concerns about the diversity and distinctiveness of the city's lifestyle and cultural amenities, the physical accessibility of many cultural assets, and a somewhat corporate, mainstream approach to the marketing of these attributes to audiences outside of the city.

There are also shortcomings with regard to the residential environments available in the city, in terms of housing options and attractive neighbourhoods that would appeal to workers in the creative and knowledge-intense sectors. Birmingham's legacy of environmental problems, concentrations of deprivation and some acute socio-economic contrasts are all impediments in this respect. The 'city living' boom of the past 10 years has helped to some degree, providing an important and popular new housing option for young professionals and creative workers whose employment is in the city centre. But this remains a relatively narrow market, geared to a mainly transient population in small, rental apartments. An important current policy agenda is planning for the development of new urban neighbourhoods that would expand the range of options for creative and knowledge workers, particularly those in their 30s and 40s, and those with young children.

Finally, in terms of tolerance, Birmingham does have a long experience of accommodating economic migrants – from other parts of the UK, Ireland, the New Commonwealth countries, and most recently from a diverse range of sources including Asia, Eastern Africa and central and eastern Europe. While there is little evidence of a direct link between this and the growth of creative sectors in recent years, the diverse, multi-cultural population that has resulted from this migration could prove a dynamic and distinctive economic asset for Birmingham in the years ahead.

The creative industries are a dynamic and growing part of the Birmingham economy, but much of the expansion in recent years has occurred in the absence of focused public sector support, and while the policy context has improved notably in the past 7 years, there remain some fundamental challenges for Birmingham if it is to fulfil its potential in these parts of the urban economy.

Many of these challenges are rooted in Birmingham's distinctive economic history and particularly its industrial legacy in recent years. Most problematically, the city's industrial experience of the twentieth century has left a considerable group of residents with low skills, educational aspirations and achievement in the labour market. The problems arising from this are likely to be experienced among some of the city's fast-growing ethnic minority communities as well as other working class families. Second, the image of industrial decline and dereliction and high levels of deprivation and unemployment remain liabilities for the visioning of the city in the twenty-first century. A core challenge remains to provide more housing and neighbourhoods that would attract and retain 'people with talent'. While Birmingham has high-quality and affluent zones and a new vibrant city centre living environment, continued out-migration of more affluent groups has exacerbated the pattern of spatial and social inequality within the city, with evident impacts on the urban environment.

A final challenge, embracing all of the above, is the complexity of policy and organisation arrangements at the city/region level, the range of strategies and actors and the effectiveness and integration of strategies for creative industries with other strategies within the city and region. A particular issue is the role of spatial policy and urban planning. This relates to creating more attractive residential environments but also the nurturing of high-profile clusters of creative industries and related activities in inner city districts. The Jewellery Quarter and Eastside/Digbeth have emerged as notable concentrations of new creative businesses and consumption activities, but they have yet to achieve their potential as prominent creative quarters that could promote Birmingham's growing strength in these sectors to wider audiences outside of the city. A more proactive planning approach to these historic areas, combining strategic public interventions with a generally subtle touch, would do much to strengthen the overall impact of the creative industries on Birmingham's broader regeneration and its image.

Dublin

If we accept that 'soft' locations factors such as tolerance, openness, diversity, and quality of life will be critical in attracting and retaining creative workers on which future economic and urban growth is dependent, Dublin has much work to do. For Richard Florida (2002, 2005), tolerant places are those where gays, bohemians and immigrants feel at home and where there is significant racial integration. Ireland's, and by inference Dublin's performance, relative to Florida's 'tolerance index' is among the lowest in Europe. The Euro-Tolerance Index is based on three measures. First, the values index 'measures the degree to which a country espouses traditional as opposed to modern or secular values' (Florida and Tinagli, 2004, p. 43). Second, the self-expression index captures the degree to which a nation values individual rights and self-expression. The final measurement is called the Attitudes Index and measures attitudes towards minority groups in the country. Ireland ranked the lowest European nation in the values index, with −8.63 points (compared to Sweden with 15 points). This low figure can be attributed partly to the sustained influence of Roman Catholic values on much of contemporary Irish society, although this has waned considerably over the last 20 years.

In recent years, Ireland has experienced a significant increase in cultural and ethnic diversity, both in terms of numbers of people and their national and ethnic origin. Much of Ireland's recent increase in cultural diversity is a consequence of migrant workers entering the country. In 1999 there were 6000 work permits issued, but over 40,000 work permits were issued in 2002 (IECD, 2005). Migrant workers have therefore played a central role in Ireland's economy since the late 1990s.

As Ireland has become one of the most affluent countries in Europe, the Irish consider themselves increasingly tolerant of their more diverse society (Cullen, 2005). However, developing a culture of pluralism is now a growing concern as, for the first time in history, Dublin is now home to many immigrant communities and reports of racist assaults have risen. While the diminution in power of traditional institutions, such as the Catholic Church, has also resulted in greater openness to alternative lifestyles, tolerance of difference in the city remains far behind other cities. The local authority has indicated a growing interest in the concept of Dublin as a creative city-region but although lip-service is paid to cultural factors, classic locational attributes still play a key role in the developing discourses. Addressing the social and cultural dimensions or 'soft factors' that have been identified as core to the creative city debate will need to underpin future growth policy if the creative city idea is to be fully embraced.

Conclusions

The three cities discussed in this chapter have been seen as models of successful public policy interventions that have transformed the economy of the city. In each case it is evident that public policy has been important but is not the sole driver of transformation. And while the effects of changes can be documented in a positive way they also have had unequal impacts. Not all existing businesses and not all sections of the population have beneffitted equally. While it is appropriate to identify the importance of policy interventions in these cities, it is also important to recognise that policy successes are linked to longer-term attributes in the case of each city. Public policy does not work with a blank canvass but in each case has built on legacies from earlier development or has operated in sympathy with existing development pathways. So, Barcelona's development has exploited its location and physical attributes, emphasised its rich cultural traditions and legacies and made use of existing strengths for example in the fashion sector's links to the older textile industry. Its position as the Catalan capital and its distinctive architectural tradition and artistic heritage have been assets. Both Barcelona and Birmingham have worked with public–private partnerships and used the strength of the private sector as well as the tradition of small businesses to reorganise their economies. Birmingham has also drawn on an exceptional history of municipal leadership and an interventionist tradition to modernise its city centre and address its image as an industrial city in decline. It has built on the legacy of university, music and the arts that were established by an earlier generation of city leaders as necessary for a leading city with the capacity to make its own future. Dublin's reorientation of its economy brings the resources associated with a strong university and education tradition and a capital city to the fore. The successful public policy interventions have built on resources that existed.

Barcelona, Birmingham and Dublin show that the re-imagining of the city can be achieved through the implementation of a wide range of strategies. The attention devoted to transforming the *image* of the city captures the relationship between image-making strategies and urban economic development under contemporary capitalism (Hubbard and Hall, 1998). In some cases, these strategies are expressed as city-based campaigns launched for the attraction of mega events such as the World Cup or the Olympics, as was the case in Barcelona during the late 1980s. In other cases, processes of urban reinvention have focused on the construction of consumer spaces such as convention centres, symphony halls, stadiums, shopping centres and other spaces that facilitate consumption, as was the case of Birmingham during the 1990s. Underlying these strategies is a broader transformation of cities from spaces of work and production to spaces of consumption. What stands out is the need for cities to appear as innovative, creative and exciting places to live, invest, work and consume in (Harvey, 1989).

As this chapter has shown, policies aimed at reinventing the image of Barcelona, Birmingham and Dublin have been crucial elements within the economic survival strategies of each city. But image-making strategies have a life cycle which, after a successful period, need revamping to include new content and new issues. For example, the Barcelona brand has been internationally positioned in a very efficient way, but after some years the image of the successful Olympic city from the 1980s is not so commanding. Nowadays efforts are being made to associate the city with the knowledge economy and there is more attention given to social cohesion.

While a range of actors and institutions have successfully marketed cities to overseas investors and other interests, the future sustainability of the cities will depend on the introduction of relevant, place-specific policies. The replication of policies that are fashionable or have worked in other places simply may not suit or be relevant to the local context. Creating cities that speak equally to entrepreneurs, residents and migrants is a difficult task and one that requires significant innovative thinking. The true test of whether Barcelona, Birmingham and Dublin succeed as a creative cities will be if they can smartly harness local knowledge and global investment to develop truly innovative approaches to future growth, marking them out from the many other 'wannabe cities' on the global stage. This will not happen without meeting challenges including those associated with increasing immigration, improving housing affordability, upgrading and developing better infrastructure to facilitate communication and transportation.

References

Barber, A. and Pareja-Eastaway,M. (2010, forthcoming) Leadership challenges in the inner city: Planning for sustainable regeneration in Birmingham and Barcelona. *Policy Studies*. London: Routledge.

Breathnach, P. (2000) Globalisation, information technology and the emergence of niche transnational cities: The growth of the call centre in Dublin. *Geoforum*, 31: 477–485.

Burnham, J. (2003) Why Ireland boomed. *Independent Review*, 7 (4): 537–557.

Cullen (2005) Same-sex couple's lawsuit a test of tolerance in Ireland. *The Boston Globe*, section: world. December 30, 2005.

Florida, R. (2002) *The rise of the creative class*. New York: Basic Books.

Florida, R. (2005) *Cities and the creative class*. London: Routledge.

Florida, R. and I. Tinagli (2004) *Europe in the creative age*. Pittsburgh: Carnegie Mellon Software Industry Center and DEMOS.

Hall, P. (1999) *Cities in civilisation*. London: Weidenfeld and Nicholson.

Hardiman, C. (2007) Centre of excellence. *Irish Independent*, Thursday, February 22. The business news.

Harvey, D. (1985) The geopolitics of capitalism. In: D. Gregory and J. Urry (eds), *Social relations and spatial structures*. London: Macmillan Publishers.

Harvey, D. (1989) From managerialism to entrepreneurialism: The transformation in urban governance in late capitalism. *Geograpfiska Annaler*, 71 (1): 3–17.

Hubbard, P. and T. Hall (1998) The entrepreneurial city and the 'new urban politics'. In: T. Hall and P. Hubbard (eds), *The entrepreneurial city: Geographies of politics, regime and representation*. New York: John Wiley & Sons.

IDESCAT (2006) *Anuari estadístic de Catalunya 2005*. Barcelona: Generalitat de Catalunya.

Ireland Embracing Cultural Diversity (IECD) (2005) *Planning for diversity. National action plan against racism.* Prepared by the Department of Justice, equality and law reform. Ireland. http://www.diversityireland.ie

MacLaran, A. (1993) *Dublin: The shaping of a capital.* London: Belhaven Press.

McNeill, D. (1999) *Urban change and the European left. Tales from the New Barcelona.* London: Routledge.

Moore, N. (2008) *Dublin docklands reinvented.* Dublin: Four Courts Press.

OECD (2006) Competitive cities in the global economy. OECD Territorial Reviews. http://www.oecd.org/document/2/0,3343,en_2649_33735_37801602_1_1_1_1,00.html. Accessed November 2008.

O'Hagan, J. (1991) *The economy of Ireland: Policy and performance* (6th edition). Ireland: Irish Management Institute.

Oliva, A. (2003) *El districte d'activitats 22@bcn.* Barcelona: Aula Barcelona.

Oliver, J. (coord.) (ed.) (2006) *Anuari Econòmic Comarcal 2005.* Barcelona: Caixa Catalunya 148.

Pareja-Eastaway, M., J. Turmo, M. Pradel i Miquel, L. García and M. Simó (2007) *The city of Marvels? Multiple endeavours towards competitiveness in Barcelona. Pathways to creative and knowledge-based regions.* ACRE report. Amsterdam: AMIDSt.

Sassen, S. (2000) *Cities in a world economy* (2nd edition). Thousand Oaks: Pine Forge Press.

Scott, A. (1988) *New industrial spaces: Flexible production, organization and regional development in North America and Western Europe.* London: Pion.

Scott, A. (1998) *Regions in the world economy: The coming shape of global production, competition and political order.* Oxford: Oxford University Press.

Sweeney, P. (1999) *The Celtic tiger: Ireland's continuing economic miracle.* Dublin: Oak Tree Press.

Trullén, J. and R. Boix (2003) *Barcelona, metropolis policéntrica en red,* Working Paper 03.03 del Departament d'Economia Aplicada, UAB.

Vives, X. and X. Torrens (2004) Estratègies de les àrees metropolitanes europees davant l'ampliació de la Unió Europea. *Col·lecció prospectiva,* 2. Pla Estratègic Barcelona.

Williams, B. and D. Redmond (2006) *Ideopolis: Knowledge city region. Dublin case study.* Dublin: The Work Foundation.

Williams, B. (2006) Fiscal incentives and urban regeneration in Dublin. Planning and environmental policy research series, working papers. Dublin: University College Dublin.

6

Institutional Change and New Development Paths: Budapest, Leipzig, Poznan, Riga and Sofia

Tadeusz Stryjakiewicz, Joachim Burdack and Tamás Egedy

Introduction

The political and socio-economic system in which cities exist, operate and are regulated is one of the key factors influencing the development of competitive, creative and knowledge-based cities. It determines the basic features of an institutional setting which may, or may not, be favourable to competitiveness and creativity. The history of Europe has seen several interruptions or discontinuities in stable, evolutionary development paths. In the twentieth and twenty-first centuries, they were most conspicuous in eastern and central Europe where the communist system (also known as a command system) was imposed after the World War II.

Path dependence is one of the most useful concepts explaining the present competitive position of cities, their institutional settings and conditions for the development of the creative knowledge sector. The notions of 'development path' or 'path dependence' are often used in a general sense to emphasise that future developments depend to a certain degree on decisions made in the past ('history matters'). There are, however, more specific formulations of path dependency models in social history and economic geography (Arthur, 1989; Margolis, 1995; Mahoney, 2000). These models stress the self-reinforcing dynamics of decisions at critical junctures. Longer periods of slow and steady development may be interrupted, at critical junctures, by sudden changes that in turn lead to new periods of more stable development. An accidentally initiated path of development may then persist due to the effects of sunk costs or high switching costs even in the face of superior alternative solutions: '... small events and random processes can shape developments during a "critical juncture", leading to the adoption of options that could not have been produced by theory' (Mahoney, 2001, p. 111). The basic argument in this explanation is that processes are highly sensitive to early events so that small contingent causes at the beginning of a development path can be of decisive importance. A self-reinforcing dynamics may start in which the costs of reversing previous decisions increase: 'Before a sufficient critical mass is reached and a path-dependent process is set in motion, there is a relatively open window that allows for contingent factors and, hence also for significant actors who are able to initiate such process and partly at least, determine its course in the formative stage. After this window of path creation, dedicated institutions are formed and path-reproduction becomes possible' (Kloosterman and Stegmeijer, 2004, p. 75).

A path-dependent trajectory often emerges when a system is in a state of instability. This instability may be caused by events outside the system (exogenous shocks) that interrupt gradual development. The development may reach a critical juncture where a number of different directions are possible. Contingent early or 'small' events may then cause an initial advantage in a particular direction. The early event is not usually anticipated from theoretical debate but is highly accidental. A self-reinforcing process emerges and the logic of increasing returns and sunk costs locks actors into the initial choice ('lock-in'). The breakdown of the communist planning economies formed an 'exogenous shock' that abruptly interrupted the post-War development paths of eastern European cities and created an unstable, open situation where many new directions of development seemed possible.

The communist system downplayed, by its very essence (e.g. the state monopoly and directive top-down regulations), the importance of competitiveness and creativeness in the development paths of both entire national economies and societies and particular cities and metropolitan regions (for a broader treatment, see Chojnicki, 1990; Parysek, 1992, 1998; Balcerowicz, 1995, 1996; Belka and Trzeciakowski, 1997; Grabher, 1997; Smith, 1997; Smith and Swain, 1998; Stryjakiewicz, 2000). This chapter focuses on the consequences of interrupted pathways and current institutional changes intended to cope with the detrimental effects of the interruption for the development of the creative knowledge sector.

The new development paths emerging in the cities of east-central Europe as a result of the systemic change started in 1989 are widely different, as are the pathways of post-communist transition. This diversity is reflected in cities referred to in this chapter:

- Leipzig – a city with a long tradition of competitive and creative development interrupted by the GDR period, immediately after 1989 incorporated into the market-oriented system and European Union (EU) regulations.

- Budapest and Poznan – cities which, having experienced a communist episode (1945–1989), went through a transition period concluded with the accession to the EU in 2004.
- Riga – the capital of a state which was part of the former USSR and regained independence only in 1991, to become an EU member in 2004.
- Sofia – another state capital under communist rule after the World War II, but with a delayed transition process and EU membership only in 2007.

The present chapter addresses two questions: whether, and how, these differences in institutional settings have affected the intensity of transition towards a creative and knowledge-based economy; whether, and how, some remnants of old, interrupted development pathways are reflected in the new economy.

It should be noted at this point that an analysis of the transition processes based on official data and indicators is far from easy, especially in the case of the creative knowledge sector. The body of statistical data for the cities in question is much more limited than for many west European countries, and economic activity classifications are not fully comparable. Statistics in east-central Europe has also been going through its own transformation intended to adjust to EU standards. This process has not finished yet, its progress varies from state to state, and this of necessity restricts comparative and dynamic analyses to descriptive and qualitative approaches.

Socio-economic characteristics of the study areas

The cities and their regions analysed in this chapter differ considerably in terms of function (state capitals: Budapest, Riga and Sofia, and second-rank cities: Leipzig and Poznan), population (from 2.4 million in Budapest to 0.5 million in Leipzig), demographic trends (growth to decline) and socio-economic structure (including the role of the creative sector).

From the point of view of the importance and level of development of metropolitan functions, certainly the highest position in the group analysed is occupied by Budapest, the capital of Hungary. Located in the central part of the country, it now has a population of 1.7 million, a decline from the peak figure of 2.1 million recorded in the mid-1980s. Budapest and its agglomeration have altogether 2.44 million inhabitants – with this figure it is the largest metropolitan region in east-central Europe. The demographic trends of the 1990s basically continued after 2001 with slight micro-level changes. As a result, the Budapest population decreased by 321,000 between 1990 and 2005, while in the wider region it grew by 25 per cent. Important features of the recent demographic trends have been a marked ageing process, social polarisation with the resultant spatial segregation and an increase in commuting.

The general level of educational attainment in the Budapest metropolitan region is much higher than the national average. In the adult age group (18 1), 54.1 per cent of the population holds secondary education (as against the national figure of 38.4 per cent), whereas the ratio of people with higher education is 13.6 per cent, nearly double the national average.

The Budapest metropolitan region is the economically most advanced area of the country. In 2004, 44.5 per cent of the national GDP was generated here (with 35 per cent in Budapest itself). The per capita GDP produced in Budapest amounted to 205 per cent of the national average.

The economic output of the Budapest metropolitan region has always been dominant within Hungary. This showed, among other things, in an explosion of the service sector and the development of high-tech industry after the change of regime in 1989–1990: the share of services on the labour market increased from 62.5 to 78 per cent between 1990 and 2006. The rapid transformation of the economy was also fostered by foreign capital investment, mainly in logistics, transportation, telecommunications, retailing and high-tech industry.

In 2005, there were 354,000 registered enterprises in Budapest – a 7 per cent growth since 1995. The majority of enterprises are small businesses with 0–9 employees and it is typical of Central Hungary that the number of medium-sized enterprises is below the national average. In terms of output and employment, the five most important branches are the chemical industry, machinery, food processing, woodworking and publishing. Within services the financial sector has been developing most intensely. Other innovative economic branches in Budapest are information and communications technologies, logistics, life sciences (medicinal production, bio- and nano-technology), creative industries and the cultural economy. The economic and spatial changes in the Budapest metropolitan region were at their most intense on the metropolitan periphery.

Leipzig (with some 500,000 inhabitants) is situated in the Free State of Saxony in eastern Germany. It is the largest city in Saxony, closely followed by the state capital, Dresden. Leipzig is one of the core cities of the metropolitan region known as Sachsendreieck (Saxon Triangle), consisting of Leipzig, Dresden and Chemnitz/Zwickau. On a smaller scale, the axis linking the adjacent cities of Leipzig and Halle forms a conurbation with about 1.5 million inhabitants. The Leipzig city region, that is the area covered by the analysis of the creative knowledge sector, embraces three surrounding districts within a radius of approximately 15 km around the core city.

The population of Leipzig declined from 562,000 in 1981 to 497,000 in 2003. This decline was due to a negative net migration and a low birth rate. Since the beginning of 2000, a small but steady consolidation and growth in population has taken place. These positive demographic developments are an exception in East Germany and can be interpreted as a sign of revitalisation.

The factors that have affected the present-day economic situation of Leipzig most crucially have been the reunification of Germany and the transition of its eastern part from a command to a market economy that started in 1990. Large parts of manufacturing industry were no longer competitive and employment in manufacturing decreased from 101,000 to about 13,000 between 1989 and 2002 (Amt für Wirtschaftsförderung, 2004). Private services, on the other hand, exhibited a rapid increase but not strong enough to fully replace the jobs lost in manufacturing. The percentage of the workforce in Leipzig accounted for by traditional industries such as machinery manufacturing and energy generation declined from 38 per cent in 1990 to 18 per cent by the end of the 1990s.

At present Leipzig's economic strategy focuses on both traditional and new sectors. The main economic activities are trade shows and exhibitions (chiefly organised by the Leipzig Fair), automotive production, retail and distribution, logistics, health care and medical engineering, biotech and life sciences, energy and environmental technology, and media and communication.

The third case, Poznan, is one of the fastest-growing cities in Poland, located in the west-central part of the country, halfway between Warsaw and Berlin. It is the capital of the Wielkopolska (Greater Poland) region where the Polish state originated more than 1000 years ago. Poznan is the fifth largest city in Poland (after Warsaw, Cracow, Lodz and Wroclaw). What gives it prominence in the national urban network is the fact that it is the seat of the Association of Polish Towns, a non-governmental organisation embracing 306 towns and cities.

The city apart, the spatial range of the Poznan metropolitan region (PMR) coincides with the boundaries of the administrative unit called Poznan poviat (district). It includes the adjacent towns and communes and has a population of 856,000, of which the city accounts for 568,000 and the poviat for 288,000.

The position of Poznan in the European network of metropolitan regions is defined by two features:

- in comparison with the biggest European cities, Poznan's metropolitan functions are not yet fully formed;
- Poznan's location halfway between Warsaw and Berlin puts the city under strong competitive pressure from those two capitals;

The economy of the PMR is mixed. Services account for 70.9 per cent of the region's gross value added (GVA). The diversification of the economic profile and the balanced growth potential (also in demographic terms) are the strongest points of the city and region. Other strong points include:

• efficient institutions and well-managed city finance;
• success in attracting foreign direct investment;
• entrepreneurship and high work standards;
• a high quality of life (in relation to other Polish metropolises);
• a recognised quality of higher education (with its 214 university students per 1000 inhabitants, Poznan ranks first among the largest Polish cities);
• a rich cultural milieu (especially music and dance);
• availability of attractive housing.

Riga is an ancient Hanseatic city and the capital of Latvia. Its population has fallen dramatically since the break-up of the Soviet Union, from more than 900,000 in 1990 to 732,000 in 2005. This means that since Latvia regained its independence in 1991, Riga has lost roughly one-fifth of its residents. The long-term demographic projection for the Riga region is assumed to follow the same trend as for Latvia, that is under-replacement of generations in the future combined with a rapid ageing of the population. There has been a dramatic absolute and relative reduction in the number of children, so that by 2020 the number of people aged 15–19 years will be half of the 2000 figure. This means that there will be a potential shortage of labour in the future. Riga is a multi-ethnic city – approximately 50 per cent of the population is ethnic Latvian, and more than 40 per cent is ethnic Russian.

The city is Latvia's main attractor of both investment and employment and by far the richest region in the country. It is the country's transportation hub and there are several infrastructural projects that will strengthen this role in the future. Riga specialises in the tertiary sector. The main services are real estate, renting and business activities; financial intermediation; as well as transport, storage and telecommunication. Since the collapse of the Soviet Union, Riga's industrial sector has undergone a substantial transformation and the industry structure has changed drastically. Large factories have either downsized their activities or closed down entirely. In contrast, the city's service industries, as well as the number of small enterprises, have grown considerably. According to the 2007 Global Entrepreneurship Monitor, Riga's level of early-stage entrepreneurial activity is among the highest in Latvia with approximately 7 per cent of the adult population involved in such activity. Not only has Riga's industrial structure changed with the fall of the Soviet Union, so has its macro-geographical position. Riga's strategic position within the Soviet Union was very strong owing to its proximity to the important Moscow–Leningrad–Minsk triangle. After 1990, Riga moved from a strategic geographical location in the hierarchy of the Soviet economic space to occupy a peripheral location in the hierarchy of the EU economic space.

The case of Sofia, the capital of Bulgaria, is slightly different from those presented above when seen in terms of institutional change. Bulgaria is the only European post-communist country that failed to make the transition in one leap. It went through two economic collapses caused by governments of ex-communists, and consequently staged two 'revolutions', first in 1989–1990 and then in 1996–1997. It was only after the latter that Bulgaria turned seriously to the business of institutional reform, in a situation of virtually zero resources and complete economic exhaustion. As a result, the country joined the EU later than most of its neighbours in the region, on 1 January 2007.

Sofia is an example of a big city with poorly developed metropolitan functions and an institutional profile which is only just 'emerging out of chaos' (Dainov et al., 2007). This also refers to the practice of institutions responsible for statistics and relying on an antiquated methodology that is lagging behind the processes of change. For example, the official population figure for Sofia is 1.4 million, but an estimated 0.5 million permanent inhabitants are not registered as residents (Dainov et al., 2007, p. 11). The same holds for economic statistics.

As in the case of Budapest and Riga, Sofia is an area of concentration of domestic employment (ca. one-fifth of the total workforce), GDP generation (ca. one-third of the national GDP), higher education (42 per cent of Bulgarian students) and foreign direct investment (56 per cent of total stock of FDI in Bulgaria). Being an old heavy-industry city, it has been changing fast into a major service centre (its tertiary sector employs 71.3 per cent of the working population and generates 70 per cent of GDP). An important role is also played by the city's communication function (three European transport corridors cross here), which is favourable to the flow of domestic and international migrants. The process of social and economic transformation in Sofia is chaotic and uncontrolled to a much greater extent than in the other cities referred to in this book. Bulgaria's joining the EU may prove the chief stimulant of institutional change.

Development pathways shaping the city profiles and the role of the systemic change

Mahoney (2000, p. 507) stated that 'path dependence characterizes specifically those historical sequences in which contingent events set into motion institutional patterns'. According to Musterd et al. (2007, pp. 13–14), one dimension of this concept 'relates to institutional and organisational change of local, regional and national political–economic systems. (...)

As Harloe (1996) argued, we cannot accept that "state socialism" was a cross-nationally identical phenomenon, or that a similarly uniform method could have been applied for the transition. (...) Institutional change in these countries also did not necessarily result in the establishment of a west European type of market economy or social and cultural milieu.' The same holds for the metropolitan regions analysed here. In the recent development pathways shaping their profiles, only two turning points have been similar:

- imposition of a command system after the World War II;
- return to the family of European cities after the collapse of the communist bloc followed by EU enlargement;

All other elements of institutional change and development paths differ from one city to the next and are described briefly below.

The development path of Budapest is closely connected with its political and administrative functions. In the past centuries there were two periods when Budapest gained a leading role in east-central Europe. During the fifteenth and sixteenth centuries, there was no other urban centre of comparable size and significance in that region except for Vienna, Prague and Cracow; and a later political compromise with the Habsburgs, in 1867, opened the second great phase of development in the history of Budapest lasting until the World War I. In population it had reached one million and the city had advanced to seventh place in Europe. Budapest exerted an economic and cultural influence stretching beyond the borders of the Austro-Hungarian Empire to the Balkans and northern Italy and it was a real competitor for Vienna in many respects. The last three decades of the nineteenth century represented the peak of urban and economic growth in the history of the city. This extensive late-nineteenth-century capitalist development turned Budapest from a provincial town into a modern, cosmopolitan metropolis. It was then that the Hungarian government decided to establish a comprehensive planning authority in the form of the Municipal Commission of Public Works. The Commission was given control over urban investments and the implementation of the government's regulations. City planning was permeated by the idea of order, with the roads and streets traced, the height of buildings set, and palaces and fountains built in an identical style.

The World War I and the dissolution of the Austro-Hungarian monarchy altered the spatial position and relationships of Budapest. In 1920, Hungary lost 71 per cent of its territory and 66 per cent of its population, and the weight of Budapest in the socio-economic pattern of the country became disproportionately large. However, the institutional mechanisms of city planning and governance did not change essentially in the interwar period.

A significant change took place after the communist takeover in 1949. The Commission of Public Works was dissolved and the central authority subordinated the processes of city development to its own ideological and economic interests. The communist political structure and the centralised management of society eliminated local self-government and local urban planning. As in the other countries of the Eastern bloc, the development of heavy-industry functions was of prime importance.

The position of the Budapest metropolitan region in the European network did not change essentially until the end of the twentieth century, that is until the collapse of the communist regime. Budapest entered the post-socialist period with a relatively good position among the east European cities. The globalisation process of the last two decades as well as its advantageous geographical location made it possible for Budapest to accumulate organising functions and to become a prime political, economic and cultural centre in central and eastern Europe. Budapest and its region have attracted nearly half of the foreign capital coming to the country after 1990; the financial and commercial sectors have developed very intensively. What can be predicted from the current trends is that the Budapest metropolitan region may become a logistic, distribution or organisation centre, but without any co-ordinating or decision-making responsibilities at the European level.

The traditional development paths of Leipzig, Poznan and Riga are closely connected with their trading functions. However, they are also examples of how institutional changes following systemic transformation can re-shape traditional development paths. Leipzig provides the best illustration here, hence it will be given more attention, the more so as this re-shaping is connected with the creative knowledge sector.

Before the World War II Leipzig was one of the most important trade centres in Germany. Much of the trade with eastern Europe was traditionally conducted in Leipzig during the two annual trade fairs. The city gained further importance as a printing and publishing centre. The growth of manufacturing industries in the nineteenth century was accompanied by rapid population growth and Leipzig became one of the largest cities in Germany at that time. It continued to hold an important position in the GDR as an international fair city. However, the city showed massive signs of decay and decline during that time due to a lack of investment in housing and physical infrastructure and a high level of environmental pollution caused in part by open-pit coal-mining and carbon-chemical industries in the region.

A new, more diversified development path opened for Leipzig after the collapse of the communist system and the reunification of Germany. In the early 1990s, public officials and marketing experts created the image of a 'boomtown Leipzig' and presented the city as an emerging international centre for East-West trade and a modern 'Messe- und Medienstadt' (city of fairs and media). The city aimed at (re-)positioning itself on the international scale. This fuelled a construction boom in the early 1990s that terminated near the end of the decade. Large amounts of public funds had also been channelled into the region in order to provide the infrastructural and technical basis for innovative technologies and international standards in the field of mobility, fair business and distribution of goods.

However, the expected growth in the business service sector did not take place, and in 2003 Leipzig had an office vacancy rate of 23 per cent, the highest among the German cities. The only business service that showed high growth rates was banking. There was some growth in the media sector (printing, publishing, film and TV productions), but other producer services lagged behind. Still, there were also signs of a recovery. The city managed to maintain the high status of the Leipzig Fair against strong competition and even the Book Fair has stood up well to its competitor in Frankfurt. The first elements of a globally oriented economy had emerged on Leipzig's northern fringe, in the shape of an airport, a motorway, a freight transport centre, a new Leipzig Fair exhibition centre and a new BMW car plant.

As mentioned before, Leipzig has a long tradition in publishing and printing. The importance of the traditional printing sector diminished considerably in the post-socialist period and hopes that publishing companies that had left Leipzig after the World War II would return did not come true. There are nonetheless some significant developments in the field of electronic media, especially movie and TV production. The development of a media cluster was to a large degree due to the involvement of the public sector, in particular the city of Leipzig and the state of Saxony. Key decisions were taken to support the growth of the cluster, for instance, subsidies for new firms and the decision to move the headquarters of the regional public TV channel MDR to Leipzig. In 1992, the Medienstadt Leipzig GmbH was formed to support the development in Leipzig of media-related activities. In 2000, the Media City Leipzig was built, a large studio and office complex for movie and TV productions. It is located right next to the headquarters of the MDR, which opened in the same year. A study of media- and communication-related activities (Bentle et al., 2002) estimates the employment in this sector at 32,800 jobs (including 9,700 self-employed persons). Some 4300 jobs are in publishing and printing and 4200 in TV, film and radio. Most of the media-related firms are very small in terms of employment, which explains their large number – 1350. Eighty-six per cent of them were founded after 1990, with a peak in the mid-1990s (Bentle et al., 2002). Leipzig is not one of the leading media cities in Germany and ranks far behind Berlin, Cologne, Hamburg and Munich. Nevertheless its media cluster is one of the strong points of the local economy.

Leipzig demonstrates that a true re-shaping of a city's development path towards a more globalised, creative and competitive profile is easier with a high level of institutional, organisational and capital involvement of the state, regional and local authorities taking advantage of public–private partnership (PPP). Unfortunately, such possibilities are unavailable in Poznan, Riga and Sofia. This does not mean, however, that there are no new development paths emerging in these cities.

The long history of Poznan city, which started in the tenth century, has been a sequence of events which provide a basis for the building of a creative region. In the fourteenth and fifteenth centuries, its favourable location on one of the major trade routes of central Europe made Poznan an important European-ranking centre of trade and crafts. As a result of the partitioning of Poland in 1793, the city was incorporated into Prussia, which greatly limited its growth. Despite the restrictive policy of the occupants, in the nineteenth century Poznan's scientific and economic life flourished, thanks to the operation of Polish institutions and private enterprises. They competed successfully with Prussian firms, and to do this the city residents had to muster their dormant resources of creativity and entrepreneurship. The regaining of independence by Poland in 1918 put Poznan again on the path of socio-economic development and enabled the creative potential of the city flourish. This manifested itself in the establishment of Poznan University (1920), the organisation of the first Poznan International Fair (1925), and the setting up of numerous banking institutions and industrial enterprises. The outbreak of the World War II curbed the city's growth. War losses and the nearly 50-year-long rule of the communist regime were not favourable to the development of the creative knowledge sector. The deteriorating socio-economic situation of the country led to an anti-communist protest of Poznan workers in 1956, the first of such protests in Poland, and later to the establishment of the Independent Self-governed Trade Union Solidarity in the early 1980s. This movement was one of the chief social initiatives releasing the creative potential of both the country and the city. People's engagement in activities directed against the communist regime led to its collapse in 1989. One should stress, however, that during the communist period Poznan was lucky enough to avoid becoming a heavily industrialised city and had developed commercial functions which later spared the city the difficult task of dealing with structural economic change.

The new political and economic situation allowed the rebirth of entrepreneurship and organisational skills among the residents of Poznan and restored the city to its traditional 'external openness' connected with its commercial and communication functions. The PMR has become one of the leaders of the socio-economic transformation. At present Poznan seems to follow two pathways to a creative and knowledge-based city. One can be termed a catch-up process imitating the development paths of Western-type metropolitan regions. The other, which can be called endogenous, utilises local tradition and resources, including human capital.

Like Poznan and Leipzig, Riga has been a centre of trade and commerce from the moment of its foundation in 1201. In 1281, it joined the Hanseatic League and for centuries its development was closely connected with trade. A significant change in Riga's development path took place from the mid-nineteenth century until the outbreak of the World War I, when the city saw heavy industrialisation and a large inflow of labour. In addition, Riga, being the third largest city in the Russian Empire, bene-fited tremendously from trade with the hinterland. Around the turn of the nineteenth century Riga could be characterised as a 'boom town'. In the early 1900s, the celebrated Art Nouveau/Jugendstil buildings were erected – build-ings that give the 'new town' its character and that are highly appreciated today.

During the twentieth century, Riga's development pathway was inter-rupted and changed many times due to external shocks including wars and the Soviet occupation. Therefore, Riga is the most glaring example of interrupted development pathways among our cities. The year 1918 saw the birth of the Latvian nation state. Riga gained political importance, but suffered from war damage as well as from the loss of the big Russian mar-ket and virtually all major industrial plants, which had been moved to the Russian interior in 1915–1916. That is why the period 1918–1940 was for Latvia, one of small-scale industry based on the country's own resources (such as woodworking and food processing) and a Western re-orientation of the economy. Probably the most advanced 'knowledge-based' company during the interwar period was VEF, which employed highly skilled engi-neers and workers to develop various 'high-tech' products, for example cameras and radio sets, that combined technological superiority with excellent design.

In the period of the Soviet occupation (1945–1991), as in the rest of the Soviet Union, Riga's economy was subordinated to central planning through 5-year plans. The Stalinist era saw a programme of rapid industrialisation putting an emphasis on the same industries for which Riga had been impor-tant prior to 1914. Many of the industries established in Riga served the entire Soviet Union. The transition period (1991–1999) following the break-up of the Soviet Union and Latvia's regaining of its independence brought about a dramatic shift in the economic structure of Riga. The change in Latvia's geopolitical situation showed considerable similarities with that of 1918. Most of the trading links with the East disappeared and industry had to re-orientate again, both in terms of trading partners and the profile of production. The service sector, underdeveloped during Soviet times, expanded rapidly during the 1990s, while at the same time the big Soviet companies either closed down entirely or downsized considerably.

The 2000s have been marked by a continuing expansion of the service sector. Financial services have grown rapidly and Riga's economy has re-oriented itself from low-skilled, low-paid jobs to ones with high value added. This has spurred a discussion about the creative and knowledge-based economy and its potential in terms of transforming the Latvian economy. So far, however, there has been much discussion on the side of policy makers, but not many concrete results. At the same time several major cultural infrastructural projects have been planned.

While Riga shows the most turbulent development path, Sofia is character-ised as lagging behind other cities of east-central Europe and simultaneously as chaotic and hard to identify clearly. Although the history of Bulgaria and its capital is very long, the Bulgarian economy in the modern mean-ing took its first steps at the beginning of the nineteenth century when the region became known for its agricultural products. Being part of the Ottoman Empire (until 1879) was a hindrance to the processes of industri-alisation and modernisation of the economy. It was only in the mid-twentieth century that the Bulgarian communist government decided to turn the country into an 'industrial giant of the Balkans' based on the Soviet heavy-industry model. This strategy applied in particular to the country's capital and for years determined Sofia's development path.

Bulgaria (and hence Sofia) was also late in entering the path of the post-communist transformation. In contrast to the other east European countries, the state maintained much of its control over the economy until the late 1990s. Privatisation was limited and corrupted, which gave rise to a 'grey' or 'shadow' economy. It was only in 1997 that Bulgaria experienced economic stability crowned, after 10 years, with EU membership. This was undoubtedly a turning point on Sofia's development path, although it is too early yet to assess the results of this change. The most readily visible consequence of the transformation has been a radical change in the city's economic structure: with more than 70 per cent of its GDP coming from the service sector, the capital is certainly no longer a heavy-industry area. From a social point of view, many international migrants have flowed to the city, forming a multinational mix. This may provide a good basis for the future growth of the creative sector.

The development path of Sofia after the World War II shows that the city has not grown according to some sound and comprehensive planning or premeditated urban policies. The plans occasionally implemented here were often based on unrealistic assumptions. In this respect little changed after 1990, current development plans of different levels (national, regional, local) are partly based on imprecise data and projections, and so they mean a continuation of the imperfect governance heritage. Undoubtedly, Sofia's economy has gone through deep restructuring over the last decade, but the 'creative' part of the economy has been entirely the outcome of private (foreign) interest and investment. Given the lack of strong traditions of planning and urban policy, it can be expected that the evolution of Sofia into a creative city will remain unplanned, chaotic and rather informally (if at all) institutionalised.

Determinants of development of the creative knowledge sector

While the development pathways of the metropolitan regions of east-central Europe differ widely, there has been a common tendency, too: a transition from manufacturing to more service-oriented and in particular to more creative and knowledge-intensive industries. In all the case studies analysed in the present chapter, the systemic change that started in the early 1990s meant an important turning point which awoke their dormant potential and opened a new 'window of opportunity' (in Sofia this took place in the late 1990s). The cities, cut off from global restructuring processes for many post-war years, had to 're-invent' themselves in the new political and socio-economic conditions. The creative knowledge sector had to develop from the ground up against a deficiency of capital, institutions and supporting policies.

In most of the metropolitan regions of east-central Europe, catching up with the creative and knowledge-based economy has been a more or less spontaneous process. Only Leipzig, successfully utilising government subsidies, provides an example of at least a partly steered development pathway in its attempt to revive the old pre-communist tradition of creative industries (such as the media or publishing), and to attract new high-tech and creative activities under state, regional and local restructuring programmes. These measures were complemented by a lively cultural scene, relatively low rents, available work spaces and thick network structures. Leipzig is often perceived by creative entrepreneurs as an 'open', unfinished city where there is still room for development.

In general, east-central European cities are in a less advantageous position than west European ones because of their inadequate level of city governance, lack of financial and organisational resources, and the weakness of innovation policy (cf. Kovács et al., 2007, p. 25). Their major competitive advantage seems to be a high level of education. Moreover, there are also some more 'localised' assets, such as the widely recognised cultural milieu of Budapest, the historically evolved entrepreneurial spirit of Poznan or the tradition of peaceful co-existence of ethnic minorities in Sofia. Unfortunately, these and other soft factors conducive to the growth of the creative knowledge sector were completely neglected before 1990, and have still not found full recognition in urban and regional development policies.

Table 6.1 Employment in the creative knowledge sector, 2004–2005.

| City region | Creative knowledge sector | | | | |
	Thousand employees	% of total employment	Creative industries	Knowledge-intensive industries	Proportion of knowledge-intensive to creative industries
Budapest	427.1	29	13	16	1.2:1
Leipzig	72	25	9	16	1.8:1
Poznan	94.3	18	7	11	1.6:1
Riga	110	29	6	23	3.8:1
Sofia	153.7	27	8	19	2.4:1

Source: ACRE reports 2.4, 2.6, 2.8–2.10 (http://acre.socsci.uva.nl/results/reports.html).

In spite of these difficulties, the development of the creative and knowledge-intensive industries in the metropolitan regions of east-central Europe within the short transition period is positive. This is evidenced by a great number of newly established, mainly small and medium-sized firms,[1] and dynamically growing employment. The employment statistics for the years 2004–2005 are presented in Table 6.1. The figures (both absolute and relative) are comparable with (and sometimes even higher than) those in west European metropolitan regions. However, they should be interpreted with care, not only because of 'twisted' statistics. In the post-communist countries, many employees in the creative knowledge sector have low-skilled, low-paid and low value-added jobs. As a result, the significance of this sector may be overestimated.

In spite of these reservations, all the analysed cities show the role of knowledge-intensive industries to be higher than creative ones. However, the proportions between them differ considerably, which makes it possible to distinguish two development profiles:

- cities with a decided dominance of knowledge-intensive industries (Riga and to a lesser extent Sofia);
- cities with a more balanced proportion of employment in creative and knowledge-intensive industries (Budapest, Poznan and Leipzig);

Looking towards the future, Budapest and Leipzig appear to have the biggest chance of developing into competitive, creative and knowledge-based cities within the European metropolitan network. Budapest's progress

---

[1] For example, in Budapest, the average employment in a creative and knowledge-based firm is 3.83 workers and in Poznan, 4.24.

in the integration with this network has been quite successful, in spite of temporary economic difficulties. If the Budapest metropolitan region proves able to use its options stemming from its geographical setting and economic endowments, it could play a gateway role in the development of the creative knowledge sector, including in particular cultural industries, in this part of Europe. The city's most serious growth limitations seem to be the overburdened public transport, affordability of service facilities, a relatively high and still growing level of prices, and social tensions (a widening gap between social strata and the position of the Roma community).

While social problems are also present in Leipzig, the future development of the creative sector in this city seems to be determined by other factors. Creative scenes and milieus play an important role here and contribute to the attractiveness of the cultural economy, although their impact cannot be fully expressed in hard economic figures. Their precarious socio-economic status reflects the instability, project-orientation and the flexibility required of this economy.

Leipzig's relatively cheap rents and living costs as well as easily accessible work space have stimulated the emergence of creative scenes and creative milieus. The existing creative scenes (core creative producers in the field of design, art, painting, fashion, film, music, architecture, photography, etc.) play a crucial, though not always visible, role in the everyday life of the city. Each of these creative scenes has its fairly individual networks, meeting places and social practices. Thus, a balance between hard and soft development factors and a system of supporting policies are the chief assets of Leipzig.

The last element, regrettably, is still poorly developed in Poznan, Riga and especially Sofia. Here hard growth factors still seem to predominate over soft ones. The key challenges in Poznan are an improvement of co-operation between the state, regional and local authorities and institutions, and between public and private sectors; and integration of the various strategic programmes and actions. Further development of the creative sector will require the strengthening of the role of cultural industries. The PMR has many solid cultural assets and a great cultural heritage, but it does not make full use of its rich offer to promote culture, for example through cultural tourism. A challenge of a different nature that has appeared after the 'old' EU states opened their labour markets to the new members is a heavy outflow of well-educated young people seeking better job opportunities in those countries (not balanced by an inflow of creative immigrants). This outflow can be both, a threat to and a chance for the development of the creative sector in Poznan. It will become a chance if those people come back after they have gained a new experience, and they will do it if on return they find comparable conditions in which to express their creativity.

The institutional context is strongly emphasised in discussions on future development paths of the creative knowledge sector in Riga and Sofia. Three challenges have been identified:

- the need to transform this sector towards activities with a higher value added;
- the need to create a political commitment to implement strategies promoting the development of creative and knowledge-based industries;
- the need for civil society to mature;

When discussing institutional change and new development paths in post-Soviet countries, it is important to emphasise that the development of the creative knowledge sector cannot proceed in a vacuum. It has to involve stakeholders other than policy makers. The recent literature on planning and regional development highlights the need to involve various stakeholders in the process, that is what Pires et al. (2001) call participatory planning. Furthermore, when discussing a new agenda there is a need for partnership among all stakeholders through a consensus between the local government, business and voluntary sectors. Such 'growth coalitions' involving and co-operating with local politicians, the media, public leaders and semi-public institutions (including development agencies, chambers of commerce, employers' federations, trade unions) with a view to generating a coherent vision and strategy, are crucial when it comes to the economic development of a city. Swyngedouw (2000) develops these arguments further and claims that failure to bring broad layers of civil society in line with the growth coalition's vision might result in conflicts that have the potential to erode the base on which successful development rests. On the other hand, North (1990) argues that the actions and behaviour of individuals as well as the functioning of institutions are path-dependent. Applied to Riga, Sofia and to a lesser extent the other cities under analysis, this means that their past might still play an important role in individual behaviour patterns and actions. According to Schrader (2004), post-communist societies face a situation where the social capital of the entire society is weak compared with western Europe. To conclude, as a result most east-central European cities face challenges different from the west European ones when it comes to developing their potential as 'creative cities'.

Conclusions

The analysis carried out in this chapter shows that the communist 'diversion' of east-central European cities from their evolutionary, 'linear' pathways assuming a priority of heavy industry and a neglect of the tertiary sector has also resulted in a late start of the creative knowledge sector.

The metropolitan regions in this part of Europe have been striving to catch up on this delay in a variety of ways and at a pace of their own. As a result, there is a mosaic of many forms of adjustment to the new conditions that have emerged after such fundamental institutional changes as the collapse of communism and the enlargement of the EU. There has undoubtedly been an increase in competition among the cities under investigation, and their future competitive advantage will largely depend on their capacity to accommodate creative and knowledge-intensive industries. The cities that have a better chance in this competition are those that are major decision-making centres (in particular state capitals), that entered the path of trans-formation relatively early, sometimes even during the communist period (Budapest), and that rely on massive government involvement in their restructuring process (Leipzig).

The case of Leipzig seems particularly promising from the point of view of the prospects for future development of a creative sector. As Bontje and Musterd (2008, p. 253) have observed, the city is struggling 'to reclaim its lost prominent position in Europe'. This indicates that even if a city's pathway has been disturbed, some remnants of earlier development paths (such as creative scenes and milieus) may still be there, although temporar-ily dormant. These remnants are a valuable asset which, supported by an appropriate policy, may be revived.

Unfortunately, unlike in Leipzig, in most east-central European cities, the problems of 'institutional thickness' and lack of coherent supporting policies are some of the more serious weaknesses hindering the accommo-dation of creative knowledge. However, a deficiency of official institutions or their antiquated style of operation is often compensated for by informal structures and activities. As a result, the dynamics of change in the met-ropolitan regions of east-central Europe is very high, although so far the directions of change from 1990 onwards have been widely different and hardly yield to generalisations. Nevertheless, two factors seem particularly important when explaining these differences: the value of old urban profiles and the present institutional setting and policies.

Acknowledgements

The authors thank Anders Paalzow (Riga) and Ivan Nachev (Sofia) for their kind and fruitful co-operation in writing this chapter.

References

Amt für Wirtschaftsförderung (2004) *Wirtschaftsbericht 2003/2004*. Leipzig: Stadt Leipzig.
Arthur, W.B. (1989) Competing technologies, increasing returns, and lock-in by historical small events. *Economic Journal*, 99: 116–131.

Balcerowicz, L. (1995) Wolność i rozwój: ekonomia wolnego rynku [Freedom and development: the economy of free market]. Kraków: Znak.

Balcerowicz, L. (1996) Polish economic reform in a comparative perspective. In: T. Baczko (ed.), *The second stage of Polish economic transformation. Transformation policy*, pp. 17–33. Warsaw: INE PAN, ICEG, PWN.

Belka, M. and W. Trzeciakowski (eds) (1997) *Dynamika transformacji polskiej gospodarki* [Dynamics of Polish economic transformation]. Warszawa: INE PAN.

Bentle, G., T. Liebert and M. Polifke (2002) *Medienstandort Leipzig IV. Studie zum Cluster Medien/Kommunikationstechnik/IT 2002*. Leipzig: Universität Leipzig.

Bontje, M. and S. Musterd (2008) The multi-layered city: The value of old urban profiles. *Tijdschrift voor Economische en Sociale Geografie*, 99 (2): 248–255.

Chojnicki, Z. (1990) The anatomy of the crisis of the Polish economy. In: A. Kukliński and B. Jałowiecki (eds), *Local development in Europe. Experiences and prospects. Regional and Local Studies* 5, pp. 55–88. Warsaw: University of Warsaw.

Dainov, E., I. Nachev, M. Pancheva and V. Garnizov (2007) *The 'Sofia Model': Creation out of chaos. Pathways to creative and knowledge-based regions*. ACRE report 2.10. Amsterdam: AMIDSt.

Global Entrepreneurship Monitor (2007) *Latvia Report*. The TeliaSonera Institute at SSE Riga.

Grabher, G. (1997) Adaptation at the cost of adaptability. Reconstructing the Eastern German regional economy. In: G. Grabher and D. Stark (eds), *Restructuring networks in post socialism: Legacies, linkages and localities*. Oxford: Oxford University Press.

Harloe, M. (1996) Cities in transition. In: G. Andrusz, M. Harloe and I. Szelenyi (eds), *Cities after socialism*, pp. 1–29. Oxford: Blackwell.

Kloosterman, R. and E. Stegmeijer (2004) Cultural industries in the Netherlands – Path-dependent patterns and institutional context: The case of architecture in Rotterdam. *Petermanns Geographische Mitteilungen*, 148 (4): 68–75.

Kovács, Z., A. Murie, S. Musterd, O. Gritsai and H. Pethe (2007) *Comparing paths of creative knowledge regions*. ACRE report 3. Amsterdam: AMIDSt.

Mahoney, J. (2000) Path dependence in historical sociology. *Theory and Society*, 29: 507–548.

Mahoney, J. (2001) *Legacies of liberalism: Path dependency and political regimes in Central America*, Baltimore: Johns Hopkins University Press.

Margolis, S.E. (1995) Path dependence, lock-in, and history. *Journal of Law, Economics and Organization*, 11: 205–226.

Musterd, S., M. Bontje, C. Chapain, Z. Kovacs and A. Murie (2007) *Accommodating creative knowledge. A literature review from a European perspective*. ACRE report 1. Amsterdam: AMIDSt.

North, D.C. (1990) *Institutions, institutional change and economic performance*. Cambridge: Cambridge University Press.

Parysek, J.J. (1992) Polski przemysłe a nowe warunki społeczno-ustrojowe [Polish industry and the new systemic conditions]. In: Z. Chojnicki (ed.), *Studia geograficzne przemian społeczno-gospodarczych [Geographical studies of socio-economic changes]*, pp. 75–88. Biuletyn KPZK PAN, 159. Warszawa: PWN.

Parysek J.J. (1998) Efekty procesu transformacji społeczno-gospodarczej w Polsce. [Effects of socio-economic transition in Poland]. In: J.J. Parysek and H. Rogacki (eds), *Przemiany spo ł eczno-gospodarcze Polski lat dziewięćdziesiątych [Socio-economic changes in Poland in 1990s]*, pp. 25–46. Poznan: Bogucki Wyd. Nauk.

Pires, A., L. Albrechts and J. Alden (2001) Conclusions: Driving process for institutional change. In: L. Albrechts, J. Alden, A. Pires and da Rosa (eds), *The changing institutional landscape of planning*, pp. 257–267. Aldershot: Ashgate.

Schrader, H. (2004) Social capital and social transformation in Russia. *Journal for Eastern European Management Studies*, 9 (4): 391–410.

Smith, A. (1997) Breaking the old and constructing the new? Geographies of uneven development in Central and Eastern Europe. In: R. Lee and J. Willis (eds), *Geographies of Economies*, pp. 331–344. London: Arnold.

Smith, A. and A. Swain (1998) Regulating and institutionalising capitalism: The microfoundations of transformation in Eastern and Central Europe. In: J. Pickles and A. Smith (eds), *Theorising transition. The political economy of post-communist transformations*, pp. 25–53. London, New York: Routledge.

Stryjakiewicz, T. (2000) Industrial transformation in Poland and its spatial dimension. In: Z. Chojnicki and J.J. Parysek (eds), *Polish geography. Problems, researches, applications*, pp. 19–39. Poznan: Bogucki Wyd. Nauk.

Swyngedouw, E. (2000) Elite power, global forces and the political economy of 'glocal' development. In: G.L. Clark, M.P. Feldman and M.S. Gerlter (eds), *The Oxford handbook of economic geography*, pp. 541–558. Oxford: Oxford University Press.

7

Changing Specialisations and Single Sector Dominance: Helsinki and Toulouse

Hélène Martin-Brelot and Kaisa Kepsu

Introduction

Globalisation and the changing 'New Economy' have created fundamental challenges for nations and metropolitan regions all over the world. For many cities, the transition to a new stage of economic development has historically been regarded as a difficult task (Porter, 1990; Porter, 1998; Steinbock, 2006). Helsinki and Toulouse are both examples of cities that have been successful in transforming their structure to a specialised high-tech economy in a relatively short period of time. Whereas the Finnish capital mainly relied on natural resources, the southwestern French metropolis was characterised by small-scale, dispersed industries producing manufactured goods in a rather rural region. In Helsinki, the ICT sector, particularly telecommunications, has been extremely successful and the main driver of the growing economy after the economic crisis of the 1990s. In Toulouse, since the 1960s specialisation has developed in aeronautics, space, electronics and ICT activities. The aim of this chapter is to explore the pathways of Helsinki and Toulouse to knowledge-driven economies. How did the shift in the economy towards high technology take place? What are the key drivers, change events and crucial institutions involved in the cities' development?

The path dependency perspective assumes that there is some kind of continuity in the process of technological change, and thus links technical innovation to past developments (Schienstock, 2004; Kovács et al., 2007). Contrary to many other European cities, neither Helsinki nor Toulouse experienced the industrial revolution. This spared them environmental damage and painful socio-economic restructuring from heavy industry and can partly explain their successful shift to a new productive system. More important is the fact that, in both cities, economic growth has been largely knowledge driven. Both regions have an exceptionally highly educated population and well-developed educational institutions – essential in creating a knowledge-based society. The focus of public policies has been on education, science and R&D aiming to create a large endogenous skilled and specialised labour force. Both Helsinki and Midi-Pyrénées regions devote an important share of their GDP for R&D expenditures (Table 7.1).

Path dependency is both temporally located and socially embedded (Schienstock, 2004). The different positions of Helsinki and Toulouse in Europe and in the national urban hierarchy, as well as their distinct environment, history and culture, have influenced the development of their economies. Institutions also play a critical part in technological change (Lundvall, 1992; Schienstock, 2004; Kovács et al., 2007). The direction of change can be shaped by conscious social choices, often triggered by a critical incident. Although the role of the state has been very important, the examples of Helsinki and Toulouse confirm that the state has changed from a control-exercising actor to a partner in policy networks of private and public actors (Schienstock, 2004). In both cities, individual decisions, individual actors and unforeseen factors have played a role in the steps towards new economic development (Kovács et al., 2007). Today, these specialised metropolises have to bear vulnerabilities associated with the dependence on a single dominant sector, and moreover, on leading global

Table 7.1 Top 15 EU regions in terms of R&D expenditure, as a percentage of GDP, all sectors, 2003.

Regions	Per cent of GDP	EUR million	Per cent of EU-27
EU-27	1.87	187708	100
Braunschweig (DE)	8.70	3595	1.9
Västsverige (SE)	6.03	3135	1.7
Stuttgart (DE)	4.66	5996	3.2
Oberbayern (DE)	4.60	7352	3.9
Pohjois-Suomi (FI)	**4.60**	**726**	**0.4**
Stockholm (SE)	4.31	3276	1.7
Östra Mellansverige (SE)	4.25	1632	0.9
Sydsverige (SE)	4.13	1490	0.8
Berlin (DE)	3.94	3096	1.6
Tübingen (DE)	3.89	1908	1.0
East of England (UK)	3.85	4595	2.4
Karlsruhe (DE)	3.83	3166	1.7
Midi-Pyrénées (FR)	**3.72**	**2283**	**1.2**
Etelä-Suomi (FI)	**3.55**	**2933**	**1.6**
Länsi-Suomi (FI)	**3.49**	**1139**	**0.6**

UK: NUTS level 1.
Exception to the reference year: East of England (UK): 1999.
Source: Science, technology and innovation in Europe. Eurostat. Statistical Books, 2008.

companies: Nokia and Airbus. There arc strong pressures for diversification of the local economy.

This chapter sets the context of the two metropolitan regions and their respective economic trajectories in a historical framework. It outlines the key features and challenges associated with their economies, and discusses the issues identified through a comparison of the development paths of the two cities.

Setting the context – Helsinki and Toulouse

Helsinki

The development of Helsinki towards its current position as a middle-sized European city began with its establishment as the capital city in 1812. This status triggered growth and resulted in the creation of the most important educational institutions in the country. In 2008, the Helsinki region accommodated almost 1.3 million people – almost 25 per cent of the total population (5.2 million) of Finland. It is unchallenged as the country's primary city: the administrative, educational and cultural centre and the only internationally sized concentration of businesses and inhabitants in the country. However, on a European scale, Helsinki is a small and peripherally located metropolis, although its remoteness is diminished through the advanced communications and transport infrastructure. The economic growth of the Helsinki region has long been faster than the growth of national economy, particularly since the shift into knowledge-intensive industries (Ylä-Anttila and Hernesniemi, 2006).

The metropolitan area holds 30 per cent of the jobs in Finland and 34 per cent of its GVA of Finland (Statistics Finland, 2008; The State of Helsinki Region – European Comparisons, 2009). The service sector dominates in Helsinki and traditional heavy industry is marginal. The manufacturing sector is specialised in electronics, particularly telecommunications, machinery and printing industry (Laakso and Kostiainen, 2007). In the creative and knowledge-intensive industries, the region's share of employment is higher, and most of the sectors are strongly clustered into the region. The Helsinki region has been the centre and the key beneficiary of the boom of the ICT cluster, the main driver for economic growth since the 1990s. More than half of the employment in ICT is concentrated in the metropolitan region (Laakso et al., 2009). Geographically, ICT employment is clustered around the Bay of Laajalahti. Many jobs are found in the centre of Helsinki, but a significant cluster of employment is located in the areas surrounding the University of Technology and the headquarters of Nokia in the city of Espoo just west of Helsinki (Figure 7.1).

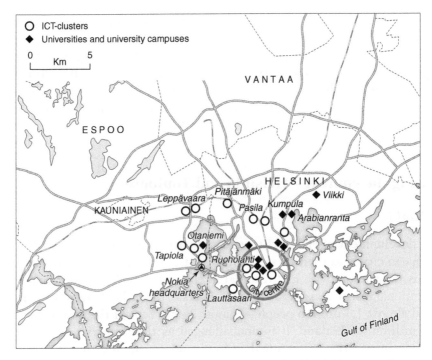

Figure 7.1   Location of ICT clusters and universities in the Helsinki metropolitan area.

Helsinki has had an extremely homogeneous population and almost no flow of foreign immigration until recent decades. Helsinki benefits from a Nordic welfare state tradition with free education, affordable health care and generous social security. Progressive taxation has helped to keep income differences among the smallest in Europe and the strong focus on education has contributed to the development into an information society (Vaattovaara, 2009).

The well-developed knowledge base is one major factor explaining why Finland and Helsinki have frequently been ranked very high in different indices measuring competitiveness, innovation and economic performance. At the beginning of the 2000s, for many years in a row, Finland was ranked the most competitive country in the world by The World Economic Forum. By 2008–2009, Finland occupied position six (The Global Competitiveness Report 2008–2009). In 2006–2007 Helsinki was positioned as number two after Brussels in the European Competitiveness Index (Centre for International Competitiveness, 2007). The Finnish educational system has also received considerable international attention: Finnish 15-year-olds have outperformed the students of other OECD countries in the PISA assessments (The *OECD Programme for International Student Assessment*) in mathematics, science and reading. The 'Finnish success story' and Helsinki's pathway to a knowledge society has unsurprisingly attracted interest abroad.

Toulouse

Toulouse is the capital of the Midi-Pyrénées, a 45,000 km² region located in southwest France. The Urban Area of Toulouse (UAT) enjoys one of the fastest rates of demographic and economic growth in the country, welcoming around 18,000 extra inhabitants each year since 1999. In 2007, the population of the urban area was estimated at 1.1 million inhabitants. The city's attractiveness can be explained by a general migration trend to the south of France and by the fact that Toulouse is the only large university and higher education centre in Midi-Pyrénées. As a major economic hub, it attracts residents from the region and adjacent regions mainly for study and job opportunities.

The structure of the economy shows the predominance of services (79 per cent of the working population) compared with industry (20 per cent) and a residual agriculture. Around 75,000 companies were located in the urban area in 2004. The growth of the number of establishments relates mainly to the building sector (+10.2 per cent between 2002 and 2004), and the services (+9 per cent), especially business services, real estate activities, health and social work. The ICT sectors (computer industry, electronics and telecommunications) have also developed strongly in recent years, providing nearly 30,000 jobs (9.4 per cent of the total working population of the urban area) in 2004 (AUAT, 2008). In terms of industrial employment, aeronautics and space building provides the metropolitan area with 17,500 direct jobs. Southeast of Toulouse, 7500 people work in the local chemistry–pharmacy–biotechnology sector. A large number of sub-contractors are linked to these main activities. The urban area also has one of the highest proportions of highly qualified jobs in France. It is notably highly specialised in research activities. High-tech industries are mostly concentrated in specialised technological parks, often close to the main higher education and research centres (Figure 7.2).

Another feature characterising the agglomeration is the high proportion of highly educated people. Twenty-six per cent of the population aged above 15 years have completed degrees in higher education in 1999 and the city ranked third in France, after Paris and Lyon, for the number of students (113,000) in 2007. The city has 3 universities, 12 engineering schools and several technical institutes. On the whole, 280 public research units are to be found in the UAT and its surroundings. With 5900 researchers in the public sector and 6800 researchers in the private sector, the Midi-Pyrénées region reaches the Île-de-France's level in terms of the number of researchers as a proportion of total salaried staff (14 per 1000 inhabitants

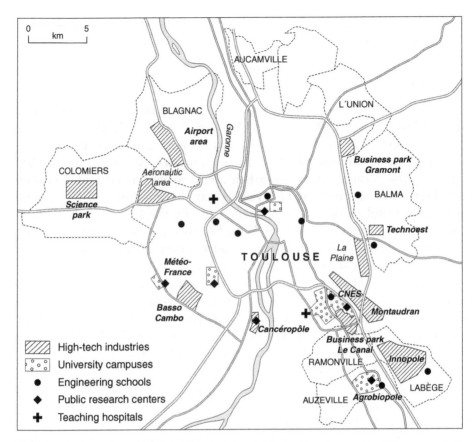

Figure 7.2 Location of high-tech industries, higher education and public research in Toulouse.

compared with 7.7 per 1000 inhabitants in metropolitan France) (Agence de Développement de la région Midi-Pyrénées, 2006). Research activities are structured around three *Pôles de compétitivité*[1] (or 'competitive clusters'). The first one created in 2005 is *Aerospace Valley*, a cluster that includes aeronautics and space activities, computer industry and electronics for airborne systems (transport, mobile phones, medical implants). It gathers 620 industrial and institutional partners over Midi-Pyrénées and Aquitaine regions, and is headed by the director of Airbus France (Toulouse). The second pole, called *Cancer-Bio-Santé*, is dedicated to the medical, pharmaceutical and biotechnology research. The latest competitive cluster

---

[1]This is a recent strategy developed by the State and implemented by DATAR (*Délégation Interministérielle à l'Aménagement du territoire et à l'attractivité régionale*) to support technological innovation. It comprises a large geographical perimeter where firms and research and education units are engaged in a partnership, in order to promote common technological projects.

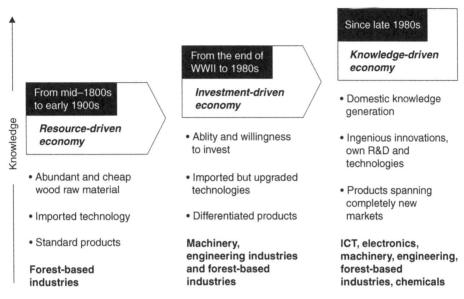

Figure 7.3 Finland's stages of industrial and economic development.
Source: Dahlman et al. (2006).

(Agrimip Innovation), created in 2007, intends to increase competitiveness in the agriculture and agribusiness sectors.

Pathways to knowledge-driven economies

Helsinki: from resource-based to ICT-driven economy

In Finland, the transformation from a factor- and resource-driven economy to a knowledge- and innovation-driven economy has happened extraordinarily quickly (Figure 7.3).

Industrialisation in Finland took off late compared with the rest of Europe. The fundamental change from an agrarian to an industrial society happened as late as in the mid-twentieth century. During most of the twentieth century industry was highly dependent on virtually the only natural resource – the forest, or 'the green gold' of the country. The rapid growth of prosperity in the early 1900s was mainly generated by increasing exports of forest-related products (Rouvinen and Ylä-Anttila, 2004). Another dominating sector of the economy was engineered metal products.[2] With the help of massive investments between 1950 and 1970, the Finnish forest industry transformed itself into a global, modern technology leader. The pulp and

---

[2]In 1970, pulp and paper accounted for 40 per cent of exports, wood products for 16 per cent and engineered metal (including shipbuilding) for 23 per cent (Porter and Sölvell, 2007).

paper cluster achieved a leading world role. The economy relied mainly on its plentiful forest resources and on imported technologies. However, the new industrial base developed during the 1970s and 1980s, and there was a strong economic boom in the 1980s.

In the early 1990s, Finland was hit by one of the worst recessions in OECD countries after World War II. GDP fell by 10 per cent and unemployment rose from 3 to 17 per cent (Ylä-Anttila, 2005). However, the deep recession was followed by a remarkable recovery. The country underwent major economic restructuring and the ICT sector was the main driver in one of the fastest growing economies in Europe. Within a few decades, Finland went from being one of the least ICT specialised countries to being the single most specialised country (Koski et al., 2002; Schienstock, 2007; Ylä-Anttila and Palmberg, 2007). In 2005, ICT-related industries had grown to account for almost 10 per cent of GDP and 20 per cent of exports.

Research has shown that a large external shock or economic crisis is often needed for efficient restructuring of the economy. That is exactly what happened in Helsinki and Finland (Rouvinen and Ylä-Anttila, 2004). In a deep crisis people are more willing to take leaps into the unknown, and accept the inevitable. The state and the City of Helsinki started to view things in a different light, and decided to adopt a knowledge-based strategy for the future. In a time of economic difficulty it was easier to build a common consensus for the new direction. The restructuring was supported by all key players in society: the government, municipalities, universities and businesses were invited and willing to join major strategic policy meetings and together invest in putting the economy back on its feet (Holstila, 2007). During the economic crisis the City Board of Helsinki adopted a new strategy which involved the future success of the city being based on science, education and innovation. Similar decisions were made in the other cities and municipalities in the Helsinki region. The situation demanded a new kind of partnership between higher education institutes, the business community and cities (Holstila, 2005).

The ICT sector took a leading role in the growing Finnish economy in the 1990s and 2000s. The new Finnish information economy was based on its strong role as a producer of information technology (Castells and Himanen, 2002). The ICT sector's GDP share increased from 4 per cent in 1990 to more than 10 per cent in 2004 (Ylä-Anttila, 2005). This growth also had a positive impact on some more traditional industries, such as pulp and paper and engineering. These industries reinvented themselves for new global markets through intensive use of ICT and rapid globalisation (Ylä-Anttila and Palmberg, 2007). Telecommunications and forestry together are world leading sectors and account for 40 per cent of exports and 8 per cent of GDP in Finland (Sabel and Saxenian, 2008).

The rapid turnaround of the Finnish economy could not have been possible without the successful rise of the ICT cluster, comprising about 6000 companies. What is the secret of this remarkable success? A knowledge-based strategy with a strong focus education, investment in R&D and innovation is the most frequent explanation. A popular conception is that Finland's outstanding economic performance and the shift in sector specialisation is directly a result of Nokia's success. Nokia, with large R&D investments and its bold internationalisation strategy (Steinbock, 2006), did play a crucial role in this transformation but the change in sector specialisation is much more complex (Moen and Lilja, 2005). Nokia had an important role as a flagship firm whose example was followed by other companies in Finland. However, these interrelated processes were built on technological capabilities that were developed in the 1970s and 1980s, and benefited from public technology and education policies (Moen and Lilja, 2005).

The ICT growth can be partly explained by developments and crucial events in telephony and telecommunications. This sector had emerged in the 1980s, as Finnish engineers and companies were engaged in basic and applied research on computer and telecom technology. A deep understanding of telecommunications and radio technology was one of the major prerequisites for building a mobile telephone system (Rouvinen and Ylä-Anttila, 2004; Gräsbeck, 2007). In the 1980s, Nokia, which already had international experience, managed to bring existing knowledge on digital telephony under one roof (Schienstock, 2007). The Nordic collaborations in developing a mobile telephone network during the 1970s and 1980s also helped Finland move to the forefront of mobile communications technology (Sabel and Saxenian, 2008). Finland was an early adopter of first NMT and then GSM technologies, which both eventually proved to be the 'winning technologies' of their time (Rouvinen and Ylä-Anttila, 2004). In 1994 the telecom sector was deregulated in Finland, which created an ideal home market for Finnish ICT manufacturing. The ICT cluster with Nokia in the forefront clearly benefited from their early entry to the global mobile market.

The fact that Finland is a small country has definitely played a part as well (Rouvinen and Ylä-Anttila, 2004; Ylä-Anttila, 2005; Ojala et al., 2006). It seems that small, homogenous countries can more quickly adjust to new technologies and other economic changes, and more easily reorient their trajectories. In Finland, the close interaction among different economic actors helped gain a consensus for rapid measures. The power of social capital has been very influential. Also, small-scale and closer networks were beneficial for the creation and diffusion of new knowledge in specific areas, including ICT.

All in all, the Finnish economy underwent a profound structural change and rapid economic growth over a few decades. However, the transformation did not just happen out of the blue and was not simply triggered by the economic crisis of the early 1990s. Although Finland was quite poor, many prerequisites for a path towards growth and industrial development were already in place. Thus, continuity and a certain path development can be stressed at the same time (Rouvinen and Ylä-Anttila, 2004; Moen and Lilja, 2005; Ojala et al., 2006). While the rise of the Finnish ICT cluster was seemingly rapid, there was a long evolutionary process behind it (Paija, 2001). The evolution of the ICT cluster was built upon a complex, self-strengthening development process (Schienstock, 2007). Significant changes are not only dependent on external shocks, but also on endogenous development processes that have historical roots (Moen and Lilja, 2005). The institutional structures, for example, had been there since the Swedish era. Well functioning banking and education systems as well as a good transport infrastructure were important from the first stages of the change until the later innovation-driven stages. Cultural factors that have contributed to the development, such as a certain mindset, and especially the attitude to work and private ownership had been there for a long time. The fact that Finland is a small nation up north, squeezed between large political blocks has affected its national identity. The nation is used to hard times, hard work and common efforts. The notion of trust is deeply embedded in Finns' mentality. In Finland, people usually trust the leaders to make the right decisions, and therefore decisions can often be made quickly (Gräsbeck, 2007). The Finnish people have been very open to technological innovations, and have been in the forefront when adopting new technology. In addition, the geographical setting has played a key role with geographical constraints that included the scarcity of factors of production and a remote location far from the centre of the international economy.

However, several developments that took place and played a role in development were beyond the control of the different actors (Paija, 2001; Rouvinen and Ylä-Anttila, 2004). Coincidence, chance and good timing may have played a larger role than sometimes thought. Even slight changes in events or their timing (such as a postponement of the deregulation of the communications sector in Finland or a later introduction of the GSM technology) could have endangered the development. Certainly many of the events around the development of mobile phones have been coincidences that were not foreseen, and they have had a major impact on the development path of the Helsinki region.

Toulouse: from a low industrial base to a high-tech skills system

Three periods can be identified in the development path of Toulouse (Figure 7.4). Until the middle of the twentieth century, with the exception of the chemical industry, the economy was characterised by small-scale, scattered industries producing mainly manufactured goods. A big change occurred in the years after 1945, when the state decided to strengthen

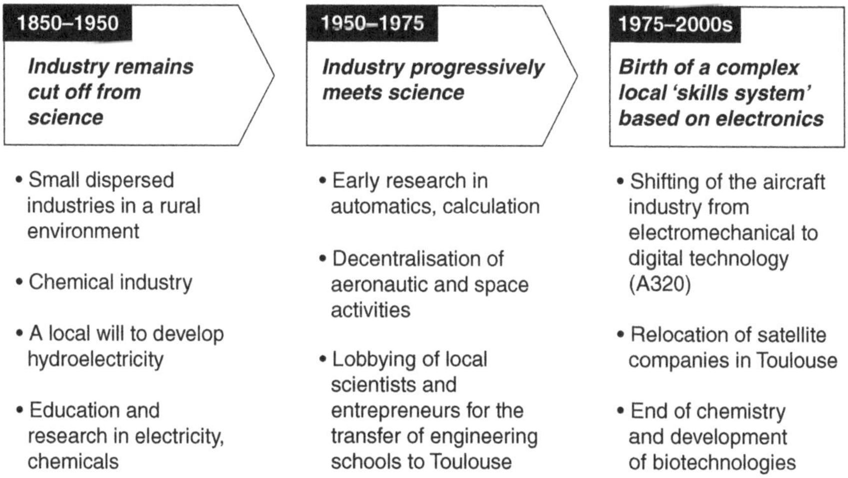

1850–1950	1950–1975	1975–2000s
Industry remains cut off from science	**Industry progressively meets science**	**Birth of a complex local 'skills system' based on electronics**

• Small dispersed industries in a rural environment	• Early research in automatics, calculation	• Shifting of the aircraft industry from electromechanical to digital technology (A320)
• Chemical industry	• Decentralisation of aeronautic and space activities	
• A local will to develop hydroelectricity	• Lobbying of local scientists and entrepreneurs for the transfer of engineering schools to Toulouse	• Relocation of satellite companies in Toulouse
• Education and research in electricity, chemicals		• End of chemistry and development of biotechnologies

Figure 7.4   Toulouse's development pathway towards a complex skills system.

aeronautical activities and decentralise several specialised education and research institutions to Toulouse. The enhanced local scientific potential was progressively associated to the growth of aeronautics and space industry in the 1970s. The following shifting of the aircraft industry from electromechanical to digital technology gave birth to the current local innovation system.

Located at an easy crossing of the Garonne river, Toulouse has been a focal point for trade between the Pyrénées, the Mediterranean and the Atlantic. Once a major metropolis of western Europe, Toulouse was a middle-sized commercial and administrative centre in the nineteenth century. Chemistry was the only large industry in Toulouse until the 1950s. The gunpowder factory employed up to 30,000 persons between 1914 and 1918, then from 1924 on, a patent confiscated from defeated Germany was utilised to produce fertilisers. The industrial landscape was mainly characterised by small dispersed businesses, employing less than 100 workers and producing large quantities of finished manufactured goods (hats, edge-tools, cutlery, bricks, tiles, faience) for external markets (Olivier, 2006). Even the production of aircraft, that developed during the World War I, was a small-scale activity that did not integrate a high level of technology. Two individual entrepreneurs of the region, Latécoère and Dewoitine, created their own business in the manufacture of airplanes and equipments for airplanes.

Parallel to this, local politicians and academics planned to implement an activity based on hydroelectricity, which was justified by the proximity of the Pyrénées. They created a university chair in industrial electricity and an electro-technical institute (1907) that grew impressively from the 1910s onwards, and entailed the creation of several engineering laboratories

(Grossetti and Milard, 1997). Another specialisation in chemical engineering due to the influence of Paul Sabatier (Nobel Prize 1912, Chemistry) emerged in Toulouse and developed in the second part of the twentieth century with the creation of the Institute for Chemical Engineering.

Despite a political will and the presence of local competences in this field, no electrical industry comparable to Grenoble's ever developed in Toulouse (Grossetti, 1995, 2001). The lack of an existing industry that could have supported the production of this energy, as well as the remoteness of the city from the mountains, explain why the dream of hydroelectricity was finally given up. Though this activity enabled the settlement of some metallurgy factories, it did not trigger the creation of local companies. The aeronautical activity also remained cut off from the faculty of science and its institutes until the 1970s. Unlike in Grenoble, businesses created in Toulouse did not profit from the local research potential and graduates had to leave the city to find work elsewhere.

An important change took place in Toulouse in the period following World War II with the emergence of a scientific research pole and the growth of aeronautics and space industry. The first development was in automatics, then a computer industry emerged, which was strongly linked with the establishment of public education and research institutions specialised in numerical calculation. At the end of the 1950s, the State decided to strengthen aeronautical activities through the decentralisation of several educational institutions that specialised in engineering and research. Local scientific leaders influenced the officials in charge of the Regional Action Plan in 1958 to transfer the National School of Aeronautics to their city. Other changes in the local higher education system occurred in the 1960s, with the transfer of the National Higher School for Aeronautical Engineering (ENSICA) in 1961 and the National School of Civil Aviation in 1968. A local branch of the National Office for Aeronautical Studies and Research (ONERA) was also created, along with a National Institute for Applied Sciences (INSA).

The decision in 1963 to decentralise part of the National Centre for Spatial Studies (CNES), created in 1961, had a great impact on the local economy in Toulouse. It has enabled industry to connect with the local research and higher education system for the first time since the beginning of the century. The CNES was indeed not only a research centre but also an industrial agency in charge of developing the national spatial industry. It had already worked with firms that later settled in Toulouse (Matra in 1979, Alcatel in 1982) and it grew by hiring a large number of local graduates and quickly connected with local laboratories (Grossetti, 1995).

The actors in the training and research system in electrical engineering, electronics and computers have played a major role in the decision to decentralise space industry to Toulouse. They also influenced the decision to settle a Motorola factory, which triggered the development of R&D activities in wireless, broadband, automotive communications technologies and embedded electronic products. The researchers' lobbying was also decisive for the shifting of the aircraft industry from electromechanical technology to digital technology, with the Airbus A320 programme.

All these major changes gave birth within a few years to a new local innovation system in Toulouse (Grossetti et al., 2006). The technological and economic take-off occurred between 1975 and 1985, as the key elements of the current system came together (Grossetti, 1995, 2001). The establishment of the 'satellite' divisions of the CNES resulted in the relocation of service companies to Toulouse. Highly specialised firms in satellite decks (Alcatel, Matra Marconi Space), satellites programmes (SPOT, Argos) or satellite imagery and localisation systems (SPOT Images, CLS Argos) as well as Météo France, with its high-tech meteorological computer centre, settled in the area of Toulouse from the 1980s onwards.

Matra and Alcatel also launched an extensive recruitment program locally. Electronic companies (Motorola, Thomson), which had settled in the 1960s mainly as large-scale mass manufacturers turned into development centres and recruited engineers.

The economic specialisation of Toulouse now relies much more on types of skill, namely in electronics and computing, than on the manufacturing of a specific product. The training and research system that has been built over the twentieth century provides the bulk of engineers and executives of high-tech industries. The transfer of the manufacturing of onboard electronics from Paris to Toulouse has strengthened and shaped the current complex industrial system that characterises the city today. With the presence of global players such as Airbus and EADS (European Aeronautic Defence and Space Company), the once sleepy southwestern centre has become known as 'Europe's capital of aerospace industry'. Digital technology allowed sub-contractors, who worked for aeronautical or automobile construction indifferently, to multiply to a point where in the 2000s it is possible to talk of a cluster taking on the format of a 'local skills system' based on competences that cut across several sectors of activity (Grossetti et al. 2006).

The explosion at a fertiliser firm in 2001 in Toulouse put an end to local chemistry industries and opened the way for the development of biotechnologies on the site of the former chemical plants (Canceropôle project) and a move towards diversification (information sciences, nanotechnology, health sector). Important activity within the fields of biotechnology and health resulted from the spread of local university laboratories (which had developed in the 1970s) and was boosted by two large pharmaceutical companies, SANOFI and Pierre Fabre. This marked the start of a second local skills system.

Knowledge driving economic development: sciences, industries and policies

Helsinki

How much of the 'Finnish success story' can be attributable to public policies? A common conclusion drawn is that the transformation into an ICT-driven knowledge economy was to a large part a business-driven process, but that policies and institutions also mattered. According to Steinbock (2006), the performance of the Finnish companies, particularly Nokia, primarily accounted for the success of the 'system'. Ylä-Anttila and Palmberg (2007) argue that there was no 'master plan' to promote the profound structural change and expansion of the ICT sector, despite the appearance.

Nevertheless, the recession in the 1990s brought with it a clear shift in policy making in Finland. High priority was given to sound macroeconomic policies to overcome recession, but at the same time there was a gradual shift to long-term microeconomic policies, that is innovation, technology and education policies. It was recognised that competitive advantage of an economy is created in firms, innovation and policy organisations and educational institutions (Schienstock, 2004; Ylä-Anttila, 2005). These policy developments explain the common conception that Finnish science and technology policy created a favourable environment for the emerging knowledge economy. Building a sound education base has been a crucial factor for the development into a knowledge economy. Human capital and skilled labour are the drivers in the generation of new technologies but on the demand side education is important as new technologies are not adopted without sophisticated users (Ylä-Anttila, 2005).

Although the change to a knowledge-intensive economy happened very quickly, the Finnish innovation system did not emerge overnight. The developments were built upon several conscious public decisions and an active innovation policy based on investments in education and R&D. Although innovation and technology has been highly emphasised in strategy only relatively recently, a clear strategy of knowledge intensity and technological know-how had already been adopted in the 1970s and 1980s, with the foundation of several science and technology policy actors including the national technology agency, Tekes. As a matter of fact, Finland was one of the first countries in Europe to adopt explicit knowledge economy strategies (Van den Berg et al., 2004). This enabled the strengthening of the university system and the development, as early as the 1970s of free, high-quality universities all over the country. The Finnish technology policy had also begun to prioritise ICT 1980s, long before the emergence of the 'new economy' (Rouvinen and Ylä-Anttila, 2004). These policies were followed up in the next decade and generated high investments in R&D[3] and increasing networking between public and private actors. For example, the Science and Technology Policy Council has been one of the most influential strategic actors in shaping the innovation system. Its unique working model includes key ministers of government, highest-level representatives of Finnish universities, industry representatives (e.g. the CEO of Nokia) and others (Castells and Himanen, 2002).

The public sector has created conditions for innovation, but the enthusiasm of private sector companies is just as important an element of the success story. The companies have also invested heavily in R&D for business reasons, which obviously have contributed to the positive development. Since the early 1990s, Nokia has been driven primarily by its own internal research and development. The close networks between economic actors have also influenced the development of the education and research system in Finland. One of the strengths in Finland has been the close science–industry cooperation with key representatives from different economic sectors involved in strategy meetings (Vaattovaara, 2009).

The role of the state diminished as the possibilities for macroeconomic direct intervention declined during the 1990s (Moen and Lilja, 2005). According to this new policy perspective, the state's role is to work as a catalyst, a supporter, a facilitator, a moderator, an organiser and an initiator. The state no longer controls the innovation process directly and this reflects the increasing fragmentation of power. The number of organisations that have important knowledge is increasing. The cooperation ability to mobilise resources in Finland for common goals has been seen as a major advantage. Finland adopted a national innovation system relatively early. A 'systemic transformation approach', stressing the interrelationship between various actors involved in innovation, has been argued to be the key to the successful transformation process.

Toulouse

Both national and local scales of political intervention form part of the explanation for Toulouse's increased competitiveness. The role of the French state, with the decentralisation of several education and research establishments from Paris to Toulouse in the 1960s, was crucial for the creation of further links between industrial and academic activities. From the beginning, the strategy aimed systematically at enhancing high-technologies sectors and supporting R&D and higher education in engineering sciences. Initially aerospace and systems technologies were mainly promoted and

---

[3]In 1982, the government raised the national investments in research and development from 1.2 to 2.2 per cent of the GDP by 1992. After that, the share was further increased to more than 3 per cent.

then diversification strategies involved airborne systems and biotechnologies applied to health (cancer treatment).

The most recent State's initiative (2005) related to competitive clusters (*Pôles de compétitivité*), a specific coordination instrument involving local public institutions. This stage of political action came after a period where Local Economic Development (LED) strategies were characterised by fragmented initiatives and multiform competition. In Toulouse, various institutional arrangements, shaping a complex system of local governance emerged. There is no single administrative and management unit at the scale of the urban area and several intercommunal bodies with quite strong identities conduct their own LED and territorial policies. However, the absence of one local government body does not prevent industrial enterprises from sharing means and resources across the territorial boundaries. At the local level, economic development strategies aim more at creating territorial resources through the intensification of relationships between existing firms than at seeking the establishment of new firms. Attention has also been paid to increasing cognitive competences in order to foster knowledge circulation.

Several studies have tried to evaluate the importance of spatial proximity in innovation processes. A study on biotechnologies in California (Zucker et al., 1994) showed that the most efficient companies were those maintaining links with academic researchers located close to them. In France, Toulouse distinguishes itself by the highest number of local relationships regarding contracts between scientific laboratories and firms. Along with Grenoble, Toulouse is the city with the highest number of companies created by researchers and jobs linked to research activities (Grossetti and Nguyen, 2001).

The notion of 'skills system' allows us to understand the importance of investing in knowledge and science. The industrial history of Toulouse shows that when one sector encounters some difficulties, local competences can be reinvested in other branches. For instance, airborne systems, promoted within a diversification strategy, benefit from the availability of a highly qualified workforce from the aeronautics, space and electronic complex. As a matter of fact, this is a way to free oneself from the dependence on a single activity and to reduce uncertainty (Grossetti et al., 2006).

The high degree of attractiveness of the metropolitan region is mainly due to a solid knowledge-based economy built over the twentieth century. The aim of local policies is less to reinvent a city development model than to ensure that current advantages benefit the highest number of people in the long term. Cultural elements are increasingly present in planification debates, and more attention is paid to 'soft' factors, but some crucial planning issues still concern infrastructural aspects, including the improvement of regional and national transport networks.

Future challenges

Specialisation

The specialised economies of Helsinki and Toulouse face many challenges. Specialisation in high-tech industries makes these cities more vulnerable in a changing and uncertain global economy. In 2008, the global projections for ICT spending were revised sharply downwards (OECD, 2008), raising concerns in both cities. Although the Toulouse case shows that an efficient local skills system reduces the risks of unemployment, the dependence on the performance of one large multinational company also creates some worry.

For Helsinki the increasing international competition in ICT is a challenge, since the effects of global competition are much larger on small open economies with limited resources such as Finland. In 2008, Nokia alone accounted for 21 per cent of the exports and 60 per cent of the market valuation of the Helsinki stock exchange (Sabel and Saxenian, 2008). Most of the company's new investments are also located outside Finland. A small country can be competitive in a few fields of science and technology. The benefits of being an early entrant to the sector are now declining (Ylä-Anttila and Palmberg, 2007). Helsinki needs new, strong industrial clusters to complement its modern ICT cluster and its traditional industries and thereby diversify its economic base. This would greatly diminish the risks associated with the considerable volatility of the global ICT business and the modest growth prospects of manufacturing. In general terms, Helsinki should become more dynamic and more innovative in order to attract not only new industries but also more domestic and foreign investments (Laakso and Kostiainen, 2005). There is also a downside to the success of the Finnish economy. In Helsinki, one recent concern is that economic success has prevented industries from reshaping their operations and the innovation system in time (Sabel and Saxenian, 2008).

In Toulouse, concerns exist about the overwhelming position of Airbus in the local economic fabric, but the local skills system serves to match the needs of flexibility and cross-sector exchange. Difficulties encountered at the end of 2006, and the significant delay in Airbus A380 programme led to reflection about how to reduce the specialisation of the industrial fabric in the aeronautical sector (Zuliani, 2008). Thanks to a refocusing on its three core activities – aircraft conception, final assembly and commercialisation of activities – the current restructuring processes in the Airbus firm worldwide do not jeopardise the organisation and structure of the productive system. The development path in the field of onboard systems, promoted by the aircraft manufacturer Aérospatiale from the 1980s on, illustrates how a 'local skills system' can be seen as a solution to over-dependence on a dominant sector (Zuliani, 2008). Based on the production of software and calculators, onboard systems are integrated into various types of machine (aircraft, space vessels, automobiles, rockets, satellites, mobile phones, rail traction systems, etc.), and thus apply to what are initially quite different activities.

Disparities

Despite their competitiveness, neither Helsinki nor Toulouse have avoided growing the social and spatial disparities in their respective territories. There is an obvious tension between the egalitarianism of the welfare state model and enhancing the competitiveness of the economy. Helsinki and Finland have been successful in the economic change towards an open, globally integrated and ICT-driven economy, while at the same time the welfare state has not had to suffer any major cutbacks. This structural mix has led Manuel Castells and Pekka Himanen (2002) to conclude that a special model of an information society has developed in Finland (Vaattovaara and Kortteinen, 2003; Inkinen and Vaattovaara, 2007). At the same time, one consequence of economic development in Helsinki has been growing income disparities and spatial differentiation (Vaattovaara and Kortteinen, 2003). The information society has whittled away at the welfare state. Current OECD statistics show that Finland tops the income disparity growth. Historically, the level of income differences has been very low in Finland, so the gap is not yet extremely wide. Nevertheless, the development is worrying.

In Toulouse, current problems also mainly relate to the tension between economic competitiveness and social cohesion. As a result of this economic specialisation, the UAT displays specific features: Toulouse is one of the urban areas with the highest household incomes in France. Disparities between incomes are greater than elsewhere in the country, in particular within the city centre as opposed to the suburbs and periurban areas (AUAT-INSEE, 2005). There is a huge contrast between well developed areas, concentrating the highly qualified workforce, and neighbourhoods with a high concentration of less educated and unemployed people (including migrants from Maghreb). The economic development model raises the issue of the professional integration of low or unqualified populations in a highly specialised urban area (Peyroux et al., 2009). In November 2005, quite violent riots have shown that underlying tensions can be aroused at any time in deprived neighbourhoods, despite the general economic welfare of the city.

Conclusion and discussion

Helsinki and Toulouse have succeeded in transforming their economic structure and creating successful knowledge-based economies in a relatively short time. The pathways to the current situation have been different in many ways, but have led to similar economic developments. Helsinki experienced a drastic turnaround of specialisations from forest products to a totally new field, ICT. However, forest industry still remains an important sector in the Finnish economy. Toulouse's economic structure shifted from the 1950s on, from a small-scale dispersed industry producing manufactured goods, to a complex skills system with high-technology industries ranging from aeronautics, space, electronics and computer engineering.

Both cities had good 'classic' conditions already in place for the transformation into a knowledge economy, and had experienced pathways which brought them into the right position for the 'next step' (Kovács et al., 2007). Neither of them carried the historical baggage of heavy industry, and the focus on education through the location of universities, higher education establishments and research institutions has created a broad knowledge base. Helsinki and Toulouse have adopted active strategies to change their development paths through major investment in higher education and research. There has also been a clear specialisation in education, with a major focus on technological knowledge. The high performance of the educational systems and production of engineers and technical scientists are common features of the two cities. In addition, there have been crucial developments of the high-tech industry at the microeconomic scale. In both cities, individual companies and entrepreneurs have been important in shaping the economic profile of the city. In Helsinki, Nokia has been a main driver for the creation of a successful ICT cluster; in Toulouse, Airbus has acted as a similar engine of growth.

Key events and political and economic 'ruptures' have strongly influenced the cities' pathways and created special trajectories. The huge economic crisis of the 1990s in Finland triggered a more active policy towards science, education and innovation which resulted in a restructuring of the economy. Also, a series of coincidences around the development of mobile phones had major impacts on the development path of the Helsinki urban region (Kovács et al., 2007). In Toulouse, the state's decentralisation policy, along with the lobbying of local politicians and scientists, has played a key role in the emergence of a scientific research pole and the growth of the aeronautics and space industry. However, the production of aircraft could have been located elsewhere in France or in Europe.

If 'context matters', does it help in understanding the possible future development of the two cities? The challenges Toulouse and Helsinki face for the future seem quite similar. Economically, the strong specialisation in a single sector is risky and makes the economies vulnerable to outside shocks. The increasing international competition in ICT products is a challenge for Helsinki, since the effects of global competition is much larger on small open economies with limited resources. It has also been widely argued that the new information society creates social inequality. It is difficult to combine a social commitment to equity and simultaneously enhance the economic performance. Both cities have already witnessed increasing income disparities and urban spatial differentiation, but the social setting makes this issue more acute in Toulouse.

Every city has different potentials and resources that reflect their development paths over time. The cities need to develop based on their own strengths and specialisations. Helsinki faces pressure to diversify its economic base. Can the economy and the innovation system transform and renew itself to meet the demands of the future? In Toulouse, there has been a focus on engineering sciences and one perspective could be that in its further development attention should also be paid to the potential contribution of human and social sciences and the cultural assets of the city.

References

Agence de Développement de la région Midi-Pyrénées (2006) *Chiffres-clés 2006*, Toulouse: Midi-Pyrénées Expansion.

AUAT (2008) *Référentiel métropolitain, Aire métropolitaine toulousaine*, 151 p.

AUAT-INSEE (2005) Revenus des ménages, les contrastes de l'aire urbaine de Toulouse. *Perspectives villes, 6 pages*, 81, June.

Castells, M. and P. Himanen (2002) *The information society and the welfare state: The Finnish model*. Oxford: Oxford University Press.

Centre for International Competitiveness (2007) *European Competitiveness Index 2006–2007*. http://www.cforic.org/pages/european-competitiveness.php (accessed 30 September 2009).

Dahlman, C.J., J. Routti and P. Ylä-Anttila (eds) (2006) *Finland as a knowledge economy. Elements of success and lessons learned*. Washington: OverviewWorld Bank Institute, 118 p.

Porter, M.E. and K. Schwab (2008) The Global Competitiveness Report 2008–2009. Geneva: World Economic Forum.

Gräsbeck, M. (2007) Innovation and urban competitiveness. In: P. Haywood (ed.), *Messages for competitive European cities. The COMPETE network final report*, pp. 63–72. Helsinki: Compete.

Grossetti, M. (1995) *Science, industrie et territoire*, Toulouse: PUM, coll. 'Socio-logiques'.

Grossetti, M. (2001) Génèse de deux systèmes urbains d'innovation en France: Grenoble et Toulouse, Réalités Industrielles. *Annales des Mines*, ESKA Paris, Février, 68–72.

Grossetti, M. and B. Milard (1997) Une ville investit dans la science: Genèse de l'Institut életrotechnique de Toulouse. *La naissance de l'ingénieur-électricien. Origines et développement des formations nationales électrotechniques*, PUF, 133–148.

Grossetti, M. and D. Nguyen (2001) La structure spatiale des relations science-industrie en France: l'exemple des contrats entre les entreprises et les laboratoires du CNRS. *Revue d'Economie Régionale et Urbaine*, II: 311–328.

Grossetti, M., J.M. Zuliani and R. Guillaume (2006) La spécialisation cognitive: Les systèmes locaux de compétences. *Les Annales de la recherche urbaine*, 101: 23–31.

Holstila, E. (2005) *Innovative Helsinki: Culminatum as a tool to govern Helsinki as a science region. Quarterly 2005*. Helsinki City Urban Facts.

Holstila, E. (2007) Finland: Towards urban innovation policy. In: L. van den Berg, E. Braun and J. van den Meer (eds), *National policy responses to urban challenges in Europe*, pp. 125–144. Aldershot: Ashgate.

Inkinen, T. and M. Vaattovaara (2007) *Technology and knowledge-based development. Helsinki metropolitan area as a creative region. Pathways to creative and knowledge-based regions.* ACRE report WP2.5. Amsterdam: AMIDSt.

Koski, H., P. Rouvinen and P. Ylä-Anttila (2002) ICT clusters in Europe – The Great Central Banana and Small Nordic Potato. *Information Economics and Policy*, 14: 145–165.

Kovács, Z., A. Murie, S. Musterd, O. Gritsai and H. Pethe (2007) *Comparing paths of creative knowledge regions.* ACRE report 3, 62 pp. Amsterdam: AMIDSt.

Laakso, S. and E. Kostiainen (2005) *Helsinki regional economy. A dynamic city in the European urban network.* Helsinki: City of Helsinki Urban Facts and the Business Development Department of the City of Helsinki Economic and Planning Centre.

Laakso, S. and E. Kostiainen (2007) *The economic map of urban Europe. A comparative study of 45 European metropolises.* Helsinki: City of Helsinki, Urban Facts.

Laakso, S., P. Kilpeläinen and V. Tähtinen (2009) *Pääkaupunkiseudun yritysraportti. Yritysten ja niiden toimipaikkojen rakenne, sijoittuminen ja muutostrendit 2000 – luvulla [Helsinki Metropolitan Area Business Report. Structure, location and trends in enterprises and establishments of business in the 2000s].* YTV.

Lundvall, B.-Å. (1992) *National systems of innovation. Towards a theory of innovation and interactive learning.* London: Pinter Publishers.

Moen, E. and K. Lilja (2005) Change in coordinated market economies: The case of Nokia and Finland. In: G. Morgan, R. Whitley and E. Moen (eds), *Changing capitalisms?* Oxford: Oxford University Press.

OECD (2008) *IT Outlook 2008.*

Ojala, J., J. Eloranta and J. Jalava (eds) (2006) *The road to prosperity. An economic history of Finland.* Helsinki: SKS.

Olivier, J.M. (2006) Les petites industries toulousaines du XIXe siècle. In: J.P. Amalric and J. Faury (eds), *L'industrie en Midi-Pyrénées de la Préhistoire à nos jours*, pp. 287–300. Toulouse: Fédération historique de Midi-Pyrénées, 444 pp.

Paija, L. (2001) *Finnish ICT cluster in the digital economy.* Helsinki: ETLA.

Peyroux E., M. Grossetti and D. Eckert (2009) Becoming a knowledge city: The example of Toulouse. *Built Environment*, 35 (2): 188–195.

Porter, M.E. (1990) *The competitive advantage of nations.* New York: Free Press.

Porter, M.E. (1998) *On competition.* Boston: HBSP.

Porter, M.E. and Ö. Sölvell (2007) *Finland and Nokia: Creating the world's most competitive economy.* Boston: Harvard Business School Publishing.

Rouvinen, P. and P. Ylä-Anttila (2004) Case study: Little Finland's transformation to a wireless giant. In: S. Dutta, B. Lanvin and F. Paua (eds), *The global information technology report 2003–2004*, pp. 87–108. New York: Oxford University Press.

Sabel, C. and A. Saxenian (2008) *A fugitive success: Finland's economic future.* Sitra reports 80. Helsinki: Sitra.

Schienstock, G. (2004) *Embracing the knowledge economy: The dynamic transformation of the Finnish innovation system.* Cheltenham, UK: Edward Elgar Publishing Ltd.

Schienstock, G. (2007) From path dependency to path creation: Finland on its way to the knowledge-based economy. *Current Sociology*, 55 (1): 92–109.

Statistics Finland (2008) *Employment statistics.* http://www.stat.fi/tup/tilastotietokannat/index_en.html . (accessed 22 December 2008).

Steinbock, D. (2006) *Finland's innovative capacity. Regional development 13/2006.* Helsinki: Ministry of the Interior.

Lankinen, L., P. Selander and T. Tikkanen (eds) The State of Helsinki Region 2009– European Comparisons *Helsinki: City of Helsinki urban facts.*

Vaattovaara, M. (2009) The emergence of the Helsinki metropolitan area as an international hub of the knowledge industries. *Built Environment*, 35 (2): 196–203.

Vaattovaara, M. and M. Kortteinen (2003) Beyond polarisation versus professionalisation? A case study of the development of the Helsinki region. Finland. *Urban Studies*, 40 (11): 2127–2145.

Van den Berg, L., P.M.J. Pol, W. van Winden and P. Woets (2004) *Helsinki in the knowledge economy.* In: A. Manninen (ed.), *Quarterly 3/2004*, pp. 22-27. Helsinki: City of Helsinki Urban Facts.

Ylä-Anttila, P. (2005) *Finland – An ICT-driven knowledge economy. ICT Cluster Finland Review 2005.* TIEKE (Finnish Information Society Development Centre).

Ylä-Anttila, P. and H. Hernesniemi (2006) *Helsingin seudun ja Uudenmaan aluetalous – selittävätkö klusterit ja erikoistuminen nopeaa kasvua? [The regional economies of Helsinki and Uusimaa – Do clustering and specialisation explain the rapid economic growth?]* In: E. Holstila (ed.), Kvartti 2/2006, pp. 36–42 [Quarterly 2/2006]. Helsinki: City of Helsinki Urban Facts.

Ylä-Anttila, P. and C. Palmberg (2007) Economic and industrial policy transformations in Finland. *Journal of Industry, Competition and Trade*, 2007 (7): 169–187.

Zucker, L.G., M.R. Darby and J. Armstrong (1994) *Intellectual capital and the firm: The technology of geographically localized knowledge spillovers.* NBER Working Paper Series, Working Paper no. 4946, NBER, Cambridge, MA.

Zuliani, J.M. (2008) The Toulouse cluster of on-board systems: A process of collective innovation and learning. *European Planning Studies*, 16 (5): 711–726.

Part III

Actors

Sofia – Creativity; the National Theatre. Photo by Pressphoto – BTA.

Dublin – Continuous construction. Photo by Philip Lawton.

8

What Works for Managers and Highly Educated Workers in Creative Knowledge Industries?

Sako Musterd and Alan Murie

Introduction

In the first chapters of this book, we indicated that it makes sense to know more about the actual behaviour and the expressed preferences of various actors who are key to the development of creative and knowledge-intensive industries. The policy actors who play a significant role are considered separately in Part IV of this book. In this part, we focus on the managers and highly educated workers whose activity is critical to the development and sustainability of creative knowledge regions. We refer to three groups: managers of creative and knowledge-intensive firms, employees with higher educational qualifications and transnational migrants who are working in creative and knowledge-based industry. The focus on these groups, in the cities we have previously discussed, enables us to test some of the assertions in the literature. From the literature we referred to in Chapter 2, it is apparent that there are plausible assertions (based on very limited empirical evidence) that those working in the creative and knowledge industries have similar objectives when choosing where to live and work. The groups we consider in this part appear to form part of what Florida refers to as the creative class: they are people with talent and we can assess how far their decisions and the reasons they give for making them accord with Florida's view of them. This part of the book draws heavily on new empirical research designed to improve our understanding of these groups and their reasons for moving, choosing and staying in the cities they live in. The evidence presented does not exhaust the debate about these issues but begins to fill a gap relating to key actors and indicates what factors are most important to them.

Theories on urban economic development are not clear about the roles of different actors, but 'classic' location theory puts a higher weight on the rational choices made by the leadership of firms – entrepreneurs, managers and owners of firms. This type of theory suggests that considerations related to conditions such as agglomeration advantages, economies of scale, tax regimes, regulations, infrastructure in its widest sense and the presence of properly skilled labour would mainly drive decisions. Considerations regarding the clustering of related activities fit in this scheme as well. Most of these conditions do not seem relevant to other actors, perhaps with the exception of infrastructure and regulation. Highly educated workers including many transnational migrants may, however, mainly be driven by the job opportunities for themselves or their partner, or by other 'hard' conditions, such as higher wages.

We also referred to other theory which suggests that, rather than being led by factors related to these hard conditions, key actors in the new and emerging creative and knowledge economy are attracted by a wider set of considerations. In this 'soft' conditions theory, key actors are seen as attracted by urban amenities and as making location decisions based on the quality of life in the places which they consider settling in. The quality of life dimension includes the level of tolerance towards 'others', a preference for diversity and 'interesting' residential conditions. We may hypothesise that these considerations might apply in a similar way for managers (and their families) and for highly educated employees and self-employed persons. This may even apply in a similar way to high-skilled transnational migrants, who may also search for an attractive place to live their lives in, even though their level of information with regard to the urban environments may be less than among non-migrants.

But there may be more. We already referred to the potential importance of personal networks, the place of study, nearness to family and friends and similar relationships that are established over time. This category of factors ('trajectories'), which is not usually referred to in the debate over the respective influence of 'soft' versus 'hard' factors in location decisions of people, has gained importance in the course of the research conducted within the project. The deliberate distinction of this category is a major result of the ACRE programme. An appropriate methodology enabled us to refine the analysis of the possible location motives of people surveyed and interviewed.[1]

---

[1] Michel Grossetti and his colleagues from the Toulouse team deserve credits for gathering and recoding the empirical data collected in each city. This enabled to show the importance of trajectory and network effects (see Martin-Brelot et al., 2009).

These individual trajectories may be highly relevant for some actors, and perhaps less important to others. They may also come to be more important factors in persuading people to stay than they ever were in attracting people to come in the first instance. For some they may even be more important than the 'classic' and 'soft' conditions referred to. For the moment, however, we must state that not much is known about the importance of these personal trajectories.

Three groups of actors and a range of conditions

In this part of the book, we address questions that relate to the drivers behind the location decisions made by various types of graduates and employees, managers and transnational migrants in selected creative and knowledge-intensive industries. These are decisions in relation to choice of where to work and live. The individual chapters address questions about the most important conditions for a range of actors. The questions include: How satisfied are they with the place where they settled? What were the reasons for moving to their current region of residence? What is the gap between their expectations of living and working in a certain region and their first-hand experience? Do they plan to move? What are the most important factors in their decision-making process? To what extent do they believe that 'soft' location factors have become more important in business location strategies compared to other location factors?

These questions may generate different answers from different categories of actors, and from different subcategories within these. The three groups of actors selected are set out in the following sections.

Workers with higher educational qualifications

Each of the theories we have referred to identifies potential drivers behind the decisions of highly educated workers in creative and knowledge-intensive industries to find and choose a location to work and live in. Perhaps this category, however, associates strongest with the concept of 'talent' and therefore associates strongest with 'soft' conditions theory in which urban atmospheres and urban amenities take centre stage. It remains to be seen whether these conditions nowadays really dominate the scene and whether such conditions can be used to attract 'talent'. In a recent study on the migration behaviour of 'talented people' in Sweden, Hansen and Niedomysl (2009) found that most migration activities of talented people relate to finishing university study, but that most of these moves are driven by job opportunities and not by places. We should also recognise the much lower mobility rates in Europe, compared with the USA. High-skilled employees in European urban regions may not be as mobile as the 'creative class' is expected to be.

We should, however, be aware of the risk of over-generalisation. There may be important differences in behaviour because of special considerations associated with specific creative or knowledge-intensive industries. Van Oort et al. (2003) investigated the role of amenities for residential behaviour of ICT employees. Their assumption was that increasing footlooseness of these employees would result in higher weights attached to amenities in the location decisions of both firms and employees. While they found that ICT employees were relatively footloose, they did not find evidence that residential preferences influenced the location decisions of ICT firms; managers and other decision-makers did not take residential preferences into account. Moreover, they argued that in the Dutch Randstad, both the firms and the employees seemed indifferent as to the level of amenities in the environment.

Managers of creative and knowledge-intensive firms

Although managers and entrepreneurs are often associated with rational behaviour, this still leaves scope for enormous variation. Rational behaviour in connection with the firm is particularly reflected in the literature discussed in Chapter 2 where we referred to agglomeration economies and clustering to take advantage of related firms, services and institutions. However, others have found that the rationality of managers is 'bounded rationality'. After an analysis of foreign direct investment location choice, which was partly based on a literature review, Buckley et al. (2007) concluded that the creation of the set of alternative locations for investment appeared to follow fairly rational rules. However, the choice of actual investment locations appeared less driven by rationality.

We believe there should also be attention for the differentiation between managers' behaviour and the size of the firm: decisions with regard to the place of settlement of larger size firms will be based on different considerations than the decisions of smaller firms. The decisions made by self-employed individuals and by managers of very small firms may more often be driven by a wider range of non-business-related considerations, such as the attractiveness of the place in terms of residential qualities and perhaps also the location relative to family and friends. It may also be the case that the balance of issues affecting decisions will vary according to the sector that is involved – for example there are likely to be different issues for those in the creative rather than knowledge-intensive sectors.

Transnational migrants

The third category we focus on is high-skilled transnational migrants. As with the other groups, the attraction of this group is seen as crucial for successful development and sustainability of creative and/or knowledge-intensive activities. Therefore, the competition for highly skilled labour continues to be fierce. Mahroum (2001) sketches the changes in policies, legislations and procedures across various EU countries and shows that EU member states not only compete with non-EU countries/regions but also among themselves in order to attract and maintain sufficient flows of highly skilled labour. The immigration policies of major industrialised economies which have experienced significant changes in recent years have moved towards more openness regarding highly skilled immigrants. He argues that there is a widespread agreement in Europe that economic competitiveness is increasingly linked to the quality and quantity of skilled human resources available for any given economy.

There is, however, a wide range of theories about what drives transnational migrants, ranging from classic push–pull models, through 'neo-classical' models of restoring the balance between supply and demand of labour, to more modern theories which stress the importance of migrant networks and personal motives such as family reunification. There are also theories more specifically dealing with high-skilled migrants. In 'The New Argonauts', Saxenian (2006) described the positive effects of international mobility of highly skilled migrants for regional development. She observed the impact of foreign talent and entrepreneurs in Silicon Valley in recent years and pointed out that the openness to foreign creative talent was one of the key factors for the success of Silicon Valley. Thus, 'soft' conditions seem to play an important role alongside 'hard'. However, Saxenian also argued that the development of ICT in Israel, Taiwan, China and India was partly due to the networks created by mobile talent which stimulated innovation, investment and trade between countries. This reflected, once more, the importance of personal ties and trajectories.

Most of the skilled international migrants migrate between large international economic centres and only stay for relatively short times – between a few months and a few years. These 'short-term' stayers are often better known as 'expatriates'. Another section of the transnational migrants settles more permanently in the new residential environment. The heterogeneity of expats increases. Apart from the seconded transferees who work in large companies, and were 'sent' by their employers to work in the firm that was already located there, an increasing share comes on their own. Due to the removal of immigration barriers for labour migration within the EU and the stronger support of student mobility, the socio-economic background and the motives of transnational migrants as well as their origins have become more mixed (Conradson and Latham, 2005). This is expected to have implications for settlement behaviour in general.

For this category as well we may wonder whether the diversifications also imply that more migrants will be settling in a place because of personal and 'consumption'-related factors and less driven by 'production'? In that regard it may again be useful to distinguish between those who are attached to creative industries and those who are related to knowledge-intensive industries.

The following chapters

In the chapters to come actors' behaviour and actors' opinions will be compared at an individual level, but also in relation to the cities and urban regions they live in. These comparisons are mainly based on three sets of information, specifically gathered to obtain comparable data for each of the three categories of actors in a set of 13 European urban regions. The key focus in this part of the book is to set out the differences between various categories of actors over what they regard to be of major importance to the decision to settle and to stay in a certain urban region. How large are the differences between different groups and between those working in creative and knowledge-intensive industries?

The development of creative and knowledge-intensive industries is sometimes presented as driven, first and foremost, by the managers and entrepreneurs. Chapter 9 considers evidence related to this for Budapest, Helsinki, Riga, Sofia and Toulouse. In all of these cases the role of firms has been important. But what was it that shaped the decisions taken by the managers and what determined their choices? How important were 'hard' and 'soft' conditions? Were personal networks and trajectories important in these decisions? These and related questions are addressed in Chapter 9.

Chapters 10–12 focus on workers in the creative and knowledge industries. Chapter 10 refers to transnational migrants in cities where this group form a significant part of the population. In Amsterdam, Barcelona and Munich, around 10 per cent of the population originates from another relatively affluent country and these cities are the place of residence for large numbers of highly educated and high-skilled transnational migrants. Much of the migration is 'brain circulation migration' (Pethe, 2006). This implies that many migrants go back and forth between country of stay and country of origin, or even hop from one country to another. Other categories seem to opt for a longer duration of stay. How these different categories of transnational migrants behave in terms of the motives for settling at a certain location, how important the various sets of conditions are to them, is the focus of attention in Chapter 10. Chapter 11 refers to young and high-skilled workers in Amsterdam, Milan and Barcelona and explores differences within this group. The concepts of 'creativity' and 'knowledge' are strongly associated with young and highly educated people. This increases the likelihood that some of their attitudes and behaviour will show strong similarities. The behaviour and location orientations and considerations are compared both within the category and between the three cities.

Finally, Chapter 12 considers important issues related to the quality of work among creative workers. The 'creative class' concept that Richard Florida (2002) uses mainly relates to individuals who are highly skilled and employed in relatively secure economic positions. This has been criticised for its focus on people with higher incomes and higher class positions and for neglecting the creativity of the poor (Wilson and Keil, 2008). However, this concept also neglects that creative employment is characterised by high levels of temporary, project-based and contract working, and very high rates of self-employment and freelancing; and that creative work is often poorly paid. Whereas some individuals might gain high-paid, high-status work, be in constant demand and have considerable power to choose where, how and when they work, this profile does not apply to all individuals or even across all sectors. Those who are less well established or have fluctuating incomes have less choice of where to live and what to do. Chapter 12 presents an analysis of work and employment conditions as well as creative workers' perceptions of 'quality of work' in Birmingham, Leipzig and Poznan to determine whether factors such as influence over work, sense of achievement and the intellectually stimulating nature of creative work do – at least partly – compensate for economic disadvantages, long work hours and feelings of job insecurity associated with creative sector employment. Not only is it important to recognise that some strategies to attract the creative class involve increasing income inequality and social polarisation, but strategies to grow the creative and knowledge sectors may involve increasing the numbers of precarious jobs as well as high-paid jobs. The issues of social inequality and insecurity arise in both cases but have different dynamics.

References

Buckley, P.J., T.M. Devinney and J.J. Louviere (2007) Do managers behave the way theory suggests? A choice-theoretic examination of foreign direct investment location decision-making. *Journal of International Business Studies*, 38: 1069–1094.

Conradson, D. and A. Latham (2005) Friendship, networks and trans-nationality in a world city: Antipodean transmigrants in London. *Journal of Ethnic and Migration Studies*, 31: 287–305.

Florida, R. (2002) *The rise of the creative class and how it's transforming work, leisure, community and everyday life.* New York: Basic Books.

Hansen, H.K. and T. Niedomysl (2009) Migration of the creative class: Evidence from Sweden. *Journal of Economic Geography*, 9 (2): 191–206.

Mahroum, S. (2001) Europe and the immigration of high skilled labour. *International Migration*, 39 (5): 27–43.

Martin-Brelot, H., M. Grossetti, D. Eckert, O. Gritsai and Z. Kovács (2009) Not so mobile 'Creative Class': A European perspective. *GaWC Research Bulletin*, 306 (A). http://www.lboro.ac.uk/gawc/rb/rb306.html

van Oort, F., A. Weterings and H. Verlinde (2003) Residential amenities of knowledge workers and the location of ICT-firms in the Netherlands. *Tijdschrift voor Economische en Sociale Geografie*, 94 (4): 516–523.

Pethe, H. (2006) *Internationale migration hoch qualifizierter Arbeitskräfte – Die Greencard-Regelung für Deutschland*. Wiesbaden: Deutscher Universitäts-Verlag.

Saxenian, A. (2006) *The new argonauts. Regional advantage in a global economy*. Cambridge: Harvard University Press.

Wilson, D. and R. Keil (2008) The real creative class. *Social and Cultural Geography*, 9 (8): 841–847.

9

Managers and Entrepreneurs in Creative and Knowledge-Intensive Industries: What Determines Their Location? Toulouse, Helsinki, Budapest, Riga and Sofia

Evgenii Dainov and Arnis Sauka

Introduction: places matter

From their inception, cities have been artificial, contrived and planned entities, seats of power, culture and creativity (Hall, 1998; Simmie, 2005). In order to thrive, however, cities constantly need to change. Globalisation, improved infrastructure and new technologies have significantly decreased the impact of distance and reduced the transportation costs of manufacturing goods (e.g. Lucas, 1988; Karlsson et al., 2008). This in turn has facilitated flows of the creative population between various cities and regions, widely acknowledged as having a positive impact on productivity (Amabile, 1983; Audretch and Feldman, 1996). Attempting to explain why economic activity and creative people group in one place and not another, recent literature has emphasised the role of supply and demand conditions.

The supply side refers to the personality and cognitive characteristics of individuals living in cities – their ability to generate new ideas and spot new opportunities and their willingness to implement these opportunities (e.g. Amabile, 1996). More recently, however, the role of the context in which people live and make everyday decisions has been highlighted as having considerable impact on the level of individuals' creativity (Florida, 2002; Rasulzada, 2007). Following this, there has been a new emphasis on aspects of the demand side of cities, referring to the 'overall quality of the city' as an element fostering the agglomeration of a creative population. Factors such as the type and quality of educational institutions, tolerance towards minorities, city size and the size of the market as well as networking possibilities and the ability to generate spillovers have been mentioned among other factors of influence (e.g. Jacobs, 1961; Glaeser et al., 2001; Florida, 2002; Fujita and Thisse, 2002).

In spite of considerable efforts to address the questions of why and how cities and regions attract people and stimulate creativity, there is still a lack of sufficiently robust empirical evidence in this regard. By exploring the attitudes and preferences of managers and entrepreneurs from creative and knowledge-based sectors, this chapter aims to contribute to the ongoing discussion of the factors fostering the flow of creative people to particular cities and regions in Europe. The cases of five very different metropolitan regions – Sofia, Riga, Budapest (East European capitals), Helsinki (a West European capital city) and Toulouse, a classic West European 'second city' operating in the shadow of the national capital – are used for this purpose.

The rest of the chapter highlights the major challenges in the existing conceptual framework, provides a brief overview of Sofia, Riga, Toulouse, Helsinki and Budapest and presents results and conclusions arising from this.

Cities and the creative class: major conceptual challenges

As has been previously noted in this book, recent debates about the competitiveness of cities have focused on the importance of the flows of people with key skills between cities. An influential position within the debate on the determinants of the flows of the creative population between cities has been the conceptual construct of the 'creative class' developed by Richard Florida (2002). There are three major points in Florida's theory. The first is that the highest value added is produced by 'creative industries' such as IT, design and arts and cities should consequently focus on these industries. Florida's second point is that, in creative industries, it is no longer the case that employees follow the company. On the contrary, creative companies tend to be located in places where the 'creative class' ('creatives' for short) congregates.

The third point is most directly linked to policymaking and planning, highlighting that 'creatives' are highly mobile, nomadic individuals who choose their location for reasons other than the classic 'hard'-factor considerations, such as rent levels, availability of office space, accessibility and transport. Instead, 'soft' factors, for example urban 'buzz', varied (sub)cultural life, ethnic diversity, availability of greenery and open water, bicycle-friendliness, friendly spaces for interpersonal communication and high levels of tolerance, are of major importance when location decisions are made. The simplified, policy-related outcome arising from this framework is obvious: a city which intends to have creative industries should first put together the right mix of 'soft' and 'hard' factors to attract the nomadic 'creatives'. The further development of the city should then follow as they move in.

In light of this discussion, it should be emphasised, however, that a multitude of critical objections have arisen regarding the Florida brand of 'creative class' theory and its policy ramifications. Steven Malanga, for example, pointed out that over a longer-term horizon, the 'most creative' US cities on Florida's list are the worst performers economically (Malanga, 2004). According to Malanga's estimates, the top 10 most 'creative' cities, for instance, experienced 17.5 per cent job growth from 1993 to 2003, while 'Florida's least creative cities' saw their job numbers grow by 19.4 per cent. Furthermore, over a 20-year period, the 'least creative' cities have been the USA's powerhouses, expanding 60 per cent faster than creative cities.

Next, in line with Florida (2002), some US-based empirical evidence has indeed indicated that amenities do matter and play a role in individuals' location decisions. The trouble here, however, is that existing empirical evidence suggests that almost every group of the population, not only 'creatives', is attracted by amenities (Clark, 2004). Furthermore, 'pipes, pavements and policing' seem, even in the USA, to remain very important in making cities attractive places. If that is the case, for example, an over-simplified Florida-derived development plan may badly misfire by misdirecting resources.

These are only a few examples of the criticism of Florida (2002) to be found in the literature. The major caveat in this discussion is that getting policy-oriented decisions wrong can have a negative impact on the future of each city. This is why the assumptions behind location theories of the 'creative class' must be constantly re-assessed. Consequently, it is reasonable to argue that updated and diversified conceptual and empirical packages are needed in order to inform policy decisions. The next sections of this chapter aim to contribute in this regard by providing empirical evidence from Sofia, Riga, Toulouse, Budapest and Helsinki, drawing on data from a survey of entrepreneurs and managers in creative and knowledge-intensive industries. Twenty-one semi-structured interviews were conducted from February–April of 2008 in each city, addressing the reasoning behind the location decisions of the managers and entrepreneurs from creative and knowledge-intensive industries. The interviews followed a common format in each city and, as briefly outlined earlier in this book, related to the same sectors of the creative and knowledge economy.[1] Before the results of the survey are discussed, however, characteristics of the cities being discussed are briefly presented as a supplement to that already presented in this book.

---

[1] See http://acre.socsci.uva.nl/results/reports.html (reports 6) for a more detailed description of methodology.

Characteristics of the cities: a brief overview

Sofia, the capital of Bulgaria and home to more than two million people, is the most concentrated urban area of the cities in the sample, still to spill over the ring road and into the surrounding countryside. In the mid-1940s this modest-sized city was recast as a Soviet-type industrial metropolis, but by the early twenty-first century Sofia had transformed itself into a city of services, which currently form more than three-quarters of its GDP. Most of the knowledge-intensive industries are concentrated in Sofia and the city is home to the bulk of the new creative industries, linked to both the IT revolution and to the new development opportunities provided by the market economy. Sofia's creative sector, comprising one-fifth of all companies located in Sofia, has grown apace, with the industries under scrutiny in this study doubling in size, and increasing their employment by three-quarters in 2004–2006 alone.

Riga, the capital of Latvia, is home to one-third of the country's population. Similarly to Sofia, Riga has long been a transport hub to the rest of the world and a centre of commerce in the region. During Soviet times, however, Riga only partly managed to escape the worst excesses of heavy industry, at the same time remaining an administrative and education centre. Although not without losses, most of its historic architecture was also spared from the invasion of 'Stalin Baroque' during Soviet times. The tertiary sector today forms the bulk of Riga's GDP, but the creative and knowledge sectors in Riga employ up to a third of the working population. The creative sector in particular has been growing rapidly since 2001.

Budapest, the capital of Hungary, can be seen as a former socialist capital 'with a difference'. More specifically, one of the results of its 1956 anti-communist revolution was that Hungary acquired the unspoken privilege not to implement the Soviet model of industry and government in the strictest of ways. Pro-market economic reforms, gradually implemented since the 1960s, ensured Budapest's smoother re-entry into the world of democracy and the market economy. Currently, Budapest is home to approximately two million people, generating 60 per cent of Hungary's total revenue. The creative and knowledge sectors boast about 112,000 companies, employing more than 420,000 people – just under one-third of total employment. During 1999–2004 alone, the creative sector in Budapest grew by 30 per cent in terms of number of companies and doubled its revenue.

To summarise, the general characteristic of these ex-socialist cities is that within living memory they suffered two major dislocations: one during the invasion of socialism in the 1940s, and another with the re-construction of democracy and the market economy during the turbulent 1990s. The 'Western' cities in the sample have been spared from these dislocations as well as from the explosive development after the end of socialism.

Regardless of this, although in the 1990s the well-planned 'Western' cities looked to be in a much better starting position as regards the development of 'creative cities', it turned out that the eastern Europe cities, chaotic in comparison, today demonstrate a similar share of employment in the knowledge-intensive and creative sectors. In terms of value creation from the creative population, however, the 'East' is still far behind the 'West'.

As for the 'Western' cities in our group, the urban area of *Toulouse* (UAT) is home to more than a million people (435,000 in the city), ranking in population size behind Paris, Lyon, Marseille and Lille. Toulouse was spared the heavy industries and environmental damage of the Industrial Revolution. It has enjoyed a clearly identifiable development path based on high technology, benefiting from the 1950s French 'decentralisation' policies, which brought Toulouse two major engineering schools (*Ecole nationale supérieure de l'aéronautique* and *Ecole nationale de l'aviation civile*) and the new *Centre national d'études spatiales*. These knowledge centres, in turn, attracted two large aerospace companies to the city, Matra and Alcatel, as well as other service companies working in the field. Recently, creative and knowledge-intensive industries have provided more than one-fifth of all employment in the UAT. Overall, unlike most of the 'Eastern' cities, Toulouse is also more attractive for researchers due to the long research tradition and the clearer development path of city-related policies.

Helsinki, the capital of Finland, is the country's leading city and dominates the national urban landscape. It houses some 24 per cent of the country's population and is Finland's only city with more than one million inhabitants. Since the 1990s, Helsinki has become a world leader in ICT and related fields, overcoming a dire economic crisis in the early 1990s. By 2004, more than 30 per cent of all employees in the Helsinki Metropolitan Area were concentrated in the creative (12.9 per cent) and knowledge (17.7 per cent) sectors. Of these, the ICT industries have produced the greatest impact on growth and employment. As in Toulouse, informed planning, greatly enhanced by stakeholder-based policymaking, has defined the city's recent development.

The starting point for the cities being discussed in this chapter is that they are as different as their histories and development paths. It is thus of even greater interest to explore whether metropolitan areas in Europe employ similar strategies to compete for creative entrepreneurs and managers, and whether there are any differences in the location preferences of this target group, as compared with the USA (e.g. Florida, 2002). Drawing on previous studies on the topic (e.g. Florida, 2002; Fujita and Thisse, 2002; Rasulzada, 2007), this chapter explores the influence of 'hard' and 'soft' factors on the location decisions of entrepreneurs and managers. The interview material drawn on enables discussion not only of why entrepreneurs and managers opted to move to a particular city and whether and in which cases capital cities are preferred to 'non-capitals' but also addresses in-city decisions, for example why they chose locations in the city centre or periphery.

Location decisions: 'individual trajectory' considerations and 'hard' factors

The interview derived data which underpin this chapter indicates that for these cities the main drivers for settlement of entrepreneurs and managers from creative and knowledge-intensive industries are linked not to 'hard' or 'soft' factors but to 'individual trajectories'. In Toulouse, for instance, as much as 75 per cent of the interviewed managers had a previous link with the city, either through family networks or networking established during their studies. Moreover, 55 per cent of the managers were born in or near the Toulouse region and 60 per cent studied in Toulouse. Very similar findings to those are also reported in the case of the Helsinki Metropolitan Area; and in Sofia, Budapest and Riga 'individual trajectory' seemed to have an even more significant impact. This is consistent with the previous comparative analysis made among the employees of the creative knowledge sectors. Nearly half of the surveyed people in our cities originate from the place where they currently live, and almost two-thirds of them also studied there (Martin-Brelot et al., 2009).

To be more specific, respondents from the knowledge-intensive industries in Sofia and Budapest reported location decisions related to 'individual trajectory' factors virtually without exception. Also, in Riga the majority of managers mentioned that their company is located in the city mainly because they were born there, have lived there in the past or have studied there, thus having relatives and friends in the city. Overall, these findings are in line with Krugman (1991) and Markusen (1996), who emphasised the place-dependency of entrepreneurial activities, arguing that entrepreneurs tend to stick to the places they know and where they have networking opportunities – very often these are the places they originally come from.

As for the influence of 'hard' factors, managers and entrepreneurs of creative companies in Toulouse cited 'market opportunity' reasons rather than 'soft' factors as having an influence on their location decisions. Opportunities to recruit skilled workers, the presence of good universities as well as size of the city seemed to considerably affect the location choices of both local and incoming managers. Furthermore, the rapid demographic growth of the UAT (about 17,000 extra inhabitants per year since 1999) is seen as a favourable factor by companies, especially those having a link with the real estate sector. Overall, these findings reflect previous empirical evidence highlighting the role of density within cities in generating knowledge spill-overs, achieved through the interaction and networking of the (creative) population and furthermore positively influencing the growth of the region

(Lucas, 1988; Grossetti, 2008; Johansson and Karlsson, 2008). It should be emphasised, however, that according to our data, 'hard' factor deficiencies are also seen, in Toulouse, as a significant stumbling block. Respondents from Toulouse, for instance, mentioned that the city is at a disadvantage due to the lack of high-speed rail connections to the capital and other strategic nodes in France and Europe. In managers' and entrepreneurs' opinion, the concentration of power and resources in Paris means that the majority of managers have to travel regularly to the capital city to meet and socialise with decision-makers.

'Hard' factors outweigh 'soft' considerations in the case of Helsinki as well. More specifically, apart from 'individual trajectory' considerations, the major drivers of entrepreneurs' and managers' location decisions here are the presence of specialised skilled labour and the concentration of customers. Furthermore, many entrepreneurs stated that nearly the whole industry is located in Metropolitan Helsinki; thus, they simply have to be there. Such claims are justified by available statistics. For example, as with other industries, the business and management consulting sector is strongly concentrated in the Helsinki area, with approximately 60 per cent of the entire sector's employment positions in Finland (Kepsu and Vaattovaara, 2008). Interestingly enough, however, none of the entrepreneurs or managers interviewed in Helsinki mentioned any 'soft' factors as important location drivers for their location in the city.

As in the case of Helsinki, 'hard' factors come just after 'individual trajectories' to play a decisive role in the decisions of entrepreneurs and managers and their companies in Budapest. The availability of an appropriate labour force, especially in financial and business activities, stands out as a crucial issue in this regard. According to respondents, Budapest, as the centre of business life and also of higher education, is an 'ideal place' to recruit. As in the other cities in our sample, however, several 'hard' factors, such as the poor state of public transportation, were mentioned as causing major dissatisfaction. Overall, the same picture with regard to the importance of 'hard factors' is reproduced by interviewed entrepreneurs and managers in *Riga* and *Sofia*, where beyond the dominant 'individual trajectory' issues, factors such as access to a qualified workforce, the concentration of the relevant industry in the city, proximity of customers, access to government institutions and networking possibilities were highlighted as having a positive role in the location decision.

Location decisions: the role of 'soft' factors

The main conclusion with regard to the influence of 'soft' factors on the location decisions of managers and entrepreneurs of creative and knowledge-intensive industries in Sofia, Riga, Toulouse, Budapest and Helsinki is that our respondents' reports fall almost entirely outside of Florida's theoretical model. More specifically, 'soft' factors were mentioned very rarely and were only emphasised as the drivers behind location decisions by isolated individuals.

Once this conclusion is lodged and still, drawing on our research interviews, it is important to introduce an analytical distinction between 'location' and 'retention' decisions. Even though the location decisions of managers in the sample are nearly free of 'soft' considerations, the decision to stay in the city is often significantly influenced by satisfaction with the 'soft' factors in place. For example, none of the respondents in Toulouse referred to a *location decision* based significantly on 'soft' considerations. Overall, the most mobile turned out to be managers in the business and management consultancy sector, over half of whom had no prior link to Toulouse, whereas web designers and managers from the games industry showed the least mobility, all of them being locals. A number of managers, however, reflected a strong affective attachment to the region by saying that they were not willing to leave the city at all. Arguably, this pattern may result from the 'individual trajectory'. However, the influence of 'soft' considerations, such as the proximity of the sea and mountains, the sunny climate and the specific atmosphere and mindset of the south of France, could be another explanation in this regard, pointing to the comparably large role of 'soft factors' with regard to managers' and entrepreneurs' retention decision.

Contrary to Toulouse, some evidence that 'soft' factor considerations inform at least a few location decisions in Helsinki emerged from the data set. The major considerations include the nearness to high-quality residential space and safety issues. Furthermore, in line with the findings of a previous sub-study on creative knowledge workers in Helsinki (Kepsu and Vaattovaara, 2008), our data from Helsinki, as well as from other cities in the sample, suggest that managers appear to value 'soft' factors, such as the ambience or 'buzz' of the city. More specifically, according to managers, various networking-related factors, such as hanging out in theatre cafés, going to movie premieres and being inspired by urban life, are of increasing importance to people. The managers' and entrepreneurs' viewpoint was that these were important factors for potential and existing employees from the whole industry. Overall, however, the 'soft' factors mentioned seem to have a greater weight in entrepreneurs' and managers' retention rather than in location decisions.

The situation regarding the influence of 'soft' factors is not very different in the former socialist cities. In Budapest and Riga, managers rarely mentioned 'soft' factors and when they did so they were largely by chance, suggesting that as far as location decisions go, 'soft' factors played no appreciable role. According to managers, 'soft' factors emerge during site selection primarily when the residence (dwelling) is also the location of the company and, in the agglomeration zone, where lower rental fees and real estate prices provide the business managers with better opportunities to consider 'soft' factors in decision-making. The importance of a calm and quiet environment was the 'soft' factor most commonly mentioned by the managers as most important. In a few cases, a neighbourhood with very poor outer appearance and social composition was also referred to as being ruled out of consideration.

The fact that very few managers from Budapest and especially from Riga explicitly discussed the role of the 'soft' factors in the location decision might support the view that 'soft' factors are not important. However, since people usually find it easier to complain than to give credit, the reason for not mentioning problems with 'soft' factors could also be due to the fact that Riga, for instance, does quite well in this regard. This notion, however, again appears to be more relevant for employees than for managers. Furthermore, as in the case of other cities, managers' and entrepreneurs' decisions to remain in Riga are more likely to be motivated by 'soft' factors than are decisions to move in.

As regards Sofia, almost uniformly companies do not see emblematic 'soft' factors, such as amenities, leisure and nightlife, or diversity as having any significance in their location decision. Of particular interest in this regard is the lack of sensitivity to cultural tolerance. Florida (2002) places great emphasis on the importance of low barriers for entry, such as barriers for self-expression (often related to tolerance towards gays and bohemians), in facilitating the flow of creatives to the city. In this light, according to the available statistics, Sofia seems to be one of Europe's most cosmopolitan and tolerant cities, with more than 17 per cent of its population being some sort of ethnic, religious or national minority (Dainov and Nachev, 2008). Yet, there was not a single respondent who saw tolerance and diversity as a factor in location decisions. It is not, therefore, surprising that in cities more homogenous than Sofia, tolerance of diversity also plays no role in location decisions.

Finally, according to our data, the importance of 'soft' considerations, especially in Helsinki, Budapest and Sofia, varies across the industries. In this light, respondents having at least some sensitivity to 'soft' factors in these cities can be found at broadcasting companies. It could be argued in this regard that while representatives of other industries, such as consultants and computer-related businesses, are almost entirely oblivious to them, broadcasters are capable of discussing and evaluating the role of 'soft' factors. One of the explanations for this phenomenon could be related to the maturity of the companies, since consultancies and computer-related businesses are at an age of infancy compared with broadcasters. Thus, the reasoning that 'individual trajectory' issues and 'hard' factors dominate when you start a business, whereas sensitivity for 'soft' factors is developed when a business matures and stabilises could make at least some sense. This is, however, something previous empirical studies have not captured to a sufficient extent, suggesting that further research is needed on the issue.

In-city location decisions

Different types of creatives tend to congregate in different locations within the urban area. While 'cultural creatives', such as artists, media and entertainment workers, scientists, teachers, designers and advertisers, usually prefer an inner-city location, managers and entrepreneurs seem to be spread much more evenly across the city (e.g. Musterd, 2004). Such differences in location decisions within the 'creative class', often influenced by 'soft' considerations, have also been pointed out by Florida (2002), especially with regard to, what are labelled by the author as 'bohemians' and 'nerds' in the USA. Whether the location preferences of creatives within the city centre or suburbs are influenced by 'soft' factors, however, is a very problematic issue in the European context. According to our findings, for example, 'soft' factor considerations play a strikingly insignificant role with regard to in-city location decisions as compared with the USA. They are mostly related to classic 'hard' factors, such as rent, access and closeness to client base. Moreover, it may be that, for whatever reason, a greater profile should be expected for soft factors in settled 'Western' cities than in the more turbulent and as yet unsettled ex-socialist newcomers to capitalism.

To be more specific, in Toulouse, for example, in-city location profiling does exist, but evidence points away from the overwhelming dominance of 'soft' factor considerations. Self-employed creatives as well as small companies (with one to nine employees), for instance, tend to settle more frequently in the periphery, where rent is lower, whereas the largest companies exclusively choose the city centre of Toulouse with no companies with 50 employees or more located in the periphery. However, companies involved in, arguably, the most creative activities, such as video, animation movie, 3D web design and computer games, seem to favour the historic core and show the most sensitivity to 'soft' factors. Here, the managers mention accessibility and flexible working hours, but location choice also relates to the image given to clients, whereas 'soft' factors are linked to atmosphere, including architecture, density of boutiques, cafés and restaurants in the neighbourhood.

Entrepreneurs and managers whose companies are located in the centre of Toulouse usually justified their choice by proximity to their own place of residence and by the fact that employees tend to live in the area. The parking difficulties and the congestion problems in the centre, however, often come up as explanations for choosing a location in the peripheral business parks. According to the survey data, the computer industry also benefits from a large density of previously existing clustered establishments. These include the aeronautics clusters in the northwest, electronic and computer clusters in the southwest as well as the space, computer and biotechnology clusters in the southeast and the multi-nodal logistic platform in the north of the city. Regardless of the sector in Toulouse, however, informal social networks linked to 'individual trajectory' factors and to the role of the earlier social insertion of the respondents in the city region were most important among the influential factors mentioned by entrepreneurs and managers.

In the case of Helsinki, and to some extent also Budapest, in general 'individual trajectories' play a decisive role with regard to the in-city location patterns of entrepreneurs and managers located outside the city centre (most companies not located in the city centre are established close to where the founding manager lives). This trend, however, is less obvious for companies which have chosen to be located in the city centre. According to our data, the main driver for the entrepreneurs and managers of these firms is the high prestige of the city centre, and 'hard' factors had the predominant influence in shaping these location decisions. It should be mentioned, however, that being located in business parks is also considered to provide a good image for the company. Overall, as in the case of Toulouse, all the managers interviewed stressed the importance of being within easy reach of the place of work and of customers. Whereas clustering was particularly valued in the film and TV industries, the factor that came up as the most decisive for all firms was the need for a supply of a specialised and skilled labour.

In the light of previous discussion, it is perhaps no surprise that 'hard' factors also dominate in-city location decisions in the case of Budapest and Riga where office price or rent seem to be of overriding importance. Furthermore problems with the availability of parking space in the centre have a significant impact, especially in Riga. Most of the managers claimed that these reasons prevented them from being located in the city centre, where desirable 'hard' factors, such as proximity to clients, would come into play. It should be emphasised, however, that at least in the case of Budapest, the issue of distance from clients has been losing significance for particular sectors, such as the ICT sector and the software consultancy subsector. Furthermore, the proximity to other research institutes rather than to customers is mentioned among the managers of companies involved in research and development in Riga.

Transport–accessibility–availability forms the next set of the most important 'hard' factors of influence in Budapest, just after the cost of office space. Entrepreneurs and managers employ various strategies to overcome the influence of such factors. In Budapest as well as in Toulouse, for example, it is common for a company to have its headquarters in an office owned by the director, thus saving on the rent. Despite such efforts, 'hard' factors still often play a decisive role. To illustrate this, most of the companies in Riga located in the suburbs, for example, do not intend to move into the centre mainly due to high rent and parking problems. The companies located in the centre, on the other hand, were generally happy with their location, but concerned about the cost of office space and the poor infrastructure: some thought that eventually this might force them to leave the centre.

Finally, our data suggest that managers in Sofia are taking deliberate in-city location decisions, in contrast with the chaotic pattern of domestic settlement of the various types of 'creatives'. As in the cases of other cities in the sample, managerial location decisions are dominated by 'hard' factors virtually to the exclusion of all other considerations, and only one company reported being at the periphery not because it is cheaper but because it is a nicer place than the centre. Furthermore, some differences with regard to inner location decisions exist across various industries in Sofia. Managers of consultancy firms, for example, generally preferred the city because of the proximity to client government institutions, whereas financial and IT consultancy companies chose the sub-centre area, near to central traffic roads for rapid movement around the city and to ensure better access for clients from outside Sofia. Moreover, for computer-related companies, prices and rents are a crucial location factor, just as they are for the ITC and software sector, where companies are young and small in size.

Capital city versus provincial city location decisions

A major – overwhelming, in effect – determinant of location decisions emerged from our interviews. This has little to do with the 'soft'/'hard' debate, but relates to whether the city in question is the national capital of a small nation (thereby attracting the bulk of its resources, qualified workforce and development potential), or a non-capital city of a big nation. According to our findings, the main trend emerging from capital cities seems to be that creative and knowledge industry managers simply found it difficult to envisage not being in the capital city. More specifically, in Helsinki, for instance, all interviewed managers were unequivocal on the issue of capital or province, usually stating that operating from other parts of the country aside from the capital city was simply not an option. According to them, the main motives for this were related to the proximity of both customers and the skilled labour force in Helsinki. The case of Budapest, where the country's creative and knowledge industries are concentrated, is very similar. In fact, the whole 'critical mass' of Hungary, in the social and economic sense, seems to be concentrated in the metropolitan region of Budapest, with branches of cultural industries being overrepresented in the Budapest area. The setting in Budapest is also favourable from the aspect of financing, as firms are better off here than in the provincial towns of Budapest. Besides, as voiced by one of the interviewed managers, tax and financial auditing is not so frequent in Budapest due to the large number of enterprises in the area, thus making life easier for the entrepreneurs. Overall, all respondents in Budapest agreed that it is absolutely necessary to be in or near the capital city to be able to take part in specific 'creative activities', such as motion picture productions, for example.

In Riga we find the same situation. Being the capital and by far the largest city not only in Latvia but also in the region (e.g. Estonia, Latvia and Lithuania), Riga is Latvia's main attractor of investment and generator of employment. Furthermore, Riga is the main educational and scientific centre of Latvia. To be located outside Riga is thus not considered to be an option by any of the companies interviewed. As mentioned by many, within Latvia, there is simply no competition from any other city.

As with Riga, Sofia enjoys the benefits of being the capital city with its concentration of the major resources of the country, including the 'power of decision-making' and the supply of qualified labour. It is obvious that many industries, almost without exception, depend on the presence and quality of these institutions; thus, it is of no surprise that managers and entrepreneurs chose to be located there. Furthermore, especially for companies that work entirely in the local market, the market size is of major importance. In this light, it should be emphasised that Sofia is several times larger than the next largest city in Bulgaria, which is of major influence on the location decisions of many entrepreneurs and managers.

In contrast to the cities explored previously, Toulouse is clearly a 'second' city, living in the shadow of the capital of France, Paris. As a result, Toulouse might seem to be attractive primarily to the industries and branches already developed in the capital city and 'moved down' to Toulouse as a consequence of the government's de-concentration policy. Otherwise, Paris is as dominant for the creative industries in France as Sofia for Bulgaria or Budapest for Hungary. For instance, 74.5 per cent of cinema, picture and video production activities are gathered in Île-de-France and 59 per cent in the only commune of Paris. More than 62 per cent of motion picture, video and TV programme production activities are concentrated in Paris and its adjacent western *département* of Hauts-de-Seine, which comes in second in most of the audiovisual sub-sectors. From these numbers it is quite clear that Toulouse's chances of directly competing with Paris are very limited.

Policymaking: 'soft', 'hard' or 'other'?

As expected, the 'Western' cities in the sample, which did not experience the severe dislocations of the 1940s as well as the 1990s, are much more prone to sustained planning and policy efforts than the ex-socialist cities. Differences, however, also exist if 'Western' cities are compared among themselves, mostly arising from the fact that one of the cities in our sample, for example Helsinki, is the capital city, whereas Toulouse is not.

More specifically, Toulouse, whose 'knowledge-intensive' profile is the outcome of national-level policies in France, seems to be lacking the local capacity to provide policy-based support for the creative sector. Here, sector managers report lack of interest and misunderstanding about new creative industries from the local policymakers as well as administrative heaviness and complications in entering local markets. Entrepreneurs and managers' demands from policymakers, however, have little to do with 'soft' factors. Instead, 'hard'-factor-related policies are requested such as improvement of transport and infrastructure, development of the business climate and easing of cumbersome administrative procedures. Furthermore, audiovisual companies claimed the need for easier access to financing. Interestingly enough, however, managers in general claimed that they would like to see policy improvement at the national rather than local level.

Being a capital city, Helsinki, on the other hand, boasts a good bottom-up policy track record. During the economic crisis of the early 1990s, government, municipalities, universities and the business community joined together to revive the economy. The key principle of the authorities has been to mobilise and join the resources of the business community, the academic community and the administrative sector. The emphasis in policymaking has been on education, research and knowledge. As a result, there is a strong enthusiasm in Finland among politicians and civil servants to work on creative knowledge strategies to foster national development.

As for 'Eastern' cities, Budapest, although for various reasons less 'Eastern' than Riga or Sofia, demonstrates a lack of effective municipal-level policy, as usually expected from non-'Western' cities. In this light, the research found that according to the viewpoint of entrepreneurs and managers, local government has virtually no role in fostering the creative sector, and that only the national government can influence the development of any creative activity. As for more specific wishes, entrepreneurs and managers highlighted the need for a more business-friendly climate at the national level. On the local level, however, 'hard'-factor-related demands were expressed, including the improvement of transport, noise, pollution, top-heavy bureaucracy in the issuing of business permits and similar areas.

When analysing policymaking practices in Riga, it should be noted that the whole concept of planning was historically discredited because of its association with the central planning of the former Soviet system. It is still symptomatic, however, that when asked about collaboration with the public sector, only one respondent out of the 21 interviewed mentioned having received support from Riga City. However, when the issue of public support or support from the European Union (EU) was brought up during the interviews, again, all but one manager in our sample claimed that no support had been received either from Latvian or from EU sources. However, there is a variety of demands from entrepreneurs and managers in Riga, primarily targeted at the central government and concerned with 'hard' factors. These include facilitation of tax administration, lowering of taxes, battling corruption, facilitation of the administration of EU projects, making education more practical and improving the business climate as such.

In the case of Sofia, the path of the city's development had much less to do with planning than application of the Aristotelian–Habermasian model, under which civic energies and habits, once awoken, spread beyond issues of governance (the end of communism, in this case) and infuse the daily lives of citizens. As a result, political initiative turned into economic entrepreneurship and established Sofia as the engine of the new national economy. Confirming this 'self-regulating pattern', all respondents reported an absence of municipal-level policies for their sectors. Strikingly enough, and uniquely for the five cities studied, the lack of policy initiatives was confirmed by the city planners themselves. To illustrate the extent of the problem, officials of Sofia Municipality refused to be involved in the research on the grounds that the Municipality had no policies whatsoever aimed at knowledge-intensive and creative industries.

National-level policies, however, such as the government's package of policies lowering taxation, are seen to be of much greater help by entrepreneurs and managers in Sofia. As with the other cities, the desirable municipal policies that were highlighted by respondents related to 'hard' factors, such as infrastructure, transportation, access to social and educational centres, security and also initiation events and happenings in the cultural life of the capital. Sadly, most of the entrepreneurs and managers seemed to be sceptical about the Municipality's capacity to deliver these outputs. At the best, respondents expressed hopes that the various administrations would simply stop getting in their way.

Conclusions and implications

Interviews with entrepreneurs and managers in five European cities suggest that location decisions are mainly driven by family and other links with cities, traditions and national identities. These findings alone lead to the conclusion that the analytical picture developed by Florida (2002) needs elaboration and, to a certain extent, redefinition. Among other things, the data from Europe suggest that, although very useful, the distinction between 'hard' and 'soft' factors is not a sufficient theoretical basis to explain the location patterns of creatives. The 'individual trajectory' considerations overwhelmingly dominated the decisions of all groups in our study and are insufficiently acknowledged in much other research. Furthermore, if we consider location decisions in the five cities in terms of the 'hard' and 'soft' dichotomy, it is apparent that traditional 'hard' factors generally reign supreme and are also important at the level of decisions to be located in a particular area inside the city.

There are areas, however, in which European 'creatives' reveal sensitivity to 'soft' factors. The vast majority of respondents from all cities in our survey reported significant levels of job satisfaction, with the emphasis placed on workplace-related factors, including a sense of achievement gained from work, the scope for innovation in the workplace and the level of influence individuals have in directing their work. At the same time, entrepreneurs and managers from creative sectors also expressed high satisfaction with 'soft' factors, such as the living environment in their district and the cultural life of the city. This supports the view that it is more important in retention of these groups than in their initial attraction.

The sensitivity of respondents in creative and knowledge-intensive industries to 'soft' issues did not turn out to drive their location decisions. These respondents simply did not behave as Florida's 'happy nomads'. A complex package of location motivations emerged instead having to do greatly with the influence of 'individual trajectory issues'. More specifically, for most of the entrepreneurs and managers, the reason for being located in a particular city had much more to do with the fact that the respondents were born in the region, had family there, had studied in the city or had moved there to join a spouse or to be in the proximity of friends than with various 'soft' considerations. Community-related rather than 'nomadic' considerations are more apparent in our study and appear to be less visible in America where individuals are more geographically mobile.

Entrepreneurs and managers in all five cities followed a 'hard' factor path of location decision-making. Costs, nearness to clients, access issues and availability of labour outweigh 'soft' factor considerations. Only a handful of isolated individuals interviewed followed the opposite, Florida-type, direction. At the same time, dissatisfaction was most frequently voiced with the 'hard' factors of a city – costs, taxes, transportation issues. This in itself means that city planners should start by concentrating on the development of 'hard'-factor-related policies, if *attracting* creative managers and entrepreneurs to the city is at least one of the priorities of their work. Our data, however, suggest that 'soft'-factor-related policies also cannot be ignored, as these considerations play a significant role in retention decisions of creatives.

According to our data, the theoretical model of city development needs to be re-drafted so as to differentiate between capital and non-capital cities. This is particularly the case with regard to less populated European countries (such as Finland, Hungary, Latvia and Bulgaria), where up to one-third of the entire population lives in the capital area and up to 100 per cent of all the nation's knowledge-intensive and (particularly) creative industries may be concentrated. The capital, being the administrative, economic, educational, political, cultural, commercial and tourist hub of a small country, can almost by default step onto the path of 'creative city'. Any city that is not a capital, therefore, would be facing an uphill battle if it decided to persuade creatives to re-locate from their nation's capital. Finally, as suggested by our study, an appreciable difference between 'Western' and 'Eastern' cities exists.

To conclude, it would be premature to 'dismiss' Florida's conceptual construct in explaining the location patterns of entrepreneurs and managers from creative and knowledge-based sectors in Europe. After all, if individual energy and creativity can compensate for structural deficiencies and push cities forward and onto the creative path, the duty of city planners is to create the optimal, favourable conditions for citizens to develop and harness their energy and creativity productively. This notion brings the discussion back, at least to some degree, to classic Florida 'soft' themes, such as the importance of the availability of friendly public and semi-public spaces for personal intercourse and networking, urban 'buzz' among other things.

Ultimately, however, it may turn out that Florida-type constructs have more relevance during 'good' times and fall by the wayside during 'bad' times. In this light, critics of Florida (2002) have long pointed out that, in the end, wages matter more than amenities, particularly during an economic recession. As managers are forced to employ 'hard' factor survival mechanisms by cutting costs and dismissing labour, even creatives see their incomes disappear or decline. The policy measures that can address the current crisis in Europe and the USA, on either a global or national level, should thus concentrate on 'hard' factors first, such as getting the financial systems kick-started and finding ways of reviving the economies of the world. Only when these issues are resolved, the policymakers can again enjoy the luxury of debating the relative merits of 'soft' factors.

Acknowledgement

The authors would like to thank Denis Eckert for his contribution to this chapter.

References

Amabile, T. (1983) *The social psychology of creativity*. New York: Springer Verlag.

Amabile, T. (1996) *Creativity in context*. Boulder, CO: Westview.

Audretch, D. and M. Feldman (1996) R&D spillovers and the geography of innovation and production. *American Economic Review*, 86 (3), 630–640.

Clark, T. (ed.) (2004) *The city as an entertainment machine*. Oxford/New York: Elsevier.

Dainov, E. and I. Nachev (2008) *The creative and knowledge class in Sofia. The managers' view*. ACRE report 6.10. Amsterdam: AMIDSt.

Florida, R. (2002) *The rise of the creative class*. New York: Basic Books.

Fujita, M. and J. Thisse (2002) *Economics of agglomeration: Cities, industrial location and regional growth.* Cambridge: Cambridge University Press.

Glaeser, E., J. Kolko and A. Saiz (2001) Consumer city. *Journal of Economic Geography,* 1: 27–50.

Grossetti, M. (2008) Proximities and embeddings effects. *European Planning Studies,* 16 (5): 613–616.

Hall, P. (1998) *Cities in civilization.* London: Weidenfeld & Nicolson.

Jacobs, J. (1961) *The death and live of great American cities.* New York: Random House.

Johansson, B. and C. Karlsson (2008) Regional development and knowledge. In: R. Capello and P. Nijkamp (eds), *Handbook of regional growth and development.* Northampton: Edward Elgar.

Karlsson, C., B. Johansson and R. Stough (2008) *Entrepreneurship and innovation in functional regions.* Working Paper Series in Economics and Institutions of Innovation 144. Stockholm: Royal Institute of Technology, CESIS – Centre of Excellence for Science and Innovation Studies.

Kepsu, K. and M. Vaattovaara (2008) *Creative knowledge in the Helsinki metropolitan area. Understanding the attractiveness of the metropolitan region for creative knowledge workers.* ACRE report 5.5. Amsterdam: AMIDSt.

Krugman, P. (1991) *Geography and trade.* Cambridge, MA: The MIT Press.

Lucas, R. (1988) On the mechanics of economic development. *Journal of Monetary Economics,* 22: 3–42.

Malanga, S. (2004) The curse of the creative class. A new age theory of urban development amounts to economic snake oil. *City Journal,* Winter 2004, http://www.opinionjournal.com/extra/?id 5 110004573

Markusen, A. (1996) Sticky places in slippery space: A typology of industrial districts. *Economic Geography,* 72 (2): 293–313.

Martin-Brelot, H., M. Grossetti, D. Eckert, O. Gritsai and Z. Kovács (2009) Not so mobile 'Creative Class': A European perspective. *GaWC Research Bulletin,* 306 (A). http://www.lboro.ac.uk/gawc/rb/rb306.html

Musterd, S. (2004) Amsterdam as a creative cultural knowledge city: Some conditions. *Built Environment,* 30 (3): 225–234.

Rasulzada, F. (2007) *Organizational creativity and psychological well-being. Contextual aspects on organizational creativity and psychological well-being from an open systems perspective.* Doctoral dissertation. Lund: Department of Psychology, Lund University.

Simmie, J. (2005) Innovation and space: A critical review of the literature. *Regional Studies,* 39 (6): 789–804.

10

Transnational Migrants in the Creative Knowledge Industries: Amsterdam, Barcelona, Dublin and Munich

Heike Pethe, Sabine Hafner and Philip Lawton

Introduction

In the last decade, the European Union (EU) and European cities and countries have developed policies to attract foreign highly skilled professionals (OECD, 2001, 2005, 2007). Labour shortages in the information technology sector and in parts of service industries such as banking and the health sector have led many states to revise what had been restrictive policies towards immigration (OECD, 2007). In Tampere, 1999 EU countries agreed to develop a common framework to manage migration and after the Hague Programme of 2004 the EU commission stated that 'legal migration will play an important role in enhancing the knowledge-based economy in Europe, in advancing economic development' (European Commission, 2007, p. 2). Three years later, a proposal for a so-called Blue Card was introduced to the public which would allow highly skilled workers from non-EU countries to gain a working and residence permit for the EU (European Commission, 2007).

Against the background of the acknowledgement of the need for a policy on highly skilled migration, European regions do not appear to be very attractive for international migrants. 46 per cent of all highly skilled migrants in the OECD countries live in the USA (OECD, 2008, p. 81), whereas only 34 per cent of all tertiary educated international migrants reside in Europe.[1] Salt estimates that the foreign national population reside in European

---

[1] Calculated from http://dx.doi.org/10.1787/247177241125 (accessed 17 April 2009).

countries in 2004 or the nearest date available 'stood at around 25.5 million people. Foreign citizens thus appear to constitute some 4.5 per cent of the aggregate population of Europe' (Salt, 2006, p. 13). Compared with the USA, the population of Europe also appears rather immobile with Americans changing their residence up to five times more often than Europeans (Favell, 2003, p. 412). Favell argues 'Eurocities remain distinctive, variable environments at the international level, and one has to compete with all the in-built advantages of the local bourgeoisie. Only in rare cases is there a critical mass of foreign residents, such that the structure of the city itself is changed' (Favell, 2003, p. 422). Consequently, the attractiveness of European countries for international, highly skilled migrants is not as high as in the USA. The remaining differences between nation states, the incompatibility of pension schemes and social security systems and other hard factors and bureaucratic obstacles as well as soft factors still affect international labour migration.

This chapter analyses the attractiveness of four second-tier metropolitan regions in western Europe: Amsterdam, Barcelona, Dublin and Munich. All of these score high in international studies of the attractiveness of business locations (Dienst Onderzoek en Statistiek Amsterdam, 2008, p. 644). The chapter presents research data on international migrants to these cities and discusses the results in the light of different theoretical frameworks.

Conceptualising transnational migrants and the creative class

The longest established way of discussing the international migration of highly skilled workers is in terms of the 'brain drain' (BD). The macro-level economic differences between countries are seen as explaining a continuing migration of highly skilled persons from less developed to indus-trialised countries. Pull/push models or world system theory are often used to explain the emigration of the educated labour force from the South to the North. Macro-economic differences in economic performance (GPD, income, foreign direct investment (FDI), labour market), and differences in factors such as tax leverage, infrastructure and working conditions are also important for international migration (Schipulle, 1973). The literature further focuses on the effects of emigration on the sending regions.

A second approach imagines the international migration of the highly skilled as 'brain exchange' (BE). Economic globalisation has led transna-tional companies to expand their network of branches (Beaverstock, 1994) and a global labour market has been created within these organisations (Perlmutter, 1969; Beaverstock, 1996b; Wolter, 1997). The companies allocate their employees due to their needs. Highly skilled personnel is seconded from the headquarters in the industrialised countries to the new branches in the developing countries (Beaverstock, 1994; Beaverstock

1996a, c). The direction of migration was opposite to the pattern in the brain drain migration. Highly skilled experts were needed to control and command the global activities of companies (Beaverstock and Smith, 1996; Boyle , 1996). They either supervised new sales offices, marketing units or new production units. Thus, the flow of highly skilled migrants was related to FDI and international trade flows (Wolter, 1997). Because it is heavily tied to the globalisation of the economy, the flow of highly skilled migrants surges and decreases in relation to economic fluctuations (Beaverstock, 1994, 1996a, b, c; Beaverstock and Smith, 1996). This migration has a strong temporary nature, because expats typically stay between 3 and 5 years. The international organisational linkages within transnational companies at the level between states and individuals are pivotal for this type of migration (Findlay and Garrick, 1990). Brain exchange research has focuses on particular occupations including accountants and managers (Beaverstock, 1994, 1996a, b, c; Beaverstock and Smith, 1996). Expatriate managers, seconded to large international cities, became the epitomy of this type of migration flow of highly skilled workers.

Both brain exchange and brain drain migration are demand driven, i.e. highly skilled migrate to places where their work is needed. This narrow conception was only one factor leading to doubts about whether these two approaches can sufficiently represent current migration flows. For example, Conradson and Latham state 'Much of the literature has focused on the economic structures driving migration. Yet what is increasingly clear is that a significant proportion of these global population flows cannot be understood within a straightforward economic rubric' (2005, p. 287). A recent review of the research on highly skilled migration also criticises the treatment of the upper echelons. 'Academically speaking, there has been relatively little "human-level" research on the diverse avatars of globalisation in the skilled, educated or professional categories' (Favell et al., 2006, p. 3). This review emphasises the need for scholarly investigation of the popular image and suggests that the lives and experiences of frequent flying, fast lane, global elites 'are better known from editorial and marketing content of glossy magazines or corporate brochures than they are from solid social science research' (Favell et al., 2006, p. 2). Where there are recent research-based accounts, they show that even demand-driven labour movements are strongly affected by the activities, networks and judgements of individual migrants (Pethe, 2006, 2007).

The new approach considers international migration in terms of economic motivations and determinants, individual selfrealisation (Conradson and Latham, 2005; Favell, 2008), individual agency (Pethe, 2007) and the effects of social, not economic networks (Favell, 2003; Conradson and Latham, 2005). The perspective emerging recognises the importance of smaller social sub-units (Favell, 2003; Conradson and Latham, 2005; Scott, 2006; Pethe, 2007); and acknowledges that the motivation, duration of residence, means of migration and migration process can differ enormously from those associated with popular version of the 'transnational capitalist class' (Castells, 2000; Sklair, 2001) whose existence is often questioned (Hartmann, 1999; Favell, 2003; Conradson and Latham, 2005; Hartmann, 2007). For example, the ability of middling transnational migrants to cope with local housing markets might be very different than that of privileged corporate movers (Favell, 2008).

Richard Florida's perspective is somewhat different from those outlined above. He starts from a view that 'The key factor of the global economy is no longer goods, services, or flows of capital, but the competition for people' (Florida, 2007, p. 16). He proposes that the constantly expanding creative class is a pivotal agent of urban change and that transnational migrants have been key to the development of the creative economy in the USA. Florida asserts that international migrants 'help build our scientific enterprises' (p. 95), account for 'a disproportionate share of most influential scientists' (p. 101), relieve the 'looming talent shortage' (p. 103), 'take American ideas and American relationships back home' (p. 110) and contribute to the entertainment industry (p. 125). In opposition to conventional theories of migration, Florida emphasises the importance of the quality of place as motivation for an international migration. He suggests that the creative class selects cosmopolitan centres with rich cultural amenities and a high quality of life, attractive living and working environments which are diverse, tolerant and open to new ideas. He describes diversity, tolerance and openness as pull-factors for migrants. The heterogeneity of ethnicity, sexuality and lifestyles in places is seen as a precondition for the inflow of new talent.

Florida (2005) sees an increasing danger that American cities lose the ability to attract and to retain talent and that American regions are losing their top position to European agglomerations. European countries and cities like the Netherlands and Amsterdam often surpass the USA. Ireland and the Netherlands have large creative workforces (Florida, 2007, p. 136) and Dublin, for example, is seen as one of the 'New Global Austins' and described as a model for a successful development of an open and cosmopolitan high-tech city (Florida, 2007, p. 176).

While Florida dwells on the importance of soft factors such as tolerance, openness and diversity, he hardly mentions hard factors. He briefly mentions the importance of economic networks for the migration of highly skilled workers but does not elaborate on this. Florida also lumps together 30 per cent of the workforce into one 'creative class' and does not distinguish between different groups of highly skilled migrants. While the brain exchange literature emphasises the strong influence of the global economy, international trade, investment relations and international networks on the migration of the highly skilled Florida emphasise the agency and judgement of the urban environment by the individual creative worker: he neglects people who are seconded or transferred or who respond to the needs of their employers. He neglects the elements highlighted in the brain exchange literature.

Given these different perspectives, this chapter considers the drivers behind the decisions of transnational creative knowledge migrants to settle in European metropolitan regions. What attracts creative knowledge migrants to European cities?

This chapter refers to four metropolitan regions and the factors shaping the flow of transnational migrants. The analysis starts with an account of the relative importance of transnational creative and knowledge workers and other immigrants and then discusses various aspects emerging as important in the migration decisions of workers in creative knowledge industry.

Places and potentials

The analysis in this chapter draws on 100 semi-structured interviews with creative knowledge workers, conducted in 2008 in Amsterdam, Barcelona, Dublin and Munich (25 interviews in each). Secondary data was also used to identify the numbers of immigrants and to profile the economy. These cities have different attributes that are relevant for migration. Amsterdam is an old globally oriented city with a tradition of attracting foreign companies through tax incentives, an excellent international traffic infrastructure and a diverse international community. The attractiveness of Barcelona is more likely to relate to its environment, weather and cultural amenities. The new 'Celtic Tiger' Dublin has been one of the fastest growing economies in Europe and has attracted foreign companies through low corporate taxes, excellent technological infrastructure, an educated labour force and an English-speaking environment (Boyle, 2006). Since Ireland had been an emigration country for the last two centuries, dense social networks with diaspora communities also exist. Munich hosts the headquarters of important global companies, but the international network and international communities are smaller than in the other cities (cf. Taylor et al., 2002) and English is rarely spoken outside academic and work-related contexts. Neither immigration laws nor tax regulations favour the settlement of international companies or employees. Before we map out how transnational creative knowledge migrants evaluate these cities, we describe the international linkages that exist in each of them. How does the migration of highly skilled migrants relate to their global linkages? How important are their economies in explaining migration and do other linkages such as family networks drive migration?

Amsterdam

Amsterdam has had a tradition of trading and international investment since the seventeenth century. Since this early period, Amsterdam has been a centre of international finance and trading. The Netherlands had colonies in various continents: most importantly Surinam in South America and Indonesia in Asia. Although international investments and immigration declined during the eighteenth and nineteenth centuries, Amsterdam and the Netherlands remained interwoven with the economies of neighbouring Western countries. Investment from abroad increased in the 1960s, first from the USA and western European countries and later from Japan. American investment later declined and Asian and European investment grew (Stec Groep, 2005; CBS, 2007). The Netherlands is one of the most open economies in the OECD with a high ratio of trade exposure and FDI flows per GPD (Hogenbirk, 2005; OECD, 2006), although these economic activities are not all related to creative knowledge industries (OECD, 2006, p. 103). Industrial sectors profited from the inflow of overseas investments in the 1960s (Smidt and Kemper, 1980; Smidt 1985) when the port function of Amsterdam declined in favour of Rotterdam which was faster to re-build and extend its harbour after the World War II (Bosscher, 2007). Logistics and trade remain important sectors of the Dutch economy, but investment has slowly shifted from the industrial (2004: 35 per cent; 2006: 28.7 per cent) to the service sector with increased investment in banking, ICT and producer services (2004: 42, 4 per cent; 2006: 48.5 per cent) (CBS, 2007, p. 38). Government regulations supported the development of regional headquarters of multinational companies: foreign workers who bring additional expertise qualify for tax reductions and corporate tax is comparatively low.[2] In addition, the high level of language proficiency in English, French and German made the Netherlands attractive for foreign companies. While these measures attracted many highly skilled migrants to the Netherlands, other immigration flows mainly comprising low skilled labour were more important. After decolonisation, immigrants from former colonies settled in two major waves in the 1950s from Indonesia and in the late 1970s from Suriname. A major movement of 'guest workers' from Turkey and Morocco entered the Netherlands in the 1960s and early 1970s. Due to a continuing family migration, the migration flows from those countries remained high. GPD growth was largely related to the increased labour supply and less related to a productivity growth (OECD, 2006, p. 32). The weak international R&D investments, low share of science and engineering graduates and foreign students as well as the high turnover of international employees and the brain drain of Dutch citizens underline the demand for foreign highly skilled labour in the future (OECD, 2004, p. 16; OECD, 2006, pp. 103–126).

   Although the Netherlands previously had an open and liberal attitude towards immigration, political tension arose around the turn of the millennium. It was felt that problems associated with control and integration of

---

[2] http://www.nfia.nl/Reasons_to_invest.html

the large numbers of former guest workers had been ignored. In 2000, a conservative government began to limit immigration. A language test and proofs of marital status and ancestry were demanded by public authorities for all incoming immigrants. The new procedures made it difficult for multinational and Dutch companies to cope with a rising labour shortage, and protests from private business and research institutions led to the introduction of a separate immigration scheme for knowledge workers in 2004. This was further changed in 2006. Although the importance of highly skilled migration was gradually recognised, immigration lawyers still regard the Dutch immigration procedure as one of the most demanding in Europe (expert interview). This legal situation contrasts with the rich social infrastructure at the local level created by private initiatives and often supported by local government and foreign investment agencies.

In 2000, 9 per cent of the workforce and 7 per cent of immigrants in the Netherlands were highly skilled (OECD). The majority of highly skilled immigrants come from non-European countries, and only 26 per cent were born in western industrialised countries including the USA, Japan, Germany and Great Britain. More important for the inflow of highly skilled workers are old immigration linkages to the former colonies or guest worker countries. Thirty-one per cent of the highly skilled workers originate from Surinam or Indonesia, another 8 per cent are first and second generation immigrants from Morocco and Turkey. Last, but not least immigration from countries with civil unrest accounted for 8 per cent of the inflow of highly educated migrants. This involves refugees from countries including Iran, Iraq, Post-Yugoslavia and Somalia. In other words, although the Dutch economy is very open and attracts international investment, international business linkages play a minor role in explaining the inflow of highly skilled migrants.

Barcelona

Immigration is a recent phenomenon in Spain. During the nineteenth century, large parts of the Spanish population left for Latin America and in the Franco period the movement came to an entire stop. After 1960, western European retirement migrants headed to the coastal areas in Spain for the good quality of life (Gonzalez, 2008). With the opening of the country and the ascendance to the EU, Spain attracted international foreign investments, first from the USA, later from other north European countries, and highly skilled migrants accompanied those investment flows (Wolter, 1997; Pareja-Eastaway et al., 2009). In 1998, only half a million foreign persons had settled in the country. A decade later, there were 5 million foreign nationals who mostly came from Latin America (33.2 per cent), Europe (West, 20.8 per cent; East, 23.3 per cent) and neighbouring African countries (17.2 per cent) (Pareja-Estaway et al., 2009, p. 45).

Opportunities for migration within the EU, economic opportunities and the social and economic linkages with Latin American countries made Spain an attractive destination for the mostly low or unskilled migrants in the last decade. The legal situation was finally adjusted with several laws after 1999 which first secured rights and legalised immigration and then took a more controlling approach to regulate the labour market. The attraction of highly skilled talent mainly aimed to reverse the ongoing brain drain of Spanish scientists to the USA. The *Ramón y Cajal* programme opened access for international researchers to strengthen higher educational institutions, because the level of R&D activities in Spain was still too low for an advanced, future-oriented knowledge economy. However, other legal efforts to support highly skilled migration failed and an EU directive which requested member countries to create a visa programme for researchers was never ratified by the Spanish parliament (Pareja-Eastaway et al., 2009). This uncoordinated legal situation was hardly a stimulus for highly skilled migration.

The unclear legal situation was mirrored by the absence of statistics on highly skilled migration. The EU countries are still the main source of highly skilled migration to Spain. EU immigrants are more highly educated than the Spanish population (40:23 per cent), and only 14 per cent of other nationals had a tertiary degree in 2006 (Pareja-Eastaway et al., 2009, p. 51). Western European and North American migrants are more often active as entrepreneurs and self-employed than other groups and account for 24 per cent of single person companies. Both groups are also overrepresented in highly qualified occupations including engineering (Gonzalez, 2008).

The Barcelona Metropolitan Region (BMR) has not profited from this inflow of highly skilled migrants to the same extent as the capital, Madrid. The share of highly skilled immigrants is lower than average in Spain and the share of entrepreneurs from EU countries or North America is also lower (Pareja-Eastaway et al., 2009). This might be caused by the strong industrial profile of BMR in contrast to the more service-oriented (banking and ICT) economic structure of the capital region. Although the share is lower in BMR, the role of European self-employed persons and engineers is striking. In the province Barcelona, western European workers are important in the education, software and financial sectors and eastern European migrants are slightly overrepresented in the ICT industry (Gonzalez, 2008). In the creative industry, foreigners are still rare although in 2008 25 per cent of the members of a well-known creative organisation in Barcelona (FAD) indicated that their parents came from abroad (Pareja-Eastaway et al., 2009).

Given the lack information, it might be too early to give a full account of immigration to the BMR. In the last decade, Spain shifted from a traditional emigration country to an immigration destination. The new inflow hardly increased labour productivity, although Latin American immigrants became increasingly important in higher educational institutions.

Currently two developments seem to be crucial. First, the migration of creative knowledge workers is influenced by the investment of mostly European and US companies which have established production branches in the region. Second, there is a high number of self-employed entrepreneurs from Western countries who appear to have located in the BMR because of the excellent quality of life and environment.

Dublin

Ireland's economy has undergone a dramatic turnabout, emerging from the depression of the 1980s to the booming 'Celtic tiger' economy of the 1990s and early 2000s (Boyle, 2006). Much of this boom followed actions by the Irish government designed to attract foreign direct investment and promote a knowledge-based economy (see Chapter 16). The knock-on effect in terms of employment has been to reverse the outward flow of migration (Boyle, 2006). Throughout much of the nineteenth and twentieth centuries, Ireland was associated with high levels of outward migration, especially to the UK and USA. In recent years, however, there has been a dramatic shift with Ireland becoming a destination country for migrants. While there has been a range of reasons for this, economic growth and associated demand for labour has resulted in a high level of immigration. Gilmartin (2007) identifies three broad groups in recent migration. Initially, immigration was marked by a return of Irish migrants who had left during the 1980s and early 1990s. Second, there was a marked increase in the numbers of migrants from countries described as 'Rest of World' (e.g. Africa, Asia and eastern Europe prior to 2004). While the USA had traditionally been a source of migration to Ireland, by 2007 the number of migrants from the rest of the world outstripped that of the USA by a factor of 10. Third, following the accession of new states to the EU in 2004, the majority of recent migration has been from countries in the European Economic Area (EEA) – 25 member states along with Norway, Iceland and Lichtenstein (Gilmartin, 2007, p. 227). From a policy perspective, the period of sustained economic growth over the last decade was marked by the promotion of labour-orientated migration (NESDO, 2006). Prior to the joining of the EU by the 10 accession states in 2004, work permits were the most common means of legal entry for employment by non-EEA nationals (NESDO, 2006, p. 11). However, from 2004 onwards, there was a significant reduction in the numbers of work permits issued, and a steady rise in migration from the new member states until 2008.

The last two decades witnessed a rapid growth in creative industries in Ireland. The numbers employed in creative industries grew by 32 per cent between 2002 and 2004 (Lawton et al., 2009, p. 12). With statistics suggesting that the Dublin region accounts for over 40 per cent of the national economy, it is possible to estimate that somewhere between 40 and 55 per cent of employees in the creative-knowledge economy are located in the Dublin region. Data limitations make it difficult to determine the exact numbers of transnational migrant workers involved in the creative-knowledge economy. However, on a broader scale, the migrant labour market is diversified according to region and country of origin. For example, in 2008, 17 per cent of migrants from the 10 EU accession states are involved in the construction industry (CSO, 2008); 17 per cent of migrants from outside of the EU (non-USA) were employed in the health sector (CSO, 2008); and migrant workers accounted for 16 per cent of people working in the financial and business sector.

Munich

Germany has been one of the most important European destinations for immigrants since the mid-1950s. However, immigration and integration have only recently become important and fiercely contested topics in German policy discussions. Since 1998 there have been important developments in immigration policy with the reform of the Nationality Act, the adoption of the Immigration Act and political measures concerning the integration of the immigration population and their descendants.

Although foreigners are underrepresented in occupations which require skill and university degrees in Munich, the proportion of foreigners with secondary and tertiary education is one of the highest of German cities (Steinhardt et al., 2008). This relatively high number of highly skilled foreign people reflects the development of Munich economy. Although there is no data available on the internationalisation of Munich's economy, a strong positive correlation between international ownerships and the employment of foreigners from developed countries can be assumed (for the case of Frankfurt see Freund, 2001). Being a German centre of the ICT industry, Munich hosts numerous firms with global activities, including Microsoft, Siemens and O2. Alongside the ICT industry, the automotive industry in particular shows a high degree of internationalisation. Munich hosts many multinationals, and BMW and MAN are both global players in this sector. Furthermore, Munich is Germany's second most important banking centre and the number one location for insurance companies. Almost 80 insurance companies have their national or international headquarters in Munich, including global players such as Allianz, Munich Re or Swiss Re. Munich also has a high concentration of firms in business-related services.

Immigration has always been important in the demographic development of the Munich region. After World War II, about 2 million refugees and displaced persons came to Bavaria (Kramer, 2008). The Munich region profited greatly from the immigration of approximately 150,000 often highly qualified ethnic German repatriates and refugees, and firms in Munich could rely on an ample and qualified labour pool (Fritsche and Kreipl, 2003).

After the integration of these German repatriatcs had almost come to an end, the recruitment of foreign workers from Yugoslavia and Turkey started in the 1960s. In the late 1960s, there was high demand for guest workers in Munich, as the infrastructure had to be developed in the run-up to the Olympic Games in 1972 (Fassmann and Reeger, 1999). In the middle of the 1970s, when the German economy slowed down and fewer workers were needed, further official recruitment of labour was stopped. As a consequence of stricter management of both labour migration and asylum for refugees, immigration declined in the mid-1990s and settled at a lower level (Fassmann and Reeger, 1999).

In contrast to other EU member states including Ireland and the Netherlands, Germany has no special programmes to recruit and facilitate the entry of foreign highly skilled workers. As the national legal framework strongly regulates the inflow of highly skilled migrants at the regional and local level, foreigners are underrepresented in highly skilled occupations. In the Munich region in 2007, foreigners represented 13.6 per cent of all employees subject to social security contributions, and in the city of Munich 15 per cent. When compared with other German cities, Munich has one of the highest proportions of highly skilled workers. Thirty-three per cent of all employees in the region, and 35.8 per cent in the city, are in highly skilled occupations. The proportion of foreigners employed in highly skilled occupations was 7.8 per cent in the region and 5.8 per cent in the city of Munich in 2007. In the Munich region, the proportion of foreign employees with university degrees increased from 6.9 per cent of all employees in 1999 to 10.9 per cent in 2007, and from 7.0 to 10.5 per cent in the city of Munich (Federal Ministry of Labour).

Most highly skilled foreigners in the region of Munich come from the EU countries: Austria, France, Italy and the UK. However, between 1999 and 2007, the proportion of citizens of the UK, the US, Turkey and Austria rose by only 10–30 per cent, whereas the proportion of citizens of the Russian Federation almost tripled, and Polish and Chinese citizens more than doubled. Remarkably, there are more highly skilled employees from China in the Munich region than from Turkey, albeit the Chinese population accounts for only a very small share of the whole population (calculated from Federal Ministry of Labour).

Scientific and student mobility plays an important role in the migration of the highly skilled in Munich: 1337 foreign scientists were working at one of the universities in Munich in 2006. So 15.3 per cent of the academic staff do not have a German passport. Most of the scientists employed at one of the universities of Munich come from EU countries. Additionally, the 25 public and semi-public research establishments draw foreign scientists to Munich and the European Patent Office appointed 3478 foreign workers mainly from France, the UK, Italy, Spain and the Netherlands (European Patent Office, 2009). In the academic year 2007/2008, 13,112 foreign students were enrolled at Munich's universities (15.3 per cent). The highest proportions of foreign students are seen in those institutions that specialise in the creative fields.

The attractiveness of European metropolitan regions

Florida asserts that 'talent is mobile, and people can and do pick where they want to go' (Florida, 2007, p. 20). However, the migration of creative knowledge workers cannot be reduced to one single factor. In Amsterdam, Barcelona and Dublin, it is evident that international investment relations have affected the migration flow of highly skilled migrants and in Munich, the headquarters of internationally important companies and research institutions draw migrants into the city. Labour shortages which are caused by the strong high-tech orientation in Munich and Dublin, lack of graduates coming from the national universities (Munich and Amsterdam) and a low wage policy (Amsterdam) also impact on the demand for highly skilled migrants. Social ties are also relevant in all cases with Dublin most prominent in this respect. Ireland has attracted return migrants from its large diaspora while the exchange between Latin America and Barcelona, between the former territories of the Soviet empire and Munich in the case of German repatriates ('Aussiedler') and between the former Dutch colonies and the Netherlands are further examples which underline how important historical ties are to explain the inflow of talent. Moreover, the political context also shapes the immigration flow. The acceptance of refugees can be recognised in Amsterdam, Munich and Barcelona. The role of supranational organisations such as the EU is another factor which affects the migration in each city (cf. Soysal, 1994; Favell, 2008). Many EU nationals find it easier to change their place of residence and are less limited by immigration procedures than other nationals; they may be most likely to behave in a Florida fashion and 'vote with their feet' (Florida, 2007, p. 240).

Although the economic, social and political context in each city is able to explain parts of the immigration flow, it is not possible to identify a single factor which is responsible for the migration movement. Nor is it possible to reject Florida's view that individuals are able to select the most convenient destination, although they might be embedded in those economic, social and political environments. Against this background we can, however, consider how individual migrants have made decisions and what factors they identify as attracting them to different metropolitan regions. What weight do individuals attach to the economic profile of each region, to hard and soft factors, international, social and professional networks and the housing market? How were these factors in the end evaluated by the creative knowledge migrants who came to the four metropolitan regions?

Amsterdam

Amsterdam is a long established international gateway with a remarkably high level of internationalisation. Since the end of 1980s, the Dutch economy has exceeded the performance of other European countries. Unemployment is a negligible problem and labour shortages represent a greater challenge for companies (Hogenbirk, 2005) in the context of the low wage policy and the high level of utilisation of the comparatively cheap labour force (OECD, 2006; Terhorst, 2008). In international business surveys, the Amsterdam region tends to score in the top 10. The high quality of life, a convenient economic climate and the availability of qualified labour create a favourable business climate (Hogenbirk, 2005; Ernst and Young, 2006; Dienst Onderzoek en Statistiek Amsterdam, 2008, p.632). Tax rates for foreign employees and employers are kept low. The level of internationalisation is high due to its ability to attract international branches of multinational corporations to the region (Stec Groep, 2005; Boston Consulting Group, 2008) and Amsterdam is one of the nodes of the international network of global cities (Taylor and Aranya, 2008). The public transport infrastructure is excellent. The Amsterdam airport ranks five by passenger turnover in Europe (Dienst Onderzoek en Statistiek Amsterdam, 2008, p. 645).

The Dutch describe themselves as an open and tolerant society and English can be used as a lingua franca in everyday situations. According to a recent survey, the Netherlands has the highest acceptance of gay culture in Europe (Keuzenkamp and Bos, 2007).

In the interviews carried out for this study, transnational knowledge migrants underlined the importance of working conditions for their decision to come to the Amsterdam metropolitan region and their evaluation of the attractiveness of the city. The migrants state that they were poorly informed about the hard and soft factors in the city. Their image of the city was based on its international importance, its historical cityscape and its size. Their migration to Amsterdam was driven by their working situation, family links and education. Self-employed creative knowledge workers often refer to family linkages as a motivation to move to the Netherlands, but expats who are seconded by their companies to the city do not have family bonds with the country although they may have undertaken parts of the education in Europe and this appears to be a positive dimension from the employers' perspective. The environment in terms of working conditions, work content and the prospect of valuable experience emerged as more important than income expectations. Job search had been uncomplicated. Nobody reported having been unemployed although some had changed their jobs for better positions. Migrants working in sectors with a strong international reputation such as design or architecture were the most enthusiastic about the ability to acquire special skills in the

Netherlands. Self-employed migrants described the ease with which they were able to set up their own company and saw this as a major advantage.

> 'There are many projects going on at the moment. Because I'm a very multidisciplinary designer, this is really perfect for me. It gives me the opportunity to take advantage of my profile. In this case – that my profile is broad – is a big plus, while in some other cases a broad profile is a minus. This is very good about Amsterdam' (Slovenian designer).

Labour market and education opportunities were important factors for settling in the Netherlands. However, later on, these opportunities were also important for staying in the Netherlands and not moving on. Here again a special Dutch profile which offered migrants a unique chance to learn special techniques was more important than internationally top rank programmes. Seconded expats with children were the most eager to discuss the education prospects for children. Although the general level of satisfaction about the working environment was very high, few reported discontent. Family migrants were the first to report difficulties in this respect. Intercultural differences in the organisation of the work and differences in the education profile were other issues of concern.

Other factors such as transport conditions or the tax regime were not seen as a motivation to move or to stay in the Amsterdam region, because their importance was seen as relatively low. Although the transport network allows frequent trips to neighbouring countries, this was not a decisive factor. The immigration procedure, however, was seen as a major barrier for non-European nationals from developing countries and it is not aligned with the international orientation of the Dutch investment policy and the importance of immigration for the future creative knowledge society.

The judgement of the soft conditions or amenities was rather divided. Although it was stated that Amsterdam offers many cultural amenities for a city of its size, the quality of many amenities was seen as insufficient. This is particularly true for restaurants, retail and personal services which did not meet the quality and the price expectations of the interviewed. A similar ambivalence was stated concerning the attitude of the Dutch towards foreigners. Many migrants underlined the international atmosphere of the city which they appreciated very much. The importance of bilingualism of the population in the AMA was, of course, put to the fore.

> 'They don't force us to talk in their language. But if you try to talk, they are very happy and try to help you. I think it's maybe the easiest country to live as a foreigner' (Turkish banker).

In terms of openness and tolerance, the answers were rather reserved. First, many observed that the attitude of the population in Amsterdam does not differ positively in terms of openness and acceptance of diversity from other countries. Compared with the working environment in which Dutch people were ready to listen and accept new ideas, they were rather reserved in the private realm. Second, immigrants often faced resentments in their endeavour to dive into the Dutch culture. Due to the pillarisation of the Dutch society, it is seen as rather inward looking and this presents problems for outsiders. Unsurprisingly many migrants refer to living in the international community rather than with Dutch citizens. Last, but not least, many challenged the need for openness and tolerance and claimed that they do not conceive this as important condition.

An issue of real concern however was the situation of the housing market. Migrants face problems in finding adequate accommodation because of the limited numbers of properties in the unregulated rental sector, the ban on short stay renting in Amsterdam (Dienst Wonen Amsterdam, 2007) and the large number of small dwellings. Seconded expats were in the most privileged position in relation to housing because their companies supported them or arranged their accommodation. However, the willingness of companies to contribute to the costs and assist in the search for accommodation appears to have decreased when compared with earlier studies (Glebe, 1986; White, 1998; White and Hurdley, 2003). In particular, multinationals from the new Asian economies do not any longer conceive this service as obligatory. Family migrants were also better able to deal with housing because they were able to move into the property of their spouse, but they were often discontented at a later stage by the limited opportunities to develop a housing career within the region. In particular, persons in creative occupations with a medium income saw their housing situation as one of the reasons for leaving even when they had settled and established themselves in Amsterdam for a long time.

In conclusion, the attractiveness of Amsterdam is not so much associated with soft conditions such as tolerance and openness but rather derives from the labour market and working conditions. Family migrants report more problems in developing their careers and immigration procedures for non-European nationals and housing present the most serious problems.

Barcelona

Although Barcelona has been an important historical Mediterranean trading centre, the internationalisation of the economy and society is relatively recent and surged after Spain joined the EU in 1986. Spain received the majority of FDI from European countries and these also became the most important trading partners. Barcelona became one of the key decision and management centres in Spain outside Madrid and 21 per cent of foreign multinational companies opened branches in the BMR. Following deregulation, large multinational companies which invested in Latin America were created and the Spanish economy became very open with Spain having 'higher FDI and more foreign subsidiaries than EC countries such as Germany and Italy, as well as the USA and Japan' (Pareja-Eastaway et al., 2009, p. 29). In other words, the economic networks of companies in Spain are likely to attract transnational migrants from the EU, the USA and Latin America who manage and control these in- and outbound investment streams. The BMR still has a strong industrial profile and profits from the allocation of industrial production plants by international investors. Increasingly knowledge-intensive units are run in the BMR, whereas labour-intensive production units are transferred to low wage countries. In this way, some previously important industrial sectors such as textile production contribute to the strength of the creative sector because they have been transformed into design-oriented companies. Other creative sectors have built international reputations. Performing arts, culture and in particular architecture have a long tradition but other sectors, such as the ICT, have only recently emerged.

International business surveys tend to indicate that the BMR has location advantages for international companies because of agglomeration economies, the high level of human capital, the low wage costs (hard factors) and the high quality of life (soft factors). Disadvantages are high transport costs, high real estate prices and the absence of tax reductions for foreign companies and the fact that Spanish instead of English is used as the most common business language (Pareja-Eastaway et al., 2009, p. 36). Apart from these economic factors, transnational migrants might be also attracted due to the strong historical link of the Spanish and Catalonian population to Latin America and Italy.

The interviews carried out in Barcelona underline the importance of soft factors for the attractiveness of the city region. Migrants in the creative knowledge industry identified the high quality of life and cultural amenities as the strongest assets of the BMR. Beautiful weather, the human size of the city, the surrounding landscape with the sea and mountains nearby contribute to the high quality of life along with the historical architecture and urban regeneration in inner city neighbourhoods. The private and public cultural offer also impressed migrants and they emphasised its variety and dynamism. Barcelona does not only have a culture-led image which is branded by regional tourist board and other private–public business organisations. It offers various opportunities through large commercial events and also hosts grassroots networks of creatives that newcomers can easily share and participate in. In addition, the expertise found in sectors such as design and architecture attracts movement to the city.

In contrast to these soft factors, the situation of the economy and the labour market are of minor importance. 'You can earn more money there [England]. But money doesn't matter, if I'm earning enough. I don't want a very good salary only to feel good. I won't go back for that reason' (Chilean architect). Migrants accept challenging working conditions or low pay or they circumvent the labour market by establishing their own business in order to live in an environment which guarantees this high standard of living and culture. This is not to say that international networks of companies and the high expertise of production and organisation in certain sectors were unimportant in the BMR. In particular, knowledge migrants came because of their companies' networks. They were often seconded by their European headquarters to command and control the branches in the BMR or to improve their knowledge in the headquarters or at related universities in Spain. Creative workers, however, often organised the international move themselves, using their private networks. Although private and professional networks were more interwoven for creative workers, private linkages were more important in their decision to migrate. Hard factors appear overall to have less importance in explaining the international attractiveness of Barcelona. The public transport system in the BMR received approval, but the level of bureaucracy which is related to immigration, entrepreneurship and the welfare state was more an object of concern.

'[In the UK] it is easy to start a business [...] and it is possible to have an income without making a big investment at the beginning. Here [Barcelona], people are discouraged from creating' (Scottish media worker).

The views expressed depended on the origin of the migrants. Whereas north Europeans were surprised by the low level of red tape, Latin American immigrants were challenged to overcome migration procedures and developed various strategies, such as enrolling in higher education, to escape immigration controls. The availability and price of housing was the largest obstacle for movement.

All of this indicates that the creative class in Barcelona cannot be seen as a unified entity – large differences exist between creative and knowledge workers, and between Latin American and European/North American immigrants. Another difference should be drawn between the use of cultural amenities and everyday culture. Barcelona is situated in Catalonia which has a distinctive culture and language from the rest of Spain. This was a surprise for many migrants. Catalonians were seen as more closed than other persons of Latin descent. The cultural difference has unexpected advantages in allowing incomers to maintain their identity and interact with a diversity of cultures.

The situation in the BMR supports Florida's view that soft factors are increasingly important to attract workers from abroad, although this statement should also be treated with caution. International economic, social and historical linkages to South America and other OECD countries also influence immigration. Finally, some doubts exist over the extent to which soft factors can boost the economy. The focus on soft factors alone bears the risk that the talent of incoming migrants is scattered and that poor working conditions do not foster the transfer of knowledge.

Dublin

Florida (2002, 2007) regards Dublin as an emerging centre of software, and other creative industries and as boasting a 'thriving artistic and cultural scene' (Florida, p. 176). This introduces an expectation that certain 'hard' factors related to the attraction of industry and labour and there is also an expectation of a 'lifestyle' in Dublin which is open to a diverse range of activities and cultural groups. Much of this transformation has been directly associated with the impact of government interventions, such as low corporation tax rates, that have boosted FDI (Boyle, 2006). Despite the existence of a highly skilled workforce, and a focus on the connection between higher education and emerging knowledge industries (Murphy and Redmond, 2008) along with a low level of unemployment, the demand for labour has outstripped availability (Boyle, 2006). As such, recent years have witnessed a high level of inward migration. Although it is not possible to determine the exact role of migrants within the creative knowledge economy in Dublin, they have formed a large portion of the financial services sector, which has become a key element of Dublin's economy with the Irish Financial Services Centre in Dublin's docklands being particularly important in promoting and attracting inward investment (see Chapters 5 and 16). However, while there is often a perception of Dublin as a booming city in both economic and social terms, recent research has indicated frustration with the general infrastructure, including transport network and broadband availability (Murphy and Redmond, 2008; Lawton et al., 2009).

The Dublin interviews demonstrated that the role of 'hard' and 'soft' factors varied according to individual trajectories. Broadly speaking, these factors could also be further divided between the initial decision to come to Dublin and factors related to experiencing the city in everyday life. While the various soft factors were seen as important, it was the hard factors which were dominant in terms of moving to Dublin. Although family networks, or the family connections of a spouse/partner, were also a dominant factor, the wide availability of employment in recent years was the predominant reason for a movement to Dublin.[3] For example, one respondent, an Indian man in his mid-fifties, described the decision to choose Dublin as follows: '*It was always going to be Dublin ... Dublin seemed to be the place to be for the simple reason that there were a large number of jobs here on the services side*'. The fact that Dublin is an English-speaking country was a secondary consideration after family and employment-related decisions.

The 'softer' factors in choosing Dublin were more often related to issues of scale. Many respondents preferred the fact that Dublin was a smaller city

---

[3] Between 2002 and 2006, the numbers in employment in the Dublin region increased by 70,000. Moreover, much of this increase was in the services sector, with a levelling out of labour within the manufacturing sector (CSO, 2006).

than cities such as London. For example, for one respondent, an American woman in her late twenties:

'England was kind of out for me just because I didn't really like the busyness of London – because London's a huge design hub – it was too big for me. So then I started looking at Edinburgh and I started looking at Dublin, simply because they are about the same size as Portland where I'm from. Visiting here previously, I just loved it. I loved Dublin in general, the atmosphere was very laid-back and was just a nice place ...'

Amongst the respondents, the issue of scale was important in terms of overall quality of life. For those living in the city centre, the compact nature of the city meant it was easy to walk around and access various amenities. For those choosing suburban areas, ease of access to the sea or mountains for various leisure pursuits was seen as a positive aspect of living in Dublin. Despite these factors, the role of hard factors was of primary importance in selecting where to live within the city. Of particular importance were considerations related to housing costs (see below) and ease of accessibility to place of employment. This was directly influenced by a wide-ranging dissatisfaction with the overall transport infrastructure of the city amongst the respondents. One respondent, a Scottish woman in her late twenties, succinctly summarised the general experience of road-based transport as follows: 'I've been on shoots and we've been driving you know for two hours when you could have walked it in twenty minutes ...'. This was related to both road-traffic congestion and the poor availability or access to hard-infrastructure systems such as rail or tram transport. Accordingly, many chose to live in proximity to the more reliable transport systems such as the Dart or the Luas, or within walking distance of their place of employment.[4]

One of the more significant 'hard' factors in Dublin was the costs associated with renting, and accessing the housing market. The housing market has played a significant role in the Irish economy in recent years. For example, in 2007, the construction sector accounted for up to 40 per cent of GDP (Lawton et al., 2009, p. 6). Throughout the era of the so-called Celtic Tiger, house prices increased at a rate of 11.4 per cent annual increase in real terms. However, in the global financial crisis, house values fell by 17.9 per cent in 2008 alone (Lawton et al., 2009, p. 6). The recent downturn combined with the current surplus of rental accommodation is seen as a positive factor by many employers in attracting mobile talent in the longer term. This was particularly evident in the emerging

---

[4] The Dart system is a commuter rail system running around the coast of Dublin. The Luas is a light rail system which was opened in 2004. At present it has two lines which run to suburbs in the South and West of the city.

computer games industry, where young single workers are looking for city centre rental accommodation. However, for many of the migrants, the high price of buying property in Ireland was a deterrent in terms of settling for a longer period of time. One respondent commented 'the housing market has been cheating people of a lot of happiness ... that's not how I want to live ... if I am not able to afford a house here I will not stay'.

The role of social networks primarily related to those of family and friends that had been made since arriving in Ireland. Many of the respondents had moved to Dublin with a spouse or partner who was from Ireland. In this regard, social networks were primarily influenced through existing contacts. Furthermore, many commented on the extent to which they had formed strong ties with people from within work. A Spanish male in his early twenties commented:

> 'This company is as well full of really young people you know, very friendly as well, like to do things together go to the cinema and go to the bar do different things. So I do think [the social] environment is important.'

However, other respondents commented on how difficult it was to build new friendships or bonds with Irish people. While people would be pleasant and courteous to a point, it was perceived that it was hard to get to know Irish people well. While some of the older or more settled respondents had strong connections through their spouse or partner, some of the younger or single respondents had built up a network amongst other transnational migrant workers living in Dublin.

As discussed above, much of the initial attraction to move to Dublin was based on a combination of family-related decisions and availability of employment. Although various soft factors, such as the scale and laid-back atmosphere of the city, along with access to various natural amenities were seen in a positive light, 'hard' factors, such as public transport, were seen as being overwhelmingly negative. However, throughout the interviews, decisions about remaining in Dublin for a long period of time varied amongst the respondents. For example, many of the younger or single respondents commented on how they would probably move in the coming years. This was particularly evident amongst those employed in the computer games and electronic publishing sector. Those who had a family or had arrived here with a partner/spouse had little intention of leaving unless the jobs market became a difficulty. This was driven by concerns that go beyond the dichotomy of 'hard' and 'soft' factors, and was more related to a desire to settle down in the same place for a number of years.

Munich

Munich is a strong economic business location with a diverse economic structure and mixture of global players and SMEs. This modern and balanced economic structure is often referred to as the 'Munich Mix' (Münchner Mischung) which is expected to absorb greater economic dislocations. Another part of Munich's success can be attributed to the existence of numerous technology-intensive and creative branches like biotechnology and pharmaceutical industry, medical technology, environmental technology, ICT, aerospace, the media and business services and insurances. Supported by numerous state and semi-state research institutions and commercialisation protagonists, the enterprises in these knowledge-intensive and creative branches form the innovative growth poles of the city region. The positive economic situation of Munich compared with other German cities is reflected in a dynamic labour market, low unemployment rates, a dynamic service sector, high purchasing power and demographic growth. The positive development of Munich's economy has been supported by a technology and innovation policy by the Free State of Bavaria since the 1950s (Hafner et al., 2007). According to the fact that the demand for labour cannot be met locally, Munich is dependent on highly skilled transnational migrants. But is Munich an attractive location for highly skilled migrants? And how satisfied are such migrants with their living and working environments?

The two groups – knowledge workers and creative workers – evaluate the job opportunities and the conditions to work and live in Munich completely differently. All interviewees in the *knowledge sector* – including researchers, employees in big firms and in the European Patent Office as well as self-employed migrants in technology- and service-orientated branches – appreciate the diverse labour market in Munich. Researches are attracted by the high quality of the diverse research facilities. Knowledge migrants can rely on an international network of business and scientific contacts. These networks can also be seen as important mobility triggers, as the following quote illustrates:

'As a researcher, you go where the research takes you. The methodology I use for my PhD thesis is based on a classification system that the World Health Organization uses and there is a World Health Organization research branch in Munich at the university. And I met someone at a conference who is sort of a leader in that area and wanted to learn more about the methodology from them, and first they said why don't you come to Munich?' (Canadian knowledge worker).

The transnational knowledge workers also enjoy privileges like an English-speaking work environment. Moreover, Munich's diverse labour market offers possibilities for dual-career couples. The self-employed migrants interviewed in the ICT and consulting sectors benefit from the technology-orientated atmosphere in the city, the high rate of venture capitalists, the good infrastructure, the supportive entrepreneurial thinking and the proximity to other European countries. In addition to these positive factors, the self-employed migrants criticised the heavy taxation and the inflexibility of government officials.

In contrast to the knowledge workers who were able to maintain or improve their social and economic status through migration to Munich, some discussion partners in the *creative sectors* stress their problems. For workers in the creative sectors access to the labour market is very difficult. Problems arise when the knowledge of the German language is not sufficient or the foreign creative workers do not get to know the right people in the field they are working in. These problems can be traced back to the fact that many activities in the cultural industries are regulated only to a limited extent through certification. Contacts to new clients come about mainly through recommendations and previous collaboration. Reputation consequently represents an important resource for self-employed creative workers and artists (von Streit, 2010). For creative workers, a wide network seems to be of pivotal importance to gain access to the market. Furthermore, the market for selling cultural products has a strong local orientation and is limited regionally. The creative industries account only for 4 per cent of exports (CBC, KWF and Prognos AG, 2009, p. 60). So, it is in the nature of things, that transnational migrants in the cultural industries cannot have an adequate business network due to the (short) duration of their stay. This might also be a possible explanation why the German creative workers are not so hyper-mobile as Richard Florida states for the American creative workers. Moving away means giving up indispensable business networks.

Although knowledge and creative workers evaluate the labour market of Munich differently, they agree on their assessment of soft factors. Most of them stress the high quality of life in the Munich region in respect of leisure and cultural opportunities. For some of them Munich is a human-scale city, the public transport system is very well developed and it is possible to get around on foot or by bike. Security and cleanliness are both emphasised by the migrants. The two international schools in Munich are of pivotal importance for them, too, because many parents regard an international education in English as fundamental for the future career of their children. But the lack of full-time childcare, which is especially important for working couples, is criticised by the migrants. Concerning the question of whether Munich is an open and tolerant city, the statements of the discussion partners were contradictory. Some describe Munich as an open and tolerant place which is more international than other German cities and where they easily made friends. But ethnic minorities in particular have experienced some different treatment in contrast to the white population: An Indian is constantly checked by the police and landlords still very often prefer Germans and discriminate against foreigners whose access to the housing market is consequently very difficult.

The accessibility of the Munich housing market is problematic for creative knowledge workers with limited economic capital. Young researchers who are at the beginning of their careers and finance their sojourns often through scholarships, or creative workers with low incomes, find that affordable housing is unavailable in the Munich city region. They often describe the search for an affordable flat or house in Munich as a 'nightmare'. In contrast to these groups of migrants, migrants with high social and economic capital have seldom reported problems. They are often supported by relocation services. To get acquainted with the German and Munich housing market, the available size as well as the layout of flats and houses is a 'learning process' for many expatriates. Many of the respondents had contacts with people or a partner who helped them find a flat or a job in Munich. Especially for those migrants who followed their partners to Munich, contacts via social networks proved to be the most important resource to find a job in the new city. But the majority of the interviewed persons in the knowledge sector did not come because of family relations; they came because of the job opportunities the city offers them.

To conclude the evaluation of Munich by the migrants: Hard factors such as jobs, and personal trajectories such as a partner in Munich, draw transnational migrants to Munich, while soft factors such as the high quality of life make them stay.

Conclusion

Richard Florida emphasises the importance of the individual agency of migrants for current migration flows. He gives an account of why and where creative knowledge migrants move. In his opinion, metropolitan regions can only take advantage from the inflow of creative talent, if they offer an attractive urban environment and a tolerant, open and diverse social climate. Thus, he highlights the pull-factors of the destination regions. If we compare his approach with other conceptions, the limits of his contribution are evident. First, he fails to inform his audience about which members of the creative class are involved in the international migration process and how they are able to migrate. Second, he is silent about the economic, social and political context which facilitate or constrain migration flows. Older accounts in terms of the international brain drain or brain exchange emphasised the influence of the economic situation in the sending and receiving countries or regions. The brain exchange literature recognised the impact of international linkages for the migration process. Although the linkages between transnational companies received most attention, reference was also made to historical, political and personal networks between source and host region. Third, other factors are underrated: the geographical position of a metropolitan region in the urban system, or national or international policy on migration. Hard factors like state regulation of immigration and taxes are given hardly any attention compared with soft factors like tolerance, diversity and openness. While Florida stresses the micro- and meso-level, he neglects the differences at the macro-level. While he underlines the pull-factors, he appears to be unaware of the push-factors.

Although all those shortcomings exist in Florida's portrayal of the international migration process, his merits should also be mentioned. The older literature was strongly demand oriented and focused too much on the economic rationales behind the migration process. Recent literature points out how important the 'human dimension' is but goes beyond Florida's preoccupation with tolerance, openness and diversity. The importance of cultural diversity in terms of language proficiency and the influence of personal networks is hardly mentioned in Florida's discussion of the soft factors. Although Florida makes a valuable contribution by underlining the influence of soft factors, his approach takes a backward step by failing to incorporate existing explanations for international highly skilled migration. This chapter has highlighted four different dimensions associated with the attractiveness of metropolitan regions for transnational creative knowledge workers: economy and labour market, hard and soft factors, social and professional networks and the housing market.

The analysis of the migration flows to each of the selected regions shows how diverse the transnational migrants in the creative knowledge industry are. Apart from the typical expats who have little choice over the country they are seconded to, the highly skilled labour pool also includes family migrants who follow their spouse, return migrants or repatriates, students who finally join the host labour market after graduation and refugees who involuntarily leave their countries of origin. The importance of each group differed in each city and labour-related migrants are also often outnumbered by others. The influence of international trade and investment activities became clear in all city regions, although Florida is right to suggest that this investment-related labour flow is complemented by other streams. One group of migrants who most seem to fulfil the characteristics of Florida's creative knowledge migrants were EU nationals with the privilege to move freely between the EU countries.

The demand for international labour is strong in Dublin and Amsterdam, because both countries have developed a policy with welcomes international foreign investment and they cannot cover the demand of highly skilled labour. This was indicated by the interviews with the transnational labour migrants who were steered to these regions due to labour-related reasons. In the case of Munich, investment-related migration was less relevant, because the German government did not support international companies with favourable tax breaks or immigration schemes. Frankfurt or Dusseldorf have developed a more international profile in Germany and are typically chosen as locations for regional branches in Germany. In Munich, various knowledge-related transnational corporations and research institutions attract international migrants to their headquarters or to their suppliers. In other words, not only international investment or trade, but also the presence of international headquarters can influence the attractiveness of urban regions for international migrants. In general, work-related reasons are still the most important drivers for transnational migrants to select a certain location.

Although it was expected that soft factors would score high in Amsterdam, and Dublin due to high proficiency of English and the high quality of cultural amenities, the interviewees did not confirm this. Their judgement of soft factors was often ambivalent and they were never the sole motivation for individual migrants to change their place of residence. In Barcelona, in contrast, the influence of soft factors on the migration process was visible and associated with the cultural scene and the high quality of life. Barcelona respondents reported that they accepted lower incomes in order to take advantage of the soft factors. This was more true for creative workers, as knowledge workers often chose the region for career-related reasons.

The history of Ireland as an emigration country and the linkages to English-speaking countries by the Irish Diaspora were important for the ability of Dublin to attract so many creative knowledge workers in such a short time. The historical and cultural linkages between the analysed regions and traditional source countries affected the migration in the other regions in a similar fashion. It was strongest in Barcelona due to the historical and cultural linkages to Latin America, but it was still relevant in Munich in the case of German repatriates and in Amsterdam which had received many highly skilled migrants from former colonies.

The housing market was conceived a pivotal barrier in all selected regions. In some regions, other inconveniences such as strict immigration procedures (Amsterdam) and the poor quality of the transport system (Dublin) were reported.

In conclusion, Florida's perspective on how metropolitan regions attract transnational migrants is rather incomplete and only works in very selective cases. Instead of focusing on soft factors alone, other factors are crucial for evaluating the international attractiveness of metropolitan regions in Europe.

First, the situation of the regional economy and labour market are far more important than Florida's soft factors. Second, hard factors such as national immigration and tax policy have a considerable impact in European regions. Although the EU as a supranational organisation aims to reduce the national regulations and wants to level out the differences in the international migration and economic policy, the differences are still pronounced when compared with the USA which consists of a unified national market. Third, family networks and traditional migration networks between countries or regions strongly contribute to the inflow of highly skilled migrants. Fourth, soft factors do have an influence on the attractiveness, but it is rather limited. Only in Mediterranean Barcelona were soft factors strong enough to attract migrants and to compensate for missing labour market opportunities.

In addition, our research demonstrates that the attractiveness of metropolitan regions depends on the different stages of the migration process. Whereas the labour market is more important to motivate immigrants to move to another place, the quality of the soft factors more often decides over the length of their stay. When transnational migrants had settled in a region, and they, as well as their employers, had invested a considerable amount of effort and capital in their new living environment and their career, soft factors are pivotal for their decision to extend their stay. In other words, local governments should not only be willing to think about ways to attract transnational knowledge migrants, but also about policies to retain them.

Furthermore, differences between subgroups are important. The creative and knowledge workers in Barcelona, Dublin and Munich used different approaches to evaluate prospective destinations. Whereas creative migrants often came under their own steam and analysed the quality of the soft factors first, knowledge migrants were more often motivated by labour-related reasons. Our research also indicates that creative migrants are not per se more mobile than knowledge workers. Often the professional network of creative workers is rooted in the local social relations at their current place of residence. If they move to other regions, they often loose those pivotal contacts. This limits their mobility. In addition, the recognition of educational credentials, and previous working experience in a foreign country, is often problematic so that some migrants end up working below their qualifications and their abilities. Instead of contributing to the regional economy as a brain gain, they suffer brain waste.

Nearly all cities experience an outmigration of skilled home nationals (Amsterdam, Barcelona and Munich) and national government implemented programmes to reverse the brain drain. In other words, the attractiveness of metropolitan regions can not only be addressed towards foreign nationals, but the needs of the 'home nationals' must be taken into account as well. It is clear that the factors involved in transnational migration and the strengths and weaknesses of cities in relation to this are complex and varied. Policy makers should be aware of such differences, if they are to develop sustainable policies.

Acknowledgments

The authors would like to thank Marc Pradel i Miquel and the ACRE team in Barcelona for their contribution to this chapter.

References

Beaverstock, J.V. (1994) Rethinking skilled international labor migration – World cities and banking organizations. *Geoforum*, 25: 323–338.

Beaverstock, J.V. (1996a) Migration, knowledge and social-interaction – Expatriate labor within investment banks. *Area*, 28: 459–470.

Beaverstock, J.V. (1996b) Revisiting high-waged labor-market demand in the global cities – British professional and managerial workers in New-York-City. *International Journal of Urban and Regional Research*, 20: 422.

Beaverstock, J.V. (1996c) Subcontracting the accountant – Professional labor-markets, migration, and organizational networks in the global accountancy industry. *Environment and Planning A*, 28: 303–326.

Beaverstock, J.V. and J. Smith (1996) Lending jobs to global cities – Skilled international labor migration, investment banking and the city of London. *Urban Studies*, 33: 1377–1394.

Bosscher, D. (2007) De oude en de nieuwe stad. In: P. de Rooy (ed.), *Geschiedenis van Amsterdam. Tweestrijd om de hoofdstad 1900–2000*, pp. 337–397. Amsterdam: SUN.

Boston Consulting Group (2008) *Hoofdkantoren een hoofdzaak. Tijd voor industriepolitiek nieuwe stijl*. Amsterdam: Boston Consulting Group.

Boyle, M. (2006) Culture in the rise of tiger economies: Scottish expatriates in Dublin and the 'creative class' thesis. *International Journal of Urban and Regional Research*, 30 (2): 403–426.

Boyle, M., A. Findlay, E. Lelievre and R. Paddison (1996) World cities and the limits to global control: A case study of executive search firms in Europe's leading cities. *International Journal of Urban and Regional Research*, 20 (3): 498–517.

Castells, M. (2000) *The rise of the network society*. Oxford: Blackwell.

CBC, KWF and Prognos AG (2009) *Kultur- und Kreativwirtschaft: Ermittlung der gemeinsamen charakteristischen Definitionselemente der heterogenen Teilbereiche der 'Kulturwirtschaft' zur Bestimmung ihrer Perspektiven aus volkswirtschaftlicher Sicht*. Bremen, Berlin: Köln.

CBS (2007) *Kerncijfers internationalisering*. Voorburg/Heerlen: Centraal Bureau voor de Statistiek.

Central Statistics Office (CSO) (2006) www.cso.ie (last accessed 2 October 22009).

CSO (2008) *Quarterly National Household Survey*: Table A2 Estimated number of persons aged 15 years and over in employment (ILO) classified by nationality and NACE Economic Sector, Dublin: Government of Ireland.

Conradson, D. and A. Latham (2005) Friendship, networks and transnationality in a world city: Antipodean transmigrants in London. *Journal of Ethnic and Migration Studies*, 31 (2): 287–305.

Dienst Onderzoek en Statistiek Amsterdam, O.S. (2008) *Amsterdam in cijfers 2008*. Amsterdam: Stadsdrukkerij Amsterdam.

Dienst Wonen Amsterdam (2007) *Short stay in Amsterdam. Woonruimte voor kort verblijf*. Amsterdam: Gemeente Amsterdam, Dienst Wonen.

Ernst and Young (2006) *The Netherlands … taking care of the future. Netherlands Attractiveness Survey 2005*. Utrecht: Ernst and Young.

European Commission (2007) *Proposal for a council directive on the conditions of entry and residence of third-country nationals for the purposes of highly qualified employment*. Brussels: The European Commission.

European Patent Office (2009) *Analysis of staff in post on 31 December 2008 by grade and nationality*. http://documents.epo.org/projects/babylon/eponet.nsf/0/ACCF7D9A6C7CFD A5C12575A000570BA6/$File/staff_analysis_nationality_2008.pdf.

Fassmann, H. and U. Reeger (1999) Einwanderung nach Wien und München. Ähnlichkeiten und Unterschiede. *Mitteilungen der geographischen Gesellschaft in München*, 84: 35–52.

Favell, A. (2003) Games without frontiers? Questioning the transnational social power of migrants in Europe. *Archives Europeennes De Sociologie*, 44 (3): 397–427.

Favell, A. (2008) *Eurostars and Eurocities*. Oxford: Blackwell.

Favell, A., M. Feldblum and M.P. Smith (2006) The human face of global mobility. A research agenda. In: A. Favell and M.P. Smith (eds), *The human face of global mobility: International highly skilled migration in Europe, North America and the Asia-Pacific*, pp. 1–22. New Brunswick, NY: Transaction Press.

Findlay, A.M. and L. Garrick (1990) Scottish emigration in the 1980s – A migration channels approach to the study of skilled international migration. *Transactions of the Institute of British Geographers*, 15 (2): 177–192.

Florida, R. (2002) *The rise of the creative class: And how it's transforming work, leisure, community, and everyday life*. New York: Basic Books.

Florida, R. (2005) *Cities and the creative class*. New York: Routledge.

Florida, R. (2007) *The flight of the creative class. The new global competition for talent*. New York: HarperCollins.

Freund, B. (2001) Hochqualifizierte Migranten im Rhein-Main-Gebiet. *Frankfurter statistische berichte*, 3: 207–223.

Fritsche, A. and A. Kreipl (2003) Industriestadt München – Eine Nachkriegskarriere. In: G. Heinritz, C.C. Wiegandt and D. Wiktorin (eds), *Der München Atlas*, pp. 160–161. Italien: Emons.

Gilmartin, M. (2007) Dublin: An emerging gateway. In: L. Benton-Short and M. Price (eds), *Migrants to the metropolis: The rise of immigrant gateway cities*. Syracuse: Syracuse University Press.

Glebe, G. (1986) Segregation and intraurban mobility of a high-status ethnic-group – The case of the Japanese in Dusseldorf. *Ethnic and Racial Studies*, 9 (4): 461–483.

Gonzalez, C. (2008) *Los otros immigrantes: Los europeos comunitarios de países ricos*. Madrid: Real Instituto Elcano.

Hafner, S., M. Miosga, K. Sieckermann and A. von Streit (2007) *Knowledge and creativity at work in the Munich region. Pathways to creative and knowledge-based regions*. ACRE report 2.7. Amsterdam: AMIDSt.

Hartmann, M. (1999) Auf dem Weg zur transnationalen Bourgeoisie? Die Internationalisierung der Wirtschaft und die Internationalität der Spitzenmanager Deutschlands, Frankreichs, Grossbritanniens und der USA. *lev.*, 27: 113–141.

Hartmann, M. (2007) *Eliten und Macht in Europa. Ein internationaler Vergleich*. Frankfurt/Main: Campus.

Hogenbirk, A. (2005) Nederland aantrekkelijk voor buitenlandse bedrijven. *Kennis en Economisch Onderzoek Rabobank*, http://overons.rabobank.com/content/images/aantrekkelijk_tcm64-74350.pdf (accessed 27 April 2009).

Keuzenkamp, S. and D. Bos (2007) *Out in the Netherlands. Acceptance of homosexuality in the Netherlands*. The Hague: The Netherlands Institute for Social Research.

Kramer, F. (2008) Aspekte der Modernisierung Bayerns. *Geographische Rundschau*, 60 (10): 10–15.

Lawton, P., D. Redmond and E. Murphy (2009) *Creative knowledge workers in the Dublin region: The view of transnational migrants*. ACRE report 6.13, Amsterdam: AMIDSt.

Murphy, E. and D. Redmond (2008) *Location factors of creative knowledge companies in the Dublin region*. ACRE report 6.13, Amsterdam: AMIDSt.

National Economic Social Council (NESC) (2006) *Migration policy*. Report 115. Dublin: National Economic & Social Development Office (NESDO).

OECD (2001) *Trends in international migration*. SOPEMI 2000. Paris: OECD.

OECD (2004) *Developing highly skilled workers: Review of the Netherlands*. Paris: OECD.

OECD (2005) *Counting immigrants and expatriates in OECD countries: A new perspective*. Paris: OECD.

OECD (2006) *OECD economic surveys: Netherlands*. Paris: OECD.

OECD (2007) *International migration outlook. Annual Report* (2007 edition). Paris: OECD.

OECD (2008) *A profile of immigrant populations in the 21st century. Data from OECD countries*. Paris: OECD.

Pareja-Eastaway, M., J. Turmo Garuz, L. Garcia Ferrando and M. Pradel i Miquel. (2009) *The magnetism of Barcelona. The view of transnational migrants*. Amsterdam: AMIDSt.

Perlmutter, H.V. (1969) The tortuous evolution of the multinational corporation. *Columbia Journal of World Business*, 4: 9–18.

Pethe, H. (2006) *International Migration hoch qualifizierter Arbeitskräfte. Die Greencard-Regelung in Deutschland*. Wiesbaden: DUV.

Pethe, H. (2007) Un-restricted agents? International migration of the highly skilled revisited. *Social Geography*, 3: 211–236.

Salt, J. (2006) *Current trends in international migration in Europe*. Consultant's Report to the Council of Europe. Strassburg: Council of Europe.

Schipulle, H.P. (1973) *Ausverkauf von Intelligenz aus Entwicklungsländern? Eine kritische Untersuchung zum Brain Drain*. München: Weltforum-Verlag.

Scott, S. (2006) The social morphology of skilled migration: The case of the British middle class in Paris. *Journal of Ethnic and Migration Studies*, 32 (7): 1105–1129.

Sklair, L. (2001) *The transnational capitalist class*. Oxford: Blackwell.

Smidt, M. de (1985) Japanese firms and the gateway to Europe. *Tijdschrift Voor Economische En Sociale Geografie*, 76 (1): 2–8.

Smidt, M. de and N.J. Kemper (1980) Foreign manufacturing establishments in the Netherlands. *Tijdschrift Voor Economische En Sociale Geografie*, 71 (1): 21–40.

Soysal, Y.N. (1994) *Limits of citizenship: Migrants and postnational membership in Europe*. Chicago: University of Chicago Press.

Stec Groep B.V. (2005) *Operations of foreign companies in the Netherlands in 2004*. The Hague: Netherlands Foreign Investment Agency.

Steinhardt, M., S. Stiller and A. Damelang (2008) *Bunt in die Zukunft. Kulturelle Vielfalt als Standortfaktor deutscher Metropolen*. http://www.hwwi.org/fileadmin/hwwi/Leistungen/ Gutachten/HVB-Bunt-in-die-Zukunft_Juni2008.pdf (accessed 27 March 2009).

Taylor, P.J. and R. Aranya (2008) A global 'urban roller coaster'? Connectivity changes in the World City Network, 2000–2004. *Regional Studies*, 42 (1): 1–16.

Taylor, P.J., G. Catalano and D.R.F. Walker (2002) Measurement of the World City Network. *Urban Studies*, 39 (13): 2367–2376.

Terhorst, P. (2008) *Amsterdam's path dependence: Still tightly interwoven with a national accumulation region*. Amsterdam: unpublished manuscript.

Von Streit, A. (2010) *Entgrenzter Alltag – Arbeiten ohne Grenzen? Das Internet und die raum-zeitlichen Organisationsstrategien von Wissensarbeitern*. Bielefeld: Transcript.

White, P. (1998) The settlement patterns of developed world migrants in London. *Urban Studies*, 35 (10): 1725–1744.

White, P. and L. Hurdley (2003) International migration and the housing market: Japanese corporate movers in London. *Urban Studies*, 40 (4): 687–706.

Wolter, A. (1997) *Globalisierung der Beschäftigung. Multinationale Unternehmen als Kanal der Wanderung Höherqualifizierter innerhalb Europas*. Baden-Baden: Nomos.

11

Attracting Young and High-Skilled Workers: Amsterdam, Milan and Barcelona

Montserrat Pareja-Eastaway, Marco Bontje and Marianna d'Ovidio

Introduction

Making competitive cities in a globalised world usually involves paying attention to the key elements that have contributed to their economic growth and are likely to determine success in the international arena. As has been pointed out earlier in this book, the expansion of creative and knowledge sectors in European cities has provided an important new reference framework for urban competition. High-skilled professionals are described as the most important class in an increasingly 'knowledge-based' economy and society (Bell, 1973). Richard Florida's creative class hypothesis seems tailor-made for high-skilled people in general and young high-skilled people in particular. The lifestyle and work ethic he ascribes to members of the creative class has many features one would associate more strongly with younger rather than older people. This includes a strong preference for inner-city living; the importance attached to culture, nightlife, sports and other leisure activities near home and workplace; the willingness to move often and across large distances to enable swift moves up the career ladder; acceptance of (and maybe even preference for) highly flexible employment; the blurring of borders between work time and leisure time and the rather informal networking practices connected to this.

Within this context, attracting talent to the creative knowledge city becomes a priority in order to increase the added value of the local GDP and improve a city's position in the global urban hierarchy. Cities with a greater share of highly educated people have grown more quickly than comparable cities with less human capital (Glaeser, 1994; Nardinelli and Simon, 1996; Simon, 1998). This suggests that attracting young and high-skilled workers contributes to a city's economic success by increasing average labour productivity. However, creative workers are not necessarily the ones with higher rates of productivity or higher salaries (Markusen, 2006). Two aspects must be stressed when analysing the dynamics of young high-skilled workers. First, their mobility must be placed in the context of the particular patterns of mobility in Europe. A range of residential mobility paradigms emerge in Europe: while Northern countries show higher rates of mobility, especially when looking at emancipation of young people (Mulder et al., 2002), Southern countries have lower rates of residential mobility even among younger age groups. While in Northern Europe, young people often leave the parental home in their early twenties, in Southern countries 'nest-leaving' is more common around the age of 30 years (Pareja-Eastaway, 2007). The residential opportunities offered by city-regional housing markets are major constraints/facilitators for such a dissimilar mobility pattern, while cultural traditions in family relations also continue to play an important role. Second, as mentioned elsewhere in this book, local factors such as personal trajectories and institutional components stimulate talented workers to remain in a city-region rather than move elsewhere.

Both of these aspects are of paramount importance in the analysis of strategies to attract talented people to cities. Following this argument, and as Glaeser (2003) points out, a city might become attractive enough for talented people if, rather than merely creating or maintaining an appealing place to live, policy strategies invested in increasing the level of local human capital.

This chapter considers the factors that determine whether or not young high-skilled people move to or stay in a certain city-region; and to what extent these factors are different than for older people in later stages of their labour market career. If Florida's perception of the young creatives being 'hyper-mobile' is justified, we might expect these early stage professionals to take strategic mobility decisions which would involve moving to 'creative' places all over the world. We also consider the influence of three categories of factors on the mobility decisions of young high-skilled workers: 'soft' factors like the offer of cultural, leisure, nightlife and retail amenities, the dwelling and the immediate living environment; 'city atmosphere' features like tolerance of ethnic, cultural and lifestyle diversity; and 'hard' factors, especially those related to salaries and working conditions.

Amsterdam, Barcelona and Milan are referred to in this chapter for three reasons. First, the city-regions of Amsterdam, Barcelona and Milan currently have a comparable status in the international hierarchy of creative knowledge centres. They form part of the next group of creative knowledge centres in Europe after the leading centres of London and Paris. Second, the city-regions of Amsterdam, Barcelona and Milan attract many young people with their rich offer of higher education. After completing their studies, many of those young people stay in the city-region, most often in or close to the core city, to start their labour market and housing market career. Third, these cities are difficult places for young highly skilled people to live in – affordable housing is hard to find (Barcelona and Milan) or hard to access (Amsterdam) and the cost of living is generally high.

The questions we address in this chapter are:

- What is the average profile of young high-skilled people in the European creative knowledge city?
- To what extent do high-skilled workers have formal (higher) education qualifications?
- Why have young high-skilled workers moved to the city-region? What are their personal trajectories?
- What is their vision of the city-region? What challenges, threats and future development perspectives do they see for the city-region?

In the rest of this chapter we give an overview of alternative theories and hypotheses on the role of the city in attracting talented workers. We then discuss the general patterns of young high-skilled workers in the 13 European city-regions as represented by our survey among creative and knowledge workers and focus on the three chosen cities stressing differences and similarities. Finally, we discuss conclusions arising from these results.

Competing for young, high-skilled workers

Competitiveness is on the agenda of local governments and takes many forms depending on the specific profile being aimed at. Innovative, economically successful and attractive are a few of many different facets of a city's positive performance. Cities compete with each other in many domains, aiming to attract high rates of private investment, expand their international markets and attract a skilled mobile population to improve their labour supply (Turok, 2004).

In the past, countries and cities benefited from low salaries and low prices to attract capital investments and companies and increase their exports to the rest of the world. While some parts of the world are still successfully using these factors for competitive advantage, European cities rather depend on '... the ability to sustain change in the factors that give rise to productivity growth (technology, human resources, etc. but also the structure of the economy and how policy seeks to shape it)' (Begg, 1999, p. 798). Several studies have provided evidence for the relationship between urban economic growth and availability of human capital: talented people and/or high-skilled workers (Brint, 2001; Glaeser and Maré, 2001; Glaeser, 2003). Thus, human capital, talent and skills are currently essential to guarantee strong positions on the competitive urban scale.

Ciampi (1996) includes inadequate human resource development and inflexible labour use among the causes of concern related to urban competitiveness. There are two possible ways for urban metropolitan regions to attract talent or human capital as a key factor for their urban competitiveness success. The first option is the provision of attractive salaries and labour opportunities together with favourable working conditions. As Kresl (1995) indicates, the creation of high-skilled and high-income jobs would emphasise the convenience and enticement of traditional 'hard' location factors to high-skilled workers and simultaneously improve urban competitiveness. Second, cities may offer a pleasant urban environment, a high standard of quality of life and possibilities to create dense personal networks and collaborative relationships to promote creativity, trust and long-term working agreements. In short, a large range of 'soft' factors oriented to make life, personal and professional, more agreeable and satisfactory. In that sense, and following Gordon and Cheshire (1998), sources of competitive advantage of cities include the 'local environment' as it influences the willingness of mobile workers to locate in the city, as well as those external, non-market influences on productivity which mainly refer to local dynamism favouring business.

The key elements attracting firms in an urban competitive environment are those that are outside the control of the firm, favouring the creation of positive externalities and innovation between firms and those that affect the input costs of employers: property prices and rents, education and training facilities, fiscal costs, quality of residential accommodation, crime rates, social cohesion and others (Begg, 1999). It is important to stress that this chapter focuses on workers' decisions and preferences rather than on firms' location decisions. However, as both choices are intrinsically related, the analysis of workers certainly reflects the conditions and possibilities of competition in urban labour markets.

Considering the economy as a whole, creative and knowledge-intensive sectors are indeed those that rely particularly highly on human capital and talent. These sectors are considered essential for urban challenges in competitiveness (Florida, 2002; Scott, 2006), and consequently an understanding of how the workers attached to these sectors make decisions about living and working is essential in developing a strategic policy to improve urban competitiveness. The mobilisation of advanced skills reflects the capacity of the city to develop and enhance the capacities of local people and/or its success in attracting talent from elsewhere (Gordon and Turok, 2005). Thus, increasing the potential of human capital in a city might follow two different paths: one based on Florida's assumption of the high mobility of the 'creative class' and the other based on the enhancement of the human capital endowments already existing in the city (Malecki, 2002). The first approach would require attractive places to live and work and high salaries to attract creative and knowledge workers to the area. The second would, in addition, command public and private investments in education and skills provision through research institutions, specialised workshops and education providers.

Youth is an additional characteristic to take into account when analysing patterns of location and mobility of creative and knowledge workers. In the beginning of the professional career, expectations of mobility are higher, especially where young people are less risk averse and value future job opportunities rather than high initial incomes. The relative importance of family responsibilities may also be less than at older ages. An analysis of the extent to which salaries and job security might be a deterrent or a stimulus in young professionals' mobility provides a clue to understanding certain decisions. In addition, young people attach a high priority to personal and family-related goals, looking for flexible jobs that better accommodate family-related exigencies. If a comfortable working environment which provides a high level of satisfaction is a common goal among new and young professionals, this may work against the expectation of higher mobility.

Some American cities have a great capacity to attract high-skilled young migrants and among the most important reasons for this are that they meet high expectations of future job opportunities, offer singular lifestyles and present tolerant environments (Glaeser, 1999; Florida, 2002). The results from our research on European cities seem to be at odds with this. At least two distinctive characteristics of European society may contribute to this difference. First, not only for creative people but for the population in general, mobility rates are much lower in Europe than in the USA. Preferences and constraints such as the tightness of the housing market, at least in some countries, might also affect this. Second, place attachment seems to be higher than in the USA as many creative and knowledge workers locate where they were born or studied, establishing and caring about their social and professional networks rather than being attracted by new offers elsewhere.

Young and high-skilled workers in European cities

The survey carried out in 13 European city-regions in 2007 (outlined in Chapter 1) enables us to take this discussion forward. This chapter focuses on differences between younger and older high-skilled workers within the survey. In each case study about 200 respondents participated in the survey and answered questions about the reasons for moving to or being in the residential satisfaction, job and workplace satisfaction, appreciation of the available amenities and living environment. Specific attention was given to the 'soft factors' highlighted by Florida and others (e.g. tolerance, city atmosphere), but we also included questions about 'hard factors' (e.g. monetary factors) and personal attachment to the area (e.g. family and friendship networks).

The main target group of this chapter are 'young' workers – workers at an early stage in both life course and employment career. We specified this group as people under 35 years old, who had embarked on a working career in the creative and knowledge-intensive sectors generally less than 10 years previously. Many of the results are presented in comparison with 'older workers' – people aged 35 years or older, generally having worked for more than 10 years in the same sectors. The discussion of research results involves a presentation of their profile (household composition and family composition); an analysis of their quality of life (in terms of use and satisfaction with the local environment); and an analysis related to their job, career and working environment. We have based our analysis on a sample of 2646 respondents, of which more than half can be categorised as 'young high-skilled workers'. In Amsterdam, Barcelona and Milan, however, we have surveyed more older workers than younger workers (Table 11.1), but in each of the cities the sub-sample of young workers is sufficiently large to analyse them separately and compare them with the older workers.

Structural profile

The family profile of young creative and knowledge workers in the ACRE survey mainly comprises couples or single people, while the older workers tend to be couples with children. The housing career is linked with age and work history, and the majority of the young workers live in a rented dwelling (and a significant portion live with their parents and have no housing costs). In contrast, most older workers (62 per cent) are home owners, with or without a mortgage. For 70 per cent of all respondents, cost is the critical factor determining the choice of dwelling and younger people are over-represented among those who think that the cost of the dwelling represents an extremely high percentage in their budget. In contrast, less than 40 per cent of the older workers emphasise housing

Table 11.1   Respondents of ACRE survey, age groups, per urban region.

	Young workers (< 35 years)	Older workers (≥ 35)	Total
Total sample, 13 cities	1,424	1,222	2,646
Amsterdam	98	137	235
Barcelona	70	134	204
Milan	106	91	197

Source: ACRE survey (2007).

costs. The vast majority of the sample, without considering age, spends between 10 and 30 per cent of their income on rent, while a little more is devoted to the mortgage.

Life in the city-region

Looking at the reasons why young creative workers live in the city-region, differences among age groups emerge, although there are also similarities. We will see in the next pages how these differences are emphasised in one metropolitan region or another. One of the most relevant findings indicates that most of the people relate their being in their residence to personal connections or study and jobs: they are in the city-region because they were born there, their family lives there, because they have studied in the city or because they have a job there. Very few of the interviewed mention 'soft reasons' such as tolerance, weather or social atmosphere of the city. Nevertheless there are differences between age groups. As we could expect, older creative and knowledge workers are more linked to family and in general personal connections (about 50 per cent of the responses are grouped around two answers: 'born there' and 'family lives there'). Nevertheless, many of them are in the city-region because of the job (21 per cent of older workers rank this as the first reason). Very few of them (8 per cent of older workers) declare that they are in the city-region because they have studied there. The young workers seem to be slightly more mobile than older workers, since 25 per cent answer they are in the city-region because of their job, followed by the fact that they were born in the region and that they have studied in the city. Young workers are slightly more interested in soft factors than the older workers. Looking more in detail and exploring the whole range of reasons why the young workers are in the city (we asked them to indicate the four most important reasons of their presence in the city in ranking order), things are more complex. While a considerable proportion of answers are still linked with hard factors, such as the opportunity of finding good jobs and the nearness to families, many others are related to soft factors – including the size of the city-region and the importance of entertainment. One third of the answers are related to proximity to friends, in particular among young workers, and a considerable proportion are concerned about housing availability and quality of life in general. Regarding the use of the city and the involvement in any activities in their spare time, generally speaking the young creative workers do not seem to be particularly involved in local social or cultural activities, although they are involved more than older workers. In any case they are pretty satisfied about this kind of activity. The opposite is true for activities related to participation in the social or political life of the community (associations, religious or community work). In general very few people are involved, but older workers are a bit more likely to be.

Working in the creative and knowledge sectors

Young workers are more often employed in companies than older workers, who are more likely to be freelancers or self-employed. This is surprising since we would have expected the young workers to have more flexible work situations, including more freelance and self-employed positions. Possibly, experience and networks play a decisive role here: it may be easier to reach clients for freelancers or self-employed persons after professional networks and market knowledge are well-developed, a process which might take lots of working experience and several years. Another aspect of flexibility of work gives less surprising results. Among the employees, age is a relevant variable for permanent contracts: as they get older, the probability of finding a permanent contract is higher. Young people are more likely than others to have short–medium term contracts, and to be in apprenticeships. The number of years working in the same company is also highly related to age: more than half of the young workers have worked for the same company for 5 years or less, and 20 per cent for 1 year or less; while 38 per cent of the older workers have worked for the same company for more than 10 years.

The creative knowledge economy is dominated by small and medium-sized enterprises. Consequently most of the sample (of all ages) works in such companies. This could also be one of the reasons why creative and knowledge workers are in general satisfied with their job – working in small companies or being self-employed may be more challenging and enable people to determine their working preferences to a larger extent than working in a large company. Three-quarters (75 per cent) of those interviewed are satisfied or very satisfied with the sense of achievement they get from their job. In general there are no large differences in age cohorts regarding the dimensions of job satisfaction. Our respondents are usually satisfied with many different aspects of their job: from the physical issues of the environment, to the chance to build networks, to the intellectual stimuli. Looking for age differences we can generally say 'the younger, the happier', especially when taking into account career improvement and training, while the opposite can be said about the possibility of having influence on their job.

Unsurprisingly, the younger workers seem more able to balance career with personal life, especially if we think about their family ties, which are not as strong as those of older workers. The expectations for the future are strongly age-related: the younger the respondent is, the less she/he will expect to remain in the same company. Two aspects must be considered here: the kind of contract and the real job expectations. Most of the young workers are employed with short-term contracts and therefore they do not expect to stay longer in the company, but there is also a tendency for young people to change company more frequently than older people. Considering only those interviewees who have a contract of more than 1 year (fixed term of 12 months or more or unlimited permanent contract), we can see the same trend: the younger they are, the higher are the expectations to change company. The main two reasons for changing company are to look for a better job and a better pay, with age differences: in general (within the young workers group) the youngest workers search for a better job, while slightly older workers look for better pay.

The Amsterdam, Barcelona and Milan city-regions

Amsterdam, Barcelona and Milan have certain similarities in their position in the European urban hierarchy and all are attractive and expensive places for young creative workers. As has been outlined elsewhere in this book, the nature and importance of the creative and knowledge-based economy differs between these three case studies. They also have different economic landscapes, path dependencies and labour market opportunities and have had distinctive trajectories in recent decades associated with contrasting roles of public policies designed to attract talented workers to the city (Bontje and Sleutjes, 2007; Mingione et al,. 2007; Pareja-Eastaway et al., 2007). The interviews completed in these city-regions provide further insight into the motivations of young and high-skilled workers.

Structural profile

The creative and knowledge workers in the three case studies are likely to be a group of young people with high incomes and good career opportunities. Household structures among young workers are broadly similar in the Barcelona and Amsterdam Metropolitan Regions while Milan Metropolitan Region has a somewhat different structure. In Amsterdam, about 87 per cent of young people live alone (40 per cent) or with a partner (47 per cent). Young households living alone or with a partner in Barcelona show the highest percentage (more than 70 per cent) compared with the rest of the population (14 per cent). In Milan, two household structures are over-represented in the young workers category: non-family households with related and non-related persons (typically two or more friends that share an apartment) and families with young people who still live in the parental home. The situation is not an exception for Milanese household structures, where young people (even those who have been working for many years) live with their parents for a long period of time (d'Ovidio, 2009). This is linked with the transition to adult life in Italy, but in particular in Milan, where economic development has caused a very fast increase in real-estate prices and has put strong pressure on the younger generations, especially women. This has begun to be recognised as a real problem, both by academics and politicians, and has consequences for the ageing of the population, the very low birth rate and a generally unbalanced demographic structure in the city. Young people tend to stay at home with their parents longer than elsewhere in Europe and they tend to have fewer children (or none at all).

The problem is typical of all the European countries, but is very strong in Italy, and particularly in Milan. In other Southern countries the problem is present (Pareja-Eastaway, 2007), but in a less extreme degree and not for all the social strata: the young creative workers in Barcelona, for instance, are more willing to exit the parental house. Nonetheless it is true that in all cities having children tends to be postponed (after 30 years old) or abandoned. This is also true for Amsterdam, but the life course before possibly starting a family looks quite different here. In Amsterdam, young people leave the parental home at quite an early age, usually around 20 years. This is especially true for students in higher education. As the regular housing market (social rental, private rental and owner-occupied dwellings) is hard to access for students and recent graduates in Amsterdam, they most often start their housing career in special student accommodation. Alternatively they rent rooms from home owners, share flats with other students, or are involved in either squatting or short-term 'anti-squatting' rental agreements. Uncertain terms of residence and frequent moves are quite common among students, recently graduated and young creative knowledge workers in the Amsterdam city-region, particularly in the core city of Amsterdam.

Living in the city-region

The strong family and friendship ties of younger creative knowledge workers are reflected also in the attachment to the place they currently live in: most of the young people have been living in the region for more than 5 years and many for more than 10 years. Those who are coming from elsewhere originate mostly from the same city-region.

While the cities thus attract relatively few long-distance migrants, it also seems that people (both young and older workers) already living there are not really willing to leave: only half of young people declare that there could be a slight possibility of leaving the city where they currently live, while fewer and fewer older workers refer to this. Moreover, in contrast with theories about the attractiveness of the creative cities and the supposed mobility of the creative class, the choice of where to live appears more related to their personal trajectories than the characteristic of the city. Of the three city-regions considered here, only Amsterdam seems a place where personal trajectories are less important, in particular for older workers: more than half of respondents in the age group 15–35 years (59 per cent) were already living in the Amsterdam Metropolitan Area before they moved to their current residence, 27.5 per cent of the young highly skilled respondents come from another part of the Netherlands, and 13 per cent from abroad. We have to keep in mind, though, that the Netherlands is a small country where regional boundaries may be crossed more easily than in Italy or Spain. In Milan only 8 per cent come from another Italian region and even less from abroad. Barcelona presents similar results, with 70 per cent of the population born in the region and slightly less than 10 per cent coming from abroad.

The Amsterdam situation can be recognised at best as a partial validation of Florida's thesis, but his thesis cannot explain why this does not occur in Barcelona. Apparently, it is not enough for a city to be creative and offer a good quality of life to attract or retain talented people. Respondents in Milan city-region indicate less satisfaction with their quality of life than those in Amsterdam or Barcelona city-regions (although our respondents still enjoy the city and are happy with leisure and cultural facilities), and regard the image of the city as not very good. It is personal trajectories that explain why they are in the city. From more in-depth enquiry (with a smaller sample of foreign workers), we know that also for foreigners, personal trajectories and relations are much more important than the other reasons to come or to stay in each studied case.

The differences among the three cities are also expressed by the fact that in Milan most of the people did not mention any of the 'soft' factors (such as quality of cultural offer, weather, tolerance) as a reason to come (or stay) in the city. In contrast, in Barcelona and Amsterdam, soft factors are often mentioned – not at a first reason, but as a third or fourth reason to come and live there (Figure 11.1).

One of the main attractions in these metropolitan regions is without doubt education: in each of the three city-regions about 80 per cent of the young creative and knowledge workers have been educated within the city-region, and very often the first reason for being there relates to the presence of a good university. Milan Metropolitan Area has very good universities with English courses and a lot of foreigners are attracted to the city by the high-level courses in fashion and design (two sectors the city is well known for). Barcelona offers universities and a broad range of post-graduate professional studies. Amsterdam offers two universities as well as art and design institutes with a strong international reputation. Having said that, it also appears that young foreigners, once they have finished their studies in the city, often leave soon afterwards and often do not become part of the local labour market. Among the older workers, the percentages of people who studied in the same metropolitan area are slightly lower: this means either that there has been greater mobility among older workers (and they have had more time to decide where to move) or that older generations studied elsewhere.

Once they are in the city (either they stayed or they arrived), young creative and knowledge workers have a diverse housing experience, linked with the different paths in the household structure. The southern

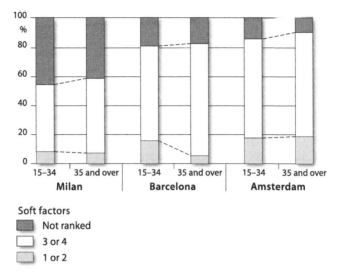

Figure 11.1 Soft factors as a reason for living in the region (in per cent).

metropolitan areas (Barcelona and Milan) have a housing market strongly dominated by owner-occupation (more than 80 per cent). This affects people in many ways. Younger age groups in particular are forced to leave the parents' nest later than in other European regions, and owner-occupation is considered as the only option. For the creative and knowledge workers interviewed, the home-ownership percentages are similar, with one important difference. While in Barcelona owner-occupation is stronger among older workers (80 per cent live in their own home, only 50 per cent of the younger generation), in the Milanese region there is no difference in housing situation between age groups. If this is linked with the difficulties that young people have in leaving the parental household, it is clear that the delay in having children and in new family building is associated with the housing market: young Milanese workers prefer to start their new families later (with a partner or alone), in order to be able to buy their own home. Most of the time, the parental family plays a crucial role in enabling them to start their home-owner project.

In all three city-regions, housing costs are considered as a major problem, although with small differences. In the Amsterdam Metropolitan Region, housing costs are the main financial bottleneck: no less than 93 per cent of the young highly skilled consider the housing costs 'very expensive' or 'expensive'. This share is very high in the older age group too (84 per cent). Housing costs are also the most mentioned item that respondents worry about: 89 per cent of the young highly skilled respondents are 'very worried' or 'worried' about housing affordability. In the Barcelona Region, more than 90 per cent of young workers considered the cost of housing as 'very expensive'. Affordability represents a less extreme problem in the Barcelona Metropolitan Region for young creative and knowledge workers than in the Amsterdam Metropolitan Region: around 48 per cent of the interviewees declare that rent or mortgage payments are just about affordable. However, 38.6 per cent of young creative and knowledge workers consider their house not easy or very difficult to afford. In the Milan Metropolitan Region, young creative and knowledge workers seem cautious with their housing expenses: the expenses for both rent and mortgage are under one third of the income for 60 per cent of young people paying a rent and for 40 per cent of young people with a mortgage and in general mortgages or rents are perceived as affordable or just about so.

Jobs in the creative and knowledge sectors

In this last section, we consider the labour market and quality of jobs within the creative and knowledge sectors in the three regions. Although there are many similarities between the cities, reflecting the strong character of the creative and knowledge economy itself, it is possible to identify a number of spheres where local features are stronger.

In Milan it is more difficult for the young generation than for older workers to find a permanent or stable job, and in general there is more flexibility than in the Barcelona region. In the Amsterdam region finding a job was generally not considered difficult in either age category. In all three regions the young working generation has fewer guarantees than older workers. If we connect this with the housing market issues, the importance of family in southern Europe becomes clear once more: the high entry level of the owner-occupied housing market, together with the flexibility of employment contracts, forces young people to rely on the parental family, thus strengthening the link with the region. The question that this raises is whether young workers can really decide where to move, or whether they are forced to stay in the region because they cannot afford a completely independent way of life? However, in Amsterdam, where young workers start their housing career much earlier, the share of respondents that have always lived in the city-region is hardly any lower than in Barcelona and Milan. Looking more deeply into the labour characteristics, especially in Milan, a peculiar situation emerges that can be called 'stable flexibility': most of the young workers have worked in the same company for many years with flexible contracts, while in Barcelona the labour market is a little more dynamic and in Amsterdam much more.

The creative and knowledge workers earn good salaries, especially when compared with the other jobs, although there are strong differences between the three regions and between the two age groups. The majority of younger creative workers in Milan and Amsterdam earn less than €2.000 per month. The situation changes with age, especially in Amsterdam, where more than 80 per cent of those older than 35 years earn

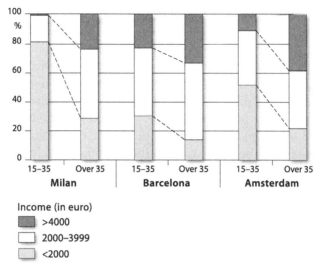

Figure 11.2 Income distribution per age group and city region.

more than €2000 per month: the older the worker, the higher the income. In the Barcelona Metropolitan Region, differences in income are less obvious between age groups although the younger group is over-represented in the lower segment of income (Figure 11.2).

As was indicated above, young workers in these three city-regions are satisfied with their jobs. Nevertheless, many think about changing them: around 80 per cent of workers think that they will change companies in the next future. This pattern is also connected with their flexible contracts, and the general flexibility ideology that permeates the contemporary economy (Sennett, 1998). In general, most of reasons for changing workplace refer to 'hard' motivations, such as having a better pay and better job conditions; the Barcelona region is the only one where a large proportion of young workers want to change their job in order to find a more interesting one.

Conclusions

This chapter confirms the hypothesis stated in the introduction of this book: personal factors matter in the attractiveness of cities in the creative and knowledge-based economy. Many young talented workers stay where they have personal connections or relationships. Therefore, they do not necessarily respond to the image of a highly mobile group who respond to the image and buzz of the city. Besides, as pointed out elsewhere in this book, public funded institutions related to higher education and research may not only contribute to attracting talented people, but also to retaining them after graduation. After all, large shares of respondents in our three city-regions have remained to start their working career in the city-region after graduating there.

The much celebrated 'soft factors' appeared less significant in attracting and retaining young creative knowledge workers. In Amsterdam, soft factors were mentioned relatively frequently compared with Barcelona and Milan, but even there, personal ties like being born or having family in the region or having studied there were much more important. These overall findings suggest that theories based on the existence of a hyper-mobile creative class do not fit the European case in so far as they imply residential mobility across large distances. Reflecting on this it may be worthwhile to investigate this hypothesis more thoroughly for the USA as well. At the same time, our survey of young creative knowledge workers provides indications of a high degree of job mobility and flexibility. Labour contracts at the start of the working career are often short-term and relatively insecure and work practices are often loose and flexible. However, these characteristics appear to generate job changes within the same city-region rather than job-hopping from city to city or even from country to country. This has important policy implications, as it might well be that investment in strengthening local resources and retaining creative workers are more likely to be effective than efforts to create an environment to attract a mobile creative class from elsewhere.

References

Begg, I. (1999) Cities and competitiveness. *Urban Studies*, 36 (5–6): 795–809.

Bell, D. (1973) *The coming of the post-industrial society*. New York: Basic Books.

Bontje, M. and B. Sleutjes (2007) *Amsterdam: History meets modernity. Pathways to creative and knowledge-based regions*. ACRE report WP2.1. Amsterdam: AMIDSt.

Brint, S. (2001) Professionals and the knowledge economy: Rethinking the theory of the knowledge society. *Current Sociology*, 49 (4): 101–132.

Ciampi, C.A. (1996) Enhancing European competitiveness. *Banca Nazionale di Lavoro Quarterly Review*, 197: 143–164.

d'Ovidio, M. (2009) Milano, città duale? In: C. Ranci (ed.), *I limiti sociali della crescita: Milano e le città d'Europa, tra competitività e disuguaglianze. Secondo Rapporto su Milano Sociale*. Milano: Maggioli.

Florida, R. (2002) *The rise of the creative class*. New York: Basic Books.

Glaeser, E. (1994) Why does schooling generate economic growth? *Economics Letters*, 44: 333–337.

Glaeser, E. (1999) Learning in cities. *Journal of Urban Economics*, 46 (2): 254–277.

Glaeser, E. (2003) *The rise of the skilled city*. Working paper 10191. National Bureau of Economic Research. Available at: www.nber.org/papers/w10191

Glaeser, E. and D. Maré (2001) Cities and skills. *Journal of Labor Economics*, 19 (2): 316–342.

Gordon, I. and P. Cheshire (1998) Territorial competition: Some lessons for policy. *The Annals of Regional Science*, 32: 321–346.

Gordon, I. and I. Turok (2005) How urban labour markets matter. In: I. Buck, I. Gordon, A. Harding and I. Turok (eds), *Changing cities*, pp. 242–264. London: Palgrave.

Kresl, P. (1995) The determinants of urban competitiveness. In: P. Kresl and G. Gappert (eds), *Urban affairs annual review, No 44: North American cities and the global economy: Challenges and opportunities*, pp. 45–68. Thousand Oaks, CA: Sage.

Malecki, E. (2002) Hard and soft networks for urban competitiveness. *Urban Studies*, 39 (5–6): 929–945.

Markusen, A. (2006) Urban development and the politics of a creative class: Evidence from a study of artists. *Environment and Planning*, 38: 1921–1940.

Mingione, E., E. dell'Agnese, S. Mugnano, M. d'Ovidio, B. Niessen and C. Sedini (2007) *Milan city-region: Is it still competitive and charming? Pathways to creative and knowledge-based regions*. ACRE report WP2.12. Amsterdam: AMIDSt.

Mulder, C., W. Clark and M. Wagner (2002) A comparative analysis of leaving home in the United States, the Netherlands and West Germany. *Demographic research*, 7 (17): 565–592.

Nardinelli, C. and C. Simon (1996) The talk of the town: Human capital, information and the growth of English cities, 1861 to 1961. *Explorations in Economic History*, 33: 384–413.

Pareja-Eastaway, M., J. Turmo Garuz, M. Pradel i Miguel, L. Garcia Ferrando and M. Simó Solsona (2007) *The city of marvels? Multiple endeavours towards competitiveness in Barcelona. Pathways to creative and knowledge-based regions*. ACRE report WP2.2. Amsterdam: AMIDSt.

Pareja-Eastaway, M. (2007) Residential opportunities and emancipation strategies in an owner occupied dominated market. *Architecture, City and Environment*, ii (5): 453–470.

Scott, A. (2006) Creative cities: Conceptual issues and policy questions. *Journal of Urban Affairs*, 28 (1): 1–17.

Sennett, R. (1998) *The corrosion of character, the personal consequences of work in the New Capitalism*. New York: Norton.

Simon, C.J. (1998) Human capital and metropolitan employment growth. *Journal of Urban Economics*, 43: 223–243.

Turok, I. (2004) Sources of city prosperity and cohesion: The case of Glasgow and Edinburgh. In: M. Boddy and M. Parkinson (eds), *City matters: Competitiveness, cohesion and urban governance*, pp. 13–31. Bristol: Policy Press.

12

Working on the Edge? Creative Jobs in Birmingham, Leipzig and Poznan

Julie Brown, Robert Nadler and Michal Meczynski

Introduction: creative work – precariousness, uncertainty and risk?

The creative industries have generated much political and academic interest in recent years, with the main focus on their economic and employment potential. According to OECD statistics, the sector now accounts for more than 5.8 million employees in the EU25 or 3.1 per cent of the total employed. Typically, these industries have contributed somewhere between 2 and 6 per cent of GDP, depending on the definitions used (UNCTAD, 2008) and are now seen as 'powerful engines driving economic growth and promoting development in a globalising world' (UNCTAD, 2008). High profile creative industries development policies have been adopted wholeheartedly by numerous cities and regions within Europe, the USA and more recently within China and other developing countries, with the express aim of boosting economic performance.

However, the raft of statistics attributed to the growth potential of the 'creative economy' disregards the 'quality of work life' of those working in the sector and the fact that much creative employment is typically 'non-standard'. While standard work is characterised by stable and continuous employment with a single employer, working full-time hours over a regular working week and being paid a wage or salary; much creative employment is temporary, short-term and project-based; contract working is the norm and there are high levels of self-employment and freelance working. Long working hours are typical (with work often spilling over into home life) and multiple-job holding in associated or different sectors is more frequent than in the general workforce. There is often frequent job changing; earnings are unequal and fluctuating and unpaid work is commonplace. In addition, there is little job protection or security; low levels of unionisation and uncertain career development pathways (Towse, 1996, 2001; Menger, 1999, 2001, 2006; Batt et al., 2001; Ross, 2002, 2008; McRobbie, 2002, 2003, 2004; Benhamou, 2003; Perrons, 2003, 2005; Oakley, 2004; Neff et al., 2005; Friebe and Lobo, 2006; Huws, 2006; Jarvis and Pratt, 2006; Reidl et al., 2006; Knell and Oakley, 2007; Throsby, 2007; Gill and Pratt, 2008). This has led many to define working conditions in the creative sector as 'insecure' or 'precarious'. Nonetheless, while a recent UNCTAD (2004, p. 3) policy report noted that, 'too often [creative industries are] associated with a precarious form of job security', observations like these remain the exception within much policy-making on the creative industries (Neilson and Rossiter, 2005).

Nonetheless, creative workers have been hailed as 'model entrepreneurs' (Florida, 2002). The 'flexible' working practices and fluid career structures characteristic of the creative sector (particularly new media) have come to be seen as representative of the 'brave new world of work' (Beck, 2000; Flores and Gray, 2000). Changes in the structure of the economy as a whole (the move from an industrial to post-industrial knowledge-based economy, globalisation, technology advances (particularly the development of the Internet) and the reform and deregulation of (Western) labour markets) have impacted on working patterns across all sectors, with jobs becoming increasingly temporary, casualised and insecure (see also Lash and Urry, 1993; Sennett, 1998; Heery and Salmon, 1999). However, it is unclear whether moves towards more 'flexible' forms of work organisation typical of the creative sector will lead to the quality of working life improvement or deterioration.

The main argument in favour of the 'non-standard' working practices adopted by the creative sector is their offer of freedom, self-governance and 'self-actualisation' (Gill and Pratt, 2008). Indeed, despite the high levels of risk and uncertainty, highly skilled (mainly young) individuals seek employment in the creative sector and in ever greater numbers. They are motivated, in part, by the 'cool', cutting-edge, dynamic image of creative work, as well as by the promise of greater autonomy, potential for self-expression and social prestige (McRobbie, 1998, 2002; Neff et al., 2005; Huws, 2006). These individuals are also said to derive enormous satisfaction from their own work and have a passionate attachment to it and to their identity as a creative worker (McRobbie, 1998). Research indicates that they value their creative freedom, the variety of (non-routine) work and the opportunity to use a wide range of their skills and talents as well as the informality and non-hierarchical nature of the work 'scene' (Leadbeater and Oakley, 1999; Huws, 2006). These aspects are often perceived as strong advantages by those working in the sector, enabling very high levels of self-exploitation and providing a justification, it has been suggested, for many to remain (unprofitably) within the sector (McRobbie, 1998).

However, the creative sector has also been described as a 'winner takes all economy' (Towse, 2002; Huws, 2006) as it leads to very low rewards to the majority of those who work in it while a few 'superstars' succeed. While some individuals might gain high paid, high status work, are in constant demand and have considerable power to choose where, how and when they work, this profile does not apply to all individuals or even across all sectors. Those who are less well established or are poorly paid and have fluctuating incomes have less choice in where they live and what they do. Furthermore, entry into the creative sector is highly competitive and increasingly reserved for those who are able and willing to work unpaid, often for months on end, as the price of entry. As Knell and Oakley (2007, p. 16) suggest, 'the reality of work in the creative industries for many is less about self-determination than it is about increasingly precarious employment in industries with an over-supply of qualified labour'.

Recent empirical evidence suggests that work in the creative sector also comes at a heavy cost to the majority of individuals (Gill, 2002; Ross, 2002; Huws, 2006; Reidl et al., 2006). Although the notion of 'flexibility' argues that the individual is able to exercise some control over when and how long they work, in practice, the needs of the project are overriding, and working hours and patterns are determined by these rather than by the needs of the worker (Ross, 2008). This often necessitates intense periods of round-the-clock working, which might then be followed by several weeks with no (creative) work (Pratt, 2000). Furthermore, the risks associated with this precarious work life are shouldered by the individual, as they must take responsibility for managing gaps between projects and for finding future work (McRobbie, 1999, 2002; Neff et al., 2005; Jarvis and Pratt, 2006; Gill, 2007). Long work hours and, in particular, non-standard work patterns also blur the boundaries between work and non-work, potentially placing pressure on social and familial relationships (Jarvis and Pratt, 2006). Significantly, despite its image as 'non-hierarchical and egalitarian' (Gill, 2007), research also indicates that new forms of gender inequalities are arising, related to many of the features of creative work that are valued (informality, autonomy and flexibility) (Perrons, 2003; Oakley, 2006; Christopherson, 2008).

The characteristics outlined above raise important questions about the social and economic sustainability of work and employment in the creative sector, which has implications for policy that argues for an expansion of employment in these industries under present conditions (Hesmondhalgh, 2006). Although academic studies which focus on and debate this topic are becoming more numerous (see, for example, *Work Organisation, Labour & Globalisation*, Winter 2006–2007; *Theory, Culture & Society*, December 2008), there is still a lack of empirical research on the nature and quality of creative employment. Further analysis is merited, given that the sustainability of work and employment in the creative industries is seen as central to ensuring the competitiveness of entire cities and regions, and the quality of living and working conditions are considered vital factors in the global location of the 'creative class' (Florida, 2002, 2005).

In this chapter we present an analysis of employment conditions and 'quality of work' in the creative sector in three European cities (Birmingham, Leipzig and Poznan), each with different labour market conditions, in order to determine the extent to which creative employment can be regarded as sustainable or insecure and whether creative workers are indeed 'living on the edge'. We address the following research questions:

- Are creative workers more exposed to 'precarious' and 'insecure' forms of employment than workers in other sectors?
- Do 'precarious' employment conditions translate into feelings of job insecurity and dissatisfaction with work, or do autonomy and self-actualisation compensate?
- Do the characteristics of work and employment in the creative sector reduce or increase gender imbalances?
- What is the effect of different labour market conditions on levels of 'precarious' employment and how does this affect feelings of job satisfaction and job 'insecurity'?

The remainder of the chapter describes the methodology and sample characteristics, introduces the three cities and the different labour market conditions operating in each and analyses the objective conditions of work and employment which represent tangible criteria for measuring the quality and sustainability of work, while allowing for a general comparison of the creative sector with the economy as a whole. Finally, there is an analysis of the more subjective opinions of workers regarding job satisfaction and conclusions are presented.

Methodology

Our analysis draws on results from 204 questionnaire-based surveys carried out with highly skilled workers (holding a first degree or equivalent level technical/vocational qualification) in selected sub-sectors of the creative industries (72.2 Computer games, Software, Electronic publishing; Software consultancy & supply; 92.1 and 92.2 Motion pictures & Video activities; Radio & TV activities; 74.4 Advertising; 74.8 Speciality Design; 74.2 Architecture) completed in 2007. Target creative sectors were outside the classical branches of the arts, and were more 'applied' sectors: advertising, architecture, graphics/design, film/broadcasting, new media and software.

Table 12.1   Socio-demographic characteristics of the sample.

City	Creative workers		
	Gender (% male)	Age(% 25–34)	Household composition (% with children)
Birmingham	50.9	62.3	20.8
Leipzig	51.4	56.4	31.5
Poznan	64.5	55.6	48.0
TOTAL	56.2	57.7	34.8

Source: ACRE survey, 2007 (N = 204: Birmingham = 53; Leipzig = 75; Poznan = 76).

Respondents were asked about their employment and working conditions including their earnings, employment and contract status and average weekly hours worked. They were also asked to evaluate their satisfaction with different aspects of their job. Finally, standard socio-demographic questions were also included. A common questionnaire was adopted for all three cities.

Male respondents outnumbered females, although this difference was most sizeable in the case of Poznan, where two-thirds of the sample was male. In each city, respondents were young, with the majority in the 24–35 age group, and in terms of household composition, just over a third of the sample had children, although this ranged from a low of only a fifth in the Birmingham sample to nearly half of respondents in the Poznan sample (Table 12.1).

The cities referred to in this chapter are Birmingham (UK), a post-industrial western European city with a deregulated, 'liberal market economy'; Leipzig (Germany), a former centrally controlled eastern German city which, with strong western German support, has already undergone transition and integration into a 'co-ordinated market economy'; and Poznan (Poland), a former eastern European city which is currently undergoing the final stages of transition from a centrally controlled command economy to a 'controlled market economy'.

While the European Union (EU) has become an integrated, more liberalised labour market, national governance systems still play an important role in shaping employment regulation, work organisation and social security and welfare policies (Christopherson, 2002; Erlinghagen, 2007). Unlike the UK which has a low level of labour market regulation policies, very low unionisation as well as low levels of social welfare protection, the less liberal German labour market is highly regulated, with strong employment protection legislation, and high levels of social welfare protection, although recent reforms have made the labour market more flexible. This western German institutional framework was transferred to eastern Germany after reunification. Indicators of the strictness of labour market regulation (such as those published by the World Bank and the OECD) show that the labour market in Poland is much more heavily regulated than the UK, but less so than in Germany, and is only marginally more regulated than the average for both the OECD and EU countries (Bukowski et al., 2008). These three different labour market characteristics create an interesting basis for comparison of 'precarious' and 'non-standard' forms of employment and which may influence, for example, perceptions of job insecurity in the creative industries sector.

Insecure, casualised or long-term, sustainable employment?

This section refers to the objective conditions of creative work, to describe the context in which creative workers find themselves when entering the labour market. The indicators 'earnings', 'employment status', 'contract type' and 'working hours' represent tangible criteria for measuring the quality and sustainability of creative work. They also allow for a general comparison of the creative sector with the economy in general.

Do creative workers earn less than other workers of comparable education and skills?

Average monthly net earnings vary considerably among the three cities: €2212 (£1492) for Birmingham;[1] €1211 (£817) for Leipzig[2] and €842 (£568) for Poznan.[3] To compare income levels for our respondents, we therefore categorised income into 'below average', 'average' and 'above average' based on the average monthly income for the city.[4]

A high proportion of our sample were poorly paid and had 'below average' earnings. This was particularly the case for workers from the two former centrally controlled cities, as 24.5 per cent of Leipzig and 44.8 per cent of Poznan creative workers earned less than the average monthly income, compared with 15.6 per cent of Birmingham workers (see Table 12.2).

In Birmingham, 'self-employed' creative workers tended to have either 'below average' or 'above average' earnings compared with 'employed'

---

[1] Based on Annual Survey of Household Earnings (ASHE), 2007 income for place of work calculated using a single person's tax allowance, and less PAYE tax and national insurance contributions, for the fiscal year 2007/8 and euro rate at 1 August 2007.
[2] Based on working group 'national accounting' Germany, 2006 data, after taxes and social contribution: http://www.vgrdl.de/Arbeitskreis_VGR/ergebnisse.asp?lang=de-DE#LA-ICM (annual data divided by 12 months).
[3] Source Poznan: Main Statistical Office, Warsaw (2009), available at www.stat.gov.pl.
[4] As incomes in the survey were grouped into bands, it is only possible to give the band in which the average income lies: €2000–2499 for Birmingham; €1000–1999 for Leipzig; and €500–999 for Poznan.

Table 12.2 Respondent average monthly personal net income in €.

City	Monthly personal net income (€)		
	Below average	Average	Above average
Birmingham	15.6%	48.9%	35.6%
	(€0–1999)	(€2000–2499)	(>€2500)
Leipzig	24.5%	52.8%	22.6%
	(€0–999)	(€1000–1999)	(>€2000)
Poznan	44.8%	43.1%	12.1%
	(€0–500)	(€500–999)	(>€1000)

Source: ACRE survey, 2007 (N = 156).

workers, suggesting that while some were economically successful others were 'self-exploiting'. However, 'self-employed' workers in the Leipzig sample were financially better off than their employed counterparts: 58.3 per cent of 'self-employed' workers had 'above average' earnings compared with only 12.5 per cent of 'employed' workers and this difference was statistically significant. There was little difference between 'employed' and 'self-employed' workers in Poznan: both had high levels of 'below average' earnings and low levels of 'above average' earnings.

Although workers on 'non-permanent' contracts in all three cities were more likely to have 'below average' earnings than their 'employed' counterparts, a well-documented phenomena, potentially relating to periods of non-work between contracts (see Menger, 1999; Throsby, 2001; Towse, 2001), these differences were not statistically significant.

Finally, there was evidence of a gender earnings gap. A higher proportion of male workers in all three cities had 'above average' earnings compared with females. In Birmingham and Leipzig, females were also more likely to have 'below average' earnings, although, interestingly, this was not the case for Poznan workers.

Are creative workers in non-standard employment with less secure work contracts?

Levels of 'self-employment' and 'non-permanent' contract working in the sample were found to exceed both the EU average and the respective national averages for each city.[5]

---

[5] In 2007, total 'self-employment' rates (men and women) for EU27 countries was 16.9 per cent. Poland had an above average rate of 24.4 per cent and both the UK (13.1 per cent) and Germany (12.2 per cent) had below average rates (Eurostat LFS, 2007). The EU27 average percentage of employees with a contract of limited duration was 14.5 per cent (13.9 per cent for males and 15.2 per cent for females). The UK had one of the lowest rates

▶

Poznan had the highest proportion of 'self-employed' (31.6 per cent), followed by Birmingham (28.3 per cent) and Leipzig (19.7 per cent), a pattern corresponding with the national picture. On the other hand, Birmingham had the highest proportion of workers on 'non-permanent' contracts (52.8 per cent) compared with around a third of Leipzig and Poznan workers. This was despite the UK having the lowest rates of contract working of our three comparative cases. Not surprisingly, a substantial majority of workers who classed themselves as 'self-employed' were employed on 'non-permanent' contracts.

Levels of 'self-employment' concealed significant differences between genders, with males more likely to be 'self-employed' than females in all three cities. Although there is little research on this topic, self-employment rates for women in the creative sector do appear to be much lower than for men, at least in the UK (see Carey, 2006 and Carey et al., 2007 for a review). Birmingham had the highest proportion of female 'self-employed' (26.9 per cent), followed by Poznan (22.2 per cent) and Leipzig (15.2 per cent). However, the largest gender difference was for Poznan (11.6 per cent) while Birmingham had the smallest difference (7.6 per cent).

Surprisingly, a higher proportion of male workers were employed on 'non-permanent' contracts in both the Leipzig (42.1 per cent male and 35.5 per cent female) and Poznan (45.0 per cent male and 35.4 per cent female) samples. Birmingham had the highest proportion of females on 'non-permanent' contracts (53.8 per cent) and was the only city where this was higher than the proportion of males.

Do creative workers have longer than average weekly working hours?

The average working time in the EU27 in 2006 was 37.9 hours a week: 41.2 for men and 33.9 for women (Eurostat, 2007). Very long hours are classed as 45 hours a week or more (Eurostat, 2007). Germany had one of the lowest weekly working hours, with an average of 35.6 hours a week (40.0 for men and 30.2 for women); while Poland had one of the highest, with an average of 40.9 hours a week (43.2 for men and 38.1 for women). The UK was in the middle, with a 36.9 hour a week average (41.8 for men and 31.3 for women).

Just under half (45.1 per cent) of the respondents in our sample worked in excess of 42 hours a week. The longest working hours were for Leipzig respondents, where 55.7 per cent worked in excess of 42 hours and 15.5 per cent worked in excess of 55 hours per week, despite Germany having the

---

of contract working at 5.9 per cent (5.2 per cent for males and 6.4 per cent for females); while for Germany, the rate was very near the EU average at 14.6 per cent (males 14.7 per cent and females 14.5 per cent). Poland was well above the EU average with 28.2 per cent (28.4 per cent for males and 27.9 per cent for females) (Eurostat LFS, 2007).

lowest national average work hours according to EU statistics. Nonetheless, 40.4 per cent of Birmingham workers and 38.4 per cent of Poznan workers also worked in excess of 42 hours a week.

There was a strong link between 'working hours' and 'employment status'. In all three cities, over half of those who were 'self-employed' worked in excess of 42 hours a week. In particular, 58.3 per cent of 'self-employed' workers in Leipzig worked more than 55 hours a week. However, there was little difference in average weekly work hours for those employed on 'permanent' or 'non-permanent' work contracts.

As expected, males were more likely to work longer hours than females. Overall, an extremely high proportion (between 66.7 and 77.8 per cent) of 'self-employed' males worked above 'average' hours. This pattern was not apparent in 'self-employed' female respondents, where around a third in all three cities worked 'below average' hours.

Summary

Our analysis of the 'objective' characteristics of creative work indicates that working conditions for a large proportion of our sample were 'non-standard' and employment could be classed as 'insecure'. A high proportion of workers had lower than average earnings, were 'self-employed' or employed on 'non-permanent' contracts as well as working 'above average' weekly hours and in each city these patterns of working were more prevalent than in the economy as a whole. These findings suggest that many of the jobs within the creative sector are unsustainable. However, a common argument in the creative industries literature is that sustainability should not only be interpreted in terms of pay, contract status or work hours in general but must be seen in terms of wider 'job satisfaction', which will be addressed in the following section.

Job satisfaction: art for art's sake?

In this section, the perspective is changed to an analysis of the more subjective opinions of workers in the sample, who were asked to evaluate their satisfaction with different aspects of their job ('rates of pay', 'job security', 'career opportunities', 'networking opportunities', 'work–life balance', 'influence over own work', 'sense of achievement' and 'intellectual stimulus'). While 'overall job satisfaction' was found to be very high (90.2 per cent 'satisfied' in Birmingham; 93.1 per cent in Leipzig and 73.3 per cent in Poznan), this analysis gives us a deeper insight into the perceptions of creative jobs which might indicate their sustainability.

Table 12.3 refers to each of the measures and indicates whether there was a significant difference in findings between cities.

Table 12.3 Job satisfaction values by city; percentage 'very satisfied/satisfied'.

	Birmingham (%)	Leipzig (%)	Poznan (%)	Significance
Overall job satisfaction	90.2	93.1	73.3	0.016*
Rates of pay	47.1	43.1	48.7	0.612
Job security	49.0	58.3	55.3	0.047*
Work–life balance	74.5	60.9	47.9	0.032*
Career prospects	52.9	41.7	37.0	0.283
Networking	72.5	66.7	58.1	0.321
Influence over work	82.4	83.3	77.6	0.261
Sense of achievement	96.1	81.7	63.2	0.001*
Intellectual stimulation	94.1	77.5	56.0	0.000*

Source: ACRE survey, 2007.

Notes: * = significant difference at the 95% level.

Table 12.4 draws on the data for these same measures but refers to three categories of workers:

1 workers on permanent and non-permanent contracts;
2 employed and self-employed workers;
3 males and females.

Data is presented where there are significant differences between the percentage of workers across the three cities who indicated they were 'satisfied' with the aspect of their job in question. These results are discussed in the following sections under the different headings in turn.

Satisfaction with rates of pay

As we have already discovered, a high proportion of our sample had 'below average' weekly earnings. Not unexpectedly, satisfaction with 'rates of pay' was also very low: fewer than half of the workers in any city indicated they were 'satisfied' with this aspect of their job. Interestingly, despite a smaller proportion of workers in the Birmingham sample earning 'below average' earnings than either of the other two cities, dissatisfaction levels were much higher: 31.4 per cent of Birmingham workers were 'dissatisfied' compared with 22.2 per cent of Leipzig and 23.7 per cent of Poznan workers. This suggests that relative as well as absolute income matters to workers. Indeed, previous studies have found that an individual's happiness not only depends on their actual income but also on some reference level (Clark and Oswald, 1996). The perception of being low paid may therefore be much more important to workers in our sample than actual

Table 12.4 Job satisfaction values by country; percentage 'very satisfied/satisfied'.

	Contract status			Employment status			Gender		
	Permanent	Non-permanent	Significance	Employment	Self-employment	Significance	Male	Female	Sig
Overall job satisfaction									
Birmingham	91.7	88.9	0.383	82.5	87.0	0.074†	96.2	84.0	0.312
Leipzig	93.0	92.6	0.946	89.2	93.8	0.974	92.1	97.0	0.375
Poznan	71.1	72.0	0.851	72.5	78.1	0.816	67.4	84.6	0.218
Job security									
Birmingham	66.7	33.3	0.050*	59.5	23.1	0.060†	53.9	44.0	0.591
Leipzig	69.8	44.4	0.143	67.3	41.7	0.456	65.8	48.5	0.223
Poznan	73.7	28.0	0.001*	64.4	41.8	0.087†	49.0	66.7	0.131
Career prospects									
Birmingham	52.2	57.7	0.844	58.3	46.2	0.141	64.0	45.8	0.152
Leipzig	47.5	44.0	0.950	46.3	41.7	0.811	59.5	28.6	0.007*
Poznan	28.6	50.0	0.165	31.7	52.2	0.366	50.0	14.3	0.012*
Work–life balance									
Birmingham	79.2	70.4	0.443	75.7	71.4	0.801	65.4	84.0	0.078†
Leipzig	58.1	55.6	0.901	62.5	53.8	0.823	55.3	60.6	0.447
Poznan	52.6	48.0	0.377	57.8	39.1	0.003*	44.9	50.0	0.567
Networking									
Birmingham	62.5	81.5	0.278	61.5	84.0	0.976	73.0	71.4	0.119
Leipzig	64.1	88.0	0.085†	81.6	48.5	0.692	72.6	78.6	0.090†
Poznan	62.2	58.3	0.851	59.2	56.0	0.415	54.6	58.3	0.400
Sense of achievement									
Birmingham	100.0	92.6	0.174	97.3	92.9	0.466	96.2	96.0	0.977
Leipzig	78.6	85.2	0.033*	80.4	92.9	0.147	81.6	84.4	0.361
Poznan	63.2	52.0	0.456	62.2	62.5	0.233	63.3	63.0	0.906
Intellectual stimulation									
Birmingham	95.8	92.6	0.233	94.6	92.9	0.640	96.2	92.0	0.589
Leipzig	76.2	77.8	0.511	77.2	78.6	0.068†	81.6	75.0	0.591
Poznan	59.5	44.0	0.470	52.2	58.3	0.876	54.2	59.3	0.913

Source: ACRE survey, 2007.

Notes: * = significant difference at the 95% level. † = significant difference at the 90% level.

income itself in terms of satisfaction levels. This resonates with findings of other studies (e.g. Parent-Thirion et al., 2007).

In all three cities, satisfaction levels with 'rates of pay' were very similar for 'self-employed' and 'employed' workers. However, workers on 'non-permanent' contracts were more satisfied with their 'rates of pay' than those on 'permanent' contracts, despite being more likely to have 'below average' earnings, although these differences were not statistically significant.

Females in our sample had lower average earnings than males, so it is not surprising that in two of the three cities (Birmingham and Poznan) females indicated lower satisfaction levels. Also, in all three cities, females were more 'dissatisfied' with their 'rates of pay' than males, particularly in Birmingham, where 40.0 per cent of females were 'dissatisfied', compared with just 23.1 per cent of males.

Job security

Exposure to more 'flexible' but insecure working does seem to translate into feelings of job insecurity, as respondents indicated low levels of satisfaction with this aspect of their job. This was especially true for Birmingham workers, with only 49.0 per cent indicating they were satisfied while a quarter (25.5 per cent) indicated dissatisfaction.

Unsurprisingly, those employed on 'permanent' employment contracts were significantly more satisfied with their 'job security' than workers on 'non-permanent' contracts in two of the three cities (Birmingham and Leipzig). This corresponds to other empirical findings (see Erlinghagen, 2007, for a review). Similarly, workers who were 'self-employed' in all three cities were less satisfied and more dissatisfied with their 'job security' than those who were 'employed', and this difference was again significant for Birmingham and Leipzig workers. Birmingham workers also indicated the highest levels of dissatisfaction: 37.0 per cent of workers on 'non-permanent' contracts and 46.2 per cent of those who were 'self-employed' were 'dissatisfied'.

Although there was little difference in satisfaction levels between males and females overall, in both Birmingham and Leipzig, satisfaction levels were lower for females who had one or more children under 16 in their households compared with males who had children and also males and females with no children. This was not surprising, given that career interruptions to have children combined with greater caring responsibilities often make labour market re-entry more difficult for women. However, females with children in the Poznan sample were more satisfied than males with children or males and females without children. It is not clear why this might be, but women might be more likely to be second earners rather than 'main breadwinners' in Poznan and therefore less affected by feelings of job insecurity than women, particularly in Birmingham, where there is more of a 'dual-earner' model.

Career prospects

Overall, fewer than half the workers in our sample were 'satisfied' with 'future career prospects' in their current job. Birmingham had the highest proportion of satisfied workers (52.9 per cent) while Poznan had the lowest (37.0 per cent). Nonetheless, a high proportion of workers in all three cities expressed a neutral feeling, which may indicate that traditional views of 'career' do not play an important role in job satisfaction for creative sector workers.

Poznan was the only city where 'self-employed' workers were more satisfied than 'employed' workers with their career prospects. This was unexpected, given that one of the potential advantages of 'self-employment' is reportedly that of a 'self-managed' career. However, this may indicate the difficulty in self-employed workers structuring a career plan. Also surprising was that workers in Birmingham and Poznan employed on 'non-permanent' contracts were more satisfied with their 'future career prospects' than those on 'permanent' contracts. This may be a feature of creative work where careers are built around 'portfolios' and so moving from one job or project to the other actually enhances career prospects.

There was, however, a gender difference as female workers in all three cities were less satisfied and more dissatisfied with their career prospects than their male counterparts, perhaps reflecting their perception of the 'glass ceiling'. Overall, 29.2 per cent of females were 'dissatisfied' compared with only 7.7 per cent of males. There was a significant difference in satisfaction levels for males and females in the two central European cities, and particularly the case for Poznan workers a third (33.3 per cent) of females were 'dissatisfied' compared with only 12.5 per cent of males.

Opportunity to network and meet fellow professionals

The importance of well-functioning industry-based peer networks within the creative industries is well documented (see, for example, Leadbeater and Oakley, 1999). Networks are thought to provide the support structure which is generally lacking in the sector due to the organisation of employment around temporary, project-based working and the prevalence of 'self-employment' and freelance working. They can also enable the sharing and exchange of ideas and promote innovation; provide skills support through knowledge transfer and peer review; facilitate collaborative projects and provide access to future work thereby reducing the risk associated with working conditions in the sector. The opportunity to network with fellow professionals is therefore an important aspect for individuals in terms of sustaining their own work and employment in the creative sector.

Overall, about two-thirds of workers in the sample were satisfied with their 'networking opportunities', but there were differences between cities: while nearly three-quarters (72.5 per cent) of Birmingham workers were 'satisfied' with this aspect of their job, only 58.1 per cent of Poznan workers were satisfied. It is reasonable to suggest that the more mature creative sector in Birmingham, and to a lesser extent in Leipzig, has lead to more established networks which facilitate greater levels of interaction between creative professionals. In Poznan, networks in the city are still new and relational patterns within them have yet to intensify.

Interestingly, workers in Leipzig and Birmingham employed on 'non-permanent' contracts were more satisfied with their ability to network than those on 'permanent contracts', and this was a significant difference in the case of Leipzig workers. Conversely, there was very little difference in satisfaction levels for 'self-employed' and 'employed' workers in each of the three cities.

Women are thought to be disadvantaged in the creative sector because the reliance on personal networking after work hours is made more difficult due to greater caring and household responsibilities (McRobbie, 2002, 2004; Oakley, 2004). Furthermore, some authors have found that these networks can be exclusionary, particularly to women and ethnic minorities (see Christopherson, 2008). However, we found that female creative workers in Leipzig and Poznan were actually more satisfied than males with their 'ability to network', while satisfaction levels were similar for both genders in Birmingham. Furthermore, female workers who had children were not significantly more dissatisfied with their 'ability to network' than males who had children or respondents of either gender who did not have children.

Ability to balance work and home life

While Birmingham respondents indicated high levels of satisfaction with their 'work–life balance' (74.5 per cent 'satisfied'), workers in the other case study cities were far less satisfied with this aspect of their job. In particular, fewer than half (46.7 per cent) of Poznan workers were 'satisfied' while nearly a quarter (22.7 per cent) were 'dissatisfied'.

There was a strong relationship between satisfaction with 'work–life balance' and 'average weekly hours worked': respondents working 'above average' hours were less satisfied and more dissatisfied than those working 'average' or 'below average' hours. This was true for all three cities, but particularly Poznan, where less than a third (32.1 per cent) of those working 'above average' hours were satisfied with their 'work–life balance'. Furthermore, workers in all three cities who were 'self-employed' or employed on 'non-permanent' contracts were less satisfied than those who were 'employed' or on 'permanent' work contracts.

Although traditional models are changing with greater female labour market participation, women still account for a larger part of caring and household responsibilities than men, and are therefore more disadvantaged by long and non-standard work hours (Perrons, 2003, 2005). Satisfaction with 'work–life balance' could therefore give an indication of whether new forms of labour organisation characteristic of the creative sector make family life and work easier to combine for women. Women in Birmingham were found to be significantly less satisfied than their male counterparts. Overall, we also found that dissatisfaction with 'work–life balance' was higher for both males and females who had one or more children under 16 in their households than those who had no children. However, dissatisfaction levels were also higher for women with children than men with children, and significantly so in the case of females working in Birmingham. This indicates that traditional caring responsibilities do disproportionately influence women's perceptions regarding their ability to balance their work and private lives.

Job content

The final indicators concentrate more on the intrinsic aspects of the job. Autonomy, personal achievement and the intellectually stimulating nature of creative work are often considered key aspects in the attractiveness of creative employment, so it is an important finding that a very high proportion of workers in all three cities were satisfied with the 'amount of influence' they felt they had over their work (average of 80.9 per cent). The 'sense of achievement' from work also elicited very high rates of satisfaction for workers in Birmingham (96.1 per cent) and Leipzig (81.7 per cent) although less so for Poznan (63.2 per cent). 'Intellectual stimulus' was the final aspect of job satisfaction we examined and this also produced high satisfaction levels, particularly for workers in Birmingham (94.1 per cent) as well as Leipzig (77.5 per cent) but again, less so for Poznan (56.0 per cent). These findings are possible indicators that, despite the increased employment opportunities in the rapidly developing creative sector, the quality of creative jobs in Poznan may be quite low.

There was a consistent pattern where workers in all three cities who were 'self-employed' or employed on 'permanent' contracts indicated slightly higher levels of satisfaction with the 'influence over their work' than those who were 'employed' or on 'non-permanent' work contracts, but these differences were not significant. While Birmingham workers who were 'employed' and working on 'permanent' contracts were more satisfied with the 'sense of achievement' and 'intellectual stimulation' from their job, workers in the two central European cities who were 'self-employed' and on 'non-permanent' work contracts were generally more satisfied with these aspects of their jobs, but again these differences were not significant. Finally, there was little apparent difference in satisfaction levels between genders.

Discussion

This chapter set out to capture a number of indicators which could provide a picture of the sustainability of work and employment conditions in the creative sector in three European cities with very different labour markets. First, we asked whether creative workers were more exposed to 'precarious' and 'insecure' forms of employment than workers in other sectors. Our analysis of the 'objective' characteristics of creative work (rates of pay, employment and contract status and working hours) indicated that this was the case – working conditions for a large proportion of our sample were 'non-standard' and could be classed as 'insecure'. Many creative workers who had lower than average earnings were 'self-employed' or employed on 'non-permanent' contracts and worked 'above average' weekly hours and, in each case study city, these patterns of working were more prevalent than in the economy as a whole. These findings lend support to other studies which note higher levels of 'precarious' working conditions in the creative sector and suggest that many of the jobs within the creative sector are unsustainable.

Following our objective analysis, we looked at the more subjective opinions of creative workers concerning 'quality of work' to see if high levels of insecure employment translated into job insecurity and feelings of dissatisfaction with work. Despite the prevalence of 'precarious' working conditions, overall job satisfaction was found to be very high among workers in all three cities. To gain a more nuanced picture, we examined in detail various factors contributing to 'job satisfaction'. Respondents were least satisfied with the more extrinsic aspects of their jobs: the high number of below average earners – particularly in the two central European cities – led to high levels of dissatisfaction with rates of pay, although significantly, the perception of being poorly paid appeared to be more important than actual income itself in the case of Birmingham workers. Exposure to more 'flexible' working also translated into a feeling of job 'insecurity', especially for individuals who were employed on 'non-permanent' contracts and those who were 'self-employed'. This was particularly the case for Birmingham workers, and perhaps provides the clearest indication of the effect of 'insecure' working conditions on the psyche of creative workers.

Satisfaction with career prospects, especially for workers in the less established creative sector in Poznan, was also particularly low. However, the large number of neutral responses to this question may indicate that traditional views of career are unimportant in the creative sector. Surprisingly, Poznan was the only city where 'self-employed' workers were more satisfied with their career prospects than those who were 'employed'. This might be regarded as an unexpected finding, given that one of the potential advantages of 'self-employment' is reportedly that of a 'self-managed' career. However, this may arise from the difficulty that self-employed workers have in structuring a concrete career plan. Another counter-intuitive finding was that workers in Birmingham and Poznan employed on 'non-permanent' contracts were more satisfied with their 'future career prospects' than those on 'permanent' contracts. This may be a feature of creative work where careers are built around 'portfolios' and so moving from one job to the other actually enhances career prospects.

Overall, about two-thirds of workers in the sample were satisfied with their 'networking opportunities', but there were differences between cities. Workers in Birmingham in particular, but also in Leipzig, were more satisfied with their 'networking opportunities' than workers in Poznan. Being well integrated in industry peer networks is an important aspect for individuals in terms of sustaining their own work and employment in the creative sector. Networks provide the support structure which is generally lacking in the sector due to the organisation of employment around temporary, project-based working and the prevalence of 'self-employment' and freelance working. They are also thought to enable the sharing and exchange of ideas and promote innovation; provide skills support through knowledge transfer and peer review; facilitate collaborative projects and provide access to future work, thereby reducing the risk associated with working conditions in the sector, so this finding is significant in terms of the sustainability of employment in the creative sector. It is reasonable to suggest that the more mature creative sector in Birmingham, and to a lesser extent in Leipzig, has led to more established networks which facilitate greater levels of interaction between creative professionals. In Poznan, networks in the city are still new and relational patterns within them have yet to intensify.

Another consequence of non-standard work and employment patterns in the creative sector is the potential blurring of the boundaries between work and home life. In the literature, there are different positions concerning this aspect of creative work. On one hand, some empirical studies have demonstrated that creative workers are able to draw a line between work and home life and that freelancing and other flexible forms of working provide the potential for greater 'work–life balance' (Henninger and Gottschall, 2007). However, others stress that work patterns demanding flexibility decrease individual autonomy regarding workload and work organisation and thus threaten the balance of work and home life (Batt et al., 2001; Perrons, 2003, 2005; Pongratz and Voß, 2003; Jarvis and Pratt, 2006; Manske, 2007). From our data, it is not possible to determine whether creative work impinged on home life, but we can state that creative workers' satisfaction with 'work–life balance' appeared to decrease when they were exposed to more flexible working patterns: those working 'above average' hours, who were 'self-employed', or employed on 'non-permanent' contracts were generally less satisfied with their 'work–life balance' than those who worked 'average hours', who were 'employed' or on 'permanent' work contracts.

Nonetheless, despite lower levels of satisfaction with the extrinsic aspects of their jobs, workers appeared to be satisfied with the more intrinsic aspects of creative work. Personal autonomy, the sense of achievement from creative work, as well as the intellectually stimulating nature of creative work, are considered key aspects in the attractiveness of creative employment, so it is an important finding that these aspects elicited the highest satisfaction levels, although again, it was the case that workers in Poznan were generally less satisfied than workers in either Leipzig or Birmingham. However, this finding lends support to previous research indicating that workers in the sector value their creative freedom, the variety of (non-routine) work and the opportunity to use a wide range of their skills and talents to such an extent that they are prepared to put up with low incomes and less satisfactory employment conditions. In our research, many of the 'precarious' conditions experienced by creative workers appeared to be offset, at least to a degree, by the fundamental satisfaction of creative work.

Our third research question asked whether the more 'flexible' forms of work and employment in the creative sector lessened gender imbalances. However, we found no support of this assertion: there was evidence of a gender earnings gap, with a higher proportion of male workers in all three cities on 'above average' incomes and in two of the cities, a lower proportion of males on 'below average' incomes compared to females. Males were also more likely than females to be 'self-employed' in all three cities. Female workers were more dissatisfied with their 'rates of pay', 'future career prospects' and 'job security' than males. Finally, females who had children and caring responsibilities were more dissatisfied than males who had children – as well as females who did not have children, with their career prospects and their ability to balance their work and home life. These findings echo those of other empirical studies (see, for example, Marcella et al., 2006). It is clear that despite their potential for addressing traditional gender imbalances, the creative industries have yet to deliver. As noted by Perrons (2005), in the creative sector, old gender inequalities are currently being reproduced and new inequalities are being created. Nonetheless, female creative workers in our sample reported equally high levels of satisfaction with their sense of achievement and the influence over their work as well as their ability to network compared to their male counterparts, so it would appear that elements of creative work may balance the more negative aspects, at least for some individuals.

Finally, we wanted to know the effect of different labour market conditions on levels of 'precarious' employment in the creative sector and how this affected job satisfaction and feelings of job 'insecurity'. Although our analysis pointed to some differences between cities, these were rather complex and there was no straightforward 'East-West' pattern as we might have expected. Our objective analysis indicated that high levels of 'precarious' and non-standard work and employment were typical of creative work in all three cities, regardless of the prevailing labour market conditions, and that differences between groups of individuals ('employed' versus 'self-employed'; workers on 'permanent' versus 'non-permanent' contracts; 'males' versus 'females') were often more striking than differences between cities. Nonetheless, the overarching labour market regulation and social welfare provision in each country may have had some influence on perceived job security. For example, the UK has the least regulated labour market and the lowest social welfare provision of the three case study countries which may have accounted for workers in Birmingham who were 'self-employed' or employed on 'non-permanent' work contracts, that is those in the most precarious employment situations, being more dissatisfied with their job security than their counterparts in the more regulated labour markets of the two central European cities. However, it is also likely that what we are seeing is the result of a complex interaction of factors at a sectoral level in terms of the degree of internal regulation and sector maturity. While the creative sector in Birmingham is less regulated, it is also more firmly established in comparison with the sector in the two central European cities. Particularly for Poznan, combined with the generally more difficult economic situation as a result of the recent transition process, this means that although the creative sector may be rapidly developing and employment opportunities are present, the market is less mature, networks are largely unformed and jobs are less secure by comparison. Furthermore, as we have already discussed, our analysis of intrinsic aspects of creative employment indicated that while the quality of creative jobs in Birmingham appeared to be high, in Poznan job quality was quite low, and dissatisfaction with these aspects of creative work could in themselves be sufficient for individuals seeking employment elsewhere (Batt et al., 2001). Nonetheless, it is difficult to separate which of these influencing aspects accounts for the overall differences in our sample. Further qualitative research is required to determine the effect of each of these conditions on the quality of creative jobs.

It is clear from our analysis that the influence of individual attitudinal characteristics is as important in subjective perceptions of job satisfaction as the quality of work life itself. As we have seen, there are people who, although they may have an unstable job and low income, enjoy their work and gain personal satisfaction and a sense of achievement from their work and so may report high levels of satisfaction. A worker with an ostensibly 'good job' which is well paid and secure may similarly report a lower level of work satisfaction. Also, although most people would regard a higher paid job as more desirable, the situation with respect to working hours, for example, is less clear-cut. A 42-hour-per-week job may be too long for some people and too short for others. There is no way of knowing without asking workers how many hours they would prefer to work. Thinking of job security, the same qualification can be applied to temporary jobs: some workers want them and others do not, and so too with freelancing and self-employment. Subjective job satisfaction in our sample is also likely to be the result of an evaluation of many factors including higher level contextual factors at the macro level (labour market regulation, state social protection system, general economic climate, etc.); at the meso level, the characteristics of the sector (maturity, competitiveness, typical job tenure and employment structure, etc.); and at the micro level, individuals' own abilities, characteristics and experiences (education and skills, life stage, age, gender, coping strategies and perceptions of risk, etc.).

Conclusions

Much of the argument for promoting creative work and employment centres on the perceived benefits of 'flexible' work practices. Optimistic accounts of creative labour point to the increased possibilities and freedoms that creative workers have (less hierarchical work structures, greater autonomy, opportunities to utilise skills, freedom to choose when and where to work, self-managed career paths and better work–life balance). However, as we have seen, creative sector workers are also exposed to more 'precarious' forms of employment than the economy as a whole: low and unequal earnings, long work hours, high levels of self-employment and freelancing and non-permanent contract working, which go hand in hand with feelings of job insecurity, a lessening of work–life balance and increasing gender inequalities. In an industry where the potential for self-actualisation through work is seen as a pay-off for increased insecurity, we would argue against both the social and economic sustainability of such forms of working practices (in the context of current policies). Indeed, many others have contested this as a reason for legitimising precarious creative labour (Gill and Pratt; 2008; Neilson and Rossiter, 2008; Ross, 2008). Such practices also suggest 'a vulnerability to the current size and scale of the creative industries, particularly in the event of economic downturn' (Knell and Oakley, 2007, p. 18) adding further implications to the long-term sustainability of employment in the sector.

As we have seen, factors such as influence over work, sense of achievement and intellectual challenges do – at least partly – compensate for the precarious nature of creative work. However, it is not clear whether these positive aspects adequately counteract the negative feelings of anxiety over job insecurity and low pay, the difficulty in juggling the demands of multiple-job holding or the stress involved in constantly looking for the next job and in moving from one project and workplace to another in an industry where you are 'only as good as your last project' (Blair, 2001). The long-term social effect of working extremely long hours on relationships outside work with friends, partners and children (and how this is unevenly affected by gender) together with what these impacts might mean for long-term physical and mental well-being are also unknown (Leadbeater and Oakley, 1999; Gill and Pratt, 2008). The negative experiences – as well as the advantages – therefore need to be analysed in order to provide a complete understanding of creative work.

Finally, although the creative industries are regarded by a growing number of policy-makers as key to improving the economic performance of an increasing number of cities and regions, the insecure nature of much employment in the sector is currently not addressed in policy frameworks for the creative economy. A recent review of policy approaches to creative labour found that 'One of the principal shortcomings has been a lack of attention to the changing nature of creative work, and the measures which foster it' (Gollmitzer and Murray, 2008, p. 24). Furthermore, a 'quick scan' review of 100 creative industries policies in 18 countries (Braun and Lavanga, 2007) found that there is rarely a comprehensive long-term strategy to build the creative labour workforce or ease the adjustments to a global creative economy. Similarly, Gollmitzer and Murray (2008, p. 45) concluded that of actual policy programmes or instruments deployed, most were directed at generating GDP from creative activities. In contrast, 'social and labour policies', which require long-term investment from governments but provide no immediate and visible economic gain, were underdeveloped. Current creative economy thinking reveals an inadequate conception of the creative labour market and there is an urgent need to rethink the model of creative employment. There are issues around how social protection could be assured while acknowledging the more fluid and individual character of creative work (which also resonates more widely with the rapidly developing global 'knowledge economy'). Addressing these issues requires a broader perspective. At the macro level, labour legislation, social security, gender equality and social inclusion policies all have a role to play. At the meso level, local welfare policies and workplace arrangements are important. Consequently, some of the most advanced of the creative economy literature has called for an entire change of creative governance, and shift to notions of 'flexicurity'. This term first emerged in the Netherlands and Denmark. Presented at the EU Lisbon Summit in 2000, it is now used across Europe to encapsulate the need to reconcile the flexibility required by the 'new economy' with the job security interests of employees (see Gollmitzer and Murray, 2008, for a review).

While there is now a growing interest in the nature of work in the creative sector, there are still significant gaps in our knowledge on the extent to which 'precariousness' affects the 'quality of work' of those employed in the creative industries (and which we were not able to address in this chapter). For example, to what extent does holding a second job outside the creative sector mitigate risk by reducing earnings inequality and perceived job insecurity? At what point does the precarious nature of creative employment trigger the decision to leave the sector to seek alternative employment? The literature suggests that the self-exploitation typical of creative work is only possible when people are young, with no responsibilities for children/family, so to what degree does life-stage influence workers' perception of risk and precarity? Research is also required to uncover the real size and impact of unpaid work in these sectors. Finally, longitudinal analysis is also required to determine whether the observed differences between national labour markets remain constant over time or whether increasing convergence or divergence can be observed.

References

Batt, R., S. Christopherson and N. Rightor (2001) *Net working. Working patterns and workforce policies for the new media industry.* Washington, DC: Economic Policy Institute.

Beck, U. (2000) *The brave new world of work.* Cambridge: Polity Press.

Benhamou (2003) Artists' labour markets. In: R. Towse (ed.), *A handbook of cultural economics.* Cheltenham: Edward Elgar.

Blair, H. (2001) You're only as good as your last job: The labour process and the labour market in the British film industry. *Work, Employment and Society*, 15: 149–169.

Braun, E. and M. Lavanga (2007) *An international comparative quick scan of national policies for creative industries.* Rotterdam: European Institute for Comparative Urban Research at the Erasmus University.

Bukowski, M., P. Lewandowski, G. Koloch, et al. (2008) *Employment in Poland 2007: Security on flexible labour market.* MPRA Paper No. 14284. Institute for Structural Research, Warsaw, Poland, Ministry of Labour and Social Policy of Poland.

Carey, C. (2006) *Characteristics of creative industries entrepreneurs: A gender perspective.* ISBE 29th Annual Conference. Cardiff, November 2006.

Carey, C., L. Martin, H. Matlay and B. Jerrard (2007) *Gender and entrepreneurship in the creative industries: What does the literature tell us?* ISBE 30th Annual Conference. Glasgow.

Christopherson, S. (2002) Project work in context: Regulatory change and the new geography of the media. *Environment and Planning A*, 34: 2003–2015.

Christopherson, S. (2008) Beyond the self-expressive creative worker – An industry perspective on entertainment media. *Theory Culture and Society*, 25: 73–95.

Clark, A.E. and A.J. Oswald (1996) Satisfaction and comparison income. *Journal of Public Economics*, 61: 359–381.

Erlinghagen, M. (2007) *Self-perceived job insecurity and social context – Are there different European cultures of anxiety?* Discussion Paper No. 688. Berlin: German Institute for Economic Research (DIW).

Eurostat (2007) *European Union labour force survey – Annual results 2007.* Brussels: Eurostat.

Flores, F. and J. Gray (2000) *Entrepreneurship and the wired life: Work in the wake of careers.* London: Demos.

Florida, R. (2002) *The rise of the creative class and how it's transforming work, leisure, community and everyday life.* New York: Basic Books.

Florida, R. (2005) *The flight of the creative class: The new global competition for talent.* New York: HarperCollins.

Friebe, H. and S. Lobo (2006) *Wir nennen es Arbeit: Die digitale Bohème oder Intelligentes Leben jenseits der Festanstellung.* Munich: Heyne.

Gill, R. (2002) Cool creative and egalitarian? Exploring gender in project-based new media work in Europe. *Information, Communication and Society,* 5: 70–89.

Gill, R. (2007) *Technobohemians or the new cybertariat? New media work in Amsterdam a decade after the web. Network Notebooks.* Amsterdam: Institute of Network Cultures.

Gill, R. and A.C. Pratt (2008) Precarity, immaterial labour and the cultural industries. Annual review. *Theory Culture and Society,* 25 (7/8): 1–30.

Gollmitzer, M. and C. Murray (2008) *From economy to ecology: A policy framework for creative labour.* Vancouver: Center for Policy Studies on Culture and Communities.

Heery, E. and J. Salmon (eds) (1999) *The insecure workforce.* London: Routledge.

Henninger, A. and K. Gottschall (2007) Freelancers in Germany's old and new media industry: Beyond standard patterns of work and life? *Critical Sociology,* 33: 43–72.

Hesmondhalgh, D. (2006) Creative labour as a basis for a critique of creative industries policy. In: G. Lovink and N. Rossiter (eds), *My creativity reader: A critique of creative industries,* pp. 59–69. Amsterdam: Institute of Network Cultures.

Huws, U. (2006) The spark in the engine: Creative workers in a global economy. *Work Organisation, Labour & Globalisation,* 1 (1): 1–5.

Jarvis, H. and A.C. Pratt (2006) Bringing it all back home: The extensification and 'overflowing' of work – The case of San Francisco's new media households. *Geoforum,* 37: 331–339.

Knell, J. and K. Oakley (2007) London's creative economy: An accidental success? *Provocation Series,* 3. London: The Work Foundation.

Lash, S. and J. Urry (1993) *Economies of signs and space.* London: Sage.

Leadbeater, C. and K. Oakley (1999) *The new independents – Britain's new cultural entre-preneurs.* London: Demos.

Manske, A. (2007) *Prekarisierung auf hohem Niveau – eine Feldstudie über Alleinunternehmer in der IT-Branche.* Munich: Hampp.

Marcella, R., G. Baxter and I. Illingworth (2006) *Women in the creative industries. A research bulletin for the European Social Fund.* Aberdeen: ABS.

McRobbie, A. (1998) *British fashion design: Rag trade or image industry?* London: Routledge.

McRobbie, A. (1999) In the culture society: Art, fashion, and popular music. London: Routledge.

McRobbie, A. (2002) From Holloway to Hollywood: Happiness at work in the new cultural economy? In: P. du Gay and M. Pryke (eds), *Cultural economy.* London: Sage.

McRobbie, A. (2003) Clubs to companies: Notes on the decline of political culture in speeded up creative worlds. *Cultural Studies,* 16: 516–531.

McRobbie, A. (2004) Making a living in London's small-scale creative sector. In: D. Power and A. Scott (eds), *Cultural industries and the production of culture.* London: Routledge.

Menger, P.M. (1999) Artistic labour markets and careers. *Annual Review of Sociology,* 25: 541–574.

Menger, P.M. (2001) Artists as workers: Theoretical and methodological challenges. *Poetics,* 28: 241–254.

Menger, P.M. (2006) Artistic labor markets: Contingent work, excess supply and occupational risk management. In: Ginsburgh and Throsby (eds), *Handbook of the economics of art and culture.* Amsterdam: Elsevier/North Holland.

Neff, G., E. Wissinger and S. Zukin (2005) Entrepreneurial labor among cultural producers: 'Cool' jobs in 'Hot' industries. *Social Semiotics,* 15 (3): 307-334.

Neilson, B. and N. Rossiter (2005) From precarity to precariousness and back again: Labour, life and unstable networks. *Fibreculture,* issue 5. http://journal.fibreculture.org/issue5/ neilson_rossiter.html

Neilson, B. and N. Rossiter (2008) Precarity as a political concept, or, Fordism as exception. *Theory Culture and Society*, 25: 51–72.

Oakley, K. (2004) Not so cool Britannia: The role of the creative industries in economic development. *International Journal of Cultural Studies*, 7: 67–77.

Oakley, K. (2006) Include us out – economic development and social policy in the creative industries. *Cultural Trends*, 15: 255–273.

Parent-Thirion, A., E.F. Macías, J. Hurley and G. Vermeylen (2007) *Fourth European working conditions survey*. Luxembourg: European Foundation for the Improvement of Living and Working Conditions.

Perrons, D. (2003) The new economy and the work life balance. A case study of the new media sector in Brighton and Hove. *Gender Work and Organisation*, 10: 65–93.

Perrons, D. (2005) Gender equality and the work–life balance: Policies and practices in the new economy. In: B. Peper, A. van Doorne-Huiskes and L. den Dulk (eds), *Flexible working and organisational change. The integration of work and personal life*. Cheltenham/Northampton: Edward Elgar.

Pongratz, H.G. and G. Voß (2003) From employee to 'entreployee': Towards a 'self-entrepreneurial' work force? *Concepts and Transformation*, 8: 239–254.

Pratt, A.C. (2000) New media, the new economy and new spaces. *Geoforum*, 31: 425–436.

Reidl, S., H. Schiffbänker and H. Eichmann (2006) Creating a sustainable future: The working life of creative workers in Vienna. *Work, Organization, Labour & Globalization*, 1: 48–58.

Ross, A. (2002) No-collar: The humane workplace and its hidden costs. New York: Basic Books.

Ross, A. (2008) The new geography of work. Power to the precarious? *Theory, Culture & Society*, 25: 31–49.

Sennett, R. (1998) *The corrosion of character*. London: W.W. Norton and Co.

Throsby, D. (2001) *Economics and culture*. Cambridge, UK and New York: Cambridge University Press.

Throsby, D. (2007) Preferred work patterns of creative artists. *Journal of Economics and Finance*, 31: 395–402.

Towse, R. (1996) *The economics of the artist's labour markets*. London: Arts Council of England.

Towse, R. (2001) *Creativity, incentive and reward: An economic analysis of copyright and culture in the information age*. Cheltenham, UK: Edward Elgar Publishing.

Towse, R. (2002) Copyright and cultural policy for the creative industries. In: O. Granstrand (ed.), *Economics, law and intellectual property*. Dordrecht: Kluwer Academic Publishing.

UNCTAD (2004) Creative industries and development. *United Nations Conference on Trade and Development, São Paulo*. Geneva: United Nations.

UNCTAD (2008) Creative economy report 2008. The challenge of assessing the creative economy: Towards informed policy-making. Geneva: United Nations.

Part IV

Policies

Birmingham – New canal housing and old canal boats. Photo by CURS.

Riga – Selling the city. Photo by Evita Dzanuskane.

13

What Policies Should Cities Adopt?

Alan Murie and Sako Musterd

Introduction

The previous chapters of this book have set out the importance of the development of the creative and knowledge-based economy for the recent and future development of European cities. They have emphasised that very different cities all exhibit some evidence of growth in these parts of the economy but that the pattern of growth is uneven: it is uneven in terms of what importance these sectors have achieved, in the rate of growth and in the relative importance of creative or knowledge-based activity or indeed the particular sectors that comprise these. In explaining these patterns of similarity and difference, particular reference has been made to path dependency and the histories of cities: capital cities and cities with strong educational traditions have been well placed to develop activities in these areas but other factors have also been identified – cities have built on international fairs and particular traditions in terms of craft and skilled work, tolerance and supportive environments for small and innovative businesses. Most of the accounts of development also feature the role of state intervention to affect various drivers of change in each city. Many aspects of the historical path have been influenced by government, and the final section of this book addresses the importance of government intervention and the role of governance and policy in the future development of the creative and knowledge economy.

What should cities do?

Much of the debate about the creative city has fuelled the development of creativity strategies and both Florida's work and critiques of it (e.g. Peck,

2005) attest to its influence on city leaders. Florida's contributions have emphasised that traditional economic development strategies based on the provision of incentives and premises to attract companies would not be effective when the key to building the creative city is nurturing and attracting talent. In his view, talent is more mobile than other factors of production and this presents a new challenge for policy and government. Florida consequently recommends that cities should invest in creativity (especially to tap the full creative capabilities of everyone through investing in the creative infrastructure, improving higher education and stimulating research and development activity), building a people climate aimed at attracting and retaining people (by remaining open to newcomers and to diversity, improving environmental quality and sustainability and improving amenities that are valued by people rather than companies) and building social cohesion (by managing inequality and diversity). Florida argues that in order to bolster a city's ability to compete for talent, it will need an approach that is tailored to its distinctive character, but it would particularly reflect analysis of its capacities in relation to technology, talent and tolerance. The outcome would be to identify strategic investments needed to address weaknesses in these, to increase openness and to provide lots of options that appeal to lots of different contributors of talent (Florida, 2005, pp. 53–54).

And the outcome of this will not be that all cities converge on a common 'Creative City' profile. Rather they will find distinctive niches, partly related to past economic strengths – the pathways referred to earlier in this book. But in order to establish and develop niches, cities have to attract and retain people whose skills and creativity they depend upon. While the strategies adopted might not be all the same they would all focus on what is needed to attract what he refers to as the creative class. It is this emphasis on the creative class and how to attract it that has generated most criticism. The various evidence we have presented elsewhere in this book casts doubt on this representation of those who work in the creative and knowledge-intensive city. At best the high earning, footloose urbanites described by Florida form a small fraction of the workers in these parts of the economy and at worst they represent a misleading caricature. Creativity strategies that put the attraction of this group at the heart of policy are bound to be deficient if they involve chasing chimeras. And they open such strategies to ridicule as modern versions of cargo cults and open to criticisms of being preoccupied with an elite, ignoring other citizens and forming part of a neo-liberal agenda dependent on trickle down (Peck, 2005).

Whatever its shortcomings Florida's contribution should not be dismissed out of hand. Florida asserts the importance of place – of cities and regions rather than countries. Because of their ability to harness creativity and foster innovation, cities have become increasingly important and 'In contrast to predictions that technology – from the telephone and the automobile to the computer and the Intranet – would lead to the death of cities the creative economy is taking shape less around national boundaries and industrial sectors and more around cities…' (Florida, 2005, p. 161). 'Place is the factor that organically brings together the economic opportunity and talent, the jobs and the people required for creativity, innovation, and growth' (Florida, 2005, p. 161). But there are contradictions even here. His concern about the availability of visas for highly skilled workers wishing to enter the USA points to the importance of national policy as well as local and although he asserts the merits of a generic view of place that asserts the interaction and interdependency between attributes and emphasises their interconnectedness he enthusiastically uses indexes that are based on quantification of assorted characteristics of cities. While there may be a role for a creative strategy that embraces the kinds of activities that Florida emphasises, the weaknesses of his analysis mean that this should not be the main or even most important part of strategies to build a sustainable creative and knowledge-intensive industry within any city.

European cities

This book has emphasised the distinctive legacies and histories associated with European cities and has highlighted the variation within the broad church that comprises people working in the creative and knowledge-based economy. It has questioned the value of the idea of a creative class and suggested instead that those working in a growing creative and knowledge-intensive industry are in different positions in terms of class, status, power, point in their life cycle and career. It has highlighted the development pathways associated with different cities and the perspectives and career paths of individuals in different parts of the broad church. Hall's (2004) sceptical view of the capacity of many cities to become creative cities is self-fulfilling if the definition of what is a creative city is exclusive enough. But in the terms used in this book Hall's view is unjustified – a wide range of cities can build on different strengths to develop creative and knowledge-intensive industry. At the same time, Hall's view of the extended timescales needed to develop the creative city or even to strengthen existing creative activity is hard to dispute. Policies need to be sustained over long periods and beyond the memory and period of office of many politicians and individual civic leaders.

If the history of cities is of importance, their age and the numbers of waves of economic development have affected the nature of each city and its assets. Older cities often have stronger traditions and practices of government intervention at local, regional and national levels than apply in younger cities, and present-day practice remains varied: the institutional forms, organisations, networks and politics that shape the governance of cities differ between cities and between countries and continents. A particular difference may exist between Europe and America. In Europe the very existence of national boundaries and differences in citizenship rights and responsibilities, even where free movement of labour applies, adds a potential barrier to entry that is not so evident in the USA. Stronger interventionist traditions associated with municipal government and the welfare state are also likely to affect the European experience. The policy areas that may affect the attractiveness of cities and regions are not just those related to economic development or creativity strategies or even the wider related areas including planning and housing. Rather they relate to wider regulation and intervention in labour markets, controls over immigration, citizenship rights, taxation and welfare provision. In view of this the caution against any simplistic universal strategy to bolster a city's ability to strengthen its creative and knowledge-based economy is particularly appropriate. If the task also relates to competing targets in different parts of the city's economy, rather than simply to some imagined creative class, there are uncomfortable and competing alternatives that will achieve different levels of support from within the diverse actors in the creative economy and outside it.

Notwithstanding this view the evidence in this book suggests a different framework for policy debate than proposed by Florida. This would relate to national, regional and local interventions and to mainstream policy activities as well as those labelled as economic development or creative. Policies related to immigration and citizenship rights are critical parts of the openness of the economy and society and the barriers to entry. Policies towards higher education are critical to the growth of skills and capacity, the attraction and retention of highly qualified workers and the sustainability of the city's economy. And policies that enable ordinary households in different occupations to access opportunities are more likely to hold households whose personal lives already provide reasons to stay in the city. In this way, whether or not the strategies to build and sustain the creative city include a superstructure of amenities and services specifically concerned with groups within different parts of the creative economy, the overarching strategy needs a firm bedrock related to basic rights and opportunities. There is a need to mainstream the agendas about 'classic' conditions, education, openness and diversity rather than to see them as special initiatives. And there is a need to directly address issues of social inequality rather than accept this as inevitable or to rely on trickle down.

Even in this context there are difficult choices for each city especially in relation to more specific questions. Should government back off and leave some or all of the creative economy to generate the environment they are comfortable with? Should it seek to engineer a creative future for the city by targeting firms and activities in selected sectors and using financial and other incentives to attract them? Should government invest in education to stimulate talent generally or should it focus on art, drama and design or other areas of study that directly feed into the creative professions? Should it seek to attract talent from other cities and countries through providing educational and other facilities and if it is to do this successfully how does it effectively lower barriers to entry? If 'networking' and 'partnership' are regarded as of key importance, how can that be facilitated? And, if government should focus on amenities, what are the arguments for supporting high profile flagship arts projects or low profile 'underground' networks and venues that are open and accessible and can be shaped by their users?

Which policy agendas?

Much of the debate about policies to facilitate the development of the creative knowledge economy naturally focuses on economic development policy. However, as the discussions elsewhere in this book have made clear, the factors that are relevant both for firms and for individuals are not restricted to this sphere. The hard factors referred to include important elements of taxation and regulation of businesses and for individuals issues related to citizenship rights and border controls are evident. A review of whether policies are conducive to the development of the creative knowledge economy would therefore include but not be restricted to policies directly relating to economic development. It would refer to policies that relate to and help shape the hard and soft factors and the clusters and personal networks that are important for different actors. It would relate to regulation and taxation of businesses (including special incentives for business set-up or relocation), labour market regulation, immigration controls and the registration of residence and individual taxation. It would also relate to representation and influence and the processes of planning and decision-making in public services and the way they impact on other sectors at a local, regional and national level. As the earlier chapters of this book have indicated it would also relate to housing provision and affordability and to other factors affecting the quality of life from the effectiveness of welfare rights and provision to the quality of neighbourhoods and environment to the quality of leisure and cultural activities (the arts, music, museums and galleries, prestige events, visitor attractions, festivals and exhibitions). The issues closer to economic development policy include transport, planning and infrastructure development, education and training and higher education, the development of science parks and support for research and development activity. Finally the core economic development activities at national, regional and local levels include those related to the provision, quality and costs of premises, city marketing, business advice and support, the promotion and development of creative quarters and prestige projects. An important part of these policies especially at a city level are activities that provide opportunities to showcase and market products and services and that help to build linkages and collaboration between businesses to operate more effectively and stimulate innovation and new products through joint working. While activities that relate to premises and physical planning are important, the less tangible activities associated with and stimulating partnership working and networks are also critical.

Networking policy

Associational working, clustering, co-operation and partnership are all recognised as important elements in successful city economies. Businesses compete but are also better able to respond to some market opportunities by joining forces and combining expertise. This emphasis on bringing individuals and organisations together poses a challenge. If government at different levels is to provide the environment which enables individuals, individual businesses and groups of businesses to prosper it will need to balance listening and learning with leading and this is also a challenge for others contributing to the wider governance of cities and regions. The dilemmas about leading or listening, engineering or enabling have been identified elsewhere in discussion of leadership of place. Economic development policy has shifted from a linear project management task involving land, infrastructure, construction and the attraction of firms towards a more holistic, integrated project to develop collaborative networking and innovation, knowledge and institution building. So the leadership task has changed. For example, Gibney et al. (2009) have argued that in the knowledge-based economy leadership of place involves leading and holding together a consortium of potentially separate interests that shape place. This presents a challenge that is very different from leading a single organisation.

This perspective connects with the arguments about policies to develop the creative economy. What is involved is the integration of what have often been seen as separate economic, social, environmental and political activities; and the development of new ways of working and networking. These involve building relationships and associational working. The key processes are characterised by interdependency, reciprocity and the pooling of resources over an extended period of time. The process of knowledge creation and exploitation are themselves dependent on the performance of cross-boundary networks and development of holistic approaches. Traditional hierarchical leadership and professional project management skills are likely to be insufficient if not counterproductive when what is needed is the skill to work with others, to lead in developing an understanding and finding an effective route through the competing alternatives (of the type referred to above) while holding all stakeholders' commitment to the place-shaping project. The skills needed are more relational and favour association, interaction and collaboration between individuals, institutions, firms and community level groups. The leadership of place in the context of the creative city needs to maintain trust between followers and other collaborating leaders. This is an inclusive, open and equitable trust that is very different from the blind-trust associated with charismatic or managerialist leadership operating within a hierarchical, unitary, organisational context. Managerialist leadership is not associated with cross or overlapping boundaries of interest beyond the unitary organisation and different tasks and skills are required when the most important elements of place shaping involve maintaining and renewing the trust, commitment to place and enthusiasm of a diverse set of individuals and organisations that could choose to move away. In their Birmingham case study, Gibney et al. (2009) refer to leadership that finds that it is having to 'lead leaders' without any formal power whilst at the same time having to navigate multiple boundaries. The challenges involved 'are about promoting collective endeavour, interdisciplinarity, and cross boundary working and sustaining all of this over a long period of time' (Gibney et al., 2009, p. 19).

The following chapters

The chapters in this section refer to the experience of policy in different European cities and address different aspects of the issues discussed above. They are, however, forward looking referring to the challenge related to the development of the creative city now and in the future. The common thread in these chapters relates to the challenges involved in fostering the development of the creative economy and how these have changed since earlier phases of economic development associated with the attraction or expansion of other parts of the economy. In the earlier phases of economic development, there were various well tested strategies, adopted at different levels of government, based on providing sites and services and incentives aimed at footloose industry as well as facilitating training and retraining the labour force. Economic development models, strategies and practices pursued by local and central government may sometimes still reflect past experience. Organisational arrangements and practices may often be legacies of the past. If they reflect their origins in an earlier economic environment they may be inappropriate or fail to obtain the response intended. Creative knowledge industry has different needs than manufacturing industry and within the creative sector there are a range of distinctive demands. Some parts of the creative sector may shy away from support from government and may see some or all forms of support as suffocating or inhibiting creativity. These parts of the creative sector are more used to, and more inclined to favour, self-generating activity and may not respond so well to formal funding and other mechanisms that grow out of the experience of supporting manufacturing. These parts of the creative economy may be suspicious of government and in some cases the absence of a high profile, overt or visible policy may be the best environment for the sector. If there is to be a strategy it may adopt a laissez faire approach providing a loose framework and encouraging innovation and variation. And in any event policy and leadership of policy in this area requires a responsive, flexible and fluid approach. The challenge is to develop approaches in an environment that is uncertain and complex and where trust has to be won and retained.

The material presented in these chapters enables questions about the role of governance and government to be addressed at different levels and using different cities to highlight the questions involved. Chapter 14 refers to the different strategic approaches put in place in Toulouse, Milan and Dublin when the development of creative and knowledge-based economic activity became a target for government. It highlights the differences in approaches adopted and some of the reasons for this and concludes that there is now some limited convergence in approaches. Chapter 15 refers to the cluster based or sectoral strategies and the wider education/planning-based strategies that were strongly promoted as building capacity and critical mass and fostering collaboration in order to increase competitiveness at local and regional levels. It refers to the alternative visions and content of policy in Birmingham, Poznan and Helsinki, and discusses the limitations of this approach. Chapter 16 reflects upon the experience of Amsterdam, Munich and Budapest and whether the policies they have pursued have been effective. It considers the experience of policies directed at individuals (emphasising soft conditions) and those more directed at firms and using hard incentives and highlights the lack of integrated policies. Finally Chapter 17 broadens the discussion to address the view that a new approach to governance is emerging and needs to be further developed if approaches relevant to the creative knowledge city are to be adopted. The record of policy towards creative sectors is poor and this partly derives form a traditional top-down policy approach that is unattractive to a sector that values creativity and independence. Ultimately this becomes a question about the style of intervention, whether government has any role in bolstering the growth of the creative economy and how it works with different professions and people.

Taken together these chapters highlight the dilemmas and challenges involved in developing appropriate strategies for creative cities. They reinforce the argument that strategies need to take account both of past economic development and the strengths and weaknesses of what cities have to offer in attracting and retaining people who work in the creative sector. They reinforce the cautions about seeking to transfer any model from elsewhere or seeking some universal approach. And they fit with a view that cities will develop distinctive niches and will not converge on some universal creative city model. In general the strategies and policies adopted by cities address part rather than all of the range of policies impacting on competitiveness. They are still closer to traditional economic development policies rather than holistic development approaches. While they address networks they are more centred on hard factors with a stronger emphasis on property, places and premises than on the wider issues associated with urban conditions.

Consistent with the general evidence in this book, these chapters suggest that the strategies adopted by different cities have to be sensitive to the variety that exists within the wide term 'creative'. In some parts of this the desire to escape constraints that could inhibit creativity means that there is a nervousness about entering full-time employment; freelance status is regarded as essential to the integrity of artistic freedom. In other parts people work within hierarchical career structures and some decisions about where they work relate to this. The variation and complexity is not easily captured in some formula that translates into a strategy that would enable all of the flowers to bloom and it is an illusion to seek such a formulaic solution. Rather the policy community has to deal with complexity and be willing to respond and adapt. Flexibility, fluidity and awareness of shifting agendas will be strong resources in delivering policy; and those involved in shaping the places where creative activity flourishes will need skills that match the complexity of the task and enable them to decide when to stand back as well as when to rush in.

References

Florida, R. (2005) *The flight of the creative class.* New York: Harper-Collins.

Gibney, J., S. Copeland and A. Murie (2009) Toward a 'new' strategic leadership of place for the knowledge-based economy. *Leadership,* 5: 5–23.

Hall, P. (2004) Creativity, culture, knowledge and the city. *Built Environment,* 30 (3): 256–258.

Peck, J. (2005) Struggling with the creative class. *International Journal of Urban and Regional Research,* 29 (4): 740–770.

14

Strategic Economic Policy: Milan, Dublin and Toulouse

Silvia Mugnano, Enda Murphy and Hélène Martin-Brelot

Introduction

This chapter compares three European cities with well-established and successful creative and/or knowledge-based economies – Milan, Dublin and Toulouse. However, each economy has different sectoral strengths and has different associated historical development paths and economic trajectories developed over varying time periods. As the national capital of Ireland, Dublin possesses several conditions that are only partly present in the regional capitals of Lombardy and Midi-Pyrénées. Dublin's economic growth in both creative and knowledge sectors has been significant in the past two decades (Murphy and Redmond, 2009); Toulouse's development relies mainly on knowledge-based activities such as aeronautics, space and electronics; Milan's success in the creative industries occurred over a prolonged period of time. Over the centuries Milan has gained national primacy by becoming the financial, economic, innovative and creative capital of Italy.

Milan and Dublin are somewhat different from Toulouse in that the former cities are well known internationally as economic decision-making centres as well as prominent historical and cultural centres. Moreover, Toulouse does not possess the same commercial influence as Dublin or Milan, where the strength of financial and business services also stems from export-oriented economic policies. On the other hand, by managing to avoid the full brunt of industrial restructuring such as that which occurred in Milan in the late 1980s and early 1990s, the French and Irish cities share an early service profile and demonstrate active innovation and technology policies, relatively good governance arrangements and well-equipped financial and organisational resources.

The number of individuals employed in the creative sectors, especially advertising, architecture and recreational services differ from one city to another with 21,000 employees in these sectors in Toulouse in 2005, 250,890 in Milan (2001) and 122,724 in Dublin (2004). Individuals employed in the knowledge sectors (Law, Information Communication Technology (ICT), Finances, R&D and higher education) also vary between the cities. These three cities have quite different past economic trajectories. Milan's regional economy is deep rooted in history with the economy of Toulouse being somewhat younger, while the development of Dublin's economy has been more recent, at least in international terms.

Bearing the foregoing in mind, the central aim of this chapter is to investigate the various policy approaches adopted in each city in the recent past and assess whether different approaches have laid the foundations for greater economic success in the creative and knowledge sectors of the economy. Moreover, the chapter also assesses whether past policy traditions and economic specialisms in each city should continue to be the focus of economic development policy in the future or whether there is some degree of convergence between the cities in terms of recent policy initiatives being adopted within the context of increased global competition.

Distinctive policy traditions

Milan's early industrial heritage was concerned primarily with iron and steel making, electricity production and developing mechanical industries. In the contemporary period, diversification and specialisation are significant features of Milan's regional economy. Exports from the region are driven mainly by creative industries such as fashion and design (including automotive design), furniture and accessory goods sectors as well as advertising. The city is also Italy's main financial centre. The *Borsa di Milano* is one of the largest European stock exchanges, with 282 listed companies and average daily trade of approximately €4.2 billion. This has positive impacts on financial services industries such as business consultancy and legal services. The financial district also attracts industries in the creative sectors: radio and television enterprises are located there together with more than 700 publishing companies (21 per cent of the national total).

As a consequence of industrial restructuring in the 1980s and 1990s, manufacturing activities have relocated from the central area to more peripheral locations in the suburbs. Political strategies aimed at regional economic development have been implemented only recently and each sector has had to reorganise considerably. At the regional level, the increasingly important role of meta-districts allows specialised enterprises and research centres to link together on a thematic basis. For example, targeting of investment in the healthcare sector has enhanced the competitiveness of local biotechnology sectors.

Turning to the Irish case, prior to the 1960s, Dublin's economy was predominantly agricultural and manufacturing based. The city's economic evolution reflects a strongly interventionist policy adopted by the state to reorient Ireland's economy towards high-technology, knowledge-based industries such as information technology, biotechnology and financial services. Additionally, in response to the recession of the 1980s, the Irish government favoured an innovative governance approach that contributed to the generation of a stable labour relations environment while also providing the country with a competitive edge for attracting foreign direct investment (FDI). Supporting small and medium sized enterprises (SMEs), developing reliable telecommunications and transportation infrastructure and favouring the proximity of new industries to universities and colleges have been some of the pillars of recent economic policy. However, rapid economic growth has not benefited all citizens and those benefiting from recent prosperity have not done so equally. In fact, after years of continued economic growth, many of Dublin's inner city areas continue to suffer from high unemployment as well as physical and social deterioration.

In terms of population and employment growth, Toulouse is currently one of the most dynamic French urban regions. Since the early 1900s, the city's development has been driven by education and research and an early specialisation in electricity. Toulouse's profile as a technopolis – specialising in aeronautics, the space sector, electronics and computer activities – is a result of both public and private sector interests. State policy has been crucial for the decentralisation of space activities (1950–1975) and also for encouraging co-operation between companies and academic institutions from the 1980s onwards. Local social networks and private companies have also played a key role in shaping Toulouse as a knowledge-intensive regional centre. The emergence of spin-off enterprises from laboratories and technological service firms in software engineering, information storage, artificial intelligence, communications and biotechnology demonstrates the city's evolution towards a 'local competency system' where most of the highly qualified workforce hails from the local academic system. Though creative industries have never been dominant, culture is being considered increasingly as part of a local urban strategy. However, critical issues remain, including concern over the agglomeration's sprawl as well as issues surrounding social segregation and functional specialisation.

The foregoing discussion has stressed the similarities and differences between Dublin, Milan and Toulouse for creative and knowledge industries in terms of their respective positions in the national and international hierarchy. The following sections outline the three separate models implemented by policymakers in each city. While Milan has adopted a bottom-up non-interventionist economic strategy, Dublin's has been a top-down highly interventionist strategic economic policy approach and Toulouse has targeted strategic economic policy focusing on selected economic sectors. Finally the chapter reflects upon the implications of trends in policy in each of these cities.

Existing strengths in creative knowledge policy

While the development of Dublin and Toulouse have been heavily influenced by top-down state-led policy initiatives the development of the creative sector in Milan has been considerably more bottom-up and direct policy initiatives have been lacking at least until very recently. Even though Dublin and Toulouse seem to have followed rather similar development paths, the two cities present some striking differences and some common elements can also be identified with development in Milan.

The first important dimension to be explored relates to the *time frame* of policy implementation. The period in which strategic economic policies were implemented is rather different in the three case studies and thus offers a possible explanation for the varying phases of economic growth in each city. Although the creative and knowledge industries have developed more or less simultaneously, the policy approaches leading to development did not.

The longest tradition of policy intervention can be found in Toulouse where the emergence of strategic economic policies promoting the growth and development of the Urban Area of Toulouse (UAT) can be traced back to the late nineteenth century. In 1870, the establishment of the Third Republic brought with it a restructuring of the French higher education system whereby, in the 1880s, universities gained considerable autonomy. At that time, many local academics and researchers saw electricity as a leading future technology. With significant financial support from the local municipality, Toulouse became an important academic centre for this specialisation. To some extent at least, this laid the skills foundation for the subsequent emergence of the early aeronautics industry. Indeed, between 1950 and 1970, state policies driven by the local Préfecture led to the further development of already existing research institutes in automatics as well as transferring aeronautical and space activities to Toulouse. In 1955, the Laboratory for Electrical Engineering of Toulouse was established by splitting the laboratory for industrial electricity founded in 1907. This laid the foundation for the future establishment of the Laboratory for Automatics and System Analyses (LAAS) in 1967. In addition, a university centre for numerical calculation was established in 1957 (see Grossetti, 1995). The National Centre for Space Studies (CNES) was transferred from Paris to Toulouse in 1968. In addition, the 1960s saw the creation of a National Office for Aeronautical Studies and Research (ONERA) and a National Institute for Applied Sciences (INSA), both located in Toulouse. This created a dual focus for industrial activity. The emergence and growth of these activities was facilitated, in no small measure, by the decentralisation of related education institutes from Paris to Toulouse over the same period. The National School of Civil Aviation, the National Higher School of Aeronautics and the National Higher School for Aeronautical Engineering were all transferred from Paris to Toulouse in the1960s. In effect, the state played a highly significant role in directing the growth of the computer and electronics industry as well as the aeronautics and space industries.

From the mid-1970s until the end of the millennium, state policy tended to focus on enhancing co-operation between academic research institutes and industry in an attempt to enhance the competitiveness of the aeronautics, space and computer industries. Several spin-off industries were created as a result of this marriage of public and private sectors interests. In the computer industry for example, the rise of high-tech industries fed the development of a number of service companies including software engineering, information storage, artificial intelligence and communication (see Scott and Zuliani, 2006). Moreover, the progressive establishment of companies specialised in integration, assemblage and testing of satellite decks for the space industry gave rise to a number of large private industries such as SPOT Image and CLS Argos (Zuliani, 1999). At the same time, many small ancillary companies were established to service the needs of a growing aeronautical sector, particularly Airbus. Thus, state policy until the turn of the millennium tended to focus specifically on the development of the UAT as a knowledge-based region.

In Dublin, the shift in economic ideals from protectionism to liberalisation over the last 50 years has been remarkable. The move coincided largely with Ireland's applications to join the European Economic Community (EEC) in 1961 and 1967 (Fitzgerald, 2000). Since the abandonment of protectionism, and with entry into the EEC in 1973, the focus of economic policy has been to attract FDI as a means of stimulating economic growth. Since the 1990s, the focus of economic policy has been to target industries associated with high-income jobs in the knowledge sectors of the economy. In this regard, Dublin has become a major financial services centre in recent years, helped in no small measure by low rates of corporation tax and a lax regulatory environment. In effect, Dublin's economic development over the last 50 years has been characterised by a high degree of state policy intervention.

In contrast to both Toulouse and Dublin, until recently Milan has adopted a non-interventionist policy approach towards regional economic development. Although Milan has been a national cultural and innovative centre since the nineteenth century, this is more as a result of organic bottom-up enterprise development rather than direct policy intervention.

Looking specifically at media and popular culture, it is important to underline the historical performance of Milan in this area. Since the beginning of the nineteenth century, Milan has been one of the most innovative centres of Italian literature, hosting the ground-breaking group of artists – 'scapigliatura' and has been home to the headquarters of several newspapers including the *Corriere della Sera*. At the beginning of the 1950s, half of Italian publishing enterprises (including Treves, Sonzogno and Hoepli, Mondadori, Rizzoli, Bompiani and Garzanti) were located in Milan. In the same period, other important 'cultural cities' such as Rome, Florence and Turin slowly lost their importance and Milan became the unquestioned media city of Italy. Much of Milan's economic success, particularly in the creative sector during 1950s–1980s, was in this way a result of independent entrepreneurial activity with little state intervention and almost a complete absence of industrial innovation policy.

Indeed, the early development of Milan's specialisation of small to medium sized industries, specialising in areas such as textiles, furniture, fashion and design, cannot be attributed to policymaking at the national or regional level. One of the reasons for this pattern is that the new economic and social changes have emerged in a period of political stalemate. In the early 1990s, a massive corruption scandal (Tangentopoli) was uncovered at all levels of political activity (Municipal, Provincial and Regional) with many senior politicians either removed from office or imprisoned. Since then, a political and institutional vacuum has existed with little integration in terms of economic or social policy between the various stakeholders in the wider metropolitan region. Ultimately, this led to a lack of political leadership in Milan for a considerable period of time. This in turn served to exacerbate the problem of weak governance in the metropolitan region. Indeed, relative to other cities in Italy, for example Turin, the Milanese authorities were slow to react to economic restructuring in the form of de-industrialisation during the 1980s and early 1990s.

The time frame of policy implementation seems to be strongly related to the policy model adopted each city. In each case it is important to explore the relationship between the State (either central or local government) and the private sector. Improving governance is a crucial step for assisting deprived individuals in society and ensuring all individuals and localities participate in economic growth. In this regard, Dublin's barriers to more inclusive governance come from the highly fragmented administrative districts within the region. As a consequence of a laissez-faire approach in Milan, public institutions have little influence over the various sectors and often favour corporate interests over the interest of the general public. In a similar manner to Dublin, the lack of a single administrative management unit operating at the scale of the UAT poses a serious obstacle for broad-based strategic policy implementation.

New strategic economic policy approaches

In the early 1990s, urban policies in Europe were influenced by a number of different factors. There was an attempt to connect the governance paradigm (Rhodes, 1987, p. 43) to a precise territorial environment and integrate the economic, political, social and technological changes that were occurring in European cities in a single interpretative grid. Or, as Le Galès (2002) asserts, European cities started to develop the ability to integrate and to give some form to local interests, organisations and social groups. At the same time, all European governments were undergoing a process of *Europeanisation* which promoted a process of multi-level or multi-layered governance (Marks, 1992, 1993; Scharpf, 1994; Hooghe, 1996). Since the emergence of the European Union (EU) in 1957 and especially since the Maastricht Treaty's convergence criteria were put into practice, the relationships between different levels of government and the traditional responsibilities assumed by the state have changed. The multi-level governance approach stresses the changes in European governance and the importance of the policy networks between the different levels of governance, without asserting the decline of the nation-state.

Within these general trends, our three cities each represents a different policy model for promoting the creative and knowledge-intensive sector.

Milan can be characterised as having a *bottom-up strategy* with little policy intervention. Despite this, and in the absence of clear policy directives, specific economic clusters have emerged in textiles, furniture, fashion and design. Institutionally, the region is highly fragmented. Its economic vibrancy is related to private entrepreneurship rather than to strategic policy. The role of public bodies has been to co-ordinate and bring together the individual actors within the economic system. At the regional level, the Lombardy Region has been active in promoting collaboration between local industries, universities and research institutes in an attempt to stimulate innovation in the creative and knowledge sectors, particularly in emerging industries such as biotechnology and ICT but also in Milan's core industries of fashion and design (Mingione et al., 2007). Furthermore, the regional strategy also sought to reinforce the clustering of industry within specific meta-districts within the region in an attempt to promote synergy and innovation within clusters. In Lombardy, industrial districts are a very important element in economic organisation. In 1991, Italy implemented a law to regulate and support industrial districts and Lombardy established criteria to identify and finance industrial districts.

While the regional authority of Lombardy holds the key to political and financial decision-making, the Province of Milan is playing an increasingly active role in the creation and promotion of a strategy for the future of the metropolitan area. Indeed, from 1999 onwards, a series of strategic plans have emerged aiming to bridge the gap between the EU discourse on innovation and the seeming lack thereof in the Milan area. The initial plan (1999–2001), which was part-financed by the EU, designed and promoted a strategic framework for industrial innovation and technology transfer. Subsequent plans have a rather different focus within the broader economic development framework. The overarching aim of the strategic plan was to provide a framework for fostering innovation and a knowledge economy as well as promoting better governance arrangements within the province. For example, the second strategic plan gave special attention to the role of so-called incubators, in which start-up companies could be housed and receive support and assistance. In particular, the Province of Milan established virtual networks to promote inter-sector policies related to the knowledge and creative sectors of the regional economy. However, a major drawback of the plans lies in the fact that they were extremely short term in scope (normally 2–3 years) which made the development of a coherent long-term economic strategy extremely difficult.

Aside from these policies, the local context is also important as the most recent policy initiatives have been at the local level. They revolve around the city of Milan's bid to host EXPO 2013 with the proposed theme focused on tradition, creativity and innovation in the food sector. Clearly then, attempts are also being made at the local level to engage more pro-actively in raising the city's profile at the global level.

The second model – Dublin – demonstrates *top-down highly interventionist strategic policymaking.* State policy interventions, de-industrialisation and global economic restructuring were crucial for the evolution of Dublin's modern economy from a predominantly agricultural and manufacturing economic base in the 1980s to one that is now service-oriented. During this period, much of the FDI in the Dublin region involved branch-plant multinational manufacturing operations characterised by low-skill assembly and low-wage workers. Competition from emerging economies in Asia highlighted the extreme vulnerability of the national economy to this type of economic base. The result was that since the early 1990s, economic policy focused firmly on establishing Ireland as a knowledge economy by attracting FDI multinational service-based industry focusing on high-skill and high-wage job creation. This change in direction was brought about by the publication of the Culliton Report on industrial policy in 1992. The report had a wide-ranging impact on subsequent policy formulation. In particular, there was increased recognition of the need to attract new emerging international growth sectors including ICT, pharmaceuticals and international financial services, as well as the need to encourage greater links between university and industry. Indeed, subsequent repositioning of Ireland on the global market placed emphasis on Dublin's perceived strengths. These included achieving recognition as a high-skill, low-taxation, low-cost gateway for FDI to EU markets with minimal regulatory and planning restrictions (Redmond et al., 2007). The establishment of the International Financial Services Centre (IFSC) in the heart of Dublin deserves particular attention. Since it was established in 1987, Ireland has become a leading player in financial services on the international stage. In fact a recent report has ranked Dublin above Paris and Amsterdam in a compilation of global financial services centres (Yeandle et al., 2008).

In 1999, the Irish Council for Science, Technology and Innovation (ICSTI) produced Technology Foresight Ireland, a report which, among other things, devised possible scenarios in relation to the development of the ICT and biotechnology sectors in Ireland and recommended certain courses of action for policy implementation. Specific reference was made to the development of a biotechnology cluster and a Centre for Advanced Informatics. The report emphasised the development of strong links with other emerging core areas of expertise including universities and the financial services sector. This initiative resulted in the consolidation of employment within the ICT sector as well as attracting high-end employment in research and development (R&D) in the biotechnology sector.

More recently, the National Development Plan (2000–2006) was heavily influenced by the Technology Foresight Ireland report with its focus on upgrading the innovation capacity of the Irish economy by investing in the hard and soft infrastructure of the country. Similar rhetoric can be found in the current National Development Plan (2006–2012). At the local level, the recent Dublin City Development Plan 2005–2011 (Dublin City Council, 2005) makes explicit mention of the dependence of the Dublin region on intellectual capital in order to develop and sustain a knowledge region. Projects such as the digital media hub in central Dublin are indicative of attempts to develop a creative employment cluster in the region. Indeed, the recent establishment of the Creative Dublin Alliance (Murphy and Redmond, 2008) is a rather overt statement of the move towards incorporating creative city ideals at the policymaking level.

The third model type – Toulouse – can be characterised as *targeted strategic policy*. The state's decentralisation policy, designed by the local Préfecture, was crucial. The local authorities (municipal and regional after 1982) have accompanied the development stemming from this policy. Undoubtedly, regional economic policy has taken direction from the state in terms of focusing on the development of knowledge-based industry in Toulouse. In the1980s, the administrative unit of the Midi-Pyrénées Region (Regional Council of Midi-Pyrénées) tried to play a role in economic development by financing theoretical and applied research and organising technology transfer through the CRITT (Centre Régional d'Innovation et de Transfert de Technologie). Until recently, financing and support for industry was provided through a number of institutional agencies often with overlapping objectives and focus. However, the recent establishment of the Regional Innovation Agency (Agence Regionale de L'Innovation), an initiative of the Regional Council, is an attempt to co-ordinate regional policy in the areas of technology transfer and support for technological innovation.

Economic development policies at the level of the UAT have complemented state and regional policy initiatives which aim at promoting specific types of industrial activity. Over the last 15 years in particular, these policies have focused on establishing centres of excellence around the aeronautics, space and electronics and computer activities. In this regard, current policy intervention is based upon two key principles: first, strengthening of the local productive system within the foregoing centres of excellence, and second, promoting diversification strategies towards airborne satellite systems and biotechnologies in the area of health research. In broad terms, these local economic development (LED) measures are aimed at creating territorial resources through the intensification of relationships between existing firms thereby fostering knowledge circulation rather than seeking the establishment of new enterprises.

While the 1990s were characterised by a high degree of institutional fragmentation at the UAT level, more coherent economic and institutional strategies emerged in the new millennium. Undoubtedly, this was facilitated by governance arrangements which allowed for greater co-operation between the public and private sector and particularly between the public sector and the large private sector industries. One notable example is the role played by stakeholders at various institutional levels in the recent development of the Airbus site for the A380. Yet it must be recognised also that enhanced co-operation between the public and private sectors has not necessarily been to the benefit of all individuals in the UAT. In particular, the drive towards economic specialisation relying on a highly skilled labour force has led to strong territorial and socio-economic disparities particularly in terms of access to housing for lower socio-economic groups who have been priced out of the housing market by high-wage labour (Peyroux et al., 2007).

Key actors in entrepreneurial cities

Several recent initiatives involve attempts to improve information processes between actors working for regional and urban regeneration or development projects. Most European cities dealt with economic restructuring and associated de-industrialisation by introducing into the political discourse issues such as globalisation, city attractiveness, and Europeanisation of policies. Cities and city regions are gaining in importance due to processes associated with globalisation and state restructuring and are becoming actors at different political levels linked together in various networks which increasingly bypass the nation-state (Le Galès, 2002). As the previous section has shown, Milan, Toulouse and Dublin, albeit in varying degrees, are promoting growth-oriented policies and new organisational structures which are highly characteristic of entrepreneurial cities (Harvey, 1989; Chapin, 2002). The term 'entrepreneurial' is used to denote a situation where the city government strategies are influenced by different actors (Hall and Hubbard, 1996; Jessop, 1998). Moreover, entrepreneurial refers to the growing influence of private sector interests on the planning and development of cities. This section will explore the role of key actors in each of the three aforementioned policy models.

In the Milanese context, the political debate continues to be focused on who will take the lead in the innovative process at the different levels of government (regional, provincial and municipal). In recent years, Italy has adopted an important decentralisation process (*devolution*). Under the Legge Bassanini and successive implementation decrees, subnational government has gained considerably more power. While the regions and local councils are playing a more important role in decision-making, the *provinces* are becoming weaker. This is particularly worrying considering that they are primarily responsible for the delivery of education as well as preserving the provincial environment (OECD, 2006, p. 129). Furthermore, Italy is more fiscally decentralised than France although it is unclear to what extend this decentralisation process has endowed Milan with the tools necessary to create more appropriate governance arrangements and allocate responsibilities within the region, province and municipality. In this context, Milan appears to have somewhat underdeveloped governance arrangements. According to a relatively recent density index of governance (Dente and Fareri, 1997), Milan suffers from a relatively loose fabric of actors and a number of potential 'flagship projects' remain isolated and are unlikely to reach maturity. In other words, for a long time Milan has been overly dependent on past heritage without investing adequately for the future development of the city region. For some considerable time, the Chamber of Commerce of Milan has been one of the most visible actors in promoting and fostering emerging design and fashion sectors. This has been achieved through targeted policy actions and by promoting the Chamber as a point of reference for the sectors. Since 2003, the Lombardy Region has become an important actor in economic development by stimulating and promoting collaboration between local industries and knowledge centres. At the provincial level, the promotion of economic incubators to support small and medium sized companies is a new development.

Two other administrative levels provide important policy actors in the Milanese context. The first, the city council, has been relatively invisible since the candidature for EXPO 2015. A candidature for such an event provides local authorities with the strength to support and co-ordinate the political, social and economic effort that these events necessitate. In other words, the council has to demonstrate the political will to build and re-enforce a system of governance, creating economic partnership and investing in the social capital of the city. In practice, however, the Council promoted a number of high-profile public–private partnerships. From this perspective, the role of private developers is considerable at influencing the urban development of the city (Memo, 2008) the landscape of Milan is changing through the 'hands' of the private developers without the control of the public body.

In the case of Dublin, the major actor is the national state and this was particularly evident in attracting FDI for economic growth. Perhaps the most pivotal turning point in Ireland's 'economic miracle' was the development of a Programme for National Recovery in 1987. The program involved the formation of partnerships between government bodies, employers and labour unions to negotiate a national wage agreement. The partnership approach to economic development provided a stable labour relations environment which afforded Ireland a competitive advantage in attracting inward investment (House and McGrath, 2004). It is interesting to note that this approach was abandoned with the onset of the economic crisis after 2007. Undoubtedly, low corporation tax (12.5 per cent) was an essential pre-requisite for many companies locating in Dublin. Complementary to the taxation policy, the aggressive marketing of Ireland as a location for business by the Industrial Development Authority (IDA) was also important together with the 1986 Finance Acts which 'effectively led to the established of the IFSC.

Innovation policy in Ireland is directed by Forfas, the enterprise agency, and is formulated by the ICSTI, an agency operating under the aegis of Forfas. As Ireland is a small, open and export-oriented economy, the nation is heavily dependent on FDI and the existence of a solid base of competitive industry. Ireland's economic future is heavily dependent on the development of an innovation-driven economy. Investment in research-related human resources and the application of new technology enabled Ireland to attract high-quality FDI. The recent National Development Plan (2000–2006) sought to significantly upgrade the innovation capacity of the Irish economy through the provision of both hard and soft infrastructure and generate key linkages between existing third level institutions and industry engaged in innovation. The future Dublin City Development Plan (2005–2011) aims to develop and sustain a knowledge economy with significant emphasis on improving related infrastructure. Future urban policies are expected to pay more attention to integrating different industrial activities. A good example is the development of the Digital Hub, a centre for new media industries that seeks to create mixed-use development consisting of enterprise, residential, retail, learning and civic space.

In Toulouse, the major actor is also the central state. It established the basis for high technology-oriented development with the decentralisation of the national space agency. The Midi-Pyrénées Région implements industrial development policies based on technology transfer and financial and start-up support for innovative firms. This policy takes place within contractual agreements between the regional authority (Regional Council of Midi-Pyrénées) and the State. Interventions are therefore conducted through state institutions such as DRIRE (Direction Régionale de l'Industrie, de la Recherche et de l'Environnement) and OSEO-ANVAR (Agence Nationale de Valorisation de la Recherche). This is viewed as a mutualisation of resources between state and region (Scott and Zuliani, 2006). Regional representatives of state institutions have become providers of consulting services as well as suppliers of loans primarily for technological SMEs. In addition, since 1970, the Midi-Pyrénées region has developed its own institutional framework to support scientific research and technological development (examples include Comité Consultatif Régional pour la Recherche et le Développement Technologique, Agence Régionale pour le Développement de la Société de l'Information and Programmes d'Action Régionale pour la Société de l'Information).

However, the Toulouse policy model does not rest on a single administrative unit. At the metropolitan level, local actors include municipalities and inter-communal structures. At the micro level, local authorities and inter-communal structures are increasingly involved with other public and private stakeholders in LED policies, in an attempt to create and establish new enterprises. The private–public partnerships often also promote planning and the development of business parks such as those specialising in aeronautics (aeroconstellation) or nurseries for firms or incubators for hosting innovative firms.

Since 2005 this multi-level policy system for fostering innovation in Toulouse has been made even more complex with the introduction of new cross-regional projects such as *Pôles de compétitivité* (competitive clusters). These clusters have been developed by the state in Aquitaine and the Midi-Pyrénées regions and are based on core regional economic competences. In the case of Toulouse, it comprises a large geographical perimeter where firms and research and education units are engaged in a partnership in an attempt to promote common technology projects. The cluster includes aeronautics and space activities as well as computer industries and electronics for airborne systems (e.g. transport, mobile phones, medical implants). It is supported by an 'Aerospace Valley' association which has 620 industrial and institutional partners. Headed by the director of Airbus France (Toulouse), the management board comprises 33 members, representing the different sectors and territories in the Midi-Pyrénées and Aquitaine regions. These new competitive clusters are characterised by new governance arrangements involving increased collaboration between private firms, and particularly large firms including Airbus, and the state sector.

Addressing barriers and obstacles

An important policy issue is how to maintain a city's evolution towards a creative knowledge economy. What are the barriers and obstacles for future development of the creative knowledge sector? Clearly, these are important issues with respect to the long-term ability of cities to attract creative knowledge industries. Failure to deal with such issues may, in the long run, lead to serious problems over the economic sustainability of the city, particularly in terms of its ability to retain large volumes of intellectual capital. There are some obstacles which are specifically related to the local context and other more general issues. More specifically, Dublin's key strength in attracting FDI appears to have become increasingly difficult. In the past, there was an emphasis on attracting ICT industries to the region and this was laid down as specific government policy in Technology Foresight Ireland. But this was mostly low value-added ICT manufacturing involving low-skilled workers. Thus, FDI in this area was originally dependent on cheap labour which left the sustainability of employment susceptible to outside competition. Recent policy shifts have been towards industrial innovation and the development of a knowledge-based economy attempting to focus on R&D and more high value-added employment in order to retain industry in the Dublin region (for example Microsoft's new data centre will be in Dublin). Although this economic development strategy has, until recently, been successful ...', new challenges are in the offing including problems with regional infrastructure and the recent crisis in the global economy and particularly financial services which the regional economy of Dublin is highly dependent upon.

Other issues appear to be common to all three cities. In the near future, most cities may need to respond to the question of where the current model of economic development is leading. City competitiveness based on a particular type of worker or industry does little to alleviate social inequality within cities. Whatever the historical background and development trajectory, industries currently being developed in these city regions predominantly require a highly skilled and flexible workforce which is mobile at the international level. These types of development, based on competitiveness policies, have deeply transformed the physical and social profiles of these cities. Solutions adopted to reduce the increasing spatial inequalities involves, at least partly, the promotion of education that better relates to local employment opportunity supply and demand.

Strong specialisations also create vulnerabilities for individuals employed in the leading local sectors. In Toulouse, development of clusters of high-technology activities relying on a highly qualified workforce has led to strong territorial and socio-economic disparities. This leads to the question whether or not the development model promoted by the creative knowledge economy is conducive to social integration. This in turn raises the issue of how to integrate low-skilled or unqualified workers into a highly specialised metropolis? Furthermore, the spatial segregation impacts of the creative economy are poorly understood and little explored. In Milan and Dublin, the idea of developing cultural quarters is gaining further ground at the policymaking level and is a deliberate model for promoting the regeneration of run-down inner cities (Montgomery, 2003, p. 294) and as a strategy of shifting the most vulnerable sectors of society from strategic parts of the city. Dublin's Temple Bar (Montgomery, 1995) or Zona Tortona in Milan are undergoing a strong process of gentrification and this is primarily state or private developer led in both cases.

In Dublin, housing affordability has been a central issue. House price escalation generated significant problems of affordability with some obvious and less obvious consequences. First, the evidence suggests that first-time buyers have affordability problems, with clear implications for the labour market and knowledge-based industries. While affordability has improved recently, the contraction of credit in the banking sector has meant that access to mortgage credit is increasingly difficult. In Dublin, a market-led approach to urban renewal was implemented in the mid-1980s and the early 1990s, based essentially on the introduction of tax incentives applied to a number of designated areas. The effect of such measures was to introduce significant risk reduction for private sector development interests, ensure far greater certainty in obtaining permission to develop and fast-track bureaucratic planning procedures. The main consequence has been large-scale property development, the physical renewal of the inner city and significant transformations in the social geography of the central area (Kelly and MacLaran, 2004). After more than a decade of tax-based incentive development, the entrepreneurial approach has been criticised for its lack of community participation in the development of many areas of the city and the consequent negative social impacts, particularly for poorer city residents (Department of the Environment, 1996).

With industrial re-conversion, the three cities are facing pressing social issues. Milan, Dublin and Toulouse are experiencing vulnerabilities due to high degrees of specialisation and changing global economic conditions and business environments. This could be the over-reliance on FDI in Dublin or the dependence on one single dominant sector such as aeronautics in Toulouse. The dependence on one particular form of economic policy or industry is less of a problem in Milan. Although it is renowned internationally as the capital of fashion and design, it has a highly diversified industrial sector.

Conclusion and new challenges

In policy terms, it appears that there is no correct strategy for developing creative knowledge industries. In the case studies considered, different policies were implemented in both Dublin and Toulouse in order to develop a knowledge-based economy while in Milan the absence of policy intervention does not appear to have hindered the development of creative industry; on the contrary, these industries have flourished. Of course, the key question is whether specific policies should be pursued in the future in order to develop a creative knowledge economy or whether policymakers should allow these industries to develop of their own accord? The lessons emerging from the cities analysed show that policymakers have been quite successful at implementing policies to develop and attract knowledge-based industry to Dublin and Toulouse. It is likely that similar policies could be pursued in Milan to develop knowledge-based industry further. However, the success of policies aimed at attracting and developing creative industries, particularly in Dublin and Toulouse, remains to be seen. Certainly in the case of Dublin, initial attempts to develop a creative industries cluster have been largely unsuccessful (Bayliss, 2007).

Previous chapters have demonstrated that the nature of creative industries is such that many tend to be rather small scale and have a tendency to spring up in unlikely locations and somewhat spontaneously. This is certainly true in the case of Milan which has one of the most vibrant creative sectors in Europe. Given that targeted policy intervention has been more or less non-existent in Milan, it would appear that targeted policy intervention in the creative sector is perhaps less important than in the knowledge sector. This conforms to the conclusions reached by Kovács et al. (2007) in their analysis of a number of European cities. Whereas policymaking has been focused on the development of economic specialisms in Dublin and Toulouse and relatively absent in Milan, there appears to be common movements in each of those cities towards the development of the 'soft' infrastructure of these cities so that they are more attractive to high-skilled workers. However, the identification of policy measures aimed at improving the relatively intangible factors of cities would appear to be a complex task and highly difficult to implement in a targeted manner.

Nevertheless, in each of the cities, some clear improvements need to be made to enhance the city liveability and competitiveness. At present, Milan is paying for 20 years of institutional stagnation. Despite recent research noting some new and positive initiatives, public institutions must counteract a long period of institutional disaffiliation and low levels of trust prevalent among firms, managers, cultural operators and the general public (Mingione et al., 2007, 2008). Creative and knowledge managers do not rely on public bodies to make Milan more competitive. The slow nature of procedures and the high level of bureaucracy have created a timing mismatch between the needs of firms and the response of public administration. For a long period, cultural operators have felt abandoned by the public institutions and in some instances they feel that the public institutions fight against genuinely positive initiatives. A bottom-up policy can only survive where the city's governance arrangements allow the economic, political and social actors to join forces to work on the transformation of the city. In order to attract new economic activity, policymakers should go beyond the idea of only implementing policies that address the hard conditions in the city (infrastructure, tax benefits, etc) and begin to think additionally about soft conditions associated with the city.

In Dublin, there is overwhelming dissatisfaction among creative knowledge workers with the level of public services being offered including health and policing while the lack of a quality transportation system is a source of particular discontent (see Murphy and Redmond, 2009). Murphy et al. (2008) have demonstrated that the inadequacy of 'hard' factors, such as transportation and accessibility, impacts negatively on all aspects of an individual's perception of living and working in the Dublin region. Clearly then, these are areas where significant efforts need to be made by urban administrators in order to improve the attractiveness of the city region for all citizens while at the same time enhancing economic competitiveness.

In Toulouse, recent surveys also revealed some dissatisfaction with the city (Martin-Brelot et al., 2008a, b, 2009). Managers in creative industries voiced the need for a change in the mindset of local leaders. Indeed, when compared with knowledge-intensive industries, the professions related to culture, arts or entertainment appear to suffer from a lack of recognition, and this could play against the attractiveness of the city in the longer term. The recently elected left-wing municipality has engaged in the enhancement of the inter-communal structure of Toulouse with a declared ambition to harmonise strategies of economic development and urban planning so that the city becomes a European metropolis. The cultural project designed for 2009–2014 insists on the promotion of creative industries as well as on a more equitable meshing of cultural resources on the whole territory.

The more recent development of the three cities under consideration tends to show that there is some degree of convergence in current urban policy. Although different policy traditions and legacies remain, they have absorbed some of the same new elements in their approaches. Examples include the influence of the EU as well as a greater awareness of economic development alternatives and of the competition between cities at the global level. There is also a common recognition of the emerging importance of soft factors for the attractiveness of cities and issues of social polarisation. Looking to the future, it seems clear that, in future strategic economic policies, whatever the different institutional and political arrangements, the three cities will need to reconcile the objective of social and spatial solidarity with the enhancement of competitiveness at the international level.

References

Bayliss, D. (2007) Dublin's digital hubris: Lessons from an attempt to develop a creative industrial cluster. *European Planning Studies*, 15: 1261–1271.

Chapin, T. (2002) Beyond the entrepreneurial city: Municipal capitalism in San Diego. *Journal of Urban Affairs*, 24 (5): 565–581.

Dente, B. and P. Fareri (eds) (1997) *Innovazione Amministrativa a Milano. AIM (Associazione Interessi Metropolitani)* quaderno n. 34, Milan.

Department of the Environment (1996) *Study of urban renewal schemes*. Dublin: Stationery Office.

Dublin City Council (2005) *Dublin city development plan 2005–2011*. Dublin: Dublin City Council.

Fitzgerald, M. (2000) *From protectionism to liberalisation: Ireland and the EEC, 1957–1966*. Aldershot: Ashgate.

Grossetti, M. (1995) *Science, industrie et territoire*. Toulouse: PUM, coll. 'Socio-logiques'.

Hall, T. and P. Hubbard (1996) The entrepreneurial city: New urban politics, new urban geographies? *Progress in Human Geography*, 20 (2): 153–174.

Harvey, D. (1989) From managerialism to entrepreneurialism: The transformation in urban governance in late capitalism. *Geografiska Annaler*, 71 B (1): 3–17.

Hooghe, L. (ed) (1996) *Cohesion policy and European integration*. Oxford: Oxford University Press.

House, J.D. and K. McGrath (2004) Innovative governance and development in the New Ireland: Social partnership and the integrated approach. *Governance: An International Journal of Policy, Administration, and Institutions*, 17: 29–58.

Jessop, B. (1998) The rise of governance and the risks of failure: The case of economic development. *International Social Science Journal*, 155: 29–45.

Kelly, S. and A. MacLaran (2004) The residential transformation of inner Dublin. In: P. Drudy and A. MacLaran (eds), *Dublin: Economic and social trends*, pp. 36–59. Dublin: Centre for Urban and Regional Studies, Trinity College, Vol. 4.

Kovács, Z., A. Murie, S. Musterd, O. Gritsai and H. Pethe (2007) *Comparing paths of creative knowledge regions*. ACRE report 3, Amsterdam: AMIDSt.

Le Galès, P. (2002) *European cities. Social conflicts and governance*. Oxford: Oxford University Press.

Marks, G. (1992) Structural policy and multilevel governance in the EC. In: A. Sbragia (ed.), *Euro-politics*, pp. 191–224. Washington, DC: The Brookings Institution.

Marks, G. (1993) Structural policy and multilevel governance in the EC. In: A. Cafruny and G. Rosenthal (eds), *The state of the European community, vol.2: The Maastricht debates and beyond*, pp. 391–410. Harlow: Longman.

Martin-Brelot, H., M. Grossetti, E. Peyroux, D. Eckert and C. Thouzellier (2008a) *Career trajectories and residential satisfaction in Toulouse. Understanding the attractiveness of the metropolitan region for creative knowledge workers*. ACRE report 5.11. Amsterdam: AMIDSt.

Martin-Brelot, H., M. Grossetti, D. Eckert and C. Thouzellier (2008b) *Main drivers for the settlement of creative industries in Toulouse: The manager's view*. ACRE report 6.11. Amsterdam: AMIDSt.

Martin-Brelot, H., C. Thouzellier, M. Grossetti and D. Eckert (2009) *Attracting and accommodating creative knowledge workers in Toulouse. The view of transnational migrants*. ACRE report 7.11. Amsterdam: AMIDSt. (It is now published.)

Memo, F. (2008) *Nuove caratteristiche del sistema immobiliare e abitabilità urbana. Alcune evidenze a partire dal caso di Milano. Sociologia Urbana e Rurale*. Milan: Franco Angeli, Vol. 84.

Mingione, E., E. dell'Agnese, S. Mugnano, M. d'Ovidio, B. Niessen and C. Sedini (2007) *Milan city-region: Is it still competitive and charming? Pathways to creative and knowledge-based regions*. ACRE report WP2.12. Amsterdam: AMIDSt.

Mingione, E., F. Zajczyk, E. dell'Agnese, S. Mugnano, M. d'Ovidio and C. Sedini (2008) *Milan: A city easy for working but difficult for living? Understanding the attractiveness of the metropolitan region for creative knowledge workers*. ACRE report 5.12. Amsterdam: AMIDSt.

Montgomery, J. (1995) The story of Temple Bar: Creating Dublin's cultural quarter. *Planning, Practice and Research*, 10 (2): 135–171.

Montgomery, J. (2003) Cultural quarters as a mechanisms for urban re generation. Part 1: Conceptualising cultural quarters. *Planning, Practice and Research*, 18 (4): 293–306.

Murphy, E. and D. Redmond (2008) *Location factors of creative knowledge companies in the Dublin region*. ACRE report 6.13, Amsterdam: AMIDSt.

Murphy, E. and D. Redmond (2009) The role of 'hard' and 'soft' factors for accommodating creative knowledge: Insights from Dublin's 'creative class'. *Irish Geography*, 42 (1): 69–84.

Murphy, E., D. Redmond and D. McKnight (2008) *The creative knowledge economy in Dublin: Understanding the attractiveness of the metropolitan region for creative knowledge workers*. ACRE report 5.13. Amsterdam: AMIDSt.

OECD (2006) *Territorial review. Area metropolitana milanese*. Report for the Chamber of Commerce and the Province of Milan.

Peyroux, E., D. Eckert and C. Thouzellier (eds) (2007) *Toulouse: Embracing the knowledge economy: Pathways to creative and knowledge-based regions*. ACRE report WP2.11. Amsterdam: AMIDSt.

Redmond, D., V. Crossa, N. Moore and B. Williams (2007) *Dublin as an emergent global gateway: Pathways to creative and knowledge-based regions*. ACRE report WP2.13. Amsterdam: AMIDSt.

Rhodes, R.A.W. (1987) *Understanding governance: Policy network, governance, reflexivity and accountability*. Buckingham: Open University Press.

Scharpf, F. (1994) Community and autonomy: Multilevel policy making in the European Union. *Journal of European Public Policy*, 1: 219–242.

Scott, A.J. and J.-M. Zuliani (2006) *L'industrie de l'informatique à Toulouse: développement, structure, enjeux*. Toulouse: unpublished paper.

Yeandle, M., A. Knapp and M. Mainelli (2008) *The global financial centres index*. London: City of London.

Zuliani, J.-M. (1999) Toulouse, métropole technologique. In: J. Philippe, P.Y. Leo and L.M. Boulianne (eds), *Services et métropoles. Formes urbaines et changement économique*, pp. 241–268. Paris: L'Harmattan.

15

Beyond Cluster Policy? Birmingham, Poznan and Helsinki

Caroline Chapain, Krzysztof Stachowiak and Mari Vaattovaara

Introduction

This chapter explores the extent to which cluster policies are necessary and sufficient to support the development of creative and knowledge industries at the local and regional levels using the example of three very different European cities: Helsinki in Finland, Birmingham in the UK and Poznan in Poland. As discussed in Chapter 2 of this book, economic cluster theory has been increasingly used to understand and foster local and regional economic development in the last 20 years (OECD, 2007; Oxford Research, 2008; CEC, 2008). The shift from macroeconomic level approaches towards the microeconomic foundations of competitiveness and growth together with the emergence of knowledge and creative industries have supported this approach as they have a tendency to cluster (United Nations, 2008; Vorley, 2008).

While the cluster concepts has been used in regional policies to a great degree (OECD, 2007; Oxford Research, 2008), it has been widely debated to a point where some authors find it confusing and unhelpful (Martin and Sunley, 2003). For example, questions arise about the possibility of delimiting clusters geographically and the extent to which clusters can be created by governments or through deliberate partnerships. In addition, there are some issues regarding the extent to which local and regional governments build on existing local and regional strengths, and over the extent to which they look for new strengths with regard to economic specialisations when developing cluster strategies. Finally, some questions emerge in terms of the degree of embeddedness of cluster strategies in broader urban development strategies and visions.

This chapter addresses these questions by examining the role of local and regional cluster policies in fostering the development of creative and knowledge industries in comparison with other local and regional initiatives and national policies in our three cities. In addition, we discuss the importance of national and local traditions in the set up of the structural preconditions to the development of creative and knowledge industries. Our three cities offer interesting contrasting examples of the development of these industries. Helsinki and Finland with the development of Nokia are celebrated as one of the best practice models for the development of the information society today (Castells and Himanen, 2002). The City of Birmingham in UK has witnessed an important process of economic restructuring in the last 20 years supported by strong local and regional policies with an important focus on creative and knowledge industries. Finally, Poznan in Poland is in a process of catching up with the knowledge and creative economy.

Our discussion involves a brief overview of the concept of cluster and cluster policy and an introduction to the three cities followed by an outline of the different cluster type policies that they have put in place and their impact on the development of their creative and knowledge industries and innovation. Special attention is given to two main characteristics highlighted in the theoretical literature on clusters – the need for a highly skilled labour force and strong networking. We then conclude with a discussion of the role of policies in fostering creative and knowledge industries in European city-regions.

The cluster policy paradigm

Vorley (2008) provides a historical review of the geographic cluster concept from the notion of geographical agglomerations introduced by Marshall in 1890 to the notion of regional innovation systems proposed by Cooke (1992). Vorley argues that in order to get the most out of the cluster concept, it is important to consider a multi-perspective approach taking into account the understanding and theories developed by authors over the years. He notes that, as a starting point, the cluster concept refers to 'a "non-random" geographical agglomeration of firms with similar or closely complementary capabilities'. Marshall was the first to recognise the importance of external economies linked to industrial agglomerations: reduction in transportation costs, availability of a specialised labour market at reasonable costs and the presence of knowledge spillovers - the technical transfer of knowledge and practical skills through primary interactions and conversations. From Marshall, cluster theories have developed to also recognise local social, institutional and inter-firm networks through which knowledge spillovers occur. Some authors also identify the need to understand that clusters are

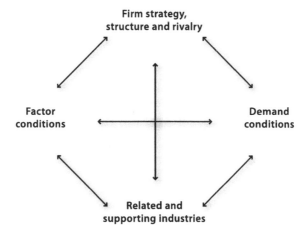

Figure 15.1 Determinants of competitive advantage.

embedded in a broader institutional matrix at the regional, national and even supranational levels (Vorley, 2008).

In the last 10 years, OECD (1999) has promoted the cluster approach, which has also been widely disseminated thanks to Porter (1990, 1998) and his diamond model (Figure 15.1). Porter's model includes four components: firm rivalry and strategy, demand conditions, related and supporting industries, factor input conditions. Porter says that the interactions between the four points of the diamond determine the productivity of firms. This 'works best where the industries are geographically concentrated' (Vorley, 2008, p. 802). The competitive advantage, as stressed by Porter (2004, p. 16) 'lies increasingly in local things – knowledge, relationship and motivation – that distant rivals cannot replicate (...) unless these microeconomic capabilities improve, macroeconomic, political, legal and social reforms will not bear full fruit'.

A review of the cluster concept by the European Commission highlights the importance of the presence of specialised firms, advance skills and competences in the labour force as well as supporting institutions and the importance of networking or 'social glue' between firms, research and higher education institutions and the public sector in the clustering process (CEC, 2008, p. 6). This confirmed work by Brenner and Mühlig (2007) who used 159 case studies to identify the factors and mechanisms causing the emergence of local industrial clusters. They found that the most frequent prerequisites for the emergence of clusters were the presence of qualified labour and strong networks between actors. These factors are also important in the self-augmenting process of a cluster. The existence of universities and public research centres was another prerequisite. Brenner and Mühlig (2007) also showed that local policies played a role in the emergence and development of some clusters.

A recent review of cluster policy in Europe identified three main categories:

1 *Cluster development policies* directed at creating, or strengthening a particular cluster.
2 *Cluster leveraging policies* that use a cluster lens to increase the efficiency of a specific instrument.
3 *Cluster facilitating policies* directed toward the elements of the micro-economic business environment to increase the likelihood of clusters to emerge.

This review by Oxford Research (2008) found national cluster policies in 26 out of the 31 European countries (including Finland, Poland and the UK); 57 per cent of these countries had regional cluster policies with smaller countries, in size and population, tending not to have regional policies.

Even though there are a variety of policies today to support existing clusters or the emergence of new clusters, 'The long-term effectiveness of such policies depends on the private sector continuing to act after a programme ends' (OECD, 2007, p. 16). The evaluation of the effectiveness of cluster policies however tends to be done either by evaluating the performance of the cluster or by evaluating the cluster initiative and its policy impact (OECD, 2007). Key indicators to evaluate the performance of a cluster relate to the strength of the networking between its different actors, the educational level of the labour force and the impact in terms of regional innovation.

In this chapter we examine to what extent cluster policies have been put in place in our three cities to foster creative and knowledge industries and if they are based on existing local and regional strengths. We also determine whether these strategies are part of broader strategies and visions and evaluate them by looking at the performance of the existing local and regional creative and knowledge clusters. Our main research question is: are cluster policies sufficient to support the development of these industries at the local and regional levels?

The state of the creative and knowledge economy

Even though Helsinki is located at the periphery of the extensive western and central European markets, it has been one of the fastest-growing regions in Europe in the last decade (see Chapter 7). For example, at the end of 1990s employment increased by 4 per cent annually, which at that time positioned Helsinki among the three fastest-growing metropolises in Europe. Since the recession of the 1990s, there has been a rapid growth in the Finnish economy, especially in the *urban regions* – first and foremost in the Helsinki region. The new economic growth has been based on an increase of private companies in *knowledge-intensive industries, telecommunication and business-to-business services*. Consequently, the country's economy has transformed itself from a north-eastern periphery, largely dependent on forestry, pulp and paper-industries and public services to one of the world's leading information societies with one of the international hubs for knowledge industries.

Today, Helsinki metropolitan region has one of Europe's leading clusters in information and communication technologies (ICT), led by Nokia, which has become the world market leader in mobile communication. More widely, the role of creative and knowledge industries is central to the development of the Helsinki Metropolitan Area. In 2004, 30.5 per cent of employees worked in sectors defined as creative and knowledge-intensive (12.2 per cent in the creative industries and 17.7 per cent in the knowledge industries). This was one of the highest proportions among cities in Europe. In general, ICT industries including manufacturing, consultancy and telecommunications, form the most important industrial segment of the Helsinki metropolitan area's economic profile.

Birmingham, with 1 million inhabitants, is the second city in the UK and is located at the heart of England in the West Midlands region (Brown et al., 2007). As seen in Chapter 2, the city grew during the industrial revolution and, with the exception of London, had overtaken longer established cities in size and importance by the twentieth century. The 1970s and 1980s saw a major decline in manufacturing in the West Midlands, and in order to cope with this economic challenge, the city of Birmingham adopted an ambitious strategy of economic regeneration and had transformed the industrial/financial/service base of Birmingham by the 1990s.

There were 27,500 jobs in the creative industries and 77,500 in the knowledge industries in Birmingham in 2006. In total, slightly more than one job out of 5 in Birmingham was in the creative and knowledge industries in 2006. The most important creative sectors in terms of jobs were Architecture, Arts and Antiques and Software whereas the most important knowledge sector was Law and other Business Services. Birmingham also has a high concentration of firms in the jewellery sector. The city is now a young, ethnically diverse city that is growing economically, but still faces challenges in terms of social deprivation. Overall, households in Birmingham have incomes below the regional and national average and some neighbourhoods display acute levels of social and health deprivation.

As described in Chapter 6, Poznan is the fifth largest city (560,000 inhabitants in 2008), and one of the fastest-growing cities in Poland. It is located in the west-central part of the country, halfway between Warsaw and Berlin. The development of creative and knowledge sectors in Poznan accelerated after Poland opened its borders in 1989. Joining the

European Union (EU) in 2004 gave rise to a host of programmes and initiatives which, with the EU financial backing, became the driving force of change in Poland. Poznan is now considered as one of the business cities and trade capitals in Poland and one of the largest Polish industrial centres in terms of employment and technological industrial progress. As a result of the loss of communist markets, the old industries have collapsed or reduced their output due to the low level of technology and competitiveness of their products. Firms that are adapting to global changes now play a key role in the economy, usually thanks to foreign investment (Parysek and Mierzejewska, 2006).

In 2005, there were a total of 30,385 jobs in the creative and knowledge industries in the Poznan metropolitan region. The city of Poznan accounted for 83 per cent of metropolitan employment in those industries. The sectors with an above-average concentration of workers in the core city included Publishing, Advertising and Architecture. In turn, the sector with the highest employment in Poznan region was Crafts with a share of nearly 57 per cent. This high figure was largely due to the neighbouring city of Swarzedz with its furniture handicraft.

Supporting the creative and knowledge economy: three approaches

Each of the cities discussed above have adopted policies to support the creative and knowledge economy. These policies and their efficiency are discussed for each city in turn.

Helsinki – a success story with emerging socio-economic issues

Helsinki and Finland are presented as an example of successful development of by knowledge industries, especially ICT, thanks to a long historic tradition of top-down centralised national policies. National policies, investments in education and creation of the welfare state have been central to the emergence of the Helsinki region as an international hub in the knowledge industries. Despite the acknowledged success of national policies, some questions are raised regarding the role of more local and regional factors. One conclusion from the studies of Finnish innovation capacities, or the ICT sector, is that there is a major divide between the national and regional parts of the Finnish innovation system. Currently, however, there are no regional governmental structures to respond to this need. Individual municipalities, by law, take care of their own residents and matters and they are only starting to facilitate regional innovation cooperation. In addition, Helsinki has become a victim of its own economic success: the lack of affordable housing is raised as an issue by creative and knowledge workers interviewed during this research.

Governance structure

Finland has a two tier government structure. The role of the national government has been key in all policy actions, including the creation of the information society. This is related to the model of the welfare state. In addition to the national government and its policies, over 400 individual municipalities are in charge of providing local services to the population. Power is not completely decentralised though, since national laws determine the obligations of the municipalities. National state grants complement the income that local governments draw from their local taxation and municipalities benefit from a local tax revenue equalisation system (Loikkanen and Susiluoto, 2006).

Economic development policies and the creative and knowledge economy

Traditionally, Finland specialised in exporting paper, pulp and engineering products. As the domestic market has always been too small for these activities, the country traded globally long before the era of globalisation and policy makers learned early on to pay close attention to the needs of large exporting corporations and to co-operate with them. Finland's enthusiasm to adopt policies fostering innovation can be seen as a continuation of this long historical approach. Since 1980, investing in innovation has become one of the strongest national policy actions and a trademark of Finland.

National policies developed to support the development of creative and knowledge industries initially mainly focusing on raising education levels. Interviews with managers of knowledge industries companies in this project highlighted this as respondents declared that *they do not have anything else in their business other than educated workers*. Helsinki and Finland as a whole have adopted a competitive strategy building upon classical urban economic development success factors: the development of competitive products by increasing the productivity of Finnish workers and firms. Unlike many other countries, Finland has not really promoted Helsinki abroad in order to attract international investment as a mechanism to counterbalance the scarcity of talents and firms. On the contrary it has grown from its own potential.

The focus on education is profound in the Finnish welfare model. The expansion of the university network from three to twenty between the 1960s and 1980s (spread around the nation) and the creation of public financing institutions for business-oriented research and development, were prerequisites for the subsequent growth of the Information or Innovation Society in the country. In addition, the Finnish educational system has provided, from early on, equal opportunities to all strata of the society. Compared with British, French or German educational systems, the Finnish system has never been very selective. On the contrary, opportunities have been provided for all social classes in all parts of Finland (Mäkelä, 1999). Education attendance and labour market participation of women have also been some of the highest in Europe. This has been noted as a unique phenomenon. One of the explanations for this has been attributed to the small size of the country and its specific geopolitical location between two great powers (Sweden and Russia). Finland could not afford to have any part of its population being left out.

Other national actors relevant to the economic development policies and the creative and knowledge economy are ministries, for example the largest and newly established Ministry of Employment and Economy (formerly Ministry of Trade and Industry). Strategic policy decisions are implemented through the National Technology Agency (Tekes), the Technical Research Centre of Finland (VTT) and 15 Employment and Economic Centres (TE- centres). Tekes, the Finnish Funding Agency for Technology and Innovation is the main government financing and expert organisation for research and technological development in Finland. Another important national actor in the sector is the Finnish National Fund for Research and Development (SITRA). It is an independent public foundation under the supervision of the Finnish Parliament. There also exist several institutions promoting networking in the field. The Finnish Information Society Development Centre (TIEKE) has an important role as a neutral and non-profit organisation in promoting the efforts of its members, within public and private sectors, to create viable tools and expertise for use in the information society. Currently, Finland is also undertaking a major structural change in its educational system to favour innovation: the establishment of a new innovation university to be called the Aalto University. This university will be created through a major merger of three existing universities: the Helsinki University of Technology (TKK), the Helsinki School of Economics (HSE) and the University of Art and Design Helsinki (TAIK).

Professor Dan Steinbock, investigating the Finnish innovation policy, cluster creation, and innovation capacity at the request of the Finnish ministry of Interior, concluded: 'the success or failure of the cluster depends on its microeconomic conditions, that is sophistication of firms, attractiveness of business environment' (2004). In his later study (2006) on *Finland's Innovative Capacity*, he noted the discrepancy between Finland's high ranking in global competitiveness and the growing sense of economic uncertainty in the country. According to Steinbock, part of the problem lays in a great divide between two views of the way the Finnish innovation system works. The conventional view is that 'this [innovation] system is policy led national top-down by government agencies, through an array of domestic public sector entities' (Steinbock, 2006). However, according to the results of his study – 'in fact, it is driven by cluster leaders, global competition, business firms and their affiliates – particularly at the R&D level'. Porter in his foreword to the same study adds that 'unless ... micro-economic capabilities improve, macroeconomic, political, legal and social reforms will not bear full fruit' (Porter, 2004).

As discussed previously, national level politics have had a profound influence in the Finnish political system. The whole creation of the welfare state relied on a kind of national uniformity. The small national elite worked with governmental bodies 'for the best of the common people'. Consequently, there is a long tradition in the Finnish political system of top-down approaches to knowledge-intensive industries and innovation policies among other things. For a long time, national political guidance to raise levels of education, standards of living, housing conditions and available services have been followed without any strong opposition by an homogenous population. It is only recently, from 1989 onwards, with the development of regional policies that the importance of differentiating regions and urban areas has received specific attention.

Finland has a two tier government and, with the increasing recognition given to regions in Europe, it would seem important to develop a city-region approach to urban and economic development to support knowledge-intensive or creative industries and co-ordinate the microeconomic conditions mentioned by Steinbock (2004). Indeed, at the time of writing the first national metropolitan policy document was under preparation. Even if there are no powerful city-regional structures of governance in Finland, the idea of the importance of city-regions, especially of the capital region has been present for some time. At the local level, several semi-private organisations act as local or regional development agencies. One of the most important of these is Culminatum Ltd., a co-operative organisation whose task is to promote technological innovation transfer from the conceptual level, through the research phase and to the production level and helps to increase co-operation between the scientific community and companies and to co-finance various projects. The shareholders of Culminatum are the Helsinki Region's universities and vocational universities, the cities and the chambers of commerce of the Helsinki Metropolitan Area and the Uusimaa Regional Council. Culminatum has been responsible for the creation of the first innovation strategy for the Helsinki metropolitan area. Even if innovation and, more widely, innovativeness bring together concepts like creativity, culture and knowledge, in Finnish documents the focus is on the knowledge industries. The contents of the first innovation strategy for the Helsinki metropolitan area consists of four pillars that are: *the international appeal of research and expertise, knowledge-based clusters and common development platforms, reform and innovations in public services and innovative activities* (Helsinki Regional Innovation Strategy, 2005, p. 5). All these pillars have a solid technologically oriented knowledge base.

The success of Helsinki economic development policy seems to be challenged today by wider socio-economic issues. The survey of creative and knowledge workers carried out in the present project show that these workers were in Helsinki mostly because of personal connections with the city ('studied in Helsinki'; 'proximity to friends'; 'family lives here') and secondly because of employment related factors ('moved here because of my job', 'good employment opportunities'). Even if a majority of the respondents were satisfied with the city, 22 per cent of the respondents thought that the quality of life in Helsinki worsened. More specifically, close to 50 per cent of the respondents were very worried about one single thing – the availability of affordable housing. In the Finnish contexts this proportion is extremely, almost revolutionarily high – see Kepsu and Vaattovaara (2008) for more details. This concern added to those about the quality of life raises questions about the retention of creative and knowledge workers in the region. This would support the ideas of Porter and Steinbock that the microeconomic conditions and capabilities need to be addressed and improved. Housing is clearly an issue that has to be solved in Helsinki.

Networking

Networking and cluster policies are not very well developed at the city-regional level in Finland. This contrasts with the national dynamic as expressed in the OECD Science, Technology and Industry Scoreboard 2007, which puts Finland in the top position in terms of firms collaborating with higher education institutions over innovation. However, Helsinki, as the urban centre of a small peripheral nation, has benefited from a peculiar national history and traditions in both policy and governance. These peculiarities are linked with long standing and continuous difficulties in both the nation building process (during the wars of 1918 and 1939–1945), and in the impact of being located between two big powers afterwards (until 1989, with the collapse of the Soviet Empire). In order to protect itself from foreign pressures, Finland has put a lot of focus on national political integration (Allardt, 1971). This national integration had to be achieved through consensual solutions, and involved decades of political and social networking, linking all fragments of the Finnish elites (the political, the economic, and the intellectual). In other words, the networking between the different fields and fractions of these elites is not recent but rather a long standing national tradition. Consequently, as 'everyone is involved', there is stronger commitment to decisions, which are also implemented more easily.

This can still be seen in current policy practices – the formulation of the Helsinki Regional Innovation Strategy (2005) constitutes a good example of this phenomenon. Over one hundred actors were actively involved in the process – including mayors of cities, heads of educational units and heads of big industries and economies. A similar collaboration can be found in the formulation of innovation strategies at the national level in which over 300 experts were involved, many of them being high level executives of key Finish organisations.

Highly skilled labour

Finland benefits from a highly skilled local workforce and Helsinki metro-politan area has the oldest and most renowned universities in Finland; about 40 per cent of the Finnish students in Finland study in the region. The University of Helsinki is an old and traditional university that was created in 1640 and was moved to Helsinki in 1828. The Helsinki University of Technology was founded in 1849 and was given university status in 1908. Since then it has been the source of many engineers and technical scientists in Finland (Inkinen and Vaattovaara, 2007). The region thus has a clear advantage in terms of education and skills. The quality of the local demand – highly qualified demanding customers in business and consumer markets – has been raised as one of the most important factors in fostering the development of innovation.

Until now, part of the success of Helsinki and Finland has come from the quality of the local and national human capital and the fact that the Helsinki region has been one of the fastest urbanising and growing regions in Europe. However, the whole nation is ageing rapidly and faster than any other European countries. The challenge now, as Porter (2004) states, is 'boosting outward internationalisation', to attract foreign capital as well as talent to the region. Today, it is not only the quality of the market but also the diversity of users that is seen as a strategic advantage to develop knowledge industries. On that front the homogenous nation and city-region of Helsinki is definitely lagging behind.

Birmingham – building on a plethora of initiatives

Creative and knowledge industries in Birmingham and the West Midlands have benefited from a plethora of sectoral or wider cluster initiatives in the past 10 years during a period when the Labour government nationally has placed emphasis on developing these industries and promoting cluster policy. While these policy initiatives have sometimes being successful and met bottom-up ones, Birmingham is still struggling to raise her profile in terms of creative and knowledge industries and to overcome some deep-seated skills challenges inherited from the past.

Governance structure

Decentralisation has been one of the priorities of the Labour government, since its election in the UK in 1997. In addition to giving more powers to

Scotland and Wales, the government set up new regional bodies in England including Government Offices in the Regions (GORs) and Regional Development Agencies to reinforce and co-ordinate the development of cities and regions. Government Offices are national government bodies that help deliver its policy in each of the nine English regions as well as gather local and regional information to feed into government's policy. GORs work with the Regional Development Agencies on behalf of the Department for Business, Innovation and Skills which focuses on economic development and trade. Regional Development Agencies' 'primary role is as strategic drivers of regional economic development in their region'. Today, there are three administrative levels in the UK: the national level, the regional level and the local level. Local and regional actors have also been encouraged to work in partnership by the national government.

Creative and knowledge cluster policy

There exist a wide variety of instruments promoting regional specialisation and cluster in Birmingham and the West Midlands as described by Brown et al. (2007). Using some research by Research House UK (2006), Brown et al. (2007) show that this policy focus has resulted in the creation of 166 organisations to support the creative industries in terms of education and skills, diversity, competition and intellectual property, business support and access to finance, technology and infrastructure in the West Midlands.

At the national level, over the last 10 years, the UK government has emphasised the knowledge and creative economy as well as the development of clusters through the Department for Trade and Industry, now the Department for Business, Innovation and Skills, and the Department for Culture, Media and Sport. With the creation of the RDA's, this national economic agenda has been brought forward at the regional level through various strategies, including the regional economic strategy and the regional cultural strategy.

Today, there exist four knowledge and creative clusters in the Regional Economic Development Strategy in the West Midlands: ICT cluster, screen, image and sound, business and service cluster, interior and lifestyle cluster (including craft). In addition, other clusters cover some research institutions involved in environmental technologies, building technologies, aerospace and medical technologies. While most clusters built on existing strengths in the region, others can be considered as aspirational clusters, for example medical technologies. One criticism of this cluster approach has been that it does not recognise the entire creative industries as a cluster but includes some creative activities under specific clusters like screen, image and sound, ICT or the lifestyle cluster diluting the marketing of the region. Nevertheless, this approach reinforces specific local and regional specialisations.

Another challenge, however, has been to reconcile regional and local strategies. The City of Birmingham has adopted a wider approach by targeting the growth of creative and knowledge industries as a whole in Birmingham's planning and economic strategies. The local vision is to foster the growth of these industries and to develop some parts of the city as prestigious, internationally renowned creative quarters and centres of excellence as well as leading edge clusters of knowledge-intensive industries (Brown et al., 2007).

Networking

Networking has been at the heart of the development of the four regional clusters which all include local and/or regional initiatives aiming to reinforce networking between businesses as well as higher education or research institutions at various geographical levels. This is the case of *Birmingham Forward*, for example, one of the local forums for professional and business services, or the *Creative Hub* located at the Custard Factory in Birmingham which supports the networking and clustering of over 300 businesses in the eastern part of Birmingham City Centre. This is the same for the *West Midlands ICT Cluster* which groups universities, research centres, national skill organisations, etc. and private actors across the region.

At the local level, there are also plenty of organisations working together to foster the cultural and creative industries; nevertheless they tend to focus on the entire sector contrary to the regional initiatives. Two examples are the *Birmingham Cultural Partnership* or the *Creative Birmingham Partnership Board* which groups key local and regional public and private actors in the sector in order to develop the cultural and creative industries and to raise the profile of Birmingham as a cultural destination (Brown et al., 2007). While this partnership working has been encouraged by the national government, this way of working also conforms to a long historical tradition in Birmingham. Using work by Ferarrio and Coulson (2005), Brown et al. (2007, p. 129) note: 'There is a well-established tradition of institutional collaboration and partnerships in Birmingham, with most local organisations working with one, or more, other organisations, usually in conjunction with Birmingham City Council, for the delivery of economic development activities.'

These local and regional public initiatives have been echoed by bottom-up ones from the industries. This is the case of the *Creative Republic* which works for people in the creative and cultural industries and aims to achieve representation, lobbying, networking and commissioning research for the sector. Another example is the *Producer Forum*, which groups producers with a track record in screen based media and film in the West Midlands and which offers networking events and training for the industry. In addition to these local and regional networks and partnerships, other initiatives have aimed to foster research and innovation in the creative and knowledge industries by linking research institutions and businesses. For instance, the Jewellery Industry Innovation Centre (JIIC), part of The Birmingham City University's School of Jewellery, was set up to assist the jewellery and silversmithing industries with new technology applications in order to develop high value products to compete with cheaper jewellery produced in Asia.

These local and regional initiatives aiming to support networking between private actors and between private and public institutions have created positive synergies in some sectors and less in others as expressed in recent interviews with creative and knowledge managers in Birmingham. People working in the creative and knowledge sectors in Birmingham and the West Midlands know each other but collaboration is dependent on the characteristics of each sector, for example the presence of influential national actors like the British Broadcasting Corporation (BBC) in the screen, media and sound sector (Brown et al., 2008).

Other wider challenges include the fragility associated with location away from London which remains a significant threat due to a perceived negative image of the work done outside the capital (Brown et al., 2008). The various cluster strategies in place regionally have all put in place initiatives fostering access to markets. However, supporting a positive image of Birmingham as a creative and knowledge city may require more than a cluster policy approach and a more general branding of the city.

Highly skilled labour

Birmingham has three universities, two higher education colleges and seven further education colleges. These institutions deliver a variety of programmes oriented towards creative and knowledge industries. Skills have been an important part of the Labour agenda since 2003 when the UK government published its first skill strategy and this has been adopted at the regional level. Recently, the local and regional organisations in charge of learning and skills have started producing sector intelligence sheets analysing the demand and supply of skills in a variety of sectors including creative industries and media, business and professional services and ICT.

Many of these sectors face some challenging local and regional skill shortages. The existing workforce in professional and financial services displays some deficiencies not only in softer generic skills, but also in a range of more technical, job specific skills (WMRO, 2006). While the creative and media sector is well supplied with graduates these lack some practical skills (LSC, 2008). Skill gaps have also been identified as an issue for ICT businesses, especially regarding highly qualified workers, in the region (LSC, 2007). These local and regional skill shortages were also highlighted in the interviews carried out with creative and knowledge managers for this research (Brown et al., 2008, p. 96).

These skill issues are not specific to the creative and knowledge industries but are part of a deeper and wider local and regional skills deficit. Up to 20 per cent of the working age population in Birmingham had no qualifications in 2006, which was higher than the regional (17 per cent) and national average (14 per cent) (WMRO, 2007). On the other hand, only 23 per cent of the working age population in Birmingham had a degree or more, compared with 24 per cent for the region and 27 per cent for England. Despite this, the region had the highest density of skill shortage vacancies and the lowest proportion of staff undergoing training in the country in 2006.

Poznan – the emergence of creative and knowledge clusters

The knowledge and creative industries have emerged in Poznan in the last decade and are developing very dynamically. This has been fostered by a boom in the education sector and increase in the number of students. To a large extent this development has had a spontaneous character, which reflects the 'natural' potential of local businesses to strive for competitiveness in the contemporary economy. Knowledge and creative industries have expanded with the strengthening of the market economy in Poland and the catching up with the West. However, their role in the local economy is yet to be fully recognised. Following the administrative decentralisation process, some local economic cluster initiatives have emerged but they have mainly come from the universities and/or transnational corporations (TNCs). In addition, the city is till struggling to co-ordinate its urban development.

Governance structure

The Polish administrative system consists of four tiers of government: national, regional, sub-regional and local. The Poznan metropolitan region coincides with the boundaries of the sub-regional unit called Poznan poviat (sub-regional district). It includes some adjacent towns and other local administrative units. Apart from its municipal and poviat administrative functions, Poznan is also the seat of the regional authority, Wielkopolska voivodeship, one of the largest in Poland in terms of area and population. It is important to note that regional bodies play a key role in the development of the city; however the local authorities have direct and decisive roles.

Economic development policies

At the beginning of the new chapter of Polish history in 1990, Poland was an almost complete 'desert' from the point of view of innovation or business networks, including those based on new information and communications technologies (ICTs). In particular, the relationships between industry, R&D centres, and science were very weak. There was no condition facilitating the development of knowledge and creative industries (Stryjakiewicz, 2002). The primary efforts of central, regional and local governments were focused on dealing with the recession caused by the initial shock of the transition period. At the time any increase in industrial output was considered a success. Consequently, state and local government policies relied mainly on short-term strategies in order to deal with the most immediate economic challenges. As the economic transition progressed, these main problems were solved and an increasing attention was paid to more qualitative aspects of development. Terms like 'clusters', 'urban knowledge systems', or 'inter-firm knowledge networks' started entering the Polish economic discourse. However, local and regional initiatives have been mainly spontaneous.

According to Stryjakiewicz (2002, p. 303), in the absence of a long-term national strategy of promotion and support for knowledge and creative industries, two local economic development paths are available: exogenous, connected with the activities of TNCs and EU institutions, and endogenous ('grass-roots'), spontaneously utilising local human capital. In the context of the unsatisfactory role of TNCs and foreign direct investment (FDI) in creating innovation networks and promoting the new economy, the development of local grass-roots ventures in this field is of special importance. The best example of such a local network can be found in the city of Swarzedz near Poznan with its artistic furniture crafts (Stryjakiewicz, 2005). Nevertheless those structures have so far been developed mainly without policy support.

Since 1990, the main strategic and planning documents developed by the Poznan local government authorities in pursuing their growth strategies have been largely general in focus. This is mainly explained by the necessity of building the market economy almost from scratch, forcing the city to tackle wider local issues like infrastructure provision. This could, over the longer term, benefit the development of the creative and knowledge sector in the city. However, today, there is no spatially and functionally cohesive policy with the objective of building a creative sector in the city and its surroundings. The survey carried out for this project revealed several major worries among creative and knowledge workers related to the quality of life– and the proportion expressing concern about this was the highest among the cities compared in this chapter (Stryjakiewicz et al., 2008a). For example, road traffic and affordability of housing appeared as two major issues for the city. To a lesser extent, some workers worried about safety, homelessness, aggressive and anti-social behaviour in the streets, and the level of crime in the city.

Despite these problems, the creative and knowledge workers interviewed had difficulty pinpointing strategies to improve the city's competitiveness through policy intervention (Stryjakiewicz et al., 2008a). They usually suggested better city promotion strategies, the improvement of infrastructure or an increase in cultural expenditure in general. This lack of ingenuity seems to be yet another hard-to-overcome legacy of communism, which tended to suppress any manifestation of creativity. That is why one of the most important tasks today is to increase the level of public awareness of the significance of the creative and knowledge sectors in the modernisation process and the development of cities.

Networking

Interviews with managers of knowledge and creative firms showed that for most firms classic hard factors, especially the nearness of the market and the labour market structure, were of paramount importance in locating in Poznan (Stryjakiewicz et al., 2008b). Nevertheless, formal and informal links among businesses were also important for their position in the market. The scale of those links determines not only the standing of a firm, but also of the city or metropolitan region where it is based. Firms with the strongest links locally but also at the supra-local and international levels were from the software and electronic publishing sector. In other sub-sectors there were no such clear interconnections among local firms or with firms outside Poznan and Poland. In general, most firms were not fully mature yet, and did not have well-developed networks. This can be partly explained by the rather poor relation between the city's high research and educational potential and its economic growth in terms of commercialisation of research results. This is evident from the small number of patent applications and licence-implementing agreements from Poznan's universities. In order to remedy this situation, the Scientific-Technological Park of the Adam Mickiewicz University (AMU) Foundation was established in the city in 1995 – the first institution of this kind in Poland to operate under market conditions. It carries out research and didactic activities and offers training and services to small and medium-sized enterprises (SMEs) (rental of space, technological consulting, production of aids, international co-operation guidance, and technology and innovation transfer guidance) as well as to the local and regional R&D sector.

More recently, there have been several initiatives aiming at a more vigorous co-operation between business and science. An example of this is the Centre for Innovation and Technology Transfer opened at AMU in 2004. In addition, higher education institutions are engaged not only in teaching but also in research activity. There are two Centres of Excellence operating at the Poznan University of Technology. Apart from universities, two other actors play key roles in networking: Poznan Supercomputing and Networking Centre (PSNC) and Centre for Advanced Information Technologies. The PSNC is the city's leading provider of information technology (IT) and network services. The state-of-the-art technologies implemented there ensure Poznan the top position among the information centres in Poland. Initially the PSNC offer was mainly addressed to the scientific circles, but today it embraces an equal proportion of other firms.

With the rapid development of knowledge-intensive industries, the city is hosting an ever-growing number of highly successful IT firms. This development is sustained by global players including Sun and Microsoft. In 2002, Sun Microsystems selected PNSC as a Sun Center of Excellence in New Generation Networks, Grids and Portals. In turn, the first Microsoft Innovation Center (MIC) in Poland was opened in the city on 1 June 2006 as a joint project between Microsoft, PNSC and the Poznan Technical University. Its chief purpose was to support innovative solutions and technologies in information security and outsourcing services. Like the other MICs in the world, the Poznan MIC is supposed to be the hub of co-operation in the field of IT research, technology and solutions among central and local government institutions, schools of higher learning, and enterprises. Its aim is an optimum application of advanced and safe Internet technologies in projects carried out by the above-mentioned units.

Highly skilled labour

Poznan benefits today from a good environment in terms of a highly skilled labour force based on strong higher education institutions. After 1989, higher education in Poland changed dramatically. Borders were opened allowing free mobility of people and autonomy of universities in curricula and management. New laws concerning higher education, convertible Polish currency, easy communication, and access to European education and research programmes made higher education more accessible. Since the beginning of the transformation period, there has been a strong focus on education both at the national and the local levels. There were 427 higher learning institutions in Poland in 2005 compared with 97 in 1989. The post-communist period has seen an increase of some 30 per cent in the number of public higher learning institutions and the creation of a very large number of private, not-for-profit institutions. Similarly, the years following 1989 saw a very rapid expansion in demand of higher education.

The rapid and mainly spontaneous development of the higher education sector in Poznan has recently been framed by some policies in order to regulate it and make it more goal-oriented. This is an important development as Poznan is the third most powerful academic and research centre in Poland. The city and the whole metropolitan region are well-prepared for the programming of the knowledge-based social and economic development due to the skills and qualifications of the local population and the capacity of existing institutional and technical infrastructures to facilitate knowledge acquisition and transfer. The area of the whole metropolitan region is inhabited by 856,000 people, one-fifth of whom has a university degree. This high level of education is ensured by 26 institutions of higher learning (including 8 state-run). Their total enrolment accounts for more than 122,000 students. The high skills and quality of the human capital explain a low unemployment rate (2 per cent) and a high level of entrepreneurship. Large foreign corporations (e.g. Volkswagen, GlaxoSmithKline Pharmaceuticals, Bridgestone, Beiersdorf) play an important role as their investment exceeds $5 billion and ensures the transfer of advanced technologies and innovations. These technologies are also developed by the 50 R&D institutions based in the Poznan metropolitan region.

Conclusions

Recent European and international theoretical and policy debates have highlighted the importance of local (city-regional) policies in the development of new innovative clusters. It is often assumed – either implicitly or explicitly – that local and regional economic policies are of particular significance in developing the structural conditions for the growth of creative and knowledge-intensive industries.

The comparison of our three European cities, Helsinki, Birmingham, and Poznan, with very different historical development and economic positions in terms of creative and knowledge industries points towards two main conclusions. The first is linked with the importance of both local/regional and national economic factors and policies in fostering creative and knowledge clusters. The second relates to the importance of wider local, regional success factors. In addition, while Helsinki is clearly an example of strong bottom-up and embedded emergence of clustering, Birmingham and Poznan allude to the possibility of developing clusters either through policies or by attracting international activities.

Helsinki demonstrates how strong national policies focusing on education and historic preconditions favouring the development of telecommunication as well as social cohesion and networking have allowed this capital of a small peripheral country to become one of the international leaders in one sector of the knowledge industries. Even if Helsinki can now be considered as mature in terms of supporting the knowledge economy with a great integration of actors and strategies around the ICT cluster, the cluster emerged initially through private sector initiative (Nokia) and was later supported by public policies. In comparison with Birmingham, Helsinki seems to have been responsive rather than proactive in terms of local and regional policies to support the creative and knowledge industries.

It is important to notice, however, that the success of Helsinki seems to be linked to a structural match (or homology) between historic national foci on both education and networking and necessary preconditions of modern cluster building. These peculiarities are linked with long standing and continuous difficulties in both nation building (during the wars of 1918 and 1939–1945) and then in the struggle for sovereignty up until the Soviet Empire collapsed. The universally accepted value attributed to higher education and related national policies, as well as the specific role of the national intelligentsia in the struggle for independence (for the nation and the people) were key factors. This was reinforced by the drive towards national political integration in the defence of the nation against foreign pressures. This was achieved through consensual solutions, over decades of political and social networking, linking all fragments of the elite (the political, the economic, and the intellectual), favouring strong networking process today.

These preconditions and historical developments seem to have contributed to a natural success and early maturation of the Helsinki region as an international hub in the knowledge industries, without the help of any specific, purposive policy intervention. While national policies have played a key role in the development of the sector, the importance of the local and regional dimensions in supporting the knowledge industries have only been recently raised. This is leading among other things to the elaboration of local and regional cluster policies around innovation and ICT. In addition, while the economic success in the knowledge economy of Helsinki is undeniable, survey evidence has highlighted the importance of a wider challenge in the retention of knowledge workers in the Helsinki metropolitan region: the availability of affordable housing. This needs to be addressed at city-regional level, if the city wants to remain competitive.

Birmingham offers a contrasting example to Helsinki. The City could be considered a perfect example of strong local and regional cluster policies aimed at developing the creative and knowledge industries in the last 10 years influenced by national priorities. This has been part of an important process of economic restructuring since the mid-1980s supported by various local and regional policies. As a result, some creative and knowledge clusters have been targeted as regional priorities. A lot of attention has been given to improving networking and skills among creative and knowledge actors. Today, the city presents a strong profile in some knowledge and creative sectors, but is lagging behind other UK cities on the creative side. The plethora of local and regional actors and the attention given to too many clusters seem to have created some political inefficiency. More importantly, local and regional policies seem to have difficulty in counteracting generally low levels of educational attainment in Birmingham and the West Midlands. While the national government put a lot of emphasis on skills and education in the last 5 years this remains a deep-seated problem in the region. It contributes to wider issues related to social inequality in the city and region and adds to the challenges of retaining creative and knowledge workers. These problems cannot only be tackled at the local or city-regional level as they are linked with a national history of strong and clear class divisions ingrained in the geography of England and enhanced by recent developments. This also explains part of the challenges related to the poor image of Birmingham as a creative city nationally. While national policies are important in sustaining the development of creative and knowledge industries in the case of Birmingham this involves more than cluster policies.

Finally, Poznan is only starting developing its creative and knowledge economy. The Polish administrative structure now consists of four tiers of government: national, regional, sub-regional and local which have refocused economic development at the local and regional level. A strong national push has been given to the development of higher education while, locally and regionally, initiatives have focused on developing collaboration between research and industry. Only recently have the notions of cluster and creative economy reached the policy scene. Poznan has traditionally been characterised as a business centre. The city has benefited from restructuring and has been growing steadily economically – and in the past 15 years, growing creative and knowledge industries. The reform of the administrative structure has resulted in the emergence of various local and regional actors, which have elaborated new policies and have put initiatives in place to support innovation and clustering in the city. Nevertheless, many of these initiatives are driven by universities in collaboration with TNCs. This raises some questions concerning their local embeddeness over the longer term and the need to better co-ordinate the city's overall urban development. While many local and regional strategies have been elaborated, there are still many that need to deal with local challenges in terms of infrastructure, housing and social issues. Consequently, policy actions are needed both at the national level to target social problems as well as at the local or city-regional level to target problems related to traffic or affordable housing.

There is at least one feature that is common to these three cities: the importance of national and local traditions, both politically and socially, in the constitution of the structural preconditions of creative and knowledge industries. Poznan, while having successfully restructured its economy since the end of communism is still trying to improve public sector processes or societal behaviour, inherited from the previous era. In Birmingham, the obstacles seem to be related to an overcrowding of policy initiatives and some skill deficiencies that were not addressed in the previous 20 years of economic restructuring as well as the existence of deep-rooted class divisions (and the social significance attached to them). Finally, Helsinki's success seems to be linked with a structural match between the historical national traditions in terms of educational level and national networking and the preconditions of modern cluster building.

In conclusion, there are some local features that are important for the development of creative and knowledge industries but cannot be effectively addressed by local decision makers or in the form of cluster policy.

Successful policy also requires there to be a reasonable match between the wider established practices and traditions of local and national governance and the requirements of the new economic success (or cluster building).

Acknowledgments

The authors would like to thank the other members of the local team in Birmingham, Helsinki and Poznan for their contributions to this chapter through their work in ACRE.

References

Allardt, E. (1971) *Yhteiskunnan rakenne ja sosiaalinen paine.* (3rd edition). Porvoo: Wsoy

Brenner, T. and Mühlig (2007) *Factors and mechanisms causing the emergence of local industrial clusters – A meta-study of 159 cases.* Paper on Economics and Evolution #0723, Germany: Max Planck Institute of Economics, Jena.

Brown, J., C. Chapain, A. Murie, A. Barber, J. Gibney and J. Lutz (2007) *From a city of a thousand trades to a city of a thousand ideas. Birmingham, West Midlands. Pathways to creative and knowledge based regions.* ACRE report 2.3. Amsterdam: AMIDSt.

Brown, J., A. Barber, C. Chapain, J. Gibney, J. Lutz and A. Murie (2008) *Understanding the attractiveness of Birmingham and the West Midlands Region for creative knowledge firms. The managers' view.* ACRE report WP6.3. Amsterdam: AMIDSt.

Castells, M. and P. Himanen (2002) *The information society and the welfare state. The Finnish model.* New York: Oxford University Press.

Commission of the European Communities (CEC) (2008) *The concept of clusters and cluster policies and their role for competitiveness and innovation: Main statistical results and lessons learned.* Annex to the communication from the Commission to the Council, the European Parliament, the European Economic and Social committee and the Committee of the Regions.

Cooke, P. (1992) Regional innovation systems: Competitive regulation in the New Europe. *Geoforum*, 23: 365–382.

Ferrario, C. and A. Coulson (2005) *Local government and economic development: The role of local government. A study of Birmingham, England, Based on 'Institutional Thickness'.* Paper presented at IRSPM IX, Milan, 6–8 April 2005.

Helsinki Regional Innovation Strategy (2005) Culminatum, Espoo. <http://www.culminatum.fi/content_files/InnovationStrategy.pdf> (accessed 11 April 2007).

Inkinen, T. and M. Vaattovaara (2007) *Technology and knowledge-based development. Helsinki metropolitan area as a creative region.* ACRE report 2.5. Amsterdam: AMIDSt.

Kepsu, K. and M. Vaattovaara (2008) *Creative knowledge in the Helsinki metropolitan area. Understanding the attractiveness of the metropolitan region for creative knowledge workers.* ACRE report WP5.5. Amsterdam: AMIDSt.

Learning and Skills Council (LSC) (2007) *Review of education and training in the ICT Sector. West Midlands.* England: LSC.

Learning and Skills Council (LSC) (2008) *Talent 2 market, review of education and training in the creative & media sector.* England: LSC.

Loikkanen, H.A. and I. Susiluoto (2006) *Cost efficiency of Finnish municipalities in basic service provision 1994–2002.* Discussion Paper No. 96/February 2006. Finland: Helsinki Center of Economic Research.

Mäkelä, K. (1999) *Valtio, väkijuomat ja kulttuuri. Kirjoituksia Suomesta ja sosiologiasta.* Gaumeamus: Tampere.

Martin, R. and P. Sunley (2003) Deconstructing clusters chaotic concept of policy panacea? *Journal of Economic Geography,* 3: 5–35.

OECD (1999) *Boosting innovation. The cluster approach.* OECD Proceedings. Paris: OECD.

OECD (2007) *Competitive regional clusters. National policy approaches.* OECD Reviews of Regional Innovation. Paris: OECD.

Oxford Research (2008) *Cluster policy in Europe. A brief summary of cluster policies in 31 European countries.* Europe Innova Cluster Mapping Project. Norway: Oxford Research.

Parysek, J. and L. Mierzejewska (2006) Poznan. *Cities,* 23 (4): 291–305.

Porter, M.E. (1990) The competitive advantage of nations. *Harvard Business Review,* 68 (2): 73–93.

Porter, M.E. (1998) *On competition.* Boston: Harvard Business School Press.

Porter, M.E. (2004) Global competition, clusters and Finland wireless alley. In: D. Steinbock (ed.), *What's next? Finnish ICT Cluster and Globalisation.* Helsinki: Ministry of the Interior Finland.

Research House UK (2006) *Scoping study: Support structures for the creative industries in the West Midlands.* Coventry, UK: Research House.

Steinbock, D. (2004) *What next? Finnish ICT cluster and globalization.* Finland: Ministry of Interior Finland.

Steinbock, D. (2006) *Finland's innovative capacity.* Finland: Ministry of Interior, Regional Development 13/2006.

Stryjakiewicz, T. (2002) Paths of industrial transformation in Poland and the role of knowledge-based industries. In: R. Hayter and R. Le Heron (eds), *Knowledge, industry and environment: Institutions and innovation in territorial perspective,* pp. 289–311. England: Ashgate.

Stryjakiewicz, T. (2005) Contrasting experiences with business networking in a transition economy: The case of Poland. In: C.G. Alvstam and E.W. Schamp (eds), *Linking industries across the world: Processes of global networking,* pp. 197–219. England: Ashgate.

Stryjakiewicz, T., E. Grzywinska, T. Kaczmarek, M. Meczynski. J.J. Parysek and K. Stachowiak (2008a) Poznan welcomes talents. Understanding the attractiveness of the metropolitan region for creative knowledge workers. ACRE report WP5.8. Amsterdam: AMIDSt.

Stryjakiewicz, T., M. Meczynski and K. Stachowiak (2008b) The attractiveness of the Poznan metropolitan region for the development of the creative knowledge sector. The managers' view. ACRE report WP6.8. Amsterdam: AMIDSt.

United Nations (2008) Creative economy report. The challenge of assessing the creative economy: Towards informed policy making. http://www.unctad.org/en/docs/ditc20082cer_en.pdf

Vorley, T. (2008) The geographic cluster: A historical review. *Geography Compass,* 2/3: 790–813.

West Midlands Regional Observatory – WMRO (2006) *Regional skills partnership sector profile 2005 Professional & Financial Services.* England: WMRO.

West Midlands Regional Observatory – WMRO (2007) *Regional skill assessment 2007. Skills and the West Midlands economy. A Birmingham and Solihull perspective.* England: WMRO.

16

Policies for Firms or Policies for Individuals? Amsterdam, Munich and Budapest

Zoltán Kovács, Heike Pethe and Manfred Miosga

Introduction

Most authors researching 'creative industries' focus on the clustering mechanisms of creative companies and the hard factors that attract them. In the same way, many of the available policy documents emphasise hard conditions and focus almost exclusively on creating favourable local conditions for such firms. In contrast, Richard Florida (2002) stated in his often-cited work that cities and regions should not focus on the creative companies, but on the people who work for these companies or might start such companies themselves. For them it is soft conditions that really matter and not the hard conditions. Florida also came to the conclusion that talent, technology and tolerance (3Ts) are important conditions. He argued that growth is powered by creative people (talent), who prefer places that are culturally diverse and open to new ideas (tolerant), and the concentration of 'cultural capital' wedded to new products (technology). Cities can formulate and implement rather different policies to create favourable conditions for attracting and settling the creative and knowledge-intensive economy. In this respect, a major strategic question is whether these policies should focus primarily on attracting firms engaged in creative activities, or is it enough to attract creative people as suggested by Florida.

To approach the dilemma for practice, this chapter discusses the examples of three European metropolitan regions of similar size – Amsterdam, Munich and Budapest. These cities have developed under very different socio-economic and political circumstances, and they followed distinctive pathways to become modern European metropolises. Their public administration and political decision-making systems have also been rather different. However, one thing is common in all three cities; they would like to attract knowledge-intensive activities and become creative cities. In order to reach this goal each city has formulated policies, over the last decade, to boost the development of the creative knowledge economy. The aim of this chapter is to summarise and compare these policies and give special attention to their goals and contents, and their success or failure. Among others the following questions are addressed:

- Do existing policies on creative and knowledge-intensive economy focus more on the location of businesses or people?
- Do the metropolitan economic development policies specifically address the conditions for attracting an international skilled labour force?
- To what extent are economic development policies in metropolitan regions connected to other policies like housing, environmental or cultural policies to attract and cater for the desired 'talent pool'?
- How are such policies influenced by the wider national and regional context?

In order to answer these questions, we first introduce the theoretical framework of the creative city and competitiveness policy debate. This is followed by a short presentation of the economic development of the cities, an account of the state of the creative and knowledge-intensive economy and a discussion of policies implemented in the selected cities to create favourable conditions for the creative economy. At the end of the chapter, the 'hard' or 'soft' factor dilemma is addressed in the light of the experiences from Amsterdam, Munich and Budapest.

Do policies help in competition? – a theoretical framework

Richard Florida captured with his phrase 'talent, technology, tolerance' the importance of individuals for the economic development of cities. He underlined that the ability to attract human capital is crucial for the economic success of metropolitan regions and that existing urban amenities such as cafes, restaurants and a vivid and diverse street life are important in this (Florida, 2002). Other researchers including Ley (1996) and Butler and Savage (1995) also noted that the demographic structure of urban areas had changed. An increasing share is academically educated and has high incomes. They were oriented towards liberal values, work in creative or knowledge-intensive occupations and often live in inner-city areas. Their presence had changed the urban landscape. Retail, housing and cultural activities were increasingly influenced by the demands of the new professional class. Urban policies were increasingly oriented to meet the demands of this well-paid stratum and to manage urban restructuring to improve the conditions for these individuals.

The American geographer Alan Scott, however, challenged this approach. In his view, attracting highly skilled individuals and 'creating a high-quality urban environment rich in cultural amenities and conducive to diversity in local social life' (Scott, 2006, p. 11) is too limited. The 'mere presence of "creative people" is certainly not enough to sustain urban creativity over long periods of time. Creativity needs to be mobilised and channelled for it to emerge in practical forms of learning and innovation' (Scott, 2006, p. 11). Scott points out that the interrelationship between the presence of creative people and regional development is more complex and more recursive. The activities of creative companies play a more important role. Scott observed that creative companies are organised in a local production system. In those production networks, companies profit from each other by exchanging information and common learning processes which revolve around the production of a certain product. They also share regional resources by relying on the same labour force, establishing common economic and social institutions. Often they also share similar values, practices and conventions. In other words, the existence of these externalities can reduce costs for regional producers. Companies also profit from the agglomeration economies, because the networks of complementary and specialised producers generate additional opportunities. Members of networks share regional facilities, they profit from each other's presence and a qualified labour market, and they participate in common learning processes (Scott, 2006, p. 8f). Scott concludes that 'Any viable developmental program focused on building a creative city must deal – at a minimum with setting up a local production system, training or attracting a relevant labour force, appropriate programming of urban space, and ensuring that all different elements involved work more or less in harmony with one another' (Scott, 2006, p. 11). In his view the support of the companies within the region is vital for regional success and competitiveness. Although he also mentions the 'programming of urban space', Scott underlines that the investments in the urban environment can only be successful when a healthy business environment exists.

In Western industrialised countries, any investment in the urban environment and actions to support companies were traditionally performed by different departments or ministries. One department was charged with some or all responsibility for economic development and policies towards firms; social and cultural policy was mainly aimed at individuals and households or neighbourhoods and was often the responsibility of one or more other departments (perhaps education) while planning or urban development departments whose remit was also related to these policy issues took on a middling position. Whereas some policy lines addressed companies directly, others such as housing or school development focused on the needs of individuals. The division of responsibilities, the aims of departments and cross-sectoral engagements have changed. Although more common integrated activities are still rare. The evolution of cultural departments illustrates this.

Public expenditure on the cultural sectors is abundant in European countries compared with the USA. The US federal agency in charge of National Endowment for the Arts (NEA) administered a budget of $115.2 million in 2002. In the Netherlands, municipalities, provinces and the national government spent €4.95 billion for culture in 2002 (CBS, 2008). In Germany, theatres, operas, museums and other cultural institutions ved €8.19 (Statistisches Bundesamt, 2008). Traditionally, this budget is used to support the individual enjoyment of high culture as it was produced by theatres, operas, museums or heritage organisations. It was mainly addressed for the individual use of culture. In the 1970s, emancipatory and educational aims came to the fore with the slogan 'culture for everybody' a common expression of equal access to culture. Art was conceived in terms of its aesthetic and social values, but not in terms of its use-value for the economy (Klamer, 1996). The reasoning about the economic value of culture entered the discussion in the mid-1980s. Then culture was not only seen in terms of individual enjoyment and education, but also as a location factor and in terms of its multiplier effects. At this stage arguments still started at an individual level. They would run like this: through the supply of cultural infrastructure, individuals in key economic position profit from the consumption of high-end culture; the image of region is improved; the elite invests in the regional economy or consumes other regional products which generate tax revenues. Thus, culture works as indirect leverage for economic development. The support of culture was justified by functional and economic arguments: culture supports innovation, it creates employment and it cushions de-industrialisation. Subsidies into the art sector, the support of civil engagement in culture and culture-led urban generation can generate economic growth in other realms (Micheel and Wiest, 2002). The old, sectoral policy was challenged by additional arguments. The production of culture does not only happen in the realm of subsidised high culture, but the privately run cultural or creative economy increasingly grows in employment and turnover. Culture and creativity have become vital for cross-sectoral innovation and the creation of new products. The sectors are more strongly interlinked at different stages of the production chain. The share of self-employed entrepreneurs steadily increases in this sector so that the distinction between companies and individuals increasingly fades away (Moßig, 2005).

In spite of these changes in activities related to culture, the discussion about a suitable policy for the creative knowledge industries is still active. Should governments invest in individuals or companies? Is the current creative knowledge policy an expression of neoliberal policy which contributes to the economic penetration of non-commercial realms as Peck and others have recently asserted (Gibson and Kong, 2005; Peck, 2005, 2007; Chapain and Lee, 2009)? Does it also support uneven development of places and does it widen social inequalities? Does the state play a new role as 'facilitator' and 'partner' in Europe in the same way that Lewis et al. (2008) described for the designer fashion industry in New Zealand? How can a new policy be developed without neglecting individuals, but recognising the new economic organisation of the creative knowledge society? How is the policy influenced by the national and regional context?

Economic development and political conditions

To what extent can policies influence the economic development and competitiveness of cities and how can the growth of the creative knowledge economy be stimulated by policy instruments? Most probably the right answer to this is that it depends on many factors including the general structure of the local economy, the long-term development of the labour market and the local political climate. We start to explore the possible answers to our main question in different European urban settings by discussing three European metropolitan regions – Amsterdam, Munich and Budapest – with contrasting development paths.

With 2.2 million inhabitants, *Amsterdam* metropolitan region is the largest urban agglomeration and primary economic centre of the Netherlands. The economic weight of Amsterdam and its region is outstanding, 17 per cent of all companies and 15 per cent of the national workforce is based on the region (Bontje and Sleutjes, 2007, p. 42). The region is characterised by a diversified service economy, which comprises 85 per cent of total regional employment (Bontje and Sleutjes, 2007, p. 45). Banking, information and communication technology, logistics and trade, tourism, higher education and the cultural economy are prominent activities.

The leading position of many of these sectors was established in the seventeenth century when Amsterdam was the second largest city in the Netherlands and the wealthiest city of the world (Tordoir, 2003, p. 108). In the so-called Golden Age, Amsterdam controlled a global colonial empire. Every second ship which made its way to Asia was carrying the Dutch flag between 1600 and 1800 (Mak, 2006, p. 129). Since then banking and trade have been important functions, and gradually Amsterdam also established itself as a cultural centre. Painters such as Rembrandt, Ruysdael and Hals shaped European baroque painting profiting from the high demand of wealthy citizens. Philosophers such as Spinoza and Descartes were attracted to the city due to its open intellectual climate. The favourable position of Amsterdam was terminated by the Napoleonic Wars. In the subsequent century, the economy mostly stagnated and the city missed the Industrial Revolution (Mak, 2006, p. 195).

After World War II, the harbour of Rotterdam surpassed Amsterdam – another clear sign of the long-term economic downturn of the city (Bosscher, 2007, p. 350). In the 1980s, the economic situation was still challenging. As Terhorst and Van de Ven (2003, p. 95) noted: 'Amsterdam was a city in crisis with a declining population, large-scale unemployment, a sky-rocketing number of people on welfare, growing crime rates associated with drug dealing ...'. The Dutch economy was badly affected by the oil crisis, low productivity and high wages and the shift from an industrial to a post-industrial economy. The region lost 21.1 per cent of its unskilled employment and gained an additional 8.8 per cent high-skilled jobs between 1970 and 1984 (Zorlu, 2002, p. 218). National urban policy focusing on the development of 'new towns' also contributed to the shrinkage of Amsterdam.

The traditional Dutch social organisations (liberal, socialist, protestant and catholic political and social communities) lost influence which lead to conflicts between old-fashioned, authoritarian representatives of the local government and members of the new social movements (Terhorst and Van de Ven, 2003, p. 93). This anti-growth coalition also blocked effective economic policy.

However, since the late 1980s, the region has experienced a long period of economic success. Gradually, problems were solved and the former disadvantages turned out to be assets. In 1982, employers, unions and the government signed the Wassenaar Accord. This deregulated labour law, limited wage increases and led to a reduction in unemployment. The close cooperation between the central state and the large cities was embodied in an urban pro-growth policy which also introduced competitive elements of revenue allocation (Terhorst and Van de Ven, 2003, p. 96). The neglected inner-city neighbourhoods were seen as important sites for state-stimulated, but preferably private investment. The communication, transport and cultural infrastructure were significantly improved. Twenty years before Florida underlined the importance of the creative class as consumers, an Amsterdam academic, Rob van Engelsdorp-Gastelaars, advised the city to accommodate the better off by stimulating culture and festivals. Amsterdam applied for the Olympic Games 1992 and became 'Cultural Capital of Europe' in 1988 (Terhorst and Van de Ven, 1995, p. 353). Private investments in the urban development were supported by tax credits for homeowners and a low real rent mortgage rate (Terhorst and Van de Ven, 2003, p. 97). Due to the diversified economic structure and the new private consumption of goods and services, the economy of Amsterdam recovered. The formerly neglected, restored historical buildings became an asset to attract highly skilled persons from outside. In addition, several cultural institutions were established by squatters contributing to the recovery of Amsterdam as a vivid creative city.

Munich is one of the most important centres of research and development, as well as high-tech industry and the media in Germany. With a current population of approximately 2.5 million inhabitants, the Munich metropolitan region has developed into one of the most dynamic and economically prosperous urban agglomerations in Europe in the post-World War II period.

Being the capital and the administrative centre of Bavaria since the fifteenth century, Munich profited from the early investment by the state in the arts, architecture and sciences. In particular, the royal patronage of the sciences in the late nineteenth century was of great importance for the early development of quality industries which capitalised on new technologies and inventions (e.g. the media, technical instrumentation). It is also important to note that, instead of becoming a heavily industrialised town, Munich became predominantly a centre of commerce, culture and higher education – which later on spared the city the painful task of post-Fordist economic restructuring.

The reconstruction of the historical cityscape after the massive devastation of World War II contributed to the gradual development of the tourist industry and the flourishing of service functions. The comprehensive modernisation of urban infrastructure (transport, public spaces, etc.) and successful organisation of the 1972 Olympic Games provided a solid basis for successful city branding in the 1970s and 1980s. Another decisive event in the post-war period was the move of Siemens Company from Berlin to Munich as it created the nucleus for the spatial concentration of other German and international companies. The post-war years also marked the beginning of the Bavarian technology policy, especially through investment in R&D as well as in the arms industry. After the oil crisis, Munich and central Bavaria developed into the leading German high-tech region during the 1980s and 1990s. The economic development was strongly supported by infrastructure policies of the Bavarian State as well as the city of Munich. The present economic situation of Munich can be characterised by a dynamic labour market, low unemployment rate, high purchasing power as well as dynamic growth in the service sector. What is the secret of this economic prosperity?

One part of Munich's strength as a business location is based on the diversity of its economic structure and the mixture of global players and SMEs. This modern and balanced economic structure is often referred to as the 'Munich Mix' (*Münchner Mischung*). This term not only refers to the mixture of big and small enterprises, but also to the diversity of economic activities what is partly the outcome of long-lasting economic policies. The economic success of Munich can be attributed to the existence of numerous clusters including biotechnology and pharmaceuticals, medical technology, environmental technology, ICT, aerospace, the media and finance, all of which constitute the foundations of a well-developed creative economy.

These activities form the innovative growth poles of the city region. The clusters are not only made up by links among enterprises of the respective branches but also by links to the numerous research institutions in the Munich area, by the networks of SMEs and large enterprises as well as links to commercialisation protagonists.

With 2.5 million inhabitants, *Budapest* and its metropolitan region is nowadays one of the largest and economically most dynamic regions east of the former Iron Curtain. The prime position of the city within the national economy is well reflected by the fact that 44.5 per cent of the Hungarian GDP was produced in the Central Hungary Region and 35 per cent in Budapest itself in 2004.

The current position of Budapest in the broader international and regional context can be traced back to the rapid economic and urban development over the last third of the nineteenth century – what is called the era of K. u K. Monarchy (*Kaiser und König*). In this period, Hungary was a rapidly modernising country of the European continent and due to its economic, commercial as well as cultural influence Budapest played an outstanding role among European metropolises (Kovács, 1994). This harmonic and dynamic development was interrupted in the following decades of the twentieth century; by World War I and the subsequent economic stagnation of the inter-war period; and then by World War II and the forceful introduction of the Soviet type state-socialist system (Enyedi and Szirmai, 1992).

During state-socialism, just like in other parts of east-central Europe, industry and industrialisation was considered the main tool for the modernisation of the economy and society. Due to the centrally planned system, economic restructuring could not take place and the structure of the economy and especially industry did not change significantly throughout the whole period. Though traditional industries (food and textiles) had shrunk and engineering strengthened, the post-industrial economic transformation was prevented by state intervention. Only the economic stagnation of the late 1970s and early 1980s forced the state-socialist regime to implement new policies that brought about a decline in factory employment and a growth in services, especially in the field of trade and tourism. As a result, the number of manual workers in Budapest fell by 23 per cent between 1975 and 1987 (Kovács, 1994).

In terms of urban development, the 1970s and 1980s were characterised by large-scale public investments on the edge of the city in the form of huge high-rise housing estates, containing a vast number of almost identical, relatively small dwelling units. At the same time the historical quarters were neglected, setting the stage for the physical decay of large parts of inner-city neighbourhoods (Kovács, 2006).

The political system changed completely after 1990. The return to self-governance and the subsequent shift of control from central (state) to local (community) level was an important component of the political transformation affecting urban development. This gave local municipalities more power to control and influence their own development. In Budapest districts suddenly became the main actors of urban development, and the planning system was switched to a very liberal and decentralised bottom-up model.

The city arrived at the gate of political changes and democratic transition with an outdated economy. Industry still employed 36 per cent of the active earners of Budapest in 1990. Due to the change of political system in 1989–1990, a deep and comprehensive economic transformation process started. The most significant trend was the collapse of heavy industry and the increasing importance of services. As a consequence of the rapid growth in commerce, tourism, business and financial activities, the ratio of services in the occupational structure increased from 62 to 78 per cent between 1990 and 2006. The rapid economic transformation was also fostered by foreign capital investments mainly in the fields of logistics, telecommunication, creative and high-tech industries (Dövényi and Kovács, 2006).

During the transformation Budapest and its urban region kept its leading position in the economic development and modernisation of the country and even further increased it in innovative activities (Meusburger, 2001). Budapest now serves as the gateway for innovation and modern technologies within Hungary, and it is the prime national centre of most creative activities (education, R&D, media, finances, etc.).

The creative and knowledge sector and policies enhancing its development

The role and structure of creative knowledge economy show significant differences among the European regions (see more details in Musterd and Gritsai, 2009). Due to their function as science and high-tech centres, some urban regions including Cambridge, Munich (Hafner et al., 2007) or Toulouse (Peyroux et al., 2007) have been described as 'technopolis' (Castells, 1989). The development of these regions was partly enhanced by large-scale public investment such as the establishment of research institutions, science parks and an excellent university infrastructure. In other European regions, despite recent economic developments, the role of the creative knowledge economy is still limited. This is the case in most of the post-socialist countries where the linkages between businesses and public institutions such as universities and research institutes are generally weak. In these countries the service economy is less developed, an alternative cultural scene is rarely tolerated and a private cultural economy is hardly present (Paalzow et al., 2007; Stryjakiewicz et al., 2007; Dainov, 2008). In addition, governments in eastern and central Europe do not always recognise the economic importance of creative industries, thus they do not place major investments in this sector.

The three cities referred to in this chapter exhibit clear differences in the role of creative and knowledge-intensive economy. Amsterdam represents the bohemian cultural hub, with distinct forms of creative and cultural industries. Munich with its aspiration of becoming science and technology as well as higher educational centre in the heart of Europe is the case of *aufstrebende Stadt*. Budapest offers the example of post-socialist city, with a rapidly changing economy within a shifting macroeconomic framework. What can these cities show up with respect to the creative knowledge economy and what are the main policies enhancing its development?

Amsterdam

The position of Amsterdam as the capital of the creative knowledge economy in the Netherlands is very strong. The number of companies has been growing since 2000, and an increasing share of new companies belongs to knowledge-intensive and creative industries. In total, 31 per cent of all companies and 26 per cent of all employees in the metropolitan region belong to the creative knowledge sector – the highest concentration in the Netherlands (Kloosterman, 2004; Bontje and Sleutjes, 2007). The importance of Amsterdam is also well reflected by the fact that 24 per cent of all Dutch creative knowledge companies are located in the Amsterdam metropolitan area, making it the prime concentration of the Dutch creative knowledge economy. Especially for certain creative industries and the 'law and other business services' sector, the Amsterdam region is dominant. The city is the financial capital of the Netherlands and the prime location of financial headquarters and stock exchange activities. The film and advertising industry as well as the most important cultural institutions of the Netherlands are also situated in the region. What is the secret of this success, and how have national and local policies contributed to the growing concentration of knowledge-intensive activities?

For a long time, the Dutch corporatist regime emphasised low wages and accepted the related slow growth of labour productivity. After labour shortages became more visible during the rapid growth of the ICT industry at the end of the 1990s, innovation-related policies came to the fore. The national government put three programmes for the creative knowledge industry on the agenda: The first scheme 'Pieken in de Delta' aimed to strengthen the core areas in the 'Randstad' for international competition (Ministerie EZ, 2004). This programme combined a spatial investment and regeneration strategy with defined key sectors in the creative knowledge economy, and invited local and regional governmen\ts as well as public and private actors to apply for national funding in the so-called *Creative Challenge Call* launched in 2006.

A second programme *Ons Creatieve Vermogen* supported the interaction between creative industries and other economic branches (Ministerie EZ and Ministerie OCW, 2005). Thus, it was mainly oriented at the business community. Different actors were brought together in a third programme called *National Innovation Platform*. This was created as a discussion platform between the public and private actors to foster the interaction between all levels of education (school, university and further education) and entrepreneurship (Innovatieplatform, 2006).

The national level took a leading position in formulating the policy in the Netherlands. Although the needs of individuals were recognised and school curricula are adapted to enable individuals to compete in the new economic environment, business-oriented programmes dominated the national strategy (Figure 16.1).

There were few initiatives at the regional level because there are no formal government institutions at the regional level in the Netherlands – and the provincial level which is the formal second tier is one level too high to be relevant for metro areas. The establishment of regional government failed in 1995 due to the lack of popular support for it (Lans, 2006). In spite of that, the *Stadsregio Amsterdam*, a collaboration of municipalities and economic organisations like the Chamber of Commerce, agreed to improve the accessibility and connectivity of the Amsterdam region by air and water and through technical networks in the so-called OPERA-plan (ROA, 2004).

The Chamber of Commerce in Amsterdam coordinated a second initiative. After proposing their own strategy *Gaan voor Goud* (Amsterdam, 2004), they developed a vision with the Chamber of Commerce Flevoland and Gooi en Eemland. The so-called *Regional Innovation Strategy* aims to improve the conditions for innovation in knowledge-intensive industries such as ICT and life sciences as well as in the creative industries (Amsterdam et al., 2006). Linkages between regional clusters are supported by creating networks and organising events. A loose collaboration of several municipalities and chambers of commerce (*Regionale Samenwerking Amsterdam* – RSA) handed in several applications for the Northern Randstad (Noordvleugel) and, for example, received funds from the national *Pieken in de delta* programme to develop a regional agency for the creative industry (www.ccaa.nl).

In November 2007, several municipalities in the region launched a new form of voluntary organisation which provided the organisational framework for regional initiatives. The collaboration of the municipalities is pragmatic, they work together either to apply for national funding or to improve their visibility outside the Netherlands. Due to the missing regional administration economic actors, such as the Chamber of Commerce often take a lead. Thus, the programmes are mostly business related, although the *Pieken in de delta* programme provides funds for urban development programmes as well.

Programmes which attract highly skilled individuals are not new in the city of Amsterdam. The regeneration of the inner-city housing stock or the investment in the cultural infrastructure (museums, theatres, etc.) has improved the liveability of the city, although those programmes did not directly address creative knowledge workers. The first reports (Musterd,

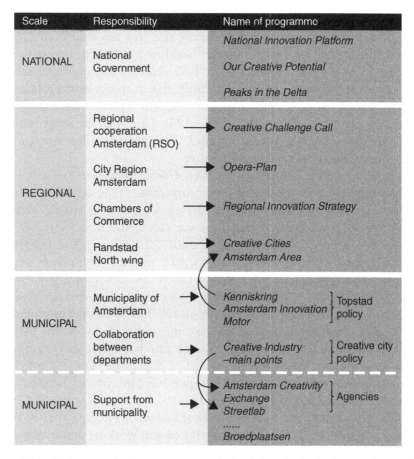

Figure 16.1 Policy lines for the creative knowledge industries in the Amsterdam region.

2002) and the proposed establishment of programmes for the creative knowledge class, however, were strongly contested in the city government and conceived as 'elitist' and socially selective by city representatives.

The city council of Amsterdam has, however, agreed two relevant policy programmes. The first is an umbrella programme for the current legislative period. *Topstad* aims to bring Amsterdam back into the top five European business locations (Gemeente Amsterdam, 2005, 2006, 2007, 2008). The *Topstad* programme is subdivided into different pillars for different policy fields. The *Kenniskring* pillar (Knowledge circle), for instance, supports the exchange and collaboration between knowledge-intensive business and educational and research institutions, and it promotes the expansion of ICT infrastructure. The *IAmsterdam* programme, in contrast, is a regional city marketing programme for tourism which aims to attract more senior affluent tourists instead of young backpackers looking for 'sex, drugs and rock 'n roll'. *IAmsterdam* also supports the allocation of new businesses, fairs, congresses and events like the Amsterdam Fashion Week and the Cross Media Congress, PICNIC. Recently, the city has also tried to police the red-light district by renting former window brothels to young talented designers from the Netherlands. The first draft of *topstad* addressed the social cohesion between different communities. It made strong reference to the previous *Wij Amsterdammers* policy which was created after the murder of an Amsterdam film director by a radical Moslem. Also the support of individual talent has become less prominent. The evolution of the programme was in a more business-oriented direction.

A second municipal programme called *Hoofdlijnen Creatieve Industrie* focuses on the creative industries. The programme is the result of collaboration between different municipal departments (economy, spatial planning, culture and society). It was passed by the city council in May 2007, and it covers the current legislative period 2007–2010 (Gemeente Amsterdam, 2007). The programme comprises six targets: the first two points improve the existing educational structure and target the development of human capital. The quality of 'creative education' is enhanced in vocational schools as well as universities. Organisations are established to involve immigrants in the creative economy. Three points are more directed towards business development. New business start-ups are provided with new consulting structures and their access to capital will be developed. Various communication platforms will be created by supporting conferences, infrastructure and cross-sectoral exchange for all businesses. Finally, international branding and international business contacts are backed. The last goal addresses spatial development. The creation of studios and working and living spaces for creative workers and artists is also mentioned as part of the development and maintenance of Amsterdam as an attractive tourist and living environment.

Many elements which are mentioned in the *hoofdlijnen* are not new. The programme rather attempts to integrate existing initiatives. The municipality of Amsterdam has assisted organisations that address and manage the needs of various creative knowledge workers. For instance, *Broedplaatsen* agency helps artists to find affordable working space in the city. The nonprofit organisations *Mediagilde* or *Waag Society* that were established by former social activists enable individuals to improve their IT skills.

The examples show that many measures in the *hoofdlijnen* and *topstad* programmes tackle problems of individuals and companies alike. Especially among the self-employed, the distinction between companies and individuals is often difficult to pursue. The business-oriented elements are, nevertheless, more pronounced. Even where programmes put the education of individuals to the fore, they also lead to the improvement of the education level of the regional labour force. The city of Amsterdam started to attract highly skilled professionals in the 1980s. This strategy is still relevant, but the business-oriented approaches have become more prominent and the group of creative knowledge workers gained more attention. The creative knowledge policy became one of the first cross-sectoral policy approaches. Departments such as culture and education which used to cover individual needs are now more open to make links with a changed business environment. The programmes were proposed by different administrations of the city. In the political arena, however, they were strongly contested and this may explain why there was less demand for a policy orientation towards the support of individuals.

Munich

Although it is not the largest city in Germany, Munich and its region can be considered as one of the prime German locations for the creative and knowledge-intensive industries. One-third of employees in the Munich region work in the creative knowledge sector, and in the city of Munich their share is even higher with 37 per cent. Over the years 1996–2004 (and despite the crises of 2001), the turnover as well as the number of firms in the creative knowledge economy grew. The high education qualifications of the population, excellent transport infrastructure and accessibility as well as the high number of public and semi-public research establishments provide a solid basis for the creative knowledge industries in the Munich region.

In recent decades, Munich has repeatedly benefited from decisions in which both the federal government and the Free State of Bavaria have been instrumental. These decisions provided new impetus for the creative knowledge hub on the Isar and improved the city's image in the eyes of creative knowledge workers.

Construction of the new airport at Erdinger Moos and the relocation of the exhibition centre to the former airport, for example, both encouraged and facilitated growth in this area. The players in the region likewise have a hand in shaping the environment in which they operate. Decisions by companies to ramp up their R&D activities in the region are one example. Initiatives launched by universities to attain a leading position in the international arena and to achieve excellence in research and education are another.

The policy of Munich on culture and arts enables art to be presented in various forms at the city's numerous museums and theatres, as well as to support artists and encourage debate about art, history and religion. Other local government departments also pursue policies that are conducive to growing and nourishing the city's creative potential. Any one policy that promotes Munich as a creative knowledge hub thus simultaneously affects an array of focused policies in other areas such as culture, housing, infrastructure, social affairs, the economy and employment. In other words, such policies fulfil a powerful horizontal function.

In Munich's sizeable labour market, highly qualified individuals benefit from plenty of job opportunities that stem from the sheer diversity of knowledge-intensive and creative companies in the region. Logically, therefore, an economic development BMR policy that seeks to attract technology-intensive companies and forward-looking industries is also a policy that promotes highly qualified individuals. Munich seeks to pursue such a policy by designating commercial space for specialised technology and business parks. Such parks exist for example in Messestadt Riem, on the southern edge of the city, and in Freiham, and in 2008, the new Munich Technology Centre is scheduled to open in Moosach. This policy also encourages the formation of industry clusters (Landeshauptstadt München, 2007).

Munich is also a popular congress venue, boasting a well-developed infrastructure for trade shows and events of all types and sizes. Leading international trade shows, large number of focused events, festivals and specialised congresses create all kinds of opportunities for creative knowledge workers to meet, communicate and build networks.

Munich operates a kind of 'home office' policy to foster tolerance and integration within its own boundaries. The city's policy puts great emphasis on keeping the peace, and integrating foreigners in the mainstream society and ensuring broad acceptance towards minorities. The recent construction of the Jewish Museum is one of the many examples in which the Bavarian capital applies itself to issues in its own history and encourages the integration of the Jewish community in the life of the city. Essentially, the city's policy focuses on anti-discrimination and equal opportunities. It aims to nurture mutual respect and recognition, encourage a positive awareness of cultural diversity, assert an across-the-board integration policy that improves access to education, vocational training and the labour market and enable foreign nationals to increase their participation in local society.

Budapest

At the end of 2004, there were 264,000 active economic organisations in Hungary in the field of creative and knowledge-intensive industries; 42.3 per cent of these firms (ca. 112,000 companies and sole proprietors) operated in the metropolitan region of Budapest and employed 427,000 people. Taking into account the number of firms, the relative weight of Budapest Metropolitan Region (BMR) within Hungary is especially outstanding in the fields of ICT (53.6 per cent), R&D and higher education (52.4 per cent). Among the different branches of the creative and knowledge-intensive industries, 81.8 per cent of the enterprises in 'motion pictures and video activities' and 71.9 per cent of 'publishing' are located in Budapest and its metropolitan region. The ratio of economic organisations operating in the field of 'reproduction of recorded media', 'software consultancy and supply', 'research & development' and 'insurance & pension funding' is also above 60 per cent (Kovács et al., 2007).

In Budapest, policies facilitating the growth of creative and knowledge-intensive industries can be identified at three different levels: national, regional and local. The most influential national policy is the 'New Hungary' Development Plan. This defines the strategy for sustainable growth and competitiveness of Hungary for the period of 2007–2013. The creative economy is emphasised among the thematic priorities. As part of the 'New Hungary' Development Plan, the national government initiated the *Budapest Innopolis Programme* which is strictly an economic development programme, primarily focusing on strengthening the knowledge-based economy. In order to increase the competitiveness of the city, the Budapest Municipality, the main universities, R&D institutions and R&D-related companies joined to establish three development poles: Information Society Technology Pole (ITT), MediPole and EcoPole. The cooperation between academics, universities and entrepreneurs provides the opportunity for each pole to integrate into the single European research and economic area. The aim is to achieve a milieu which is attractive for foreign investors and also boosts the local actors' innovation capacity, increasing the importance of high added value activities represented locally.

Being a unitary state, regional level governance has traditionally been weak in Hungary. Only recently the Regional Organisation and Development Act (No. 21/1996) introduced a regional level: Hungary was divided into seven statistical planning regions made up by counties. Budapest and Pest County together form the Central Hungary Region. However, regional identity and cohesion is generally weak in Hungary. Not surprisingly, the collaboration between the city and municipalities lying in the metropolitan region is problematic. On the regional level, the development of R&D and creative industries also enjoys high priority in policy documents like the support scheme of the EU funded *Operational Programmes*. The Central Hungary Operational Programme aims to increase the international competitiveness of the region and to strengthen the growth of the knowledge-based economy. In this respect, the most significant targets are the stimulation of cooperation between the players of knowledge-based economy, the development of creative and cultural industries in the region producing high added value and the creation of new innovative jobs. Within the Operational Programme, the role of Budapest is highlighted as that of a development pole, integrating R&D and innovation activities in Hungary.

On the local level, the Medium-term Urban Development Programme for Budapest (the so-called *Podmaniczky Programme*) provides a clear orientation and priorities for the development of creative and innovative industries (cultural life, knowledge-based economy, IT sector). The programme outlines concrete projects within the full spectrum of sustainable urban development and aims to strengthen the position of Budapest amongst the competing metropolitan regions of Europe. The main priorities include the establishment of 'technopolis' areas in the northern and southern part of Budapest, the establishment of links between university, governmental and commercial bodies, and the creation of technology clusters, the support of the development of science parks and urban 'technopolis' quarters, the development of key organisations of a knowledge-based society (education, libraries, e-government, etc.). These policies focus nearly exclusively on the development of 'hard' factors creating space and infrastructure for the knowledge-based economy, improving higher education and stimulating research and development. These activities are definitely part of the creative economy but they are not equated with it. Substantial parts of the creative sector like arts, media, publishing, entertainment or creative business services are hardly addressed in policy documents. These parts of the creative sector are more used to self-generating activity and they do not generally respond so well to formal funding and other supportive mechanisms. Indeed, this is the case in Budapest where festivals, art events, design, media or creative entertainment activities develop within the loose framework provided by the highly decentralised public administration system. A good example is the spread of 'ruin bar' culture in the inner part of Budapest. 'Ruin bars' have been established in abandoned residential buildings in the dilapidated inner-city neighbourhoods since the end of the 1990s. These venues regularly host different cultural events, fashion shows, art exhibitions, musical performances and promote a vivid cultural scene. They have become focal points for particular groups of consumers often including those involved elsewhere in creative activities and cultural industries. Ruin bars as a distinct cultural phenomenon is the result of post-socialist transformation of Budapest. The transformation since 1990 has created countless 'loose spaces' in the city where alternative forms of public life and creative reuse could evolve due to weak planning control (Kovács, 2006).

Conclusions

There are significant differences between the three cities discussed in this chapter in terms of the mechanisms, goals and contents of competitiveness and creative strategies. The differences derive partly from their distinctive development pathways and partly from their wider political conditions. Due to their historical development and global connectedness, Amsterdam and Munich have much better points of departure to become creative cities than Budapest. While state-socialism meant a serious obstacle for post-industrial development in Budapest, Amsterdam and Munich transformed their economy steadily in the 1970s and 1980s. They could formulate their urban economic policies to create an attractive business environment for global players, and they also implemented policies (e.g. urban regeneration, city marketing) which influenced competitiveness much earlier than Budapest.

Another dimension of difference is associated with the political systems of the respective countries. Munich has been developed in the framework of a federal state in the post-World War II era, where the federal level (*Bundesland*) had a much stronger control over sectors which had a direct impact on the growth of the creative knowledge economy (higher education, R&D, culture, tourism). In this respect, we can also say that Amsterdam and Budapest have been more dependent on national policies than Munich. This is especially true for Budapest, since post-socialist transformation and EU accession in 2004 provided little room (and money) for local incentives to develop the creative knowledge economy.

The public administration and thus political decision-making system in the three cities are also substantially different. In Amsterdam and Munich, the city council is a strong player with direct influence over every aspect of life in the city. In Budapest, a two-tier administrative system was introduced in 1990 and the decision-making power was substantially shifted from the city to district level. Local governments of districts became very influential and they could elaborate their own policies in many fields including housing, health and social care. The decentralised public administration system has brought about many conflicts and problems in Budapest, but as has been noted the lack of strong central control (and policy) can provide favourable conditions for certain creative activities to flourish.

We can also observe clear similarities in our three cities. In each case, the main emphasis of competitiveness policies rests on the improvement of the basic infrastructure of knowledge creation. This normally includes new technology centres, science parks, university facilities and research laboratories. Development of long-distance transport, especially airport, facilities are also frequently on the agenda. All these developments are clearly aimed at creating new enterprises and improving knowledge transfer, and not so much the attraction and retention of creative people. The primary objectives of national, regional and local policies in our three cities relate to provision of hard factors that are seen as enhancing competitiveness. Soft factors are considered to be important only at the local (city or urban district) level, and policies (initiatives) aimed at attracting talented people in these cities are either weak or absent.

References

Amsterdam, K.v.K. (2004) *Gaan voor goud. Aanvalsplan voor de Noordvleugel van de Randstad als krachtig internationaal economisch centrum*. Amsterdam: Kamer van Koophandel Amsterdam.

Kamers van Koophandel Amsterdam, Flevoland en Gooi- en Eemland (2006) *Regionale innovatiestrategie Noordvleugel conferentie*. Amsterdam: Kamer van Koophandel Amsterdam.

Bontje, M. and B. Sleutjes (2007) *The Amsterdam metropolitan area: Towards a creative knowledge region? Pathways to creative and knowledge-based cities: The case of Amsterdam*. Amsterdam: AMIDSt.

Bosscher, D. (2007) De oude en de nieuwe stad. In: P. de Rooy (ed.), *Geschiedenis van Amsterdam. Tweestrijd om de hoofdstad 1900–2000*, pp. 337–397. Amsterdam: SUN.

Butler, T. and M. Savage (eds) (1995) *Social change and the middle classes*. London: UCL Press.

Castells, M. (1989) *The informational city: Information technology, economic restructuring, and the urban–regional process*. Oxford, Cambridge, Mass: Basil Blackwell.

Centraal Bureau voor de Statistiek, CBS (2008) *Overheid; uitgaven cultuur, sport en recreatie*. www.cbs.nl accessed on 28th November 2008.

Chapain, C. and R. Lee (2009) Can we plan the creative knowledge city? Perspectives from western and eastern Europe. *Built Environment*, 35 (2): 157–164.

Dainov, E. (2008) *The creative & knowledge class in Sofia. Understanding the attractiveness of the metropolitan region for creative knowledge workers*. Amsterdam: AMIDSt.

Dövényi, Z. and Z. Kovács (2006) Budapest: Post-socialist metropolitan periphery between 'catching up' and individual development path. *European Spatial Research and Policy*, 13 (2): 23–41.

Enyedi, Gy. and V. Szirmai (1992) *Budapest: A central European capital*. London: Belhaven Press.

Florida, R. (2002) *The rise of the creative class*. New York: Basis Books.

Gemeente Amsterdam (2005) *Onderzoek internationale concurrentiepositie regio Amsterdam*. Amsterdam: Gemeente Amsterdam.

Gemeente Amsterdam (2006) *Amsterdam topstad*. Amsterdam: Gemeente Amsterdam.

Gemeente Amsterdam (2007) *Hoofdlijnen programma creatieve industrie 2007–2010*. Amsterdam: Gemeente Amsterdam.

Gemeente Amsterdam (2008) *Werkprogramma Amsterdam topstad 2008*. Amsterdam: Gemeente Amsterdam.

Gibson, C. and L. Kong (2005) Cultural economy: A critical review. *Progress in Human Geography*, 29 (5): 541–561.

Hafner, S., M. Miosga, K. Sickermann and A. von Streit (2007) *Knowledge and creativity at work in the Munich region. Pathways to creative and knowledge-based regions*. Amsterdam: University of Amsterdam, AMIDSt.

Innovatieplatform (2006) *Kennisinvesteringsagenda 2006–2016. Nederland, hét land van talenten!* Den Haag: Innovatieplatform.

Klamer, A. (ed.) (1996) *The value of culture. On the relationship between economics and arts*. Amsterdam: Amsterdam University Press.

Kloosterman, R.C. (2004) Recent employment trends in the cultural industries in Amsterdam, Rotterdam, The Hague and Utrecht: A first exploration. *Tijdschrift Voor Economische En Sociale Geografie*, 95 (2): 243–252.

Kovács, Z. (1994) A city at the crossroads: Social and economic transformation in Budapest. *Urban Studies*, 31 (7): 1081–1096.

Kovács, Z. (2006) Social and economic transformation of historical districts in Budapest. In: G. Enyedi and Z. Kovács (eds), *Social changes and social sustainability in historical urban centres. Discussion Papers Special*, pp. 39–64. Centre for Regional Studies of Hungarian Academy of Sciences. Pécs.

Kovács, Z., T. Egedy, Zs. Földi, K. Keresztély and B. Szabó (2007) *Budapest. From state socialism to global capitalism. Pathways to creative and knowledge-based regions*. ACRE report 2.4. Amsterdam: AMIDSt, University of Amsterdam. 119 p.

Landeshauptstadt München (2007) *München – Standortfaktor Kreativität*. Veröffentlichungen des Referates für Arbeit und Wirtschaft. Heft Nummer 217. München.

Lans, J. v.d. (2006) *Kleine geschiedenis van de stadsregio Amsterdam*. Wormer: IMMERC.

Lewis, N., W. Larner and R. Le Heron (2008) The New Zealand designer fashion industry: Making industries and co-constituting political projects. *Transactions of the Institute of British Geographers*, 33 (1): 42–59.

Ley, D. (1996) *The new middle class and the remaking of the central city*. Oxford: Oxford University Press.

Mak, G. (2006) *Amsterdam. Biographie einer Stadt*. Munich: btb Verlag.

Meusburger, P. (2001) The role of knowledge in the socio-economic transformation of Hungary in the 1990s. In: P. Meusburger and H. Jöns (eds), *Transformations in Hungary*. pp. 1–38. Heidelberg: Physica-Verlag.

Micheel, M. and K. Wiest (2002) Kulturförderung im föderalen Staat – Länder und Gemeinden. In: I.f.L. Leipzig (ed.), *Nationalatlas Bundesrepublik Deutschland – Bildung und Kultur*, pp. 132–135. Heidelberg: Spektrum Elsevier.

Ministerie EZ (2004) *Pieken in de delta*. Den Haag: MinEZ.

Ministerie EZ and Ministerie OCW (2005) *Ons creatieve vermogen*. Den Haag: MinEZ, MinOCW.

Moßig, I. (2005) Die Branchen der Kulturökonomie als Untersuchungsgegenstand der Wirtschaftsgeographie. *Zeitschrift für Wirtschaftsgeographie*, 49: 99–112.

Musterd, S. (2002) *De nieuwe Amsterdamse kernvoorraad; Woonmilieus in de creatieve culturele kennisstad*. Amsterdam: Bestuursdienst.

Musterd, S. and O. Gritsai (2009) Creative and knowledge cities: Development paths and policies from a European perspective. *Built Environment*, 35 (2): 173–188.

Paalzow, A., R. Kilis, V. Dombrovsky, D. Pauna and A. Sauka (2007) *Riga: From Hanseatic city to a modern metropolis*. Amsterdam: University of Amsterdam, AMIDSt.

Peck, J. (2005) Struggling with the creative class. *International Journal of Urban and Regional Research*, 29 (4): 740–770.

Peck, J. (2007) The cult of urban creativity. In: R. Keil and R. Mahon (eds), *The political economy of scale*. Vancouver: University of British Columbia Press.

Peyroux, E., D. Eckert and C. Thouzellier (eds) (2007) *Toulouse: Embracing the knowledge economy. Pathways to creative and knowledge-based regions*. ACRE report WP2.11. Amsterdam: AMIDSt.

Regionaal Orgaan Amsterdam (ROA) (2004) *Ontwikkelings Plan Regio Amsterdam*. Amsterdam: ROA.

Scott, A.J. (2006) Creative cities: Conceptual issues and policy questions. *Journal of Urban Affairs*, 28 (1): 1–17.

Statistisches Bundesamt (2008) *2007: Kulturausgaben der öffentlichen Hand 8,1 Milliarden Euro*. Pressemitteilung Nr.339 vom 09.09.2008. Wiesbaden: Statistisches Bundesamt.

Stryjakiewicz, T., T. Kaczmarek, M. Meczynski, J.J. Parysek and K. Stochowiak (2007) *Poznan faces the future. Pathways to creative and knowledge-based regions*. Amsterdam: University of Amsterdam, AMIDSt.

Terhorst, P. and J. Van de Ven (1995) The national urban growth coalition in the Netherlands. *Political Geography*, 14: 343–361.

Terhorst, P. and J. Van de Ven (2003) The economic restructuring of the historic city centre. In: S. Musterd and W. Salet (eds), *Amsterdam human capital*, pp. 85–101. Amsterdam: Amsterdam University Press.

Tordoir, P. (2003) The Randstad: The creation of a metropolitan economy. In: S. Musterd and W. Salet (eds), *Amsterdam human capital*, pp. 105–125. Amsterdam: Amsterdam University Press.

Zorlu, A. (2002) *Absorption of immigrants in European labour markets. The Netherlands, United Kingdom and Norway*. Amsterdam: Universiteit van Amsterdam.

17

New Governance, New Geographic Scales, New Institutional Settings

Bastian Lange, Marc Pradel i Miquel and Vassil Garnizov

Introduction

Throughout this book, and especially where the nature and role of public policy has been discussed, it has been apparent that the new concern to promote the creative knowledge city has posed a challenge for many approaches and traditional arrangements in all of the cities referred to. These relate to the difficulty of making appropriate responses because of the strength of traditional practices and boundaries – administrative, professional and public/private sectoral boundaries. Against this background, this chapter sets out key considerations related to the emergence of new forms of governance within the framework of creative and knowledge industries. It pays special attention to new geographical scales as well as new institutional settings. The evidence presented elsewhere in this book and related publications demonstrates that new governance arrangements (or in some cases a lack of governance arrangements) related to creative and knowledge industries can be detected in cities in very different contexts. New concepts and ways of governing metropolitan regions are called for in order to promote creative and knowledge economies and address the wider issues raised by their expansion. This chapter defines a theoretical framework on the emergence of creative as well as new economic actors and discusses the issues arising from this, using examples from three cities and three different contexts.

We derive the concept of governance first of all from a traditional way of understanding governance concepts and modes: Governance is thus seen as collective action by private, public and corporate agents regarding public goods, spatially relevant resources, cultural values and action resources (Heinelt, 2004; Healey, 2006). In general what is meant by the use of the concept 'governance' is a mode of decision-making which does not only follow top-down patterns, but that also includes horizontal or bottom-up processes. The groups of players (decision-makers) are usually represented by a triangular scheme, with *state, economy* and civil society on its three points forming collaborative strategies by handling unequal spatial resources. This concept allows the examination of collective action as well as the spatial positioning. Moreover, local decision-making processes are not isolated from the national context in which cities are involved, and it is necessary to analyse governance taking into consideration the role of national and supranational scales influencing local action. Governance strategies in the field of creative and knowledge industries have to be seen as negotiation-based approaches by new, often less established and therefore young agents in city-regions. Negotiations are necessary in forming alliances and social networks guaranteeing visibility and attention in public administration as well as within the private sector. At the same time, formalised and established public–private networks are often critically discussed because of their distant attitude towards these creative agents and their informal networks. The formal networks within creative and knowledge industries, being new, often lack evaluation and transparency (Balducci, 2004; Kunzmann, 2004). The structure of creative and knowledge industries brings new forms of urban management to the fore: informal alliances between private and public stakeholders, self-organised networks to promote new products in new markets and context-oriented forms such as branding of places, represent new forms of managing urban areas. Thereby, cities become the places where different actors participate in the negotiation of future markets.

In this way governance refers to new relationships between state and society that imply a blurring of traditional boundaries of governmental agency (Jessop, 1995; Rhodes, 1996; Stoker, 1998). The discussion of steering and organisational arrangements related to creative and knowledge industries has recently been analytically related to organisational changes within micro and small enterprises (Grabher, 2004; Rae, 2004; Neff et al., 2005; Wilson and Stokes, 2005; Scott, 2006; Lange, 2007). New combinations of innovative and creative 'knowledge' activity itself restructure the economy but in turn change public administration, entrepreneurship and the relationships between different sectors and agencies.

Building on these approaches we argue that creative and knowledge industries are best considered as new organisational forms that are modifying and creating new forms of governance arrangements both in their institutional and scale dimensions (Lange et al., 2008; Lange et al., 2009). After presenting conceptual prerequisites, two contrasting sketches of new governance modes will be discussed referring to Leipzig (Germany), Barcelona (Spain) and Sofia (Bulgaria).

Conceptual prerequisites: understanding governance in creative and knowledge industries

Governance strategies are mainly seen as new negotiation-based approaches by various agents in city-regions – recognising that in practice negotiation may be located on a continuum from real bargaining to token. At the same time such strategies are often critically discussed because of their lack of creativity and, being new strategies, because they are not based on experience and lack of proof (Balducci, 2004; Kunzmann, 2004). Alternative approaches emerging from within creative and knowledge industries might present fresh perspectives and involve more innovative, self-steering and self-promoting practices applied by new professional agents. Who could these new professional agents be?

The emergence of new economic fields is accompanied by new entrepreneurial agents and this applies in the field of creative and culture production (Lange, 2005a, b). Yet, from an analytical perspective, these new agents are confronted with structural paradoxes that affect their entrepreneurial practices (Thelen, 2003; Zhang, 2004; DeFillippi et al., 2007; Kosmala, 2007; Lange et al., 2008). When speaking about new modes of labour and the procedural forms of market access by new agents, we should look at the social and work practices they are faced with. Very generally speaking, two paradoxes play a crucial role in their work practices: the 'Globalisation Paradox' and the 'Identity Paradox'. The first addresses the tensions between local-based creativity, transnational networks of production systems and localised production networks that are driven by an ethos of creativity and adhere to an 'artistic mode of production'. The 'Globalisation Paradox' also addresses the ambivalence between new knowledge milieus and their territorial embedding practices. Being able to operate worldwide in socio-spatially integrated 'communities of knowledge' (Wenger, 1999) gained more and more relevance and thus provides the necessary embedding ground for translocal knowledge workers. The 'Identity Paradox' addresses the ambivalence between individual and collective careers, identities, and reputations. Because mavericks and outsiders as well as independent creative artists play the major role in this dynamic and rapidly changing market (Steyaert and Katz, 2004), it is inappropriate to rely on static concepts of entrepreneurs in analysing this economy and strategies for it.

Based on these substantial paradoxes, different governance modes can be presented, highlighting the degree of irritation, the different interests and separated logics of action, when promoting creative and knowledge industries and their creative agents. These issues, or structural paradoxes, demonstrate how the institutional set-up 'creative industries' is constituted and how difficult it is to invent marketing and place-based strategies to promote creative and knowledge industries.

New governance dimensions

One of the key urban, cultural and economic developments in creative and knowledge industries is the emergence of a new hybrid of both cultural and entrepreneurial agents, the so-called culturepreneurs (Lange, 2007). While this new development has led to a substantial reconsideration of 'entrepreneurship' in respect to space (Steyaert and Katz, 2004), it has also led to a new line of thinking with regard to the notion of economic progress and professionalisation within entrepreneurial networks (Rae, 2002; Sydow et al., 2004). The term culturepreneur is a compound of culture and entrepreneur and was first suggested by Davies and Ford (1998, p. 3), following Pierre Bourdieu's typological notion of an entrepreneur as someone who embodies various forms of capital (Bourdieu, 1986, p. 241). Davies and Ford (1998) have characterised this as people who, in structural terms, are communicative providers of transfer services between the sub-systems' 'business-related services' and 'creative scene'. In doing this they seem to satisfy a necessary demand by operating in flexible social networks. In effect they generate new modes of self-governance.

The formation of new social networks by new professions demonstrates the unintended rise of distinct segments of creative knowledge industries – at least from the point of view of the government. This opens up the opportunity to examine the emergence of such segments since top-down support initiatives by the state or public administration hardly existed prior to 2000. Most emerged without external support. In this ambiguous situation, the catchword of a 'new entrepreneurship' alludes to a variety of practices. These may include individualised marketing strategies, self-promotion and social hardships, but also to skilful alternation between unemployment benefit, temporary jobs, self-employment structures and new temporary network coalitions – as practiced by numerous young agents in the field of cultural production. Social capital becomes an existential value for exchanging relevant information. Performing intense 'multiple and constantly shifting transaction structures in cultural-products industries means that much of the workforce becomes enmeshed in a network of mutually dependent and socially coordinated career paths' (Scott, 2006, p. 13). Only recently this new work ethos has been celebrated ironically with the term 'digital bohème' (Friebe and Lobo, 2006).

The high number of creative knowledge workers that have recently emerged is based on spontaneous informal social bonds as well as network alliances that have enabled the appearance of new creative milieus. New practices concerning the temporary organisation of projects are intertwined with the production of new social places for the exchange of experiences, knowledge and expertise. Since the mid-1990s, new forms of project-based cooperation (Grabher, 2002a, 2006) as well as specific spatial practices had to be invented in order to economically, culturally and socially focus on targeted markets. Especially in harsh transformation contexts such as post-socialist Leipzig and Sofia, there was very little experienced expertise, few tools of application and few strategic guidelines. However, new agents have been developing their practices in an unclear, unstructured and unstable market realm (Thomas, 1997; White, 2002). Within the framework of what is called the creative industries, they collaborate, interact and network with other agents, while at the same time being confronted with the risk of losing their initial capabilities for innovation. Gernot Grabher in particular has identified this inner-organisational dimension and the emergent network-based project ecologies and entrepreneurial and socio-spatial practices in these industries (Grabher, 2002b; DeFillippi et al., 2007). Rapidly changing project-based activities within flexible network formations pose structural constraints. Learning is problematic when teams are constituted only for a short period of time and team members have few opportunities to learn what are understood as 'traditional', long-standing learning cultures (Cameron and Quinn, 1988, p. 8; Grabher, 2004).

Professionalisation – self-regulation and self-governance of new professions

Creative industries are often based on 'communities of practice' (Lave, 1991). These are groups or networks of professionals who cooperate, exchange views and ideas, and inform each other about trends of professional, political and practical concern. The fate of these creative communities of practice is shaped and partly driven by professionalisation for the simple reason that they have to survive economically. Thus, professionalisation has become a limiting context restriction that can restrict creativity. Professionalisation can be viewed in a narrow and a wider sense (Mieg, 2008). Professionalisation in the narrow sense denotes the transformation of an occupation into a profession, that is an occupation with a certain autonomy in defining and controlling the standards of the work of its members. Professionalisation in the wide sense denotes the transition towards paid work that is subject to binding quality standards. In this wide sense, people and activities can be professionalised, gaining in professionalism. Professionalisation has turned towards the notion and phenomenon of professionalism (Freidson, 2001). Freidson understands professionalism as a third organisational logic of work alongside the market logic and the logic of planning or bureaucratic administration. In contrast to these, professionalism means self-organisation, self-regulation and self-governance of experts.

The paradoxes of creativity (DeFillippi et al., 2007) can also be reconsidered from the perspective of professionalisation research. The so-called difference paradox of 'crafting or standardising policies' relates to the two linked sources of professional competence: individual skills and competencies that are built up and the evaluation of these by the professional community. The distance paradox of 'whether to couple or decouple routine work' also refers to a phenomenon that is common in professionalisation research: the coupling of private life and profession – simply because of passion for the particular professional work. Perfect examples are doctors' families, especially community physicians. The globalisation paradox of 'whether to reconcile or separate local and global arenas of activity' and the identity paradox of 'creating individual or collective identities, reputations and careers' can be considered as expressions of the fact that individual professionals are members of a potentially global profession. Similarly professional knowledge tends to be shared globally.

In creative industries, professionalisation serves several functions (Lange and Mieg, 2008): a control function, an evaluation function and an expert function. The inherent *control function* of professionalised work currently is one of the main topics of discussion in the sociology of professions (Freidson, 2001; Evetts, 2003). Professionalised action is generally subject to the self-control of professionals. In professional work, other common forms of organisational or institutionalised control are replaced by self-control. Professional self-control is also at work in organisations: new forms of human resource management even assume self-control from employed professionals. Here organisational control takes on the form of 'control at a distance' (Fournier, 1999, p. 280) – that is internalised self-control.

The second function, *evaluation*, is closely linked to the first one. If there is today an enduring source of legitimisation for professions, then it has to be based on the institutionalised control of evaluation standards for particular professional work. Classical professions (such as the medical profession) as well as new professions or professional groups (such as in the field of web design or patent auctions) attempt to define standards for professional work in their domain and to establish systems of evaluation that include standards for professional training. Thus, professions have certain basic, socially accepted criteria for defining work in their domains. These criteria are variable and subject to the dynamics of changing jurisdiction in the 'system of professions' (Abbott, 1988).

The third function, the *expert function* of professionalised work, plays a decisive role in the domain of creative industries from two perspectives. We see not only an external expert function (towards clients and the public), but also an internal one (in the network). The internal expert function serves to differentiate and legitimate evaluation processes by identifying those professionals who set new quality standards and – equally important – who are renowned trainers or coaches in that particular professional domain. The attribution of the 'experts' in the field also determines the direction of 'collective' competence development in local creative economies (as professional groups). Therefore professionalisation has to be considered as a process. Professionalisation involves the transformation of trust regulation (from trust in single experts to trust in qualifications), the transformation of learning (from erratic individual learning to a more academy-like training) and the transformation of quality control (from individualised trust to quality reflections in globalised professional networks). The last argument in particular raises the issue of scale and its importance for the development of governance perspectives among creative knowledge industries.

Towards new geographical scales?

In his work, Florida stresses the relevance for economic development of the city and the region rather than the country. Moreover, most of the existing literature on the creative city focuses mainly on local governance and the role of local actors in promoting policies to foster the creative and knowledge economy. Nevertheless these policies and governance arrangements – at least in the European context – are strongly influenced by the national context. European countries show different degrees of centralisation and the degree of autonomy of the city differs widely from one country to another. Thus, in many countries central governments are playing a role in the promotion and development of local strategies for economic growth.

Furthermore, some of the factors that Florida considered relevant for the attraction and promotion of creativity and knowledge are within the sphere of central government, for example migration policies or welfare provision. Thus, national policies have an impact on the strategy of the city. For instance, in Barcelona, the retention of knowledge workers in medium and large companies is sometimes difficult because of bureaucratic problems with their residence and working permits and this directly involves the central state. The European Union also plays a role that affects national policies and influences local practices through funding and regulations. Thus, a focus on governance in the European context has to include a multi-scalar perspective. Against this background the research underpinning this book has referred to 13 cities with different roles in their national contexts, including capitals and non-capitals as well as large metropolitan regions and medium-sized cities. The analysis of governance strategies takes into account the national context and the influence of different levels of government on policies related to the creative and knowledge industries.

The promotion of creative knowledge industries interacts with the inherited economic and social features of industrial metropolitan regions. The changes affecting these regions in the 1960s and 1970s had encouraged attempts at policy coordination between municipalities and other levels of government. With the hegemony of neoliberalism, after the 1970 oil crisis, most of these attempts were dismantled. At the same time, the crisis of fordism increased social and economic segregation not only between cities but also within them (Geddes and Bennington, 2001). Consequently metropolitan regions are now experiencing increased diversity both in social and economic terms but lack robust governance mechanisms to coordinate policies and actions. Although some coordination for the provision of infrastructures and basic services exists, for instance the creation of public and private transport infrastructures, there is a lack of coordination regarding policies for the promotion of creative industries. In some cases this leads to the emergence of similar projects in different municipalities or neighbourhoods of the same metropolitan region.

As has been stated, in structural terms, 'culturepreneurs' and professionals differ from 'industrial workers', and informal social networks play a major role in the consolidation of creative and knowledge markets. That generates an even more complex scenario, in which the hierarchical practices of governance at the metropolitan scale can hinder the role of these networks and the consolidation of creative knowledge industries in the city. Conversely, the absence of any coordination from the public administration makes formal and informal networks weaker and does not allow the development of creative knowledge industries.

Summarising, whereas the logic of urban competitiveness demands major coordination between public and private actors at different scales, a growth strategy based on the creative industries' demand for plural governance in which formal and informal networks of actors must be taken into consideration (Markusen, 2006; Pareja-Eastaway et al., 2007). In regard to this situation, local public administrations are looking for new forms of governance that allow coordination with other scales and the emergence of social networks. As we shall see in the three following cases, these attempts have appeared recently, when city councils have included the creative industries in their policy agenda, although knowledge was already the main growth engine.

The inclusion of creativity as a cornerstone of urban growth is also blurring the limits between geographical scales in a peculiar way. Our research shows that formal and informal networks of actors in the creative sectors at a local level can be connected with other networks in other cities or places, framing knowledge and resources. Thus, the city and the metropolitan region – understood as places for social relations and economic exchange – are being complemented with connected networks that allow for new ways of producing goods and services and generating innovation. In terms of governance that means that the scenario of competitiveness between cities and regions in a global framework is only partially true. Economic actors in cities look for ways of cooperation and seek new arrangements to profit out of the complementary economies of their cities. Higher scales (national and European) play a key role in this coordination, for example, through the creation of transport infrastructures and standardisation of formal qualification degrees and qualified training. This reveals that creative and knowledge economy can benefit from new geographical scales based on networks of cities in which there are different specialised nodes.

Finally, in this framework, it is necessary to emphasise again the role of national governments in policies that configure the framework of opportunities for cities. In this regard the regulation of the labour market and migration reduce the scope for attraction of talent to the cities. Whereas it seems that nation states have assumed knowledge as a priority for the development of cities and regions, creativity plays a more timid role in the agenda at national scale in most of the European countries which means less funding for the development of projects. As we will see in Barcelona, Leipzig and Sofia, the promotion of knowledge has determined the possibilities for development and organisation of creative industries.

Governance approaches in Barcelona, Leipzig and Sofia

Barcelona, Leipzig and Sofia are referred to in this chapter both because of their differences and their similarities. They all have different institutional backgrounds. Even though all of these nation states are currently based on a capitalist economic system and a democratic political system, their pathways to this current state have differed. Today, they play an important role in their national economies and are attempting to compete in the creative knowledge economy.

Barcelona

Although there has been a recent economic transformation to a service-oriented economy, the Barcelona Metropolitan Region (BMR) is one of the most important industrial regions of Spain (Trullen et al., 2002). Barcelona itself has developed a service-oriented economy, but the rest of the region remains mainly industrial. The region has a polycentric shape with a diversified economy, where traditionally the small and medium cities played a significant role through industrial specialisation. The network of cities that forms the BMR includes more than 4.4 million inhabitants and 164 municipalities in an extension of 4320 km^2. One of the main features of the transformation of Barcelona is the key role of the governance coalition in the city, featured by the strong role of the city council and its openness to private and civil society agents (Pareja-Eastaway et al., 2007).

The consolidation of that governance model took place during the 1980s and allowed for the success of the city in the organisation of the 1992 Olympic Games, which speeded urban renewal and opened the city to European and global markets. The Olympic Games also made culture a resource for economic growth and the attraction of visitors, and introduced a specific policy for cultural industries.

After the success of the Olympic Games, the Barcelona city council put knowledge at the centre of its policy for the next phase, while continuing to foster the existing sectors that were expanding – mainly services linked directly or indirectly to tourism. The city council proposed a new strategy to complete the urban renewal of the city and, at the same time, create the conditions for the growth and consolidation of the knowledge economy. The idea was to transform the former industrial district of the city into an innovative industrial district for the knowledge economy, mixing housing, space for knowledge companies and equipment and services. At the same time the city council expanded the practice of strategic planning from the urban to the metropolitan level, enabling coordination and making the urban and economic transformation of the city a motor for the transformation of the whole region. Nevertheless, the first stage of development, from 1996 to 2006, was characterised by negotiations and some conflict with private agents and neighbours in the districts, and actions by the rampant construction sector, who were leading protagonists for transformation. The emerging knowledge companies were already settled in other parts of the city and did not participate actively in this development. Nevertheless, some of them started to move to the new district and companies from abroad, such as Microsoft or Yahoo!, were invited to settle. Moreover, to avoid undesirable economic development, the city council listed the economic activities that would be allowed in the district under the label '@ activities': these included knowledge and services sectors. After this first stage, the public–private partnership leading the project started to promote four strategic clusters: biomedicine, energy, ICT and media. More recently, since 2007, design has been promoted as a new cluster. The leaders of the project also attempted to cluster companies that were already settled by creating formal networks of companies and informal meetings as spaces to share experiences. Moreover, efforts were made to engage the companies in the daily life of the neighbourhood, involving them in social and civic activities.

The whole strategy represents a strong top-down governance approach with a strong role for public bodies at different scales. It involved efforts not only in terms of urbanisation and direct investment but also in moving companies and institutions linked to knowledge to the district. Public and private universities have also moved faculties related to the strategic clusters and their postgraduate schools to the district. Thus the 22@ project means an effort from different administrations to create an environment attractive for companies in the 'new economy' including not only knowledge-intensive industries but also some creative sectors that need a specific infrastructure. One of the main elements of this approach is that it promotes the creation and attraction of new businesses and, because it is not based on the existing economic activity, is seen by the existing companies as marginalising them (Pareja-Eastaway et al., 2008a, b).

Although culture and cultural industries have played a key role in the development of the city since the Olympic Games, the approach to the cultural milieus and the conditions for the generation and fostering of creative industries were not taken into consideration until the end of the 1990s. Emerging creative sectors such as design or software development were strongly based on self-regulation. As our research shows, entrepreneurs and workers in these sectors do not feel engaged in the strategy of the city (Pareja-Eastaway et al., 2008a, b). Nevertheless, in the new strategic plan of culture of 2006, agents from the creative industries as well as representatives of artistic workshops in the city agreed common objectives and policies for the future. The plan included an active policy to promote bottom-up initiatives. The most relevant example was the creation of 'factories of creativity' – places where young artists could develop their projects. The final objective was to generate a creative environment that would improve the whole economic system. The shift in the discourse has taken place after strong complaints from creative industries, civil society and the artistic sectors that they had not played any role in the strategy for the city during the 1990s. The most relevant example is the creative cluster in Poblenou. After being almost completely concentrated into the knowledge 22@ district through a top-down process, the city council is now trying to promote the same kind of clusters in the whole city (Martí and Pradel, 2008). Moreover, as has been stated, some activities such as design have been integrated in the policy agenda of the 22@ as a transversal strategic cluster, widening the aims of the 22@ district which now is promoted as the 'innovation district' instead of the 'knowledge district'.

Two main distinctive, but complementary, strategies for the attraction of knowledge and creativity have been observed. In the case of knowledge, there is a strong policy for the attraction of excellence through major investments and the generation of a knowledge cluster through a top-down process. Some creative industries needing strong investments (including media industries) were included in this strategy. For creative industries, a more bottom-up policy based on fostering networks of creative actors and their participation in the cultural project of the city is now being promoted after strong opposition from the creative industries to being the recipients of policies emanating from a classic governance approach. The case of 22@ district shows that a lack of coordination of these two strategies can hinder possibilities for one sector or another. Discourses on both strategies without a clear coordination can generate conflict and waste.

Barcelona also shows that more coordination is needed at the metropolitan scale to avoid a lack of coordination between municipalities. In this regard, most of the municipalities in the region are developing their own knowledge parks or neighbourhoods with no direct coordination with other projects. Moreover, the promotion of the knowledge economy is a key element for the municipalities of the region, because they remain mainly industrial. However, strategies to foster creativity through bottom-up policies are only visible in the city of Barcelona, where classic industry disappeared during the 1980s.

Leipzig

Leipzig is situated in the Free State of Saxony in eastern Germany. It is the largest city in Saxony, closely followed by the state capital, Dresden. The city of Leipzig itself has a population slightly exceeding 500,000 (30 June 2008). The transition to a market economy brought about by German reunification in 1990 quickly led to the widespread collapse of the traditional economic structures. In order to overcome lasting high rates of unemployment (16.0 per cent in March 2009), brain drain and economic stagnation, there were huge investments in new economic fields along with investment in transportation infrastructure, but these did not stop Leipzig's socio-economic decline.

Apart from other labour markets, the city of Leipzig demonstrates a very positive performance in creative and knowledge-intensive industries and positive growth rates in jobs as well as in GDP growth rates (SMWA, 2008, p. 17). The media industry is embedded in a broad institutionalised knowledge and educational landscape, with university, polytechnic college, several extra-university research centres and various art, music and technical schools. Policies and state-subsidised transfer facilities and incubator schemes in combination with ultra-modern technical, mobility infrastructures make Leipzig a competitive location: attractive urban qualities, open-minded social milieus, active civil society and cultural facilities in various fields stimulate its economic competitiveness.

Although huge federal and state financial investment has been directed towards forward-looking fields of knowledge (mobility, R&D, high-tech infrastructure and communication technologies), research outputs (numbers of patents, research funding, etc.) do not yet fully justify the financial investment. Officially, the city administration has selected five economic clusters based on their performance since 2000 (see Stadt-Leipzig, 2006). These clusters are media and creative industries (since August 2008), life sciences, biotechnology and medical technology, energy and environmental technologies, vehicle and components industry, enabling technologies and business services, especially logistics.

The city's policy objective was to steer new knowledge industries by acquiring state, federal or EU subsidies for establishing and accommodating these knowledge clusters. By founding new private but still state-led institutions to organise the promotion of clusters (e.g. Aufbauwerk GmbH), the city administration acted top-down as a leading agent. Furthermore, the local authorities were stimulating intermediary structures (round tables, fairs, conferences) aiming at increased communication and exchange between knowledge workers.

Knowledge-intensive industries are marked by a lack of entrepreneurship, low rates of spin-offs, and a lack of international or national headquarters with strong decision competencies. This and other factors explain the largely top-down policy approach adopted in Leipzig, drawing on the administrative and financial help of the state. The rupture with the socialist past forced the local administration to make great efforts to establish a privately organised knowledge industry structure. But in a situation where R&D and large parts of the education system had been organised by state authorities, there was a lack of established SMEs in R&D and the service-oriented enterprises, and knowledge industry was weak. This added to the reasons for adopting a top-down approach. The failure of larger knowledge-intensive enterprises to position themselves in Leipzig as national or regional headquarters even stigmatised the city-region as economically weak and as constantly relying on external European or national subsidies. Consequently a strong role continued to be taken by the local and national government in decision-making to establish knowledge industries.

Creative industries in general have only been identified as a strategic field of action by the local government in the city of Leipzig since 2008. Although there has been positive performance of this field (primarily in the media industry, in art and design), integrative public–private partnership strategies and a coherent urban and economic policy cannot be identified before 2009 and the development of this sector cannot be attributed to targeted policies.

A first and important step occurred in 1992 when the MDR (Mitteldeutscher Rundfunk, the regional broadcasting corporation serving the states of Saxony, Saxony-Anhalt and Thuringia) opened its headquarters in Leipzig. Shortly afterwards, a media development agency entitled *Medienstadt Leipzig GmbH* was set up to support the growth of media-related activities. About 4300 jobs are in publishing and printing, along with 4200 in TV, film and radio (Bentele et al., 2006). Most of the media-related firms are very small, explaining why there are so many (2100 companies in the year 2007; see Bentele et al., 2008).

Apart from formally top-down and politically induced crises-solving policies, informal networks have proved essential in order to promote creative industries and play an ever-increasing role in shaping creative professions in Leipzig. The city's social networks provide numerous ways of self-organising and of improving better access to small markets. Though the formal labour market is weak, inaccessible or unattractive for highly qualified people in this industry, many of them have launched their own rather unusual entrepreneurial start-up business in the midst of the substantial crisis in Leipzig. Informal networks have provided an important backbone in order to cope with minimal financial income, hardly any venture capital or similar formal and 'known' support structures (Bismarck and Koch, 2005; Steets, 2005, 2008). In combination with their existing cultural capital, which had survived the GDR times (such as painting, photography and design), cultural scenes became more and more visible and so regained importance not only for the heterogeneity of cultural life, cultural consumption, but also as a professional opportunity for making their living. In the course, architectural offices (such as L 21, KARO and URBIKOM), artistic collectives (such as NIKO 31, Spector), gallery agglomerations in the former Spinnerei in Plagwitz in East-Leipzig, a leading cultural centre called naTO in Südvorstadt as well as a prospering media and film-related experimental creative scene emerged in the mid-1990 (Bismarck and Koch, 2005). The structural crisis of the city after unification thus led to creative actions by different agents and has in the course also informed and stimulated different knowledge institutions. For example, the Academy for Visual Arts reacted to the professional situation of its alumni and repositioned its curriculum, urban engagement and institutional role (Bismarck and Koch, 2005).

Governance practices are mainly about communication and about certain discourses between various public, civic and entrepreneurial agents and three phases can be detected between 1993 and 2008 in Leipzig.

The first phase dates from 1993 to 2006. After unification the city administration had to reorganise its administrative structures as well as the relationship between high culture and the administration for cultural affairs. Many civil society initiatives claimed an independent role for their programmes. A strong emphasis was placed on the way an independent cultural sector can serve a newly liberated society. Culture was seen as a mainly independent sphere of action without market and political restrictions. Government acted in close contact to a heterogeneous and lively cultural scene, which broke new ground after the state-led milieus disappeared from the official sphere. Parallel but decoupled from this development, there were huge financial efforts aimed at developing knowledge industries although these have not yet led to establishing a strong knowledge industry base.

The second phase started in 2007. First scientific and empirical studies were completed referring to the potential for creative industries to form a new economic segment in Leipzig. These studies paved the way for a broader and less 'traditional' sector-oriented discussion not only within the public authorities but most importantly between official and market representatives. A major cornerstone was the title in the city magazine 'Kreuzer', if Leipzig will become a creative city. The magazines top story asked for the economic options for the city in the field of creative industries and, slowly it was acknowledged that negotiations could start with representatives and new stakeholders in informal networks. These bottom-up initiatives stand in contrast to the continuing top-down efforts by local and state authorities to promote knowledge-intensive industries.

The last phase, starting in 2008, is characterised by the fears, expressed by leading public figures and market representatives, that the discursive hype on the issue of creative industries and creative city policies will not lead to any substantial improvement in the actual situation of mainly self-organised creative and entrepreneurial practices. The ongoing discourse about Leipzig's distinct profile, suitable policies and concerted investments in urban eco-nomic policies is likely to lead to the formulation of a report on the creative industries as well as to further cooperation between heterogeneous market representatives, aiming to improve their precarious socio-economic situation.

Sofia

After the collapse of the pro-Soviet communist regime in 1989, Sofia under-went rapid socio-economic transformation from totalitarian to democratic society, from planned to market-based economy, from an isolated to an integrated position in the world economy, from an industrial to post-indus-trial (service) economy and society. Twenty years after the beginning of this transformation, the city produces more than one-third of the national GDP and attracts almost 70 per cent of all direct foreign investment. Over 70 per cent of Sofia's GDP come from the service sector, while 20 per cent of the companies active in the city operate in the creative sphere. Thus Sofia is Bulgaria's economic, administrative and creative knowledge capi-tal, being home to 100 per cent of all Bulgarian information agency and market research companies, and Bulgarian magazines; 80–90 per cent of all Bulgarian music (including shops) and publishing companies; 60–70 per cent of all Bulgarian insurance (and 78 per cent of life insurance), human resources and training, and hardware companies; 50–60 per cent of all Bulgarian software, computer service, engineering and TV companies, and antique dealers; 40–50 per cent of all Bulgarian advertising, architec-tural and design, radio, fashion design and printing companies.

Moreover, the city hosts the principal academic institutions, financial services and public services, 23 theatres, 30 museums, 115 municipal cultural centres called 'Chitalishte', 512 libraries. The cultural her-itage is also mainly concentrated in Sofia – in the Museum of National History, in the Archaeological Museum, the Ethnographic Museum, the National Art Gallery and others, and these accumulate the most impor-tant regional collections from all over the country. A major part of the Bulgarian universities as well as almost the entire research base of the Bulgarian Academy of Science is also situated in Sofia.

The concentration of cultural, educational and research resources is entirely path dependent and results from centralised socialist planning, exalted by the spontaneous effect of the invisible hand of the market. Thus Sofia became an example of an economically unregulated post-communist capital city.

Knowledge-intensive industries in regard to governance perspectives

Regardless of the concentration of institutions and professionals, knowledge-intensive industries are a priority neither at a national nor local level. Their development rests completely on market principles and self-organisation.

During the post-socialist transformation property, rights were the main theme of the policies, debates and scandals in Sofia. In 1989, with the exception of parts of domestic residences, almost the entire property in the city was owned by the state. Subsequently part of it was returned to the citizens, part was privatised by the state and part was transferred to the city, which on its part also adopted privatisation. Other than promoting the restructuring of property, most government decisions were focused on the construction sector and infrastructure development. The domination of these two agendas – restructuring and construction – tightened the space for interaction between the city administration and the citizens and the administration and the businesses that together privatise, grant concessions and build. At this stage Sofia had not considered developing a city of regional competitiveness, creativity, knowledge-based economy, creative and knowledge-based clusters. When candidates had raised this issue during pre-election debates, they had later lost the elections.

Consequently, the city administration had not started developing active sector or territorial policies. Nor were these adopted at other levels: the districts, into which the city is divided, did not have competences and resources to make policies, and they were not interested in doing so; the regional administration (for the economic hinterland of Sofia) was a decentralised branch of the central government and did not take decisions on economic and territorial policies; the Southwestern district for development, created for the purposes of the European Regional policy also did not plan measures and actions to support regional competitiveness or the development of a creative and knowledge-based economy; the national authorities conduct national sector policies without territorial or cluster aspects (including Sofia). This political agenda is dominated by the concepts of the fordist era: the government has recently created a public company, which would build industrial zones in the country.

Not only did the central and local authorities miss the opportunity of having a greater role in guiding the development of Sofia, but the knowledge-intensive sector itself did not show signs of self-organisation and self-regulation. After the transition, the scientific institutions demanded and received autonomy from the state and later asked for higher government subsidies without accepting the conditions, programmes and policies suggested by the authorities (e.g. the recent scandal concerning the activities, the results and the status of the Bulgarian Academy of Science). Foreign companies in the field of R&D stand outside these events – they attract low-paid qualified workers, in order to develop applications for the global market (e.g. the research departments of Siemens).

Similar processes have taken place over creative industries. Twenty years ago the players in this industry demanded and were granted independence from the public authorities. Nonetheless, the state and the city council retained the property of key cultural institutions, seized control over the programmes, but also decreased their sponsorship, the idea being that the market would fill the gap. Local authorities retained their property rights over the Chitalishta. According to tradition it acts as a training centre for arts and cultural events as well as a knowledge centre, e.g. for learning foreign languages and running technical workshops.

Local authorities also support some cultural events but such activities are not based on strategies, programmes or clear criteria, and in most cases are PR events used by the mayor or the president of the city council. In general, the creative industries in Sofia were left to develop in the spirit of Neoliberalism. Some attempts for structuring and self-organisation can be observed in some sectors, but without success (e.g. the press agreed on standards and a code of conduct for professionalism, but lacked a clear mechanism for its implementation).

As has been seen, the dominant governance mode of the knowledge-intensive and cultural industries in Sofia is one of self-organisation outside the activities of the state and local authorities. Where institutions that are independent of the state and the municipality are the primary actors in any request for greater funding and support for culture and science, this is treated as unique to that sector and not as an instrument for development. The answer of the state and the local authorities is also part of the discourse and practice of 'the residual principal' (whatever amount is left in the budget after the financing of other priorities). The absence of any coordination from the public administration makes formal and informal networks weaker and does not allow the development of creative knowledge industries.

Conclusions

In this chapter we have focused on the emergence of new governance approaches to foster the creative knowledge economy in cities and metropolitan regions and the insights presented suggest six main conclusions.

First, despite the existence of complex governance mechanisms, government still matters, and classic government approaches are being developed in some fields strongly dependent on the public sector. This is relevant for instance in the case of policies to foster media industries, which are strongly dependent on the public sector in the Barcelona and Leipzig.

Second, especially in core creative branches such as design and art, there is strong notion of self-governance as a mode of organising professions and professional standards bottom-up. In contrast to these high demands for self-organisation, knowledge-intensive industries are still organised, to a large extent, top-down and have much more formalised professional constellations than some experimental segments of creative industries.

Third, in knowledge-intensive and creative industries, it is critically important that actors have various ways of sharing knowledge and ideas. In this, professional networks are a key to promoting innovation and new projects and businesses. Whereas in the knowledge industries, these networks are sometimes promoted top-down, generating spaces for exchange and formal professional networks, in the creative industries existing very informal networks appear to from the basis for activity. In this case, the members of networks are wary of the efforts of public administration; they consider that public intervention can hinder autonomy and the innovative impulse that their professional networks provide.

Fourth, governance approaches to foster creative industries are increasingly based on generating a creative environment in which informal professional networks will emerge. One example is the promotion of cultural or creative events to foster a creative atmosphere. In other cases governance is based on a more classic approach, trying to generate 'clusters' and agglomeration economies. A good example of this kind of policy is the creation of technologic or scientific parks.

Fifth, the great variety of governance modes, branches, actors and place-specific constellations indicate the absence of a common and overall approach to how to develop suitable policies promoting creative and knowledge-intensive industries. The distinctive city-regional institutional fabric has to be considered as a central cornerstone from where to derive suitable policy approaches.

Finally, existing policy approaches to stimulating creative and knowledge-intensive industries can roughly be differentiated in two ways: context-sensitive and direct-steering policies. By 'context-sensitive' we mean approaches that take into account the specificities of social place and the particular ways that certain milieus or economic segments are constituted. Direct-steering approaches refer to more traditional forms of economic development such as where entrepreneurs obtain direct funding for a certain period of time. Direct-steering to further develop creative industries are suitable for segments such as film, TV or architecture but would fail in the art segment, where the returns from financial aid are less easily quantified.

A context-sensitive approach takes into account the very fact that the creative and knowledge-intensive industries as well as their milieus expect a suitable social, cultural and economic environment. Communication, exchange and innovation processes depend on these contexts in order to have an opportunity to flourish.

Acknowledgements

The authors would like to thank Kornelia Ehrlich for her contribution to this chapter.

References

Abbott, A. (1988) *The system of professions*. Chicago: The University of Chicago Press.

Balducci, A. (2004) Creative governance in dynamic city regions. *DISP*, 158: 21–26.

Bentele, G., T. Liebert and R. Fechner (2006) *Medienstandort Leipzig: Eine Studie zur Leipziger Medienwirtschaft 2005/2006*. Dresden: Sächsische Staatskanzlei Dresden/Amt für Wirtschaftsförderung der Stadt Leipzig.

Bentele, G., T. Liebert and R. Fechner (2008) *Medienstandort Leipzig VI: Eine Studie zur Leipziger Medienwirtschaft 2007/2008*. Dresden: Sächsische Staatskanzlei Dresden/Amt für Wirtschaftsförderung der Stadt Leipzig.

Bismarck, B. v. and A. Koch (eds) (2005) *Beyond education. Kunst, Ausbildung, Arbeit und Ökonomie*. Leipzig: Revolver – Archiv für aktuelle Kunst.

Bourdieu, P. (1986) The forms of capital. In: J. Richardson (ed.), *Handbook of theory and research of the sociology of education*, pp. 241–258. Westport: Greenwood Press.

Cameron, K. and R. Quinn (1988) Organizational paradox and transformation. In: R.E. Quinn and K. Cameron (eds), *Paradox and transformation*, pp. 1–18. Cambridge: Harper & Row.

Davies, A. and S. Ford (1998) Art capital. *Art Monthly*, 1 (213): 12–20.

DeFillippi, R., G. Grabher and C. Jones (2007) Introduction to paradoxes of creativity: Managerial and organizational challenges in the cultural economy. *Journal of Organizational Behavior*, 28 (5): 511–521.

Evetts, J. (2003) The sociological analysis of professionalism. *International Sociology*, 18 (1): 395–415.

Fournier, V. (1999) The appeal to 'professionalism' as a disciplinary mechanism. *Social Review*, 47: 280–307.

Freidson, E. (2001) *Professionalism: The third logic*. Cambridge: Polity.

Friebe, H. and S. Lobo (2006) *Wir nennen es Arbeit: die digitale Bohème oder: Intelligentes Leben jenseits der Festanstellung*. München: Heyne.

Geddes, M. and J. Bennington (2001) *Social exclusion and partnership in the European Union*. London: Routledge.

Grabher, G. (2002a) Cool projects, boring institutions: Temporary collaboration in social context. *Regional Studies*, 36 (3): 205–214.

Grabher, G. (2002b) The project ecology of advertising: Tasks, talents and teams. *Regional Studies*, 36 (3): 245–262.

Grabher, G. (2004) Learning in projects, remembering in networks? Communality, sociality, and connectivity in project ecologies. *European Urban and Regional Studies*, 11 (2): 103–123.

Grabher, G. (2006) Trading routes, bypasses, and risky intersections: Mapping the travels of 'networks' between economic sociology and economic geography. *Progress in Human Geography*, 30 (2): 1–27.

Healey, P. (2006) Transforming governance: Challenges of institutional adaptation and a new politics of space. *European Planning Studies*, 14 (3): 299–320.

Heinelt, H. (2004) Governance auf lokaler Ebene. In: A. Benz (ed.), *Governance – Regieren in komplexen Regelsystemen*, pp. 29–44. Opladen: Leske + Budrich.

Jessop, B. (1995) The regulation approach, governance and post-fordism. *Economy and Society*, 24 (3): 307–333.

Kosmala, K. (2007) The identity paradox? Reflections on fluid identity of female artist. *Culture and Organization*, 13 (1): 37–53.

Kunzmann, K.R. (2004) An agenda for creative governance in city regions. *DISP*, 158: 5–10.

Lange, B. (2005a) Landscapes of cultural scenes: Socio-spatial emplacement strategies of 'Culturepreneurs' in Berlin. In: A.-M. d'Hauteserre and T.S. Terkenli (eds), *Landscape of a new cultural economy of space*, pp. 41–67. Dordrecht: Kluwer Press.

Lange, B. (2005b) Socio-spatial strategies of culturepreneurs. The example of Berlin and its new professional scenes. *Zeitschrift für Wirtschaftsgeographie (Special Issue: Ökonomie und Kultur)*, 49 (2): 81–98.

Lange, B. (2007) *Die Räume der Kreativszenen. Culturepreneurs und ihre Orte in Berlin.* Bielefeld: Transcript Verlag.

Lange, B., A. Kalandides, B. Stöber and H.A. Mieg (2008) Berlin's creative industries: Governing creativity? *Industry and Innovation*, 15 (5): 531–548.

Lange, B., A. Kalandides, B. Stöber and I. Wellmann (2009) Fragmentierte Ordnungen. In: B. Lange, A. Kalandides, B. Stöber and I. Wellmann (eds), *Governance der Kreativwirtschaft. Diagnosen und Handlungsoptionen*, pp. 11–32. Bielefeld: Transcript.

Lange, B. and H.A. Mieg (2008) Professionalisierungswege und Konstituierungen von 'Märkten' in den Creative Industries. *Geographische Zeitschrift*, 94 (4): 225–242.

Lave, J. (1991) Situating learning in communities of practice. In: J.M. Levine, L.B. Resnick and S.D. Teasley (eds), *Perspectives on socially shared cognition*, pp. 63–82. Washington, DC: American Psychological Association.

Markusen, A. (2006) Urban development and the politics of a creative class: Evidence from a study of artists. *Environment & Planning A*, 38: 1921–1940.

Martí, M. and M. Pradel i Miquel (2008) *Urban creativity in the spaces of capital: The case of Poblenou artists in Barcelona.* Paper presented at ISA Forum, 6–8 September, Barcelona.

Mieg, H.A. (2008) Professionalisation. In: F. Rauner and R. Maclean (eds), *Handbook of vocational education research.* Dordrecht: Springer.

Neff, G., E. Wissinger and S. Zukin (2005) Entrepreneurial labour among cultural producers. 'Cool' jobs in 'Hot' industries. *Social Semiotics*, 15 (3): 307–334.

Pareja-Eastaway, M., J. Turmo, M. Pradel i Miquel, L. García-Ferrando and M. Simó (2007) *The city of marvels? Multiple endeavours towards competitiveness in Barcelona.* Amsterdam: AMIDSt.

Pareja-Eastaway, M., J. Turmo, M. Pradel i Miquel, L. García-Ferrando and M. Simó (2008a) *Main drivers for settlement in the Barcelona Metropolitan Region: The managers' view.* Amsterdam: AMIDSt.

Pareja-Eastaway, M., J. Turmo, M. Pradel i Miquel, L. García-Ferrando and M. Simó (2008b) *Why in Barcelona? Understanding the attractiveness of the metropolitan region for creative knowledge workers.* Amsterdam: AMIDSt.

Rae, D. (2002) Entrepreneurial emergence: A narrative study of entrepreneurial learning in independently owned media businesses. *The International Journal of Entrepreneurship and Innovation*, 3 (1): 53–60.

Rae, D. (2004) Entrepreneurial learning: A practical model from the creative industries. *Education + Training*, 46 (8/9): 492–500.

Rhodes, R.A.W. (1996) The new governance. *Political Studies*, 64: 652–667.

Scott, A.J. (2006) Entrepreneurship, innovation and industrial development: Geography and the creative field revisited. *Small Business Economics*, 26 (1): 1–24.

SMWA (ed.) (2008) *1. Kulturwirtschaftsbericht für den Freistaat Sachsen*. Dresden: Sächsisches Ministerium für Wirtschaft und Arbeit.

Stadt-Leipzig (2006) *Leipzig Facts 2006*. Leipzig: Dezernat für Wirtschaft und Arbeit.

Steets, S. (2005) Doing Leipzig. Räumliche Mikropolitiken des Dazwischen. In: H. Berking and M. Löw (eds), *Die Wirklichkeit der Städte*, pp. 107–122. Baden Baden: Nomos Verlagsgesellschaft.

Steets, S. (2008) *'Wir sind die Stadt!' Kulturelle Netzwerke und die Konstitution städtischer Räume in Leipzig*. Frankfurt am Main: Campus.

Steyaert, C. and J. Katz (2004) Reclaiming the space of entrepreneurship in society: Geographical, discursive and social dimensions. *Entrepreneurship and Regional Development*, 16 (3): 179–196.

Stoker, G. (1998) Governance as theory. *International Social Science Journal*, 50 (155): 17–28.

Sydow, J., L. Lindkvist and R. Defillippi (2004) Project-based organizations, embeddedness and repositories of knowledge: Editorial. *Organization Studies*, 25 (9): 1475–1490.

Thelen, K. (2003) The paradox of globalization: Labor relations in Germany and beyond. *Comparative Political Studies*, 36 (8): 859–880.

Thomas, M. (1997) Voraussetzungsvolle Passagen Neuer Selbständiger im ostdeutschen Transformationsprozeß. In: M. Thomas (ed.), *Selbständige – Gründer – Unternehmer*, pp. 14–57. Berlin: Berliner Debatte Wissenschaftsverlag.

Trullen, J., J. Llados and R. Boix (2002) Economía del conocimiento, ciudad y competitividad. *Investigaciones Regionales*, 001: 139–161.

Wenger, E. (1999) *Communities of practice*. Cambridge: Cambridge University Press.

White, H.C. (2002) *Markets from networks: Socioeconomic models of production*. Princeton u.a.: Princeton University Press.

Wilson, N. and D. Stokes (2005) Managing creativity and innovation. The challenge for cultural entrepreneurs. *Journal of Small Business and Enterprise Development*, 12 (3): 366–378.

Zhang, X. (2004) Multiplicity or homogeneity? The cultural–political paradox of the age of globalization. *Cultural Critique*, 58 (Fall 2004): 30–55.

Part V

Synthesis

Barcelona – Leisure, culture, Olympics. Photo by Montserrat Pareja-Eastaway.

Munich. Photo by Puikang Chan.

18

Synthesis: Re-making the Competitive City

Sako Musterd and Alan Murie

Introduction

The previous chapters of this book have worked through a very wide agenda about the competitive city and the development of the creative knowledge city. We have drawn on a wide range of sources but added to what is available elsewhere by using evidence generated through a major international comparative research programme. Through this we have introduced new data that begins to test some assertions and fill some gaps. We have also referred more fully to European cities – and to a variety of cities and avoided both the focus on a small number of special places and on American cities. The cities we have chosen each have its own special features but its strength is in the variety of histories and roles that they have rather than in their representativeness. They are presented as case studies that enable us to test the plausibility of arguments and see if they stand up in such diverse contexts. Where they do it does not establish them as proven and where arguments do not stand up to this plausibility test they are not disproved – but in both cases we are able to confirm whether these arguments can reasonably continue to be regarded as robust or how far they should be treated with scepticism.

This book has referred to 13 distinctive European cities but reflects a more sustained research effort in each of them than lies behind much of the debate about creative knowledge cities. The data has been purposively generated to address basic propositions in the field and has included the examination of historical and secondary sources as well as original empirical research that begins to test assertions about the motivations of key actors in the creative knowledge industries. All of this research was designed to take full account of the relevant literature – of what was known already – and to use as far as possible common approaches so that the combination of factors that composed the unique account for each city represented real variation and was not simply a result of the idiosyncratic ways in which the research had been carried out. So, for example, the interviews referred to throughout the book were carried out to a common design and format and those selected for interview were drawn using an agreed framework and largely from the same sectors of the industries concerned. We believe that the systematic nature of this approach makes the material we have presented robust and reliable. In any international comparative research of this type, however, the individual character of each city and its economy and differences between the perspectives of researchers and their resources in implementing the research design present a challenge. The discussions of the results of the research have not, therefore, asserted too much. In some respects what we have are rich city studies generated through the application of a common template and enabling comparisons of key dimensions of the competitive city.

The aims of this book were set out in Chapters 1 and 2 and relate to a wide academic and policy-related literature. Against some expectations, all of the cities we have referred to have seen the modernisation of their economies through the growth of knowledge and creative industries. These sectors have not developed to the same extent or in the same way and confirm that the creative city cannot be made overnight by adopting a Florida-type formula or indeed any other formula. There is path dependency and successful developments can generally be linked to some historical roots. At the same time, our city studies counsel against the overly sceptical view that it is a waste of time for any but a few special cities to aspire to developing their competitiveness by fostering creative knowledge industry. A more robust middle view is that strategies to grow these sectors need to take account of the histories, assets and barriers facing different cities and would not anticipate the same form of success in all cases. The discussion at the outset of this book referred to the view that some cities were better placed to build creative knowledge industry and the work we have reported confirms that capital cities and those with histories as centres for the arts and culture and of university education can build on these resources. But the cities that fit this mould each have very different histories and outcomes; and each of the cities that do not fit this mould have built on other assets that are just as critical in explaining the scale and nature of their emerging creative and knowledge economies.

Some of the difference between cities that explains their distinctive pattern of development in this area relates to public policy. One perspective is that cities without favourable 'natural' attributes have developed more energetic policies to compensate. And there is a deeper debate that historical cities with strong established vested interests have been less likely to be centres of innovation. Perhaps this is an important part of the explanation for differences in the role of policy in the past as well as today. And this relates to the important discussion in the final section of this book – referring to the limitations of traditional policy approaches and the challenges for policy makers in deciding how best to support growth and innovation in sectors that value independence and self-regulation and are wary of bureaucratic interference. The skills needed in this context are not only to avoid using a formula borrowed from elsewhere but to adopt an approach that maintains probity but is responsive and builds working and social relationships rather than relying on form filling and formality.

Throughout this book we have referred to the reality, for European cities, of the growth of the creative and knowledge sectors of the economy. This does not imply that the consequences of growth in terms of inequality and the strains of restructuring are unimportant. Indeed, increasing the attention given to social cohesion and to issues related to housing and living conditions are an essential aspect of policy related to the creative knowledge city. The evidence is that we are a long way from achieving holistic and integrated policies. It is also important to recognise that the development of the creative knowledge city does not simply pose challenges because those outside it will not share in the wealth and opportunities it creates. The precarious nature of work for many of those within the creative sector has been emphasised. This further adds to the case to reject the discourse of the creative city associated with a creative class. The engagement with this image of a new higher-paid, hyper-mobile class throughout this book has cast doubt on its value. Some of those working in knowledge-intensive and creative industry may conform to this stereotype but most do not and are neither higher paid nor hyper mobile. They are often anchored (often willingly so) in career paths and personal networks and these are often enmeshed with the places that they live in and where their work and family networks are centred on. While the perspective advanced so heroically by Richard Florida should not be totally dismissed, his emphasis on soft factors and on talent, tolerance and technology should be put in perspective. This means that they form part of the explanation of what drives competitive cities along with the classic and other factors emphasised by others.

A city is not a T-shirt

Making competitive cities is not an activity that can be carried out by applying recipes that have been written down by a single professional. It is not something you can make or re-make like a standard product with the help of a common set of tools and instruments. Cities and urban economies are not T-shirts that can be produced in much the same way across the world.

But why not?

The main element in answering this is that a city is mainly 'context'; it is about the individual and collective histories and about networks that have developed in a differentiated way over a longer time path. In the words of evolutionary economic geography we could say that contexts, as soon as they have been developed, tend to have a continuous impact on future developments (Frenken and Boschma, 2007). These contexts tell us what kinds of transformations are feasible. Cities are multi-dimensional, multi-temporal and multi-scalar entities, often existing for thousands of years and they have been built upon and for a wide variety of societies. The resulting variations and diversities cannot be neglected when urban change is on the agenda. There is not one formula with which to change the city to the good and there is not one set of policies that would produce the 'competitive city'. This book, with the title *Making Competitive Cities*, therefore, is not aimed at formulating a prescription for how to make competitive cities. It does, however, clarify what dimensions are important if we intend to understand some of the current urban economic transformations and opportunities. These dimensions include the various contexts that have changed over time and continue to change. The dimensions also refer to the social and professional networks that exist, including those that are connected with the presence of centres of education. These networks of friends, family, colleagues and 'youth and study turf' emerge as major conditions for continued economic initiatives and orientations. Of course, these conditions are also affected by current and previous policy interventions. Policy has contributed in various ways to shaping the forms and functions of cities, but they have not determined them.

In this unique book we have made efforts to better understand the behaviour of key actors in sections of the creative and knowledge-intensive industries. We call this volume 'unique' since we believe that the authors have had the special opportunity to develop an empirical research project which is unsurpassed in its kind. Supported by funding from the European Commission, we were granted the freedom to work on this project for a period of 4 years, with 13 high-skilled university research teams from as many urban regions in Europe, to investigate empirically which pathways these urban regions went through, to figure out what kind of conditions would be important to different kinds of actors to settle and stay in the urban area where we found them and to register what kinds of policies were being developed in various contexts. We were able to include insights from a range of theories while testing various hypotheses. We did not restrict our analyses to tests of the 'New Conventional Wisdom' (see Gordon and

Turok, 2005) that strongly builds on the three T's (talent, tolerance and technology) Richard Florida referred to in his work on the Creative Class, but decided to include concepts, hypotheses and ideas from cluster theories (Porter, 1998), from 'classic' location theory (Sassen, 2002) and from theories in which personal ties and individual trajectories were highlighted (Grabher, 2004).

Evidence was collected on the basis of an integrated methodology, so we did not simply collect findings from individual case studies, but instead we developed joint survey lists, item lists, interview strategies, cohorts to be interviewed and sector selections for creative industries and knowledge-intensive industries. Subsequently, we applied these joint strategies in each of the 13 urban regions involved. Although comparisons are always difficult in a diversified environment, this offered the best possible way for confronting the empirical outcomes for the urban regions with each other. It provided the opportunity to come with stronger empirical evidence about a range of assumptions that have dominated the public and academic debates in many places across the globe. The narrow theoretical foundation and the thin empirical support that form the base for current debates and interventions may already have had serious negative implications for the development of urban policies aimed at enhancing the competitiveness of urban regions. It was our ambition to come up with a broader theoretical foundation and more solid empirical analyses of the crucial assumptions, thus providing the elements for developing better understanding and more adequate policies aimed at enhancing urban economic positions in the longer run.

In this final chapter we will try to highlight the most important findings of this study as reflected in the three main parts of the book. In the next three sections we pay attention to the importance of different contexts and pathways, the opinions and behaviours of various actors and to policies.

Multi-layered cities: the importance of pathways

The contributions in this volume indicate that it is impossible to 'Make the Competitive City' overnight, or even within the time span of a couple of decades, that is to say: in a sustainable form. Although there are examples of efforts made in that direction, it seems either very difficult to break with the past or very difficult to create new and proper sustainable balances to make the city sufficiently attractive to work and live in. Path dependence, the rootedness in rich or poor urban histories, continues to play a major role in future opportunities for cities and for those who create and recreate them. The historically grown structures and urban cultures may help or may prevent the city from flourishing in a certain time-space framework. These frameworks are changing, as short and long economic cycles show us. The more structural changes may have particularly serious effects on the development of the city, as we have experienced in the past. An era in which mainly manufacturing industries and port activities were driving urban economies – as was the case in many European cities from the nineteenth century onwards – can change into an era in which trade, consumer and producer services and technology are the combined new engines. As a result inflexible, standard ways of production were replaced by more flexible processes. This has had major consequences for urban structure and urban life. Economic restructuring is not the only deeply rooted driver of change; large technological, political, cultural and institutional changes will have major implications for urban transformation in turn. A relatively recent example of significant change has been formulated by Manuel Castells (1989), who saw that the telecommunication revolution would transform information exchange and this would, in turn, have major impacts on cities. Spaces of flows in various networks would become dominant over the classic spaces of places. New urban realities would be better understood when looking at the city's embeddedness in a range of (global) networks (Krätke, 2003; Scott, 2006). Even though people and firms did not become really footloose, and even though the spaces of flows did not make the spaces of places redundant (as many initially thought they would), the importance of networks has been acknowledged and still seems to be increasing. Similar changes may be connected with major shifts in the type of welfare state that cities are embedded within and with other major political changes (the rise and fall of the Iron Curtain and connected state systems, the consolidation of democracy in Spain, admission of new Member States to the European Union).

Those cities that are best able to change their profile from old to new will become the winners of their time. However, to be able to make the appropriate change, certain conditions have to be met. In this volume, in Part II on Pathways, examples have been given that show that cities have built on distinctive legacies and traditions but that a varied economic structure represents an important asset. Sofia, which was forced to become specialised in heavy manufacturing industries under communism and was late to develop a post-communist economy, Birmingham, identified with manufacturing industry from the early years of the Industrial Revolution onwards and the city and region of Barcelona, that experienced the last wave of industrialisation rather late, are cases in point. Superficially, these can be represented as cities with an urban history dominated by a manufacturing industry. But on closer examination they are much less monolithic and uniform with roles as capital city or regional cultural and educational centre or as a centre for innovation and proactive local government enriching the assets of each city. Consequently, even these cities cannot be treated as similar or disadvantaged. In Birmingham, for example, many who were employed in manufacturing industries were high-skilled and the role of small and medium-sized enterprises, skilled craftsmen and artisans offered a good basis for the development of creative industries. In Barcelona, where labour was predominantly lower skilled, albeit diversified, there were strong traditions related to fashion and textiles and arts and architecture. While the low-skilled labour force offered good opportunities to the building industry, the diversity of industry also offered opportunities for the development of new creative and knowledge-intensive industries. And in both of these cities there were strengths that emerged in their size and the capacity to adopt active and effective policies to re-invent the city.

Capital cities, cities with a long history as a centre of culture, cities that were not built on a narrow manufacturing industry profile and cities that had strong positions as control centres for wider, perhaps even global, networks, have assets that attract new creative and knowledge-intensive industries. This seems to apply to Amsterdam, Munich and Budapest, and perhaps also Dublin. These cities are characterised by political power that was established long ago, by a differentiated economy, not a reliance solely on manufacturing industry, an established position in major economic networks and they are known as historical cultural centres with a preserved urban core. But cities with some of these elements in their histories should not assume that their histories will guarantee their futures – they may have to address barriers and develop new practices in the same way as others.

What emerges is a differentiated reality in which accumulated economic, social, political, cultural, physical and functional structures play an important role and are crucial for stable and continued development. This also implies that, in contrast, it will be very difficult to create a new sustainable city with no reference to its past. Urban histories and multiple urban layers simply add to the variety of the city. This does not mean that all layers will be good or helpful at any point in time, but the presence of multiple signs and remnants of urban structures, forms and functions may offer opportunities for a wide array of producers and consumers, and will provide opportunities for re-use when society is changing once again. This is about re-inventing the city and re-using crucial elements of the old urban social, economic, institutional and functional fabric (Bontje and Musterd, 2008). In this volume we included experiences in a range of urban regions that have been under communist rule until 1989. The breakdown of the communist planned economies resulted in instability and opportunities for changes in future direction – starting along new pathways. However, some of these urban regions have been able to maintain crucial characteristics of their older, pre-communist, profiles. Budapest (with its once central position in the Austro-Hungarian empire) and Leipzig (as a rich economic and cultural centre before communism, with major fairs, and being an important publishing and printing centre) have been able to capitalise on elements of their rich histories, including their 'reclaimed' geographical position. What is important, though, is that each of these histories (and those of Poznan, Riga and Sofia) has their own character that has to be recognised individually to be able to 'make the most out of it'; and all need significant support from public and private investors to overcome their turbulent recent histories. These kinds of support are not equally available in practice. Although there are some common threads between some of the cities – this was the basis for bringing them together in the various chapters in the first place – the unique pathways, histories and assets of the cities and their urban regions mean that they must also be considered one by one. This also means that any strategies and policy approaches must be tailored in an individual way to fit each city – and this perspective also holds for each of the other urban regions.

What most cities and urban regions do have in common, though, is that contemporary urban leaders often regard themselves as key actors who are responsible for current urban affluence. However, the real foundations for successful economic development were often established long ago. Toulouse and Munich had created the basis for their scientific and technological development in the nineteenth century, and other local conditions contributed to the cross-fertilisation of research and industry. Current leaders and policies may have enhanced their potential, but they did not (have to) invent them completely and could build upon them. Similarly, those who intend to get involved in the study of urban transformation in Amsterdam cannot do so without proper knowledge of what happened to the city in the seventeenth century, the so-called Golden Age. At that time the city became a global city *avant-la-lettre* and foundations were laid for trade and for the financial and insurance sectors. Milan's strong position in fashion and design also seems to be deeply rooted. Traces go back in textile and silk production and trade as far as the late Middle Ages; the city's wealth was based on these activities (and was spent on luxury goods). Alongside this, Milan's rise as a cultural city is rooted in the Renaissance. The two developments together are of key importance to the current fashion and design industry and therewith form an important element in the profile of the contemporary city.

Some cities have had economies that have experienced sharper discontinuities. This applies to cities and urban regions that developed a strong connection with manufacturing industry. Birmingham and Barcelona have pathways that were clearly different from those of Munich, Milan or Amsterdam. Whereas the latter were able to substantially capitalise on their historical legacies, Birmingham and Barcelona have shorter histories to draw on. But even in these cases the roots of the contemporary creative knowledge city are in the past. For Barcelona the role as Catalan capital and distinctive traditions in trade and architecture have been assets and these have been enhanced by public policy activity and strong urban leadership that has self-consciously built on these foundations. Although Birmingham has to dig deep to find a history much before the eighteenth century, its size and energetic invention of what is needed by a major city meant that by the beginning of the twentieth century the best governed city in the world had established enviable public services, a university and an economy that became the assets for subsequent transformation. Both of these cities show elements of catching up – of building assets that do not eliminate the gap with longer established cities but narrow it in some respects. And this process of catching up is also observable in other cities including those in east and central Europe and in Dublin's repositioning itself as a major location for multinational firms in Europe.

Revolutionary changes in the urban region also occur; however, even in these cases emerging patterns often reflect, to some extent, pre-existing arrangements. Although such situations may seem attractive, because new initiatives may not be hindered by urban legacies and can start, more or less, from a blank sheet, this is often an illusion. It will also be extremely difficult to build a successful economy that makes no use of the legacy of skills and other resources that reflect past patterns and can be utilised in the future. And where such revolutionary invention of the competitive city does occur, the risks associated with a lack of embeddedness in a rich and varied economic structure are evident. Although Helsinki is not a perfect example of this type, it is the closest example referred to in this book. That city and wider urban region, or perhaps even the country, are highly dependent on the ICT firms, with Nokia as the flagship. Vaattovaara (2009) noticed that in 2002, 62 per cent of Finland's investments in R&D came from that one single firm. The single ICT layer that developed has brought a very high-skilled population, significant economic growth, world-class positions and affluence and resulted in multiple spin-offs. Yet, the lack of variety simultaneously implies that there is a fragile basis for further development. If Nokia fails, the city of Helsinki will be seriously affected. If the wider ICT sector gets into trouble, the city will be hit even harder. It remains to be seen whether the other layers, such as the fact that Helsinki is the political and educational centre of Finland, create sufficient counterbalancing forces.

The urban region of Toulouse is sometimes said to have a comparable single sector dominance in technology but here the economic roots in history seem to be deeper. Toulouse was already known as a major crossing for trades between the Mediterranean and the Atlantic, and the economic base reflecting this history is more diversified.

Because each city's history and the legacies from history are important influences (but not determinants) on their future, development policy approaches quite rightly tend to involve efforts to build upon the past. There is a reluctance to destroy urban cultural heritage. Cities with a more limited number of layers (e.g. rapidly grown new towns, characterised by economic and urban structures that reflect the time when they were built) run a greater risk of becoming the problem areas of the future, because they do not have the 'fall back' options associated with richer, layered legacies. The multi-layered character and rich urban histories of many European cities would – in the longer run and in general – impart an advantage compared with the currently booming cities in China or compared with the formerly booming but single-layered cities in some parts of the USA.

The importance of development pathways does not imply that local government and policies are completely unimportant. What it does say is that the impact of the pathways and path dependence cannot be neglected. The histories will enable certain developments or they will block or obstruct certain changes, and thus they result in a variety of successes and failures. Of course, actors and strong leaders often can make a difference as well, but based on the research shown in this volume, they cannot tell the whole story and those who intend to change the city will have to have and make use of very good knowledge of the historical development of the city and its region. Moreover, that development will have to be taken into account, because it may offer new and more opportunities when current initiatives can be connected to some of the achievements from the past, especially when they offer unique comparative advantages that are difficult to copy.

Personal actor networks: key conditions

Cities are made and transformed by a wide range of actors, not least the people who work, and live in them, and those who use the city for recreation or who simply pass through the city – whether they enjoy it or hate it. In current debates there is a controversy about their actual roles and 'positions'. Some scholars, notably Florida (2002), believe that these actors are the golden element that creates the urban economy: residents and employees and managers in particular shape the future of the city and the economy develops in response to (talented) actors. The implication of this view is that these actors are the primary target for attention and, as they would typically be attracted by soft conditions or 'amenities', such as tolerance, diversity, openness and 'nice environments', these attributes become the key to the competitiveness of the city. If the city is successful in attracting talent firms will follow the employees and (potential) managers.

Others, however, say that this is a naïve way of thinking about how urban economies function. As Storper and Manville (2006) state, 'the notion that skills have driven growth, and that skilled workers locate according to some set of exogenously determined preferences and therefore determine the growth's geography, is less convincing than a theory that the preferences of firms – i.e. agglomeration economies – give rise to growth' (p. 1254).

In this view, firms are the key issues and cities have to try to facilitate the firms; they have to build on past performance and enable the development of clusters with related economic activities and the accompanying institutions. Space, connections and tax climates would be among the major instruments to use when trying to realise the initiatives. So, these would be the important factors to start with. Employees and (potential) managers would follow the firms!

In Part III of this book we analysed these relations and presented empirical evidence about opinions and experiences with a range of potential conditions of various key actors. The conditions distinguished included personal trajectories, their relations in networks of friends, family and professional colleagues; but also 'classic' hard conditions, such as available space, accessibility, tax-regimes, etc.; and so-called soft conditions, in which tolerance to other people, diversity, openness and an 'attractive' urban climate were mentioned as key factors. The actors we distinguished included employees with higher educational qualifications, managers of creative and knowledge-intensive firms and transnational migrants working in creative and knowledge-based industry.

The behaviour and attitudes of higher-skilled employees in creative and knowledge-intensive activities were explored through a large survey carried out in the ACRE programme (see Chapter 1). The overall opinions about what were the most important considerations for living in the urban region under consideration are summarised in Table 18.1. Generally, it is individual connections or trajectories that are mentioned as the most important conditions.

For most high-skilled employees in most of the cities so-called hard conditions are also important, although generally to a lesser extent and with more variation. Exceptions are Leipzig and Munich, where hard conditions are more often ranked first. What is striking is that the soft conditions, which formed the key building blocks for the Florida hype, are very rarely mentioned as ranking first. Here Amsterdam is an exception, although hard conditions and individual trajectories also score higher in this city.

A closer inspection of the scores provides even more insight. In the current debates between soft conditions believers and their opponents, four key concepts appear to be crucial:

- The first is the importance of the presence of employment opportunities.
- The second is the level of openness and tolerance.
- The third is the level of diversity and a positive attitude to it.
- The fourth is the role of personal networks, relations and connections.

In order to consider these four dimensions, again, on the basis of the rankings provided in the interviews, we have adopted the following procedure.

We first selected relevant conditions that fit the key concepts.

Table 18.1 Percentage of responses that ranked indicators as the most important (from a list of 26 indicators), classified as indicators for trajectories, hard and soft factors, per urban region.

	Trajectories	Hard conditions	Soft conditions	Total percentage	N
Amsterdam	38	35	26	100	221
Barcelona	62	27	11	100	200
Birmingham	57	38	5	100	165
Budapest	71	24	5	100	197
Helsinki	51	39	10	100	191
Leipzig	43	50	8	100	159
Munich	30	60	10	100	178
Poznan	74	23	3	100	155
Riga	80	17	4	100	132
Sofia	91	10		100	200
Toulouse	47	42	10	100	191
Milan	64	32	4	100	183
Dublin	57	42	1	100	201
Total	58	34	8	100	2,373

Source: ACRE survey, 2007.

The measurement of employment opportunities was based on three indicators:

- moved to the city because of a job;
- moved to the city because of a job of the partner;
- lives in the city because of good employment opportunities.

If a respondent ranked at least one of these three indicators as very important (in position 1 to 4 out of 26), we registered that the respondent scored on 'employment opportunities'.

We followed the same procedure for the three other dimensions.

The level of openness and tolerance was based on whether the respondent included any of the following among the four most important conditions for living in the urban region:

- the openness to different people in terms of race, colour or ethnicity;
- the open minded and tolerant urban atmosphere; and the gay and lesbian friendliness.

The level of diversity and positive attitude towards it was measured by whether the respondent included any of the following among the four most important conditions for living in the urban region:

- diversity of leisure and entertainment;
- 'cultural diversity'.

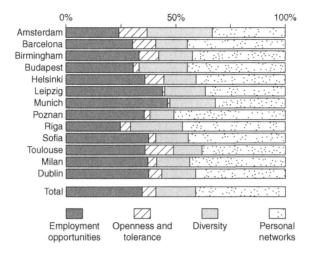

Figure 18.1 Relative share of respondents that ranked indicators as among the four most important from a list of 26 indicators, assembled in specific dimensions, per urban region.

The importance of personal relations was measured by whether the respondent included any of the following among the four most important conditions for living in the urban region:

- they were born there;
- their family lived there;
- their friends were nearby;
- they studied there.

For each city we then calculated the proportion of respondents that regarded these four dimensions important and presented this relative to each other in Figure 18.1. In Barcelona, for example, 82 per cent of all respondents said that personal relations were of key importance to them to be in that city; 56 per cent of the respondents said to be there because of employment opportunities; only 19 per cent mentioned the openness and tolerance; and 27 per cent mentioned diversity as important. These scores were made relative (total 100 per cent) to allow for an easier comparison between urban areas.

The results clearly show the importance of individual networks and of employment opportunities in particular. These findings are in support of those who argue that individual networks are key to understanding people's location behaviour. This also holds for highly skilled employees in creative and knowledge-intensive firms. Furthermore, job opportunities are still of crucial importance. Diversity and tolerance, on their own perhaps 'values' to be nurtured, do not seem to be highly relevant for the attraction of 'talented people'.

These general statements also seem to hold for the potentially even more 'urban' oriented people, the younger ones.

It is valuable to look more closely at three cities known for their creative position and regarded as attractive to young people in particular and to consider the importance of soft and hard conditions and personal relations among the young and highly skilled. These cities are Amsterdam, Barcelona and Milan. At first sight the findings for these three cities do not differ that much from the general findings: job opportunities and personal networks also turn out to be key factors for the young. If the 13 metropolitan areas are considered together, 72 per cent of young respondents say they are in the city because of job opportunities; 81 per cent because there are personal ties; only 10 per cent mention diversity and 38 per cent refer to openness and tolerance. In Amsterdam, however, young respondents (compared with all areas) are almost twice as likely to mention openness and tolerance, and this is the only metropolitan region where less than 50 per cent say that job opportunities were of key importance.

A remarkable finding was that even the young and highly skilled employees in creative and knowledge-intensive industries did not show a very high residential mobility rate. In that respect European cities clearly differ from those in the USA. The 'mobile creative class' did not appear to be very mobile at all. However, the difference between the two continents may actually have nothing to do with the young and highly mobile creative class. Mobility differences between young and high-skilled employees in European and American cities may just be a reflection of the general differences in residential mobility between the two continents.

In this volume we were also able to show that the frequent talk about 'talent' and the 'creative class', about the 'young and mobile' or about the 'competitive city' is not all about glitter and glamour. The evidence presented for Birmingham, Leipzig and Poznan showed that in all of these contexts, with clearly different labour market situations, there is a downside to the economic development of jobs in creative industries and this pattern also applies elsewhere. Much creative employment was temporary, insecure, short-term, contract work, characterised by long working hours; there was often a need to have multiple jobs, and many employees frequently changed job; unequal and insecure payments were also no exception. It remains to be seen whether the freedom, self-actualisation and self-governance connected to the type of jobs and frequently mentioned as contributing to the overall job satisfaction will in the longer term outweigh the negative characteristics of these precarious jobs.

When the attention is shifted from the employees to the managers and entrepreneurs, a similar pattern emerges in relation to the type of conditions that shaped their decision-making process. Based on a range of face-to-face, semi-structured interviews with these actors, the conclusion was again that individual trajectories or networks were the main drivers for settlement in a specific urban region. In Toulouse, for example, 75 per cent of the managers had an existing link with the city (family, study, being born there); similar results were found in the other cities as well. This is very much in line with findings by Krugman (1991) and Markusen (1996); they refer to place attachment and dependence on networks once they have been established. Moreover, just as with the employees, for managers it was hard conditions that came second and so-called soft conditions were hardly referred to. The approximately 300 managers of creative and knowledge-intensive industries, who were interviewed in the project underpinning the findings in this book, strongly confirm that Florida's theoretical model must be brushed aside.

However, there is one 'but'. A distinction must be made between the conditions that are relevant for the decision to settle somewhere – in which soft conditions do not feature strongly – and the decisions to stay after settlement. The retention side of the process seems to be more inter-linked with amenities available in the urban area. But even then other considerations play a very significant role as well.

Transnational migrants formed the third category of actors we specifically focused upon. In the summer and autumn of 2008, at least 25 interviews were completed with transnational migrants in each of the urban regions we have referred to in this volume. The interviews were designed to identify what kind of conditions were most important in their location deci-sions. In this volume the comparison focused on four cities: Amsterdam, Barcelona, Dublin and Munich. In Amsterdam the responses indicated a similar pattern to those of employees and managers: soft factors were not driving the decisions; instead, labour market opportunities are more important, together with hard conditions such as immigration policies. In Dublin and Munich employment opportunities were mentioned as among the most important factors, but together with family relations or other personal trajectories. In Barcelona, however, soft conditions were clearly mentioned as primary, although there too personal linkages with relatives and others from elsewhere (overseas) were mentioned as of key importance.

As for the managers, also for migrants, soft factors seem to gain impor-tance for the decision to stay after settlement. However, the decision to settle somewhere is much more driven by employment opportunities and personal relations of those who migrate to a new place to live in. These results suggest that the distinction between factors influencing key actors to come to a city and those influencing them to stay should receive more attention – as well as looking at 'those who go'. The latter category, migrating out of the urban region often also appear to be high-skilled persons, and the relative quality of life elsewhere may be a factor affect-ing decisions – although in line with the evidence reported here it would rarely be the key factor.

New governance approaches

In the research reported in this book, a large number of questions were asked about policies aimed at 'making competitive cities'. What do policy makers see as the most relevant strengths and weaknesses of their metropolitan regions with respect to international competitiveness? To what extent do local and regional governments in the case study regions aim to build on existing regional strengths, and to what extent do they look for wholly new economic specialisations? To what extent are the economic development strategies and visions embedded in and aligned with broader public policy activity at different spatial scales? Are economic development policies connected to regional spatial development policies, housing market policies and/or policies to attract and cater for 'talent'? What is the role of 'soft' location factors in metropolitan economic development strategies when compared with the more traditional, 'hard' location factors? How do policy makers respond to ideas about clustering economies? What is the role of creativity, innovation and knowledge in the metropolitan economic development strategies and visions? Do the metropolitan economic development strategies specifically address the conditions for attracting an international skilled labour force? How, if at all, are policy makers coping with the knowledge that personal networks appear to be highly important in the decision-making processes of highly skilled employees, managers and transnational migrants? Are there sufficient skills among policy makers to capitalise on relations, associations, interactions and collaborations between individuals, institutions and firms? How does policy aim to build trust, commitment to place and enthusiasm? To what extent can we speak of an integrated regional strategy, and on what geographic and administrative level?

Part IV of this volume suggests that the answers to these questions are not the same for all urban regions. What appears to be effective in one context does not seem to help in others. However, this does not imply that there are no situations where more or less similar strategies may work. Awareness of the differences and similarities is, however, a necessary condition for the organisation of future economic development policies. The experiences outlined in Parts II and III of this volume point to the need for policy makers to pay attention to at least five fields.

- First of all, policy makers should know their cities and the assets they can draw upon. This may seem trivial, but what we mean is that strategies and policies must connect with the urban history of the region, in its wider setting within various networks. The pathways the city went through and the legacies from this partly shape what can be achieved and over what timescales. If cities have rich and multiple-layered histories, and if cities are firmly embedded in multiple networks, enormous competitive advantage may be reached when proper use is made of these qualities. If these histories and networks are more restricted, an awareness of that may help to evaluate investment options and to make well-judged decisions. In either case, understanding the pathways cities went through and the networks they are embedded in is a more robust foundation for policy and strategy than any template adopted from elsewhere.

- The second field policy makers should consider carefully is that 'classic' location factors, such as accessibility, tax policies, availability of good infrastructures and communication facilities, and various factors that enable clustering are still key factors for various actors to build their decisions upon. Although these conditions should not be the only points of attention, their relevance is still huge.
- The third field regards the complicated finding that personal networks appear to be of key importance for all actors in creative and knowledge-intensive industries when they are to decide where to settle down. This condition came out strongest in the empirical research that underpins this volume. This is a complicated finding, since the policy challenge is to facilitate and enable these networks to become stronger and urban region focused and the question is: how?
- The fourth field relates to urban amenities. Urban amenities appear to play an important role – not so much in decisions to settle in the city, but more so in the decisions to stay, taken by those who have already settled in the city. This holds for all citizens and poses general challenge for policy makers and politicians to be fully aware of. These amenities are a necessary condition and require attention; but they neither represent the primary condition nor a sufficient condition to make the city more competitive.
- Finally, it is essential that the policies that are seen as relevant to the development of the creative knowledge city are not too narrowly defined in terms of local or economic development policies. Policies related to migration and citizenship, anti-discrimination and equal rights and how safe and secure newcomers feel may be particularly important for some groups but may relate more to the decisions of national than local governments. And policies relating to planning and transport may be more determined at a regional level. Intensive local efforts related to economic development could be undermined by policies in other spheres and at other levels of government. The need to align, integrate and co-ordinate policy is easy to identify but barriers of professional and organisational practice may not be easily overcome.

Current urban policies pay attention to each of these five fields, albeit with different weights attached to each and with different degrees of integration between policies that are the responsibility of different levels of government, different departments and sections within any one level of government and different professions. In some cases there is a plethora of strategies but less evidence that these affect delivery or really shape the creative knowledge city. Policies generally seem to be more concerned with what we have called hard conditions, including initiatives that help to create agglomeration advantages. Cluster policies, advocated by Porter (1990) and subsequently by the OECD (1999), have also been widely adopted. However, cluster theory appears to be developing and more and more attention is given to networking and relations between firms and other institutions (e.g. education and government). This was picked up in many cities, as is illustrated with the cases of Helsinki (recently) and Birmingham in this volume. Policy strategies aimed at creative and knowledge-intensive industries have become more varied. Education and networking play a bigger role now, together with clustering strategies. Overall, there appear to be limited policies aimed at soft conditions and economic development practice may not have come to recognise these as having a contribution to make or to recognise their greater importance for retention of key residents. There are also few policies aimed at strengthening personal relations; and balanced or rounded policies that take account of the full range of factors that influence decisions are not apparent at all.

There is differentiation between cities in their approaches to policy and strategy. This is related to different contexts and different histories. One legacy of distinctive histories relates to the organisation and dynamics of urban government and governance. The importance of that has been illustrated in this volume through Barcelona and Leipzig. Both of these cities have introduced new approaches to governance but in each of them government still matters. The discussion of governance suggests, however, that successful interaction between government and key actors in different sectors is unlikely if there is no variation in approach. It was suggested that while knowledge-intensive industries may respond to more top-down and formal policy mechanisms these will not be so well received by those working in creative industries where autonomy, creativity and self-reliance are valued and more bottom-up and responsive policy processes are needed. In both settings, however, networks are very important; more informal in the creative industries and more formal in the knowledge-intensive sphere. Promoting networking is therefore of major importance. Events are among the favourite tools to achieve this in the creative industries, whereas cluster formation is favoured in the knowledge-intensive sectors.

There are important examples in this volume of cross-boundary working that is essential if different levels of government and different activities are to complement one another. In both Barcelona and Toulouse, the story of successful policy interventions is partly about co-operation between adjacent municipalities and effective partnerships within the public sector and between public, private and third sectors. Institutional development and funding has also been important in Leipzig and the removal of the barriers associated with the Soviet block has had a general impact on cities previously affected by these. The difference between policy strategies, related to different histories of development, is also visible in a comparison between policy models adopted in cities Barcelona, Sofia, Milan, Dublin and Toulouse; these models range from bottom-up strategies with hardly any policy intervention (Milan, Sofia), through targeted strategic policies (Toulouse), to top-down highly interventionist strategic policy making (Dublin, Barcelona). It seems that the absence of policies in Milan and Sofia has not hindered the development of creative industries. The development of knowledge-intensive industries (albeit of a different character) in Dublin and Toulouse, however, seems to have benefitted much from the targeted policies applied there. Again this suggests that there is greater certainty about the policies developed when knowledge-intensive activities are aimed for; and less certainty about the role or form that policies should take when creative industries are the target. This uncertainty adds to the case for arguing that the development of the creative knowledge city is generating a new urban governance and new leadership. The traditional forms of government and top-down approaches are not equipped to deal with the complexity, diversity and pace of change of the new economy and effective leadership will involve listening and responding and building networks and partnerships. It may involve leadership without leading in the traditional sense.

Conclusion

This book has addressed pathways, actors and policies related to making competitive cities. We have presented insights derived from four theoretical fields that partly overlap: theories that stress the importance of agglomeration advantages and clustering, theories that illuminate the relevance of soft conditions, 'classic' location theories that elaborate on hard conditions, and theories in which relations and networks take centre stage. Based on the empirical evidence, we pointed out that whatever the theoretical position one takes to understand current urban economic transformations, cities' development pathways are of crucial importance. Beyond that we have been able to show that in each of the European regions we investigated, a mixture of factors is relevant to understand the various behaviours and attitudes of key actor groups. Having said that, the soft conditions, on which most of the recent debate on creative cities has focused, turned out to have some significance but to be the least important! Classic conditions seem to function as a necessary condition and in some urban regions, such as Leipzig and Munich, their importance may even be stronger. But most important seem to be the existing relationships and networks that have been built up in the past. Individual trajectories of key actors almost always have reference to these relations and networks. We should be aware, however, that several indicators that underline the importance of relationships and networks also refer to some of the other theoretical fields. This touches upon agglomeration theory and cluster theory, since the advantages derived from agglomerations and clusters are also strongly linked to various kinds of relationships. But also in 'classic' theory there are elements that relate to networks and individual trajectories and relationships. When key actors, for example, state that they went back to the place where they studied, this may be regarded as an individual study turf relationship; but this is also enabled by the presence of institutions for education, which feature in 'classic' theory. Therefore, the dividing lines between the different theoretical orientations should not be drawn too rigidly.

Yet, it was striking to find that issues like tolerance, openness and diversity were not regarded to be the key factors in the decision-making process to settle for a time or to stay longer in a specific city. The fact that some cities have an image that meets these criteria may not harm them, but it does not imply that these are necessary condition for future economic development and they are certainly not a sufficient one. A more powerful policy strategy would rather seem to stimulate the awareness about the characteristics of one's own urban history, the pathways these urban regions have gone through and to see what this offers in terms of opportunities when future developments are considered. In addition, it may be challenging to think about the multiple ways to facilitate a range of networks that appear to be crucial for the individual decision-making process of employees, managers and labour force from abroad. This requires creativity and knowledge as well as a flexible mind. The result may be a more diversified approach to urban economic development, away from 'models' and 'best practices'.

Our evidence also established that key actors are much less mobile than some of the literature, notably Florida (2006), would like us to believe. Mobility rates among key actors in Europe do not seriously differ from more general mobility rates and this may also be the case in the USA (where the general mobility rate is much higher than in Europe). The 'competition for talent', therefore, seems to be much more difficult and we have serious doubts that promoting diversity, tolerance and openness will create bigger flows of talented people to the cities that aim for that. This is not to say that structural problems in cities will have no negative effects in the long run. If there is a structural problem of lack of access to affordable housing in the regional housing market of a city, or lack of proper amenities, this may in the end result in driving away those who were already settled in the city. With regard to the housing market, a lack of affordable housing supply may initially – perhaps – be seen as a sign of success of the city (there is much demand!); however, in the longer run, this may turn into a disadvantage and thus an adequate response is of crucial importance to sustain the competitiveness of the city and region. The high costs of housing and other premises may also have a particular impact on the creative sector where incomes generated are not high – and there is some sense that this is the case in Milan and Munich for example.

One dimension tends to be underexposed when debates on *Making Competitive Cities* are at play; that is the question about the 'effects' of urban economic development. This book has only briefly referred to these effects although it has referred to the precariousness and the quality of the jobs in creative and knowledge-intensive sectors. The growth of the creative knowledge city is associated with increasing income inequality and this in turn contributes to housing affordability and other issues. Even where the welfare state has remained vigorous and the tradition of limiting inequality is strongest (Finland is a good example), inequality has increased and presents a challenge. It is not apparent that the best response to this is to resist the growth of the creative knowledge city and actions to address inequalities may be more appropriate. Nevertheless, it is essential that there is a policy response of some kind. For two major reasons, this is an important field for further exploration. First of all, societies have to be aware of the impacts of urban economic development. Second, the effects, especially the social and social inequality effects may also, in the end, become relevant dimensions in the entire set of path-dependent conditions for economic development. Studying the interrelations between the social and the economic may thus become a crucial new challenge in the research arena that focuses on *Making Competitive Cities*.

References

Bontje, M. and S. Musterd (2008) The multi-layered city: The value of old urban profiles. *Tijdschrift voor Economische en Sociale Geografie*, 99 (2): 248–255.

Castells, M. (1989) *The informational city: Information technology, economic restructuring, and the urban-regional process*. Oxford/Cambridge, MA: Basil Blackwell.

Florida, R. (2002) *The rise of the creative class*. New York: Basis Books.

Florida, R. (2006) The flight of the creative class. *Liberal Education*, 92 (3): 22–29.

Frenken, K. and R.A. Boschma (2007) A theoretical framework for evolutionary economic geography: Industrial dynamics and urban growth as a branching process. *Journal of Economic Geography*, 7 (5): 635–649.

Gordon, I. and I. Turok (2005) Moving beyond the conventional wisdom. In: N. Buck, I. Gordon, A. Harding and I. Turok (eds), *Changing cities*, pp. 265–282. New York: Palgrave Macmillan.

Grabher, G. (2004) Learning in projects, remembering in networks? Communality, sociality, and connectivity in project ecologies. *European Urban and Regional Studies*, 11 (2): 103–123.

Krätke, S. (2003) Global media cities in a world-wide urban network. *European Planning Studies*, 11 (6): 605–628.

Krugman, P. (1991) *Geography and trade*. The MIT Press, Cambridge, MA.

Markusen, A. (1996) Sticky places in slippery space: A typology of industrial districts. *Economic Geography*, 72 (3): 293–313.

OECD (1999) *Boosting innovation. The cluster approach*. Paris: OECD Proceedings.

Porter, M.E. (1990) The competitive advantage of nations. *Harvard Business Review*, 68 (2): 73–93.

Porter, M.E. (1998) Clusters and the new economics of competition. *Harvard Business Review*, 76 (6): 77–91.

Sassen, S. (2002) *Global networks, linked cities*. New York: Routledge.

Scott, A.J. (2006) Creative cities: Conceptual issues and policy questions. *Journal of Urban Affairs*, 28 (1): 1–17.

Storper, M. and M. Manville (2006) Behaviour, preferences and cities: Urban theory and urban resurgence. *Urban Studies*, 43 (8): 1247–1274.

Vaattovaara, M. (2009) The emergence of the Helsinki metropolitan area as an international hub of the knowledge industries. *Built Environment*, 35 (2): 204–211.

Index

Lightning Source UK Ltd.
Milton Keynes UK
UKOW07n1850200516

274671UK00001B/5/P